# MACHIAVELLI

# MACHIAVELLI

## THE CHIEF WORKS AND OTHERS

### TRANSLATED BY ALLAN GILBERT

#### VOLUME TWO

*Non in exercitu, nec in robore . . .*

*Duke University Press   Durham and London   1989*

# TABLE OF CONTENTS

## VOLUME ONE

## VOLUME TWO

## *VOLUME THREE*   Page

# ILLUSTRATIONS

# TEXTS USED IN TRANSLATING

TUTTE LE OPERE STORICHE E LETTERARIE DI NICCOLÒ MACHIAVELLI, *a cura di Guido Mazzoni e Mario Casella, Firenze 1929.*

TUTTE LE OPERE *di Niccolò Machiavelli, a cura di Francesco Flora e di Carlo Cordiè, 1959, 1960 (to be completed).*

LE OPERE DI NICCOLÒ MACHIAVELLI, *per cura di P. Fanfani e di L. Passerini e di G. Milanesi, Firenze 1873-77 (incomplete).*

OPERE DI NICCOLÒ MACHIAVELLI, *Italia 1813.*

OPERE MINORI DI NICCOLÒ MACHIAVELLI, *con note di F. L. Polidori, Firenze 1852.*

IL PRINCIPE DI NICCOLÒ MACHIAVELLI, *Firenze (Giunta) 1532.*

IL PRINCIPE DI NICCOLÒ MACHIAVELLI, *Rome (Blado) 1532.*

DISCORSI DI NICCOLÒ MACHIAVELLI, *Firenze (Giunta) 1531.*

LIBRO DELLA ARTE DELLA GUERRA DI NICCOLÒ MACHIAVELLI, *Firenze (Giunta) 1524.*

COMEDIA DI CALLIMACO & DI LUCRETIA, [*Firenze ?*] [*1524 ?*].

MANDRAGOLA, *a cura di S. Debenedetti, Strasburgo (Bibliotheca Romanica).*

NICCOLÒ MACHIAVELLI, ISTORIE FIORENTINE, *per cura di Plinio Carli, Firenze 1927.*

*Niccolò Machiavelli,* LETTERE FAMILIARI *pubblicate per cura di Edoardo Lisio, Firenze 1883.*

*Niccolò Machiavelli,* LETTERE FAMILIARI, *a cura di Gerolamo Lazzeri, Milano 1923.*

*Machiavelli,* LETTERE, [*a cura di Giuseppe Lesca*], *Firenze 1929.*

*Niccolò Machiavelli,* LETTERE, *a cura di Franco Gaeta, Milano 1961.*

*Oreste Tommasini,* LA VITA E GLI SCRITTI DI NICCOLÒ MACHIAVELLI, *vol. 2, parte 2, Appendice, Roma 1911.*

*Pasquale Villari,* NICCOLÒ MACHIAVELLI . . . *illustrati con nuovi documenti, Milano 1912-1914.*

*VOLUME TWO*

# THE LIFE OF CASTRUCCIO CAS⁄TRACANI OF LUCCA, WRITTEN BY NICCOLÒ MACHIAVELLI AND SENT TO ZANOBI BUON⁄DELMONTI AND LUIGI ALA⁄MANNI, HIS VERY DEAR FRIENDS

[*Written during a visit to Lucca in 1520.*

*The narrative is founded on fact but is essentially a work of fiction; no detail is to be taken as true without verification. Important is the interest in military affairs, suggesting passages in* THE ART OF WAR, *published in 1521. Other passages are akin to parts of* THE PRINCE, *for Castruccio knew how to gain and hold power. Undisturbed in his admiration by Castruccio's hostility to Florence, Machiavelli nevertheless does not present him as a man who might early have united Italy. In his last speech, Castruccio reviews the difficulties of attempting to unite even part of Tuscany under one government; had he been content with Lucca and Pisa only, his dominions would have been more secure. The work has as a unifying idea the power of Fortune. Cas⁄truccio was aided by her; yet on the other hand even Virtue could not free him from her power; she gave him neither the judgment to recognize the best course nor the long life needed to carry out his ambitious though mistaken plans.*]

## [The Power of Fortune]

Those who consider it, my dearest Zanobi and Luigi, think it wonderful that all, or the larger part, of those who in this world have done very great things, and who have been excellent among the men of their era, have in their birth and origin been humble and obscure, or at least have been beyond all measure afflicted by Fortune. Be⁄cause all of them either have been exposed to wild beasts or have had fathers so humble that, being ashamed of them, they have made themselves out sons of Jove or of some other god. Who these are, since many of them are known to everybody, would be boring to repeat and little acceptable to readers; hence, as superfluous, I omit it. I well believe that this comes about because Fortune, wishing to show the world that she—and not Prudence—makes men great, first shows her forces at a time when Prudence can have no share in the matter, but rather everything must be recognized as coming from herself.

### [Castruccio an example]

So then, Castruccio Castracani of Lucca was one of those who, according to the times in which he lived and the city where he was born, did very great things—and like the others, did not have a more fortunate or better-known beginning[1]—as will be plain in my narration of the course of his life. I have chosen to bring him back to the recollection of men, since I have found in his life many things, both as to ability and as to Fortune, that are very striking. And I have chosen to address it to you, as to those who, more than other men I know, delight in noble acts.

### [The Castracani family]

I say, then, that the Castracani family is counted among the noble families of the city of Lucca, although in these times, according to the way of all mundane things, it has disappeared. Into this family long ago was born a son named Antonio, who, becoming a priest, was Canon of St. Michael of Lucca, and as a mark of respect was called Messer Antonio. He had no near relatives except one sister, whom he early married to Buonaccorso Cennami, but after Buonaccorso was dead and she was left a widow, she came to live with her brother, intending not to marry again.

### [The finding of the infant Castruccio]

Messer Antonio had behind his house a vineyard, into which, because it was bordered by many gardens, it was possible to enter from many directions and without much trouble. It happened one morning soon after sunrise when Madonna Dianora (for that was the name of Messer Antonio's sister) was walking about in the vineyard and, according to the custom of women, gathering certain herbs with which to make seasonings, she heard a rustling under a vine among the foliage, and turning her eyes toward it, heard a

---

1. *The clause seems uncertain between the two forms: He was like the others in having an unfortunate and obscure beginning; and: His beginning was not more fortunate and well known than that of the others; that is, the other great men above alluded to.*

sound like weeping. So, moving toward it, she saw the hands and face, surrounded by the leaves, of a baby boy who seemed to ask for help. Partly astonished, partly frightened, full of compassion and amazement, she took him up and, carrying him to the house and washing him and wrapping him up in white cloths according to custom, presented him to Messer Antonio on his return home. He, hearing what had happened and seeing the little boy, was not less filled with wonder and pity than was the woman, and after considering between themselves what plan they ought to adopt, they determined to bring him up, since Antonio was a priest and his sister had no children. Taking a nurse into the house, then, they took care of him with the same love as though he were their own son. And having had him baptized, in memory of their father they gave him the name of Castruccio.

### [*Castruccio a natural soldier*]

In Castruccio charm increased with the years, and in everything he showed ability and prudence, and quickly, according to his age, he learned the things to which he was directed by Messer Antonio, who, intending to make him a priest and in time to turn over to him his canonry and other benefices, according to that purpose taught him. But he had found a subject wholly alien to the priestly character, for as soon as Castruccio reached the age of fourteen and began to get a little courage in respect to Messer Antonio and not to fear Madonna Dianora at all, laying churchly books aside, he began to busy himself with weapons; he took delight in nothing else than in handling them or, with his companions, in running, jumping, wrestling and similar sports, in which he showed the utmost strength and far surpassed all others of his age. If he did read at any time, no other reading pleased him than that which dealt with war or with things done by the greatest men. On account of this, Messer Antonio suffered immeasurable unhappiness and distress.

### [*Francesco Guinigi adopts Castruccio*]

There was in the city of Lucca a gentleman of the Guinigi family named Messer Francesco, who in riches and affability and vigor far exceeded all the other Lucchese. His business was war, and under the Visconti of Milan he had long been campaigning; and since he was a Ghibelline, he was esteemed above all the others who

belonged to that party in Lucca. Being in Lucca and talking every
evening and morning with the other citizens under the Loggia of the
Podesta, at the head of the Public Square of St. Michael, the chief
square in Lucca, this man many times saw Castruccio with the
other boys of the neighborhood in those exercises which, as I say
above, he practiced. And since it seemed to him that, in addition to
outdoing them, he had over them a kingly authority, and that they
in a certain way loved him and respected him, he became very eager
to know about his situation. Being informed about it by the by-
standers, Messer Francesco burned with greater desire to have him in
his service, and one day calling the boy, he asked him where he
would prefer to live, in the house of a gentleman who would teach
him to ride and to handle arms, or in the house of a priest where he
would never hear anything other than holy offices and masses. At
once Messer Francesco realized how happy Castruccio was when he
heard mention of horses and arms. At any rate, after a little bashful
hesitation, being encouraged by Messer Francesco to speak, he replied that if it pleased his sire, he could have no greater pleasure than
to leave the studies of a priest and take up those of a soldier. To
Messer Francesco this reply was very pleasing, and in just a few days
he so managed that Messer Antonio gave the boy over to him; to
which he was driven more by Castruccio's nature than by anything
else, judging that he could not long retain him as he had been.

### [Castruccio's accomplishments]

So Castruccio was transferred from the house of Messer Antonio
Castracani the canon into the house of Messer Francesco Guinigi the
general; it is an extraordinary thing to contemplate in what a very
short time after that change he fully possessed all those capabilities
and habits that are expected of a true gentleman. First of all, he
made himself an excellent rider, managing even the most fiery horse
with the greatest skill; and in jousts and tournaments, though he was
a mere boy, he was more notable than anybody else, so that in every
feat, whether of strength or skill, no man could be found who surpassed him. To this should be added his manners, in which was
seen a modesty beyond belief, because he was never seen to do a deed
or heard to speak a word that was displeasing. And he was respectful
to his elders, modest with his equals, and gracious with his inferiors;

these things made him loved not merely by all the Guinigi family but by all the city of Lucca.

## [*Castruccio's first campaign*]

It happened in those days, Castruccio being then eighteen years old, that Guelfs drove the Ghibellines out of Pavia; to the aid of the latter the Visconti of Milan sent Messer Francesco Guinigi, with whom went Castruccio, as the one who had the responsibility for his whole company. In this expedition, Castruccio showed so many signs of his prudence and courage that no one in that campaign gained such favor with everybody as he carried off. And not merely in Pavia but in all Lombardy his name became great and honored.

## [*He is envied in Lucca*]

Returning then to Lucca, much more esteemed than on his departure, Castruccio did not fail to make friends as much as he could, practicing all the methods necessary for gaining men's friend⁄ship. Messer Francesco Guinigi, dying and leaving a son thirteen years old, named Pagolo, left Castruccio as guardian and adminis⁄trator of his goods, for before his death he sent for him and begged him to consent to bring up his son with the same devotion as Castruccio himself had been brought up, and asked that those indications of gratitude which he had been unable to show to the father he would show to the son. So Messer Francesco being dead, Castruccio, as director and guardian of Pagolo, increased so much in reputation and power that the good will he was accustomed to have in Lucca changed in part into envy; hence many slandered him as a man to be feared and of a tyrannical spirit. Among these the chief was Messer Giorgio degli Opizi, head of the Guelf party. Since this man hoped that on Messer Francesco's death he would be left as it were prince of Lucca, he feared that Castruccio, who was in that position through the favor that his qualities gave him, had taken away his own opportunity; therefore he kept spreading gossip that would put Castruccio out of favor. The latter first felt anger at this, to which fear was soon added, because he believed that Messer Giorgio would never rest until he had brought him into disfavor with the vicar of King Robert of Naples, who would drive him from Lucca.

### [*Uguccione della Faggiuola captures Lucca*]

Pisa at that time was ruled by Uguccione della Faggiuola of Arezzo, who first had been chosen by the Pisans as their general, and then had made himself their ruler. With Uguccione there were some Lucchese exiles of the Ghibelline party, with whom Castruccio was scheming about bringing them back with Uguccione's help; and he also made known his plan to his friends inside the city, who could not endure the power of the Opizi. So having made arrange‐ ments for what they were going to do, Castruccio cautiously fortified the Onesti tower and filled it with munitions and with a store of food, so that if he had to, he could defend himself in it for some days. When the night came on which he had agreed with Uguccione, he gave the signal to that leader, who had arrived with a large force on the plain between the mountains and Lucca; on seeing the signal, Uguccione came to Saint Peter's Gate and set fire to the barbican. Castruccio within the wall raised the alarm, calling the people to arms, and mastered the gate on the inside, so that Uguccione and his men, coming in, occupied the city and killed Messer Giorgio with all the members of his family and with many of his friends and supporters, and drove out the chief magistrate; they reorganized the city government as Uguccione desired, with very great damage to the place, because it is reported that more than a hundred families were then driven out of Lucca. Of those who fled, one group went to Florence, another to Pistoia; these cities were ruled by the Guelf party and therefore were hostile to Uguccione and to the Lucchese.

### [*Florence makes war on Uguccione*]

Since the Florentines and the other Guelfs believed that the Ghibelline party in Tuscany had gained too much power, they agreed to restore the exiled Lucchese. And having raised a great army, they came into Val di Nievole and took Montecatini; next they laid siege to Montecarlo, in order to have free passage to Lucca. Meanwhile Uguccione, having assembled many Pisans and Luc‐ chese, and in addition many German cavalry which he had brought from Lombardy, advanced toward the Florentine army; the latter, hearing that the enemy were coming, had left Montecarlo and taken position between Montecatini and Pescia. Uguccione placed him‐ self near Montecarlo about two miles distant from the enemy. For a

few days, there were some slight skirmishes between the cavalry of
the two armies, because, Uguccione having fallen sick, the Pisans
and the Lucchese avoided fighting a battle with the enemy.

### [*In Uguccione's absence, Castruccio takes command*]

But since Uguccione's illness grew worse, he withdrew to Montecarlo in order to be cared for and left to Castruccio the care of the
army. This caused the overthrow of the Guelfs, because they took
courage, since they supposed the hostile army left without a leader.
Castruccio realized their belief and for some days attempted to
strengthen them in it, making a show of being afraid and not letting
anybody leave the fortifications of the camp. On the other hand, the
Guelfs, the longer they saw his fear, the more they kept growing
arrogant; so every day, drawn up for battle, they presented themselves
before Castruccio's army. He, thinking he had given them enough
confidence and having learned their order, determined to fight a
battle with them. First with words he gave firmness to the spirit of
his soldiers and put before them victory as certain, if they were willing
to obey his orders.

### [*Castruccio's tactics*]

Castruccio had seen that the enemy put all their strongest men
in the center of their array and the weaker soldiers on their wings.
Therefore he did the opposite, putting on the wings of his army his
bravest men and in the center those of less value. Going out of his
camp in this order, as soon as he came within sight of the hostile
army, which arrogantly, according to its custom, was coming to
offer him battle, he ordered the squadrons in the center to go slowly
and those on the wings to move rapidly. Hence, when they began
close combat with their enemies, the wings alone of both armies were
fighting, and the squadrons in the center were standing still, because
the soldiers at Castruccio's center had kept so far back that those at
the enemy's center did not meet them, and so it came about that the
strongest of Castruccio's soldiers were fighting with the weakest of
the enemy, and their strongest were standing still, without being able
to injure those they had opposite them or to give any aid to their
companions. Hence, without much difficulty, both wings of the
enemy were put to flight, and those in the center—denuded of their
flanking forces, without having had any chance to show their valor

—fled. The defeat and the slaughter were great; in that battle more than ten thousand men were killed, with many leaders and great knights of the Guelf party from all Tuscany, and in addition many princes who had come to their aid, such as Piero, King Robert's brother, Carlo his nephew, and Filippo lord of Taranto. Yet on Castruccio's side they did not amount to three hundred, among whom died Francesco, Uguccione's son, a young man and ardent who was killed in the first charge.

*[Uguccione, jealous, attacks Castruccio; is thwarted]*

This defeat made Castruccio's name very great. Hence Uguc-cione came to have so much jealousy and fear of Castruccio's position that he meditated on nothing else than how he could destroy him, feeling that victory had not given him sovereignty but had taken it away. And while he continued in this belief, awaiting a justifiable opportunity for acting on it, it happened that Pier Agnolo Micheli, a man of quality and highly esteemed, was killed in Lucca, and his slayer took refuge in Castruccio's house, where the officers of the chief of police, when they went to arrest him, were held off by Castruccio, so that through his aid the homicide escaped. When Uguccione, who was then at Pisa, learned this, he believed he had just cause for punishing Castruccio; so he sent for his son Neri, to whom he had earlier given the rule of Lucca, and charged him that, under pretense of inviting Castruccio to a banquet, he should arrest him and put him to death. Hence Castruccio, going to the ruler's palace in a friendly way, not fearing any harm, was first detained for supper by Neri and then arrested. But Neri, fearing that if he put him to death without any trial the people would revolt, kept him alive, in order to learn better from his father how he wished him to proceed. Uguccione, condemning his son's sluggishness and cow-ardice, in order to finish the thing left Pisa with four hundred horse-men to go to Lucca. And he had not reached the Bagni before the Pisans took up arms and killed Uguccione's vicar and the others of his household who had remained in Pisa; and they set up as their ruler Count Gaddo della Gherardesca. When Uguccione, before he reached Lucca, learned what had happened in Pisa, he thought it unwise to turn back lest the Lucchese, after the Pisan example, should also close their gates against him. But the Lucchese, when they heard of the events in Pisa, even though Uguccione had come into Lucca, finding an opportunity in Castruccio's liberation, began first in groups in the public squares to speak without restraint, and next to make an uproar, and after that they took to arms, asking that Castruccio be set free, so that Uguccione for fear of worse took him out of prison. Whereupon Castruccio, quickly gathering his friends, with the aid of the people attacked Uguccione, who, seeing that he had no defense, fled with his friends and went into Lombardy to enter the service of the Lords della Scala, where he died in poverty.

### [*Castruccio becomes prince of Lucca*]

But Castruccio, no longer a prisoner but as it were prince of Lucca, managed in such a way, with the help of his friends, and with the new support of the people, that he was made leader of their soldiers for a year. Having accomplished that, in order to give himself reputation in war, he set out to regain for the Lucchese many towns that had rebelled after Uguccione's departure. So with the aid of the Pisans, with whom he was leagued, he invested Sarzana. In order to attack the town, he built nearby a fort which, later fortified by the Florentines, is today called Sarzanello; and in two months he captured the town. Then, by means of the reputation gained there, he conquered Massa, Carrara, and Lavenza, and in a very short time conquered all Lunigiana, and in order to close the pass that from Lombardy leads into Lunigiana, he seized Pontremoli, and drove out Messer Anastagio Palavisini, who was her ruler. Returning to Lucca after this victory, he was welcomed by all the people. Since Castruccio had concluded that he should not defer making himself prince, with the help of Pazzino dal Poggio, Puccinello dal Portico, Francesco Boccansacchi, and Cecco Guinigi, then of high reputation in Lucca, who were bribed by him, he made himself ruler, and formally and by the decree of the people was chosen prince.

### [*Castruccio champion of the Tuscan Ghibellines*]

At this time Frederick of Bavaria, King of the Romans, came into Italy to take the crown of the Empire. Castruccio allied himself with him and visited him with five hundred cavalry. In Lucca he left as his deputy Pagolo Guinigi, to whom, for the sake of his father's memory, he showed as much consideration as though he were his own son. Castruccio was received by Frederick with honor and many privileges were given to him; and he made him his viceroy in Tuscany. And because the Pisans had driven out Gaddo della Gherardesca and for fear of him had gone to Frederick for aid, Frederick made Castruccio ruler of Pisa, and the Pisans in their dread of the Guelf party, especially of the Florentines, accepted him. Since after this Frederick went back to Germany and left a viceroy in Rome, all the Ghibellines of Tuscany and Lombardy, who belonged to the party of the Emperor, took refuge with Castruccio, and all of them promised him the sovereignty over their native cities, if with his aid they themselves could get back into them again. Among these were Matteo Guidi, Nardo Scolari, Lapo Uberti, Gerozzo Nardi, and Piero Buonaccorsi, all Ghibellines and Florentine exiles. Planning by their means and with his own forces to make himself ruler of all Tuscany, Castruccio, to raise his reputation, made an alliance with Messer Matteo Visconti, prince of Milan, and organized the whole city and the country around her for military service. And because Lucca had five gates, he divided into five parts the surrounding district and armed them and arranged them under leaders and banners, so that quickly he could get together twenty thousand men, besides those who could come to his aid from Pisa. When he was surrounded, then, by these forces and by these friends, it happened that Messer Matteo Visconti was attacked by Guelfs of Piacenza, who had driven out the Ghibellines, and in whose aid the Florentines and King Robert had sent their soldiers. Hence Messer Matteo requested Castruccio to attack the Florentines, in order that they, obliged to defend their homes, would call their soldiers back from Lombardy. So Castruccio with many soldiers attacked the Valdarno and occupied Fuccechio and San Miniato, with the greatest damage to the country. Hence the Florentines through this necessity called back their soldiers, who scarcely had returned to Tuscany when Castruccio was obliged by another necessity to return to Lucca.

### [Rebellion in Lucca; Castruccio's ruthlessness]

For in that city the Poggio family, powerful because it had made Castruccio not merely great but prince, and thinking it had not been rewarded according to its merits, united with other families in Lucca to make the city revolt and to drive out Castruccio. And taking an opportunity one morning, they made an armed attack on the deputy that Castruccio had there in charge of justice, and killed him, and when they were about to go on to raise the people in a riot, Stefano di Poggio, an old and peaceful man who had not taken part in the conspiracy, came before them, and with his influence impelled his family to lay down their arms, offering himself as mediator between them and Castruccio, to see that they got what they wished. They did, therefore, lay down their arms, with no more prudence than they had shown in taking them up, because Castruccio, hearing of their uprising and not letting any time go by, went to Lucca with part of his soldiers, leaving Pagolo Guinigi as leader of the rest. Finding the riot subsided, contrary to his expectations, and thinking it would be very easy for him to make himself safe, he stationed his armed partisans in all the suitable places. Stefano di Poggio, who supposed that Castruccio must feel under obligation to him, visited him, and did not beg for himself—because he judged he had no need to—but for the others of his house, begging that he would pardon many things to youth, many to the long-standing friendship and obligation he had to their family. Castruccio replied graciously, and exhorted him to be of good courage, making him think that he himself was much more pleased at finding the disturbances calmed down than he had been indignant at their beginning. And he exhorted Stefano to have them all come to him, saying that he thanked God that he had a chance to show his clemency and kindness. Having come, then, on the faith of Stefano and of Castruccio, along with Stefano they were imprisoned and put to death.

### [*Truce with the Florentines*]

It had happened meanwhile that the Florentines regained San Miniato. Thereupon Castruccio decided it would be a good thing to end that war, having concluded that until he made himself certain of Lucca, he must not go far from home. And sounding the Florentines as to a truce, he easily found them inclined to one, because they too were worn out and eager to put a stop to their expense. They made, then, a truce for two years, and by it each one was to hold what he was holding. Freed from war, then, Castruccio, in order not to run again into the dangers that he had run into before, with various excuses and pretexts got rid of all those in Lucca who through ambition might aspire to the princedom; he did not spare anybody, depriving them of country, of property, and—for those he could get his hands on—of life, affirming that he had learned through experience that none of these could be loyal to him; and for his greater security he built a fortress in Lucca and made use of material from the towers of those he had driven out or killed.

### [Castruccio takes Pistoia]

While Castruccio was suspending hostilities against the Floren-tines and was fortifying himself in Lucca, he was not failing to do such things as he could, without carrying on open war, to add to his grandeur. So having a great desire to occupy Pistoia—since it seemed to him that as soon as he gained possession of that city he would have one foot in Florence—in various ways he made all the Mountain[2] friendly to him, and with the parties in Pistoia he con-ducted himself in such a way that both of them confided in him. At the time, that city was divided, as she has always been, into Whites and Blacks. The head of the Whites was Bastiano di Possente; of the Blacks, Jacopo da Gia; each one of these had very secret dealings with Castruccio, and each of them wished to drive out the other. Hence the two, after many doubts, came to arms. Jacopo fortified himself at the Florentine Gate, Bastiano at the Lucchese Gate; and since both of them trusted more in Castruccio than in the Floren-tines, because they judged him more rapid and better equipped for war, they sent to him secretly—both of them—for help. And to both Castruccio gave promises, telling Jacopo that he would come in person, and Bastiano that he would send Pagolo Guinigi, his foster son. And giving them the time exactly, he sent Pagolo by the Pescia road, and he himself went straight to Pistoia, and at mid-night—for so Castruccio and Pagolo had agreed—both of them were at Pistoia, and both were received as friends. As soon as they had got inside, when it seemed the right time to Castruccio, he made a signal to Pagolo, after which one killed Jacopo da Gia and the other Bastiano di Possente; and all their partisans were either captured or killed. Castruccio took Pistoia without further opposition. Having thrown the government out of the Palace,[3] he compelled the people to give him allegiance, making them many remissions of old debts and many promises. And so he did to all the surrounding country,

2. The mountainous country north of Pistoia.
3. The city hall, where the chief magistrates resided during their term of office.

which in great part had run to see the new prince, so that everybody, full of hope and moved in great part by his abilities, became quiet.

### [*Castruccio in Rome*]

It happened in those days that the Roman people rebelled on account of the high cost of living, alleging as its cause the absence of the Pontiff, who was living in Avignon, and blaming the German authorities. Hence every day there were homicides and other troubles, which Henry, the Emperor's deputy, could not deal with. So there came upon Henry a great fear that the Romans would call in King Robert of Naples and drive him out of Rome and give her back to the Pope. Not having any nearer friend on whom to call than Castruccio, he sent to beg him that he would be so kind as not merely to send help but to come in person to Rome. Castruccio judged that it was not to be put off, both to repay his obligations to the Emperor and because he judged that whenever the Emperor was not in Rome, he himself could take no other course. Leaving, then, Pagolo Guinigi at Lucca, he went with six hundred cavalry to Rome, where he was received by Henry with the greatest honor. In a very short time his presence brought such great reputation to the Emperor's party that, without bloodshed or other violence, everything was assuaged; because by having a large amount of grain come by sea from the region of Pisa, Castruccio removed the cause of the disorder. Then, partly by admonishing, partly by punishing the chief men in Rome, he brought them willingly under Henry's government. Castruccio was made Roman senator and given many other honors by the Roman people. This office Castruccio assumed with the greatest pomp, putting on a toga of brocade, with letters on the front that said: "That is which God wills"; and behind they said: "That shall be which God shall will."

### [*The Florentines begin war on Castruccio*]

Meanwhile the Florentines, indignant that Castruccio in times of truce had made himself master of Pistoia, were considering how they could make her revolt; because of his absence they judged it an easy matter. Among the Pistolese exiles in Florence were Baldo Cecchi and Jacopo Baldini, both men of influence and ready to put themselves into any peril. They schemed with their friends at home, so that with Florentine aid they entered Pistoia at night and drove out

Castruccio's partisans and officials—part of them they killed—and restored liberty to the city. This news greatly vexed and angered Castruccio; taking leave of Henry, by long days' journeys he came with his followers to Lucca. The Florentines, when they heard of Castruccio's return, surmising that he would not be likely to stand still, decided to forestall him by leading their soldiers into the Val di Nievole ahead of him, judging that if they occupied that valley, they could cut the road by which he would retake Pistoia. And having brought together a great army of all the friends of the Guelf party, they came into the territory of Pistoia. On the other side, Castruccio with his men came out to Montecarlo. And having learned where the Florentine army was, he decided not to meet it in the plain of Pistoia nor to wait for it in the plain of Pescia but, if he could do so, to encounter it in the pass of Serravalle, judging that if such a plan should succeed, he would gain from it a sure victory, because he had learned that the Florentines had altogether thirty thousand men, and he himself had from his own selected twelve thousand. And though he trusted in his own diligence and their efficiency, yet he feared that if he joined battle in a wide plain he would be surrounded by the multitude of his enemies.

### [Castruccio prepares for battle at Serravalle]

Serravalle is a fortified town between Pescia and Pistoia, situated on a hill that shuts in the Val di Nievole, not in the pass itself, but above it two bowshots. The place where one passes over is more narrow than steep: in either direction it rises gently, but it is so nar-row, especially on the hill where the waters divide, that twenty men side by side would fill it up. In this place Castruccio had planned to encounter the enemy, both because his few men would have an advantage and because he would not need to reveal the enemy to his soldiers before the fight, since he feared that, seeing the multitude of their opponents, they would be frightened. At this time the lord of Serravalle was Messer Manfred, a German by birth, who, before Castruccio became master of Pistoia, had been left untouched in his town as a place common to the Lucchese and the Pistoians. Nor after that had anybody had reason to attack him, since he promised them all to be neutral and not to bind himself to either of them. So for this reason, and because he was in a strong place, he had been kept in power. But when this event came about, Castruccio became

Serravalle. The road on which the combat took place is still lower down than the houses at the bottom of the picture. The steepness of the hill is emphasized by the switchback at the right. Castruccio's army came up to the road's summit, below the town, from the left; the Florentine forces came from the right. Castruccio's detached force descended the hill from the town. (Alinari photograph)

eager to take that place. And having a close friendship with a citizen, he so arranged with him that during the night before he was going to join battle his friend should receive four hundred of his men and kill the ruler.

### [Castruccio defeats the Florentines at Serravalle]

And being so prepared, he did not move his army from Montecarlo, in order to give the Florentines more confidence to cross the hill at Serravalle. They, wishing to remove the war from Pistoia and take it into Val di Nievole, encamped near Serravalle, with the intention of crossing the hill the next day. But Castruccio, having in the night without uproar taken Serravalle, about midnight left Montecarlo and in silence arrived with his soldiers in the morning at the foot of the hill. Thus at the same time the Florentine army and he, each from his own direction, began to climb the slope. Castruccio had directed his infantry by the main road and had sent a band of four hundred cavalry to the left hand toward the town. The Florentines, on the other side, had sent four hundred cavalry ahead, and then had moved their infantry and, behind them, their men-at-arms. They were not expecting to find Castruccio on the hill, because they did not know that he had mastered the town. Hence the Florentine cavalry, having climbed the slope, unexpectedly beheld Castruccio's infantry; the cavalry were so near as scarcely to have time to lace their helmets. Since, therefore, the unprepared were attacked by the prepared and the well ordered, with great spirit Castruccio's soldiers pressed upon the Florentines, and the latter resisted with difficulty; yet some of them made a stand. But as the report went down through the rest of the Florentine army, everything fell into complete confusion. The cavalry were crowded by the infantry, the infantry by the cavalry and the baggage; so narrow was the place that the leaders could not go either forward or backward. Hence nobody, in such confusion, knew what he could do or ought to do. Meanwhile the cavalry, who were at close quarters with the hostile infantry, were being killed and defeated without being able to defend themselves, because the adverse nature of the site did not allow it. Yet more through necessity than through valor they were resisting, because, having at their flanks the mountains, behind them their friends, and in front of them their enemies, there was left to them no road open for flight. Meanwhile Castruccio, having seen that his men were not strong enough to make their enemies turn about, sent a thousand infantry by way of the town. When he had them come down with the four hundred cavalry that he had sent earlier, they struck the enemy on the flank with such fury that the Florentine soldiers, unable to resist their charge, and defeated more by the place than by their enemies, fled. The flight began with those who were in the rear toward Pistoia, and as they scattered through the plain, each man, where best he had a chance, provided for his own safety. This defeat was great and very bloody. Many leaders were taken, among whom were Bandino de' Rossi, Francesco Brunelleschi, and Giovanni della Tosa, all noble Florentines, with many other Tuscans and inhabitants of the Kingdom, who, having been sent by King Robert to aid the Guelfs, served with the Florentines.

### [Castruccio approaches Florence]

The Pistolese, hearing of this defeat, without delay, after driving out the party friendly to the Guelfs, gave themselves up to Castruccio. He, not content with this, took Prato and all the towns in the plain, both across as well as to the north of Arno. He stationed himself with his soldiers in the plain of Peretola, two miles from Florence; there he remained many days to divide the plunder and to rejoice over the victory gained, in derision of the Florentines having money coined and races run by horses, by men, and by harlots. Nor did he fail to try to bribe some noble citizens, so that at night they would open the gates of Florence. But since the conspiracy was discovered, Tommaso Lupacci and Lambertuccio Frescobaldi were arrested and beheaded.

### [The Florentines take as their lord King Robert of Naples]

Terrified, then, by their defeat, the Florentines did not see any means by which they could preserve their liberty. To be more certain of help, they sent ambassadors to Robert King of Naples to offer him the city and sovereignty over her. That King accepted, not so much because of the honor done him by the Florentines, as because he knew of what importance it was to his position that the Guelf party should retain control in Tuscany. Having agreed with the Florentines that he should have two hundred thousand florins annually, he sent to Florence his son Carlo with four thousand cavalry.

## [*A plot against Castruccio in Pisa*]

Meanwhile the Florentines were somewhat relieved from the soldiers of Castruccio, because he had been obliged to leave their territory and go off to Pisa in order to put down a conspiracy formed against him by Benedetto Lanfranchi, one of the chief men of Pisa. This man, unable to endure having his native city enslaved by a Lucchese, conspired against him, intending to take the citadel and, after driving out the garrison, to kill Castruccio's partisans. But—since in these affairs if a small number is enough for the secret, it is not enough for the execution—while he was seeking to bring over more men to his determination, he happened upon one who revealed his plan to Castruccio. Nor did this revelation come about without infamy to Bonifacio Cerchi and Giovanni Guidi, Florentines banished to Pisa. Castruccio, therefore, laying hands on Benedetto, killed him, and sent all the rest of that family into exile and beheaded many other noble citizens. Since he knew that Pistoia and Pisa were not very loyal, with sagacity and force he tried to make himself sure of them.

## [*The Florentines again attempt war on Castruccio*]

This gave time to the Florentines to regather their forces and allowed them to await Carlo's arrival. When he came, they decided not to lose time and brought together a great many men, because they summoned to aid them almost all the Guelfs of Italy, and formed a very large army of more than thirty thousand infantry and ten thousand cavalry. And after debating which they ought to attack first, Pistoia or Pisa, they decided on attacking Pisa, as a plan more likely to succeed because of the recent conspiracy in that city, and of more value, since they judged that when Pisa was theirs Pistoia would of her own accord surrender. Coming out, then, with their army in the beginning of May, 1328, the Florentines rapidly captured Lastra, Signa, Montelupo and Empoli, and came with their army to San Miniato.

## [*Castruccio's military plans*]

Castruccio, on the other hand, learning of the large army that the Florentines had moved against him, not terrified in any way, believed that this was the hour when Fortune was going to put in his hand dominion over Tuscany, assuming that his enemies would not be able to make a better showing in the territory of Pisa than they had at Serravalle, and besides that they would not this time have any hope of reorganizing as then. So assembling twenty thousand foot‑soldiers and four thousand cavalry, he placed himself with his army at Fucecchio, and Pagolo Guinigi with five thousand infantry he sent into Pisa. Fucecchio has a stronger site than any other walled town in the territory of Pisa, being between the Usciana and Arno and somewhat raised above the plain. If he were there, in no way could the enemy, unless they divided themselves into two parts, impede the coming of supplies from Lucca or from Pisa. And they could not, except with disadvantage to themselves, either attack him or go toward Pisa, for in the latter case they would be placed between Castruccio's soldiers and those in Pisa; in the other, having to cross Arno, they could not do it with the enemy upon them, except with great danger. Castruccio, in order to give them courage to adopt this plan of crossing, had not stationed himself with his soldiers on the bank of Arno but near the walls of Fucecchio, and had left much space between the river and himself.

### [*The Florentines attempt to ford the Arno*]

The Florentines, having taken San Miniato, discussed what was to be done: whether to go to Pisa or to attack Castruccio. After estimating the difficulties of the two plans, they determined to assail Castruccio. At that time the Arno River was so low that it could be forded, but not, however, to such an extent that infantry would not get wet up to the shoulders and horses up to the saddles. When the morning of June 10 came, then, the Florentines, drawn up for battle, began the crossing with part of their cavalry and a force of ten thou‑sand infantry. Castruccio, who was prepared and alert for what he had in mind to do, attacked them with a force of five thousand infantry and three thousand cavalry. Nor did he give them time for all of them to come out of the water before he was in combat with them. A thousand light infantry he sent along the bank down Arno and a thousand upstream. The Florentine infantry were weighed down by the water and by their equipment, and not all of them had climbed up the bank of the river. The horses, after some of them had crossed, since they had broken up the bottom of Arno, made pas‑sage by the others difficult. As a result, many, getting into the ruined ford, fell on their riders; many were so stuck in the mud that they could not get out. Hence the Florentine generals, seeing the difficulty of crossing at that place, sent them back higher upstream, in order to find the bottom unspoiled and the bank more favorable for receiving them. To them were opposed the infantry that Castruccio had sent up along the bank; these, lightly armed with shields and with galley-darts in their hands, with loud shouts wounded the horses in the face and in the breast, so that frightened by the wounds and the shouts, not wanting to go ahead, they fell one on top of another.

## [*Castruccio's tactics*]

The fight between Castruccio's men and those who had crossed was fierce and terrible, and on either side many fell, and each army tried as hard as it could to defeat the other. Castruccio's men attempted to plunge them back into the river; the Florentines attempted to shove them back, in order to give room for the others, so that on coming out of the water they would be able to fight. To this stubbornness were added the officers' exhortations. Castruccio reminded his men that these were the same enemies that not long before they had beaten at Serravalle; and the Florentines reproached their men that the many were letting themselves be beaten by the few. But Castruccio, seeing that the battle was continuing and that his men and their adversaries were already exhausted, and that everywhere there were many wounded and dead, pushed forward another band of five thousand infantry, and, bringing them close behind his men who were fighting, ordered those in front to open out and, as if they were taking to flight, to retire, half of them to the right and half of them to the left. This being done, it gave some space for the Florentines to push forward and gain some ground. But the fresh troops coming to blows with the tired ones did not delay long before they drove them into the river. Between the cavalry on either side there was not yet any advantage, because Castruccio, knowing that his were inferior, had ordered his officers merely to resist the enemy, since he hoped to defeat the infantry and, when they were defeated, then more easily to beat the cavalry. This happened according to his plan; because, seeing that the hostile infantry had retired into the river, he sent the remainder of his infantry against the hostile cavalry. The infantry with spears and javelins wounding them, and his cavalry also pressing upon them with greater fury, they put them to flight. The Florentine leaders, seeing the difficulty their cavalry had in crossing, attempted to have infantry cross at a place farther down the river, in order to make a flank attack on Castruccio's soldiers. But since the banks were high and their tops were held by his men, they tried in vain.

### [The Florentines defeated]

So the army was defeated with great honor and glory for Cas/ truccio; and of so great a multitude there escaped not a third. Many leaders were taken; and Carlo, King Robert's son, together with Michelagnolo Falconi and Taddeo degli Albizzi, Florentine com/ missioners, fled to Empoli. The booty was large, the slaughter very large, as in so great a conflict can be expected, because of the Floren/ tine army there were killed 20,231; but of Castruccio's men 1,570 were killed.

### [Castruccio's mortal illness]

Yet Fortune, hostile to his fame, when it was time to give him life, took it from him and broke off those plans that he for a long time before had been intending to put into effect, nor by anything other than death could he have been impeded. All that day in the battle Castruccio had been toiling; then when it had come to an end, all weary and soaked with sweat, he stood still near the gate of Fucecchio to wait for his soldiers who were returning from the victory, and in person to receive them and to thank them, and partly that if anything should still be undertaken by the enemy, who in some place might have assembled a force, he would be prompt in dealing with it—judging it the duty of a good general to be the first to mount his horse and the last to dismount. Hence, standing ex/ posed to a wind that generally at midday rises from up Arno and is almost always unhealthful, he grew cold as ice. This, not being regarded by him, as one who was used to such discomforts, was the cause of his death, because the next night he was attacked by a very severe fever. Since this kept increasing and the illness was thought mortal by all the doctors and Castruccio learned of it, he called Pagolo Guinigi and spoke to him these words:

### [*Castruccio's dying regrets*]

"If I had supposed, my son, that Fortune was going to cut off in the middle of my journey my path for moving on to that glory which I through my many successful actions hoped to attain, I would have toiled less and to you would have left, if a smaller state, fewer enemies and less envy. Because, contented with the rule of Lucca and of Pisa, I would not have subdued the Pistolese, and with so many injuries stirred up the Florentines; but, making both of these two peoples my friends, I would have carried on my life, if not longer, of a certain more quietly, and I would have left you a state, if smaller, without doubt more secure and more solid. But Fortune, who is admitted to be arbiter of all human things, did not give me so much judgment that I could early understand her, nor so much time that I could overcome her.

### [*Castruccio's gratitude*]

"You have learned, for many have told you, and I have never denied it, that I came into the house of your father while still a youth and lacking all those hopes that ought to dwell in every noble spirit, and that I was brought up by him and loved by him much more than if I had been born of his own blood; then that I, under his training, became valiant and capable of attaining that fortune that you yourself have seen. And because, when he was about to die, he entrusted you and all his property to my loyalty, I have brought you up with the same love and increased the property with the same loyalty by which I was bound and now am. And so that you should have not merely what was left you by your father but also what Fortune and my ability have gained, never have I been willing to take a wife, in order that love of children should not so hinder me that I could not in every way show the family of your father such gratitude as I believed myself bound to show.

### [*The weakness of Castruccio's Tuscan empire*]

"I leave you, therefore, a large state, at which I am much pleased; but because I leave it to you weak and insecure, I am very sorry. You control the city of Lucca, which never will be satisfied to live under your authority; you control Pisa, where men are by nature fickle and full of deceit. That city also, though accustomed at various times to servitude, nevertheless will always disdain having a Lucchese ruler. Pistoia is also yours, hardly loyal, through being divided, and angered against our family by recent injuries. You have as neighbors the Florentines, embittered and in a thousand ways injured, but not destroyed—whom the news of my death will please more than would the conquest of all Tuscany. In the princes of Milan and in the emperor you cannot trust, because they are far off, slow, and their assistance late. You must not, therefore, trust in anything except your own cleverness and the memory of my ability, and in the reputation brought to you by the present victory. The last, if you can use it with prudence, will aid you in making an agreement with the Florentines, who, since they are terrified by the present defeat, will certainly be eager to accept your terms. As to them, where I sought to make them my enemies and thought their hostility must bring me power and glory, you must with every effort seek to make them your friends, because their friendship will bring you security and ease.

### [Know thyself]

"It is in this world of great importance to know oneself, and to be able to measure the forces of one's spirit and of one's position. He who knows that he is not suited to war ought by means of the arts of peace to endeavor to reign. To them, in my opinion, it is well that you apply yourself, and that you strive in this way to enjoy the results of my labors and dangers. In this you will succeed easily if you will accept as true these reflections of mine; and to me you will have two obligations: one that I have left you this realm; the other that I have taught you how to keep it."

### [Castruccio dies; Pagolo's failure]

Then having summoned those citizens of Lucca, Pisa, and Pistoia who were serving under him, and having spoken to them in behalf of Pagolo Guinigi and made them swear obedience to him, he died, leaving in all those who had heard him mentioned a high regard for his memory, and in those who had been his friends as great regret for him as for any prince who ever died at any time. His funeral was celebrated very honorably and he was buried in San Francesco in Lucca. But Ability and Fortune were not so friendly to Pagolo Guinigi as to Castruccio, because not much later he lost

Pistoia and then Pisa, and with difficulty kept the sovereignty of Lucca, which remained in his family until the time of Pagolo his great grandson.

### [*Castruccio's qualities and opinions*]

So, then, Castruccio, according to all that we have learned, was a man unusual not merely for his own times but also for many by, gone times. In his person he was of more than ordinary height, and every limb was in proportion with the rest. He was so gracious in his bearing and received men with such kindness that never did anybody who spoke with him go away dissatisfied. His hair tended toward red, and he wore it cut above his ears, and always and at every time, even when it rained or snowed, he went with his head bare. He was gracious to his friends, to his enemies terrible, just with his subjects, not to be trusted by foreigners. Never when he could win by fraud did he attempt to win by force, because he was accustomed to say that the victory, not the manner of the victory, would bring you renown. Nobody was ever bolder about entering into dangers, or more wary in getting out of them. He used to say that men ought to try everything, not to be afraid of anything; and that God is a lover of strong men, because we see that he always punishes the powerless by means of the powerful.

### [*Castruccio's sayings*]

He was also wonderful in giving answers with a bite in them, either sharply or courteously, and as he did not in this way of speaking spare anybody, so he was not angry when others did not spare him. Hence many things are recorded that he said sharply, and many that he heard with patience.

When he had bought a partridge for a ducat, and one of his friends reproved him, Castruccio said: "You would not have paid more than a soldo?" And when the friend answered that he spoke truly, he replied: "For me a ducat is much less important."

Once when he had a flatterer in his presence, and in contempt had spit on him, the flatterer said: "The fishermen to take a little fish let themselves be thoroughly wetted by the sea; I shall certainly let myself be wetted by a little spit in order to catch a whale." Cas, truccio not merely listened patiently to the man but also rewarded him.

Someone having censured him because he lived too splendidly,

Castruccio said: "If this were a vice, there would not be such splendid banquets at the feasts of our saints."

Passing through a street, and seeing a young man coming out of the house of a harlot all blushing because Castruccio had seen him, he said to him: "Do not be ashamed when you come out of there, but when you go in."

When a friend gave him a knot to untie that was very carefully entwined, he said. "Oh fool, do you think I want to loosen something which, when it is fastened, gives me so much trouble?"

When Castruccio said to one who professed to be a philosopher: "You are like the dogs, that always come around him who will give them something good to eat," the man replied: "On the contrary, we are like the physicians, since we go to the houses of those who most need us."

When he was going from Pisa to Livorno by water and there came up a dangerous storm, by which Castruccio was much dismayed, one of those with him rebuked him for timidity, saying that he himself was not afraid of anything. To whom Castruccio returned that he did not wonder at it, because each man values his life for what it is worth.

Being asked by someone what he needed to do to make himself esteemed, he said: "Be sure, when you go to a banquet, that one block of wood doesn't rest on another block."

When somebody was boasting that he had read many things, Castruccio said: "It would be better to boast of having kept many of them in mind."

When somebody was boasting that, though drinking a great deal, he did not get drunk, he said: "An ox does just the same thing."

Once there was a young woman with whom Castruccio associated intimately. For this, being reproached by a friend of his who said especially that it was bad for him to let himself be taken by a woman, "You are wrong," said Castruccio; "I have taken her, not she me."

Also when someone scolded him for using too delicate foods, he said: "You would not spend on them as much as I do?" And the man saying that he told the truth, he replied: "Then you are more avaricious than I am gluttonous."

Once he was invited to supper by Taddeo Bernardi of Lucca, a man very rich and greatly given to display. After he arrived at the house, Taddeo showed him a room all decorated with tapestries and having a floor made of fine stones which with their different colors, differently combined, represented flowers, branches and similar verdure. Then Castruccio, having gathered much saliva in his mouth, spat it all in Taddeo's face; when Taddeo showed offence, Castruccio said: "I did not know where I could spit so as to annoy you less."

Being asked how Caesar died, he said: "God grant that I may die as he did."

Being one night in the house of one of his gentlemen, where many ladies had gathered to enjoy themselves, as he was dancing and having a good time more than fitted one in his position, and was reproved for it by one of his friends, he said: "He who is thought wise by day will not be thought foolish by night."

When a man came to ask a favor, and Castruccio gave the appearance of not hearing, the man threw himself on his knees on the floor. Castruccio rebuking him for it, the man said: "You are the cause of it, for you have your ears in your feet." As a result, he obtained double the favor he was asking.

He used to say that the road for going to Hell was easy, since one went down hill with closed eyes.

When a man asked a favor from him with many and superfluous words, Castruccio said to him: "When you want something more from me, send somebody else."

A man of the same sort, having bored him with a long speech and having said at the end: "I have perhaps by too much talking wearied you," he replied: "Not at all, because I have not heard a thing you have said."

He used to say of one who had been a handsome boy and later was a handsome man, that he did too much damage, for earlier he had taken the husbands from the wives and now he was taking the wives from the husbands.

To an envious man who was laughing, he said: "Are you laughing because you are doing well or because another is in trouble?"

Being still under the control of Messer Francesco Guinigi, and one of his companions saying to him: "What do you want me to give you for letting me slap your face?" Castruccio replied: "A helmet."

Having put to death a citizen of Lucca who had been a cause of his greatness, and being told that he had done wrong in killing one of his old friends, he answered that they were deceiving themselves, because he had put to death a new enemy.

Great praise was given by Castruccio to men who selected wives and then did not marry them, and likewise to those who said they were intending a voyage and then did not go on it.

He used to say that he wondered at men who, when they buy an earthenware or glass dish, sound it first, to see if it is good, and then in taking a wife are content only to look at her.

Someone asking him, when he was about to die, how he wished to be buried, he answered: "With my face turned down, because I know that when I am dead this country will turn topsy-turvy."

Being asked if in order to save his soul he ever considered making himself a friar, he answered that he had not, because it seemed to him strange that Brother Lazarus should be going to Heaven and Uguccione della Faggiuola to Hell.

Being asked when it was good to eat in order to keep in good health, he answered: "If a man is rich, when he is hungry; if a man is poor, when he can."

Seeing a gentleman of his who was having one of his servants lace up his clothing, he said: "I pray God that you have him feed you too."

Seeing that a man had written on his house in Latin letters: "May God guard it from the wicked," he said: "That requires that he shan't go in there himself."

Passing through a street where there was a little house that had a big door, he said: "That house will run away through that door."

Being told that a foreigner had ruined a boy, he said: "He must be a Perugian."

Having asked what city had a reputation for cheaters and grafters, he was told "Lucca, where by nature they were all of that sort except Buontura."

When he was debating with an ambassador of the King of Naples about the property of some exiles, and getting somewhat angry, the ambassador said to him: "So you aren't afraid of the King?" Castruccio replied: "Is he good or bad, this King of yours?" And on the ambassador's answering that he was good, Castruccio retorted: "Why, then, do you want me to fear good men?"

It would be possible to report many other things said by him, in all of which would be seen wit and dignity, but I believe these are enough in witness of his great qualities.[4]

### [*Always great*]

He lived forty-four years and in all fortunes he acted the prince. And as of his good fortune there appear many memorials, so he wished that of his bad some should also appear. Hence the hand-cuffs with which he had been chained in prison are to be seen even today fastened up in the tower of his dwelling, where they were placed by him in order that they might always give assurance of his adversity. And because when living he was inferior neither to Philip of Macedon, Alexander's father, nor to Scipio of Rome, he died at the age of both; without doubt he would have surpassed both if instead of Lucca he had had for his native country Macedonia or Rome.

4. *Machiavelli may have written this with amusement. Most of the sayings are taken from Diogenes Laertius'* LIVES OF THE PHILOSOPHERS; *one (the choice of a wife) is from Tegrimi's* LIFE OF CASTRUCCIO; *one from Dante (on Buontura or Bontura).*

# THE ART OF WAR

## List of Books

[*Published in Florence in 1521, THE ART OF WAR, like MAN-DRAGOLA, was printed during its author's lifetime. If, as seems likely—though the matter has not been adequately studied—Machiavelli corrected the proofs, we have here the most correct text among all his writings; often we cannot be sure that he considered his manuscripts ready for printing.*

*The work is an outgrowth of a paragraph in the last chapter of THE PRINCE. Can there be armament and tactics that will give an Italian army an advantage over the soldiers of invading forces? Further, how can the Italians avoid reliance on mercenary troops, and provide for defense with their own hands?*

*Though Machiavelli had no personal experience as a soldier, as an agent of the Florentine government he had abundant opportunity for observation, and had actually borne responsibility for Florentine war against Pisa. He was the prime mover in organizing a militia in the city's rural territory, and executed many of the details of administration. He had read the standard books on military affairs and had meditated on them. The result, as set down in THE ART OF WAR, is a mixture of the unworkable and the highly important. Of all his compositions, this is perhaps the one most limited to the years in which it is written. He did not set out to predict the future of warfare but to urge what could be done in his own day. Yet that even for the future he was not wholly unsuccessful is shown by the history of his work; for example, before any of his other writings, this one was put into English, as useful for English soldiers. Failure to realize this limited purpose has led to such absurdities as rating him for not seeing what artillery would become as technical knowledge advanced with the centuries. It has even been asserted that he despised cannon. But it is impossible to turn many of the following pages without finding them referred to; they were always in his mind as part of the equipment of an army, and his estimate of their value at the date when he wrote is a reasonable one. Because of the effect of artillery fire in battle, he modified even the Roman tactics he admired.*

*Searching through antiquity and through his own times for the best infantry equipment, he decided on a combination. Part of his soldiers he armed with the long pikes of the Macedonians and of the sixteenth-century Swiss. Part he armed with shields and swords derived from the Romans and from the Spanish of the battle of Ravenna. The first equipment is evident enough.*

The second had not been tested as had the Swiss weapon; it is not the characteristic Spanish armament for Italian wars. Moreover, like most writers before and after him, Machiavelli did not realize that the Roman sword was effective because combined with the Roman pilum—known to him but given no importance. The Roman invention was a heavily armed soldier, standing in order such that the legion was the rock at the center of a Roman battle, yet provided with missile weapons, two pila or javelins. A Roman body of one hundred men would launch two hundred of these formidable weapons before coming to close quarters with their opponents.[1] If we suppose that only one-tenth of the pila struck home, the effect on adversaries was terrible. A Macedonian formation, suddenly reduced twenty per cent, would be vulnerable to swordsmen who could not make a successful attack when the order of leveled spears was unbroken. Moreover, the Roman soldier had the mobility permitted by a short weapon that demanded less group action than did long spears. Machiavelli deserves great credit for early seeing a military need, if we recall that Napoleon at Waterloo sent forward his guards in heavy columns with slight fire power, to be destroyed by the bullets of the more lightly ordered English. But Machiavelli's solution was not what practical soldiers were slowly and haltingly to work out. From all his Roman imitation comes no more than the importance of Roman discipline— but that is no slight matter.

Important for battle tactics is his realization of the power of artillery over massed and motionless bodies of either infantry or cavalry. The best instance of this, the battle of Ravenna in 1512, he actually names only in the DISCOURSES. His remarks might be taken as the precursor of Wellington's disgust at the position of the Prussian infantry, exposed to French artillery, at Ligny. The tactics in the LIFE OF CASTRUCCIO CASTRACANI, in this matter essentially part of THE ART OF WAR, are hardly realistic. The last battle represents Castruccio as repelling the Florentines in their attempt to ford Arno. Then Machiavelli says that the Florentine army was destroyed with heavy loss. Yet such a victory is impossible unless Castruccio's army crossed Arno in the face of the large Florentine force which had not been engaged. Machiavelli does not mention such a crossing.

In insisting on the primary importance of infantry and the secondary value of cavalry, Niccolò was in harmony with European practice for many years

1. The belief cannot be escaped that the Romans in rear ranks threw their javelins over the heads of those in front ranks. This demanded perfect timing, the result of long training. See H. M. D. Parker, THE ROMAN LEGIONS (1958), pp. 16, 251.

*after his time. Nothing but commendation can be given to his insistence on the value of reserves, though his tactical method is hardly practicable.*

*Like certain more recent theorists, he emphasizes the importance of battle. Success or failure there can negate everything else. But unlike some proponents of the offensive, he will have his general fight only when he can hope to succeed, and will advise him to avoid battle if he can gain the results he wishes without fighting.*

*His opposition to the mercenary system is complete. The hired soldier cannot be well chosen and is likely not to fight; if he does fight and win, he is as dangerous to his employer as the enemy would have been. Only an army of citizens or subjects, loyal because well governed, is a secure defense.*

*So the farther Machiavelli goes from the details of war and the more he considers its political connections, the more stimulating he is. His picture of the commanding general, though in part derived from his reading, is presented with conviction, inasmuch as that general is actually the Machiavellian man of* virtù, *brave, wise and with a sense of responsibility for the happiness of the citizens of his native land.*]

# THE ART OF WAR

PREFACE BY NICCOLÒ MACHIAVELLI, FLORENTINE SECRETARY AND CITI⁄ZEN, FOR THE BOOK OF THE ART OF WAR, TO LORENZO DI FILIPPO STROZ⁄ZI, FLORENTINE PATRICIAN

*[Dedication; military habits; lessons from antiquity]*

In the past, Lorenzo, many have held and now still hold this opinion: that no two things are more out of harmony with one another or differ more from one another than civilian life and mili⁄tary life. Because of this we often see one who plans to excel in the soldier's calling at once not merely changing his dress, but also in habits, manners, voice and presence departing widely from every civilian custom, because he does not believe that civilian dress can be worn by one who strives to be active and ready for any and every violent deed. Nor can civilian habits and manners be used by one who thinks those habits effeminate and those manners not helpful in his activities; nor does it seem suitable for him to retain normal bearing and speech when with his beard and his curses he intends to make other men afraid. This makes the opinion I have mentioned seem in these times very true. But if we consider ancient ways, we shall not find things that are more closely united, more in con⁄formity, and of which one, necessarily, so much loves the other as do these,[1] because all the arts that are provided for in a state for the sake of the common good of men, all the statutes made in it so that men will live in fear of the laws and of God, would be vain if for them there were not provided defenses, which when well ordered, preserve them, even though they themselves are not well ordered. And so, on the contrary, good customs, without military support, suffer the same sort of injury as do the rooms of a splendid and kingly palace, even though ornamented with gems and gold, when, not being roofed over, they have nothing to protect them from the rain. And if

1. *Civil and military life.*

for every other order of men in cities and kingdoms every diligence should be used to keep them faithful, peaceful, and full of the fear of God, in the army it should be redoubled. Because from what man ought his native land to expect greater fidelity than from that one who has to promise to die for her? In whom ought there to be more love of peace than in him who can get nothing but injury from war? In whom ought there to be more fear of God than in a man who every day, being exposed to countless perils, has great need for his aid? This necessity, well considered both by those who give laws to empires and by those who are put in charge of military training, would bring it about that the life of soldiers would be praised by other men and with great zeal followed and imitated. But since military customs are wholly corrupted and have greatly diverged from ancient methods, about them have sprung up injurious opin, ions, which make everybody hate soldiering and avoid association with those who engage in it.

But judging from what I have seen and read that it is not impos, sible to bring military practice back to ancient methods and to restore some of the forms of earlier excellence, and wishing not to pass these my times of leisure without doing something, I have determined, for the pleasure of those who love ancient deeds, to write out what I have learned about the art of war. And though it is a rash thing to treat material with which one has not dealt professionally, nonethe, less, I do not believe I err in holding with words alone an office that many, with greater presumption, have held with actions, because the errors I make as I write can without damage to anybody be cor, rected; but those which the others make as they act cannot be recognized except through the ruin of their governments. You, then, Lorenzo, will consider the qualities of these labors of mine and give them, according to your judgment, such censure or such praise as you think they merit. These I send to you both to show that I am grateful—though my capability does not measure up to the benefits I have received from you—and also because, since it is the custom to honor with such works those who through nobility, riches, intelli, gence, and liberality shine brightly, I know that in riches and nobility you do not have many equals, in intelligence few, and in liberality none.

## BOOK 1. [*THE CITIZEN SOLDIER*]

### [*Cosimo Rucellai*]

Because I believe that without censure every man can be praised after his death, since all cause and suspicion of flattery have disappeared, I shall not hesitate to praise our Cosimo Rucellai, whose name I shall never remember without tears, since I have observed in him those qualities strongly desired in a good friend by his friends and in a citizen by his native city. I do not know what possession was so much his (not excepting, to go no further, his soul) that for his friends he would not willingly have spent it; I do not know of any undertaking that would have frightened him, if in it he had perceived the good of his native land. And I confess, freely, that I have never met, among all the men I have known and dealt with, a man whose spirit was more on fire for things grand and magnificent. At his death he complained to his friends of nothing except that he was born to die young in his own house, and unhonored, without according to his desire having assisted anyone, because he knew that nothing else could be said of him than that he died a good friend. It does not for that reason follow, however, even though deeds did not appear, that we, and any others who like ourselves knew him, cannot put faith in his praiseworthy qualities. Still it is true that to him Fortune was not so hostile that he did not leave some short record of his active intelligence, which appears in some love poems of his; for though he was not in love, yet in order not to waste his time until Fortune should lead him on to higher activities, in his youth he exercised himself in such writings. From these we learn with certainty how aptly he would have set forth his conceptions, and how much fame he would have won in poetry if he had practiced it as his chief interest. Since, then, Fortune has deprived us of association with so able a friend, I know we can find no other recourse than as much as possible to enjoy his memory and to repeat whatever he said with keenness or discussed with wisdom.

### [*The discussion in Cosimo's gardens*]

Because there is nothing of his fresher than the discussion which in very recent times Lord Fabrizio Colonna carried on with him in his gardens (for that gentleman held forth at length on military affairs and Cosimo keenly and wisely asked a great many questions), it has seemed good to me, since I, with some other friends, was present, to put it on record. Thereby the friends of Cosimo who were there assembled can, as they read, refresh their recollection of his excellent qualities. Any others will on the one hand have to regret that they were not there; on the other, they can learn many things useful not merely in military but in civilian life—sagely discussed by a very sagacious man.

### [*Fabrizio and his audience*]

I say, then, that when Fabrizio Colonna returned from Lombardy, where he had long been campaigning for the Catholic King with great glory to himself, he decided, as he was passing through Florence, to rest some days in that city in order to visit His Excellency the Duke and to see again some gentlemen with whom in the past he had been acquainted. Hence Cosimo thought it proper to invite him to a banquet in his gardens, not so much to exercise his own liberality as to have a reason for speaking with him at length, and from him hearing and learning various things such as from a man of that sort can be hoped for, since it seemed to Cosimo a chance to spend a day in talking about those matters that brought satisfaction to his own spirit. So Fabrizio came as Cosimo wished and was received by him along with other faithful friends, among whom were Zanobi Buondelmonti, Batista della Palla and Luigi Alamanni, all young men loved by him and zealous in the same studies, whose good qualities, because every day and every hour they are their own praise, we shall omit. Fabrizio, then, according to the times and the place, was by all of them honored with the greatest possible honors.

### [*The ancients to be imitated in vigor*]

But when the pleasures of the banquet were over, and the tables were cleared and every sort of festivity had been concluded—something that in the presence of noble men whose minds are intent on honorable thoughts is concluded quickly—since the day was long and the heat great, Cosimo thought that in order better to satisfy his desire it would be well, using the excuse of escaping the heat, to go to the most secluded and shady part of his garden. When they had arrived there and taken seats, some on the grass, which is very fresh in that place, some on the seats arranged in those spots under the shade of very tall trees, Fabrizio praised the spot as delightful, and observing the trees closely and failing to recognize some of them, he was puzzled. Observing this, Cosimo said: "You perhaps do not know some of these trees; but do not think it strange, because some of them were more renowned by the ancients than today they are by common custom." And having told him their names and how Bernardo his grandfather had busied himself with such cultivation, he was answered by Fabrizio: "I was thinking that it might be as you say, and this place and this avocation were making me remember some princes of the Kingdom, to whom these ancient plantings and shades give pleasure." And pausing in his remarks at this point and sitting for a while as though inwardly intent on something, he added: "If I thought I should not give offense, I would tell you my opinion of it, but I do not believe I shall offend, since I am speaking with friends, and in order to discuss things and not in order to censure them. How much better they would have done (be it said with due respect to all) to seek to be like the ancients in things strong and rough, not in those delicate and soft, and in those that are done in the sun, not in the shade, and to take their methods from an antiquity that is true and perfect, not from that which is false and corrupt, because as soon as activities of this sort satisfied my Romans, my native land went to ruin." To which Cosimo replied—But to escape the bother of having to repeat so many times *He said* and *The other answered*, I shall give only the name of him who speaks, without repeating anything else. So then said

*[Men imitating antiquity would be thought peculiar]*

COSIMO. You have opened the way to a discussion that I was wishing for, and I pray you to speak without reservation, because without reservation I shall question you. And if in asking or replying I excuse or accuse anybody, it will not be for the sake of excuse or accusation but to learn from you the truth.

FABRIZIO. And I shall be very glad to tell you what I under⁄ stand of all you ask; as to whether it be true or not, I shall resign myself to your judgment. And to me it will be pleasant to have you ask, because I am just as ready to learn from you when you ask as you are from me when I answer, because many times a wise questioner makes one consider many things and come to know many others, which, if one had not been asked about, one would never have known.

COSIMO. I wish to turn to what you said first, that my grand' father and those princes of yours would have been wiser to imitate the ancients in things harsh rather than in those delicate; but I wish to offer excuse for my side, because I shall leave the excusing of the other to you. I do not believe there was, in his times, any man who so much detested soft living as he did and was such a lover of that severe life you praise. Yet he realized that neither in his own person nor in those of his children could he follow it, because he was born in an age so corrupt, in which one who wished to depart from the usual habit would be defamed and spoken against by everybody. Because if a naked man, in the summer, under the midday sun should stretch out on the sand, or in the winter in the coldest months on the snow, as Diogenes did, he would be thought crazy. If any' one, like the Spartans, should bring up his children in the country, should make them sleep in the open air, go with their heads and their feet bare, bathe in cold water, in order to bring them to be able to bear distress and to make them have less affection for life and less fear of death, he would be mocked and held to be rather an animal than a man. If anyone also fed on vegetables and despised gold, like Fabricius, he would be praised by few and followed by none. Hence, dismayed by our methods of living at present, he abandoned the ancients, yet whenever he could without causing great astonish' ment imitate antiquity, he did so.

### [The Romans to be imitated in public affairs]

FABRIZIO. You have excused him in this matter with great vigor, and certainly you speak the truth. But I was not referring so much to those severe methods of living as to other methods, more humane and more in harmony with the life of today, which I do not believe that one counted among the leading men of a city would find it difficult to introduce. I shall never depart, in giving examples of anything, from my Romans. If we consider their life and the organization of their republic, we shall see there many things not impossible for introduction into any state in which there is still left something good.

COSIMO. What are these things you would like to introduce that are like the ancient ones?

FABRIZIO. To honor and reward excellence, not to despise poverty, to esteem the methods and regulations of military discipline, to oblige the citizens to love one another, to live without factions, to esteem private less than public good, and other like things that could easily fit in with our times. About these customs, it is not difficult to be persuaded when one thinks about them enough and takes them up in the right way, because in them so plainly can be seen the truth that every public-spirited nature is capable of receiving. He who accomplishes such a thing plants trees beneath the shade of which mankind lives more prosperously and more happily than beneath this shade.

COSIMO. I do not intend to reply to what you have said in any way, but I wish to let the decision about it be turned over to those who easily can judge it; and I shall direct my speech to you who blame those who in serious and great actions do not imitate the ancients, believing that in this way my intention will be more easily fulfilled. I should like, then, to learn from you why it is that on one side you condemn those who in their acts do not imitate the ancients, and that on the other, in war, which is your profession and in which you are considered excellent, we do not see that you have used any ancient methods, or any showing some likeness to them.

### [Ancient example for warfare]

FABRIZIO. You have appeared just where I expected you, because my speech did not deserve any other question, nor was there any other that I desired. And though I might acquit myself with an easy excuse, nevertheless, for my own greater satisfaction and yours, since the time is propitious, I wish to enter into a longer discussion. Men who wish to do anything ought first with all diligence to make preparations, in order that when an occasion comes, they may be ready to carry out what they have intended beforehand to do. And because when preparations are made cautiously they are not known about, no man can be accused of any negligence, if his plan is not revealed before that occasion. But when it comes, if nothing is done, he appears as not having prepared himself enough to be adequate or as in some respect not having made decisions. Because no occasion has come to me for showing the preparations I have made for bringing the soldiers back into their ancient courses, if I have not brought them back, neither by you nor by others can I be censured. I believe this excuse enough for a reply to your accusation.

COSIMO. It would be enough, if I were sure the occasion had not come.

FABRIZIO. But because I know that you can doubt whether this occasion has come or not, I intend, if you are willing patiently to listen, to discuss at length what sort of preparations must be made beforehand, what sort of occasion has to arise, what sort of difficulty keeps the preparations from being effective and the occasion from coming, and how this thing at the same instant, though the terms seem contrary, is very difficult and very easy to do.

COSIMO. You cannot do, both for me and for these others, a thing more pleasing than this, and if it is not irksome for you to speak, never will it be irksome for us to hear. But because this discourse must be long, I want aid from these friends of mine, with your permission; and they and I beg from you one thing: that you will not be annoyed if sometimes we interrupt you with some urgent question.

FABRIZIO. I am very willing that you, Cosimo, and these other young men should here question me, because I believe that your youth makes you more interested in military matters and readier to believe what I shall say. Men of another age, with their hair white and the blood in their bodies turned to ice, are commonly some of them enemies of war, some beyond correction, believing that the times and not bad customs force men to live thus. So ask questions of me, all of you, with assurance and without hesitation; this I wish both because it will give me a little rest and because I shall be glad not to leave in your minds any uncertainty.

## [*Professional soldiers cannot be good men*]

I wish to begin with your words, in which you said to me that in war, which is my profession, I have not used any ancient methods. On this I say that because this is a profession by means of which men cannot live virtuously at all times, it cannot be practiced as a pro-fession except by a republic or a kingdom; and neither of these, when they have been well regulated, has ever allowed one of its citizens or subjects to practice it as a profession, nor has any good man ever engaged in it as his special profession. Because he will never be reckoned a good man who carries on an occupation in which, if he is to endeavor at all times to get income from it, he must be rapacious, fraudulent, violent, and must have many qualities which of necessity make him not good; nor can men who practice it as a profession, the big as well as the little, be of any other sort, because this profession does not support them in time of peace. Hence they are obliged either to hope that there will be no peace, or to become so rich in time of war that in peace they can support themselves. And neither one of these two expectations is to be found in a good man, because from the desire to support themselves at all times come the robberies, the deeds of violence, the murderous acts that such soldiers commit as much against their friends as against their enemies; and from not wishing peace come the deceits that the generals practice against those by whom they are employed, in order that a war may last; and if peace does come, it often happens that the generals, being deprived of their stipends and of their living, lawlessly set up their ensigns as soldiers of fortune and without any mercy plunder a region.

*[Mercenary soldiers by example]*

Is it not in your historical records that when there were many soldiers in Italy without pay because the wars were finished, several groups joined together, which were called Companies, and kept exacting money from the cities and plundering the country, and there was no remedy? Have you not read how the Carthaginian soldiers, at the end of the first war they had with the Romans, under Matho and Spendius, two leaders rebelliously chosen by them, waged a more dangerous war against the Carthaginians than the one they had finished with the Romans? In the time of our fathers, Francesco Sforza, in order to be able to live sumptuously in times of peace, not merely deceived the Milanese by whom he was employed, but took away their liberty and became their prince. Like him have been all the other soldiers of Italy who have practiced warfare as their personal profession, and if they have not, by means of their evil deeds, become dukes of Milan, they merit so much the more to be blamed, because without so much gain, they all, if you examine their lives, have the same faults. Sforza, the father of Francesco, forced Queen Giovanna to throw herself into the arms of the King of Aragon, having suddenly abandoned her and left her unarmed in the midst of her enemies, merely to satisfy his ambition or to exact money from her or to take away her kingdom. Braccio, with the same efforts, tried to occupy the Kingdom of Naples, and if he had not been defeated and killed at Aquila, would have succeeded. Such outrages do not come from anything else than that there have been men who practiced the trade of the soldier as their special profession. Do you not have a proverb reinforcing my reasons that runs: "War makes thieves and peace hangs them?" Because those who do not know how to live by any other occupation and do not find anybody who will support them in soldiering and do not have so much ability that they can join together to carry out an honorable villainy, are forced by necessity to rob on the highway, and justice is forced to wipe them out.

### [*The professional general may become a tyrant*]

COSIMO. For me, you have made this profession of the soldier become almost nothing, and I had thought it the most excellent and the most honorable there could be. Hence, if you do not explain it better, I shall not be satisfied, because, if it is as you say, I do not know whence comes the glory of Caesar, of Pompey, of Scipio, of Marcellus, and of so many Roman generals whom fame praises as though they were gods.

FABRIZIO. I have not yet finished discussing all that I have laid out, for there were two things: one, that a good man is not able to carry on this activity as his profession; the second, that a well-ordered republic or kingdom would never permit her subjects and her citizens to make it their profession. About the first I have said all that has occurred to me. It remains for me to speak of the second, in which I shall arrive at an answer to this last question of yours. So I say that Pompey and Caesar and almost all the Roman generals after the last Carthaginian war gained fame as brave men but not as good ones, while those who lived before them gained fame as brave and good. This came about because the latter did not take the waging of war for their profession, and those I first named did practice it as their profession. And while the republic continued without reproach, no great citizen ever presumed, by means of such an activity, to retain power in time of peace, so as to break the laws, plunder the provinces, usurp and tyrannize over his native land and in every way gain wealth for himself. Nor did anybody of low estate dream of violating his oath, forming parties with private citizens, ceasing to fear the Senate, or carrying out any tyrannical injury in order to live at all times by means of warfare as a profession. But the generals, satisfied with their triumph, eagerly returned to private life; and those who were privates laid down their arms with greater eagerness than they took them up, and each one turned to the occupation by means of which he had supported his life. Nor was there ever anybody who hoped by plunder and by means of this profession to make his living. About this one can make, as to the great citizens, an obvious inference by means of Regulus Attilius, who, when he was general of the Roman armies in Africa and had almost conquered the Carthaginians, asked from the Senate leave to return home to take care of his fields, which were ruined by his laborers. From this it is clearer than sunlight that if he had practiced war as his profession and by means of that had expected to gain profit, he would not, when he had as booty so many provinces, have asked leave to return to take care of his fields, because every day he would have gained more than the value of all of them.

### [*A well-governed state has only citizen soldiers*]

But because these good men, who did not practice war as their profession, did not expect to get from it anything except labor, peril, and fame, when they were famous enough, they wished to come home and live by their profession. As to the men of low rank and the mass of soldiers, it is evidently true that each one was in the same condition, for everyone gladly left such a pursuit and, when he was not soldiering, was willing to be a soldier, and when he was soldiering, wanted to be dismissed. This is verified in many ways, and especially because among the chief privileges the Roman people gave to a citizen was that he would not be forced against his will to serve as a soldier. Rome, then, while she was well governed (which was up to the time of the Gracchi) did not have any soldier who took up this pursuit as his profession, and for that reason she had few bad ones, and all of those were severely punished. A well-ordered city will then decree that this practice of warfare shall be used in times of peace for exercise and in times of war for necessity and for glory, and will allow the public alone to practice it as a profession, as did Rome. Any citizen who in such an activity has another purpose is not a good citizen, and any city that conducts itself otherwise is not well governed.

## [*Kings should find soldiers among their subjects*]

COSIMO. I am well pleased and satisfied with what you have said up to now and am much gratified with this conclusion you have drawn, and so far as it deals with a republic, I believe it is true, but as to a king, I do not at all know, because I should suppose a king would wish to have around him those who would especially take as their profession this pursuit.

FABRIZIO. So much the more will a well-governed kingdom avoid such professionals, because they alone are the ruin of its king and are altogether servants of tyranny. Do not bring up to me in reply any kingdom of the present. I shall deny that they are well-governed kingdoms, because the kingdoms that have good laws do not give absolute command to their king except in their armies; in this place alone sudden decision is necessary, so in it there must be one and only one authority. In other things he cannot do anything without consultation, and they are obliged to fear—those who give him advice—that he will have somebody near him who in time of peace will desire war, being unable to get his living without it.

But I wish to carry this matter a little further and not to seek out a kingdom wholly good but one like those that exist today, where likewise the king needs to be afraid of those who for their profession take warfare, because the might of armies, without any doubt, is their infantry. Hence if a king does not manage in such a way that his infantrymen in time of peace are glad to return home and live by their occupations, he will necessarily be ruined, because there is no more dangerous infantry than that composed of men who carry on war as their profession, because you are obliged either to make war always,[2] or to pay them always, or to be subject to the danger that they will deprive you of your kingdom. To make war always is not possible; to pay them always is not possible; so necessarily you run into danger of losing your power.

## [*When Rome turned to professional soldiers, she fell*]

My Romans, as I have said, while they were wise and good, never allowed their citizens to take this pursuit as their profession, notwithstanding that they would have been able to support them at all times, because at all times they made war. But to avoid the injury that

2. *For a moment, Machiavelli addresses the prince directly.*

could be done them by this continual employment, since the times did not vary, they varied the men, and they observed the time in such a way for their legions that always in fifteen years they had renewed them; and thus they made use of men in the flower of their lives, that is, from eighteen to thirty-five years, a time in which the legs, the hands and the eye are in harmony with one another, nor did they wait until their vigor decreased and their malice increased, as later they did in corrupt times. Because Octavian first and then Tiberius, thinking more about their own power than about the public advantage, began to disarm the Roman people in order to command them more easily and to keep those same armies continually on the frontiers of the Empire. And because they still did not judge that they would be enough to hold in check the Roman people and Senate, they set up an army called Praetorian, which remained near the walls of Rome and was like a castle over that city. Because they then freely began to allow men chosen for those armies to practice soldiering as their profession, these men soon became arrogant, so that they were dangerous to the Senate and harmful to the Emperor. The result was that many emperors were killed through the arrogance of the soldiers, who gave the Empire to whom they chose, and took it away; sometimes it happened that at the same time there were many emperors established by various armies. From these things resulted, first, division of the Empire, and finally its ruin.

[*Good soldiers wish to return to peaceful pursuits*]

Hence kings, if they wish to live securely, make up their infantry of men who, when it is time to make war, gladly for love of them go into it, and when peace comes, more gladly return home—which will always happen when a king selects men who know how to live by some other profession than this. So he must see to it that when peace comes his chief men return to rule their peoples, his gentlemen to the management of their property, and the infantry to their individual occupations. Each one of these will gladly make war in order to have peace, and will not seek to disturb the peace in order to have war.

[*Few soldiers find military employment in time of peace*]

COSIMO. Truly this reasoning of yours seems to me well considered. Nevertheless, since it is almost opposite to what I have up to now supposed, my mind is still not purged of every doubt, be, cause I see many lords and gentlemen support themselves in time of peace by means of the pursuits of war, such as those like yourself who receive pay from princes and from republics. I see also almost all the men-at-arms steadily getting their pay. I see that there are many infantrymen in the garrisons of cities and fortresses. Hence it seems to me that there is a place, in time of peace, for everybody.

FABRIZIO. I do not believe you believe that in time of peace everyone has his place, because, supposing that no other reason could be brought forward, the small number of all those who remain in the places mentioned by you would answer you. What fraction of the infantry needed in war are those used in time of peace? Be, cause the fortresses and the cities that are guarded in time of peace, in war are guarded much more; and to them are to be added the soldiers kept in the field, of which there are a large number, all of whom in peace are dismissed. And as to governmental garrisons, a small number, Pope Julius and you have shown to everybody how much to be feared are those not willing to carry on any other occupation than war; such men because of their arrogance you have rejected from your garrisons, and you have put there Switzers, since they were born and brought up under laws and chosen by their free states, with genuine selection. So hereafter you will not say that in peace there is a place for every man. As to the men-at-arms, since all of them in peace continue to get their pay, any solution of their case seems more difficult. Nevertheless, he who carefully considers the whole finds the answer easy, because this way of keeping the men-at, arms is a method that is corrupt and not good. The reason is that they are men who make war their profession, and every day they would cause a thousand disorders in the states where they are, if supported by a body of sufficient size; but since they are few and unable by themselves to make up an army, they are not so often able to cause grave damage. Nevertheless they have done it many times, as I explained to you about Francesco, and Sforza his father, and Braccio da Perugia. So as to this custom of retaining men-at-arms, I do not approve of it, for it is corrupt and can cause serious troubles.

### [*The citizen army*]

COSIMO. Would you plan to do without them, or, if you re, tained them, how would you plan to retain them?

FABRIZIO. By the method of the citizen army; not like that of the King of France, because that is dangerous and unjust like ours, but like that of the ancients, who raised cavalry from their subjects and in time of peace sent them to their homes to live by their occupations, as I shall set forth more at length before this discussion is over. So if now this part of the army is able to live by military activity, even though there is peace, it comes from corrupt method. As to the pay that is reserved for me and the other leaders, I say that this in the same way is a very corrupt method, because a wise republic would not be giving it to anybody; on the contrary it ought to use its citizens as leaders in war, and in time of peace have them return to their professions. So, too, a wise king either ought not to give such pay, or if he does give it, the causes should be either that it is reward for noble deeds or that he wishes to make use of a man as much in peace as in war.

Because you bring up my case, I wish to use myself as an example. I say that I have never practiced war as my profession, because my profession is to govern my subjects and to defend them, and, in order to be able to defend them, to love peace and to know how to make war. And my king rewards me and esteems me not so much because I understand war as because I also can advise him in peace. No king, then, ought to allow around himself anyone who is not of my sort, if he is wise and intends to conduct himself prudently, because if he has around him either too great lovers of peace or too great lovers of war, they will make him err. I cannot, in this my first discourse and according to my proposals, speak further on this; and if what I have said is not enough for you, you must find somebody who will satisfy you better. You can at least see how difficult it is to bring ancient methods back into present wars, and what sort of preparations a wise man ought to make and what opportunities he can hope for that will let him carry them out. But you will gradually understand these things better, if the discourse does not weary you, as we compare some parts of the ancient ways with modern methods.

### [*The importance of battle in war*]

COSIMO. If at the beginning we wished to hear you discuss these things, truly what up to now you have said of them has redoubled our desire; so we thank you for what we have had, and for the remainder we ask.

FABRIZIO. Since you are pleased to have it so, I intend to start my treatment of this material at the beginning, so that it may be better understood, for it is possible by that method to explain more at length. The purpose of him who wishes to make war is to be able to fight with any enemy in the field and to be able to win a battle. If he expects to do this, it is necessary to draw up an army. In order to draw up the army, it is necessary to find men, to arm them, to organize them, to train them both in small and in large bodies, to furnish them with quarters, and at last, either by remaining quiet or by marching, to bring them into the enemy's presence. These affairs comprise all the labor of field warfare, which is the most necessary and the most honored. In a man who well understands how to offer battle to the enemy, the other errors he may make in affairs of war will be bearable; but he who lacks this knowledge, though in other particulars he may be very able, will never carry on a war with honor, because a single battle that you win cancels all your other bad actions. So in the same way if you lose one, all the good things you have earlier done have no value.

### [*The selection of citizen soldiers*]

Since then the men must first be found, it is necessary to come to their selection, for so the ancients called it. We call it drafting, but in order to call it by a name more honored, I wish us to keep for it the name of selection. It is the opinion of those who have given rules for warfare that men should be chosen from temperate countries, in order that they may have spirit and prudence, because a hot country produces the prudent but not the spirited, a cold one the spirited but not the prudent. This rule is well given to one who is prince of all the world and therefore has the opportunity to take men from such places as seem good to him. But if we wish to give a rule that anybody will be able to use, we must say that every republic and every kingdom must draw its soldiers from its own countries, hot or cold or temperate as they happen to be. Because ancient examples show that in every country training can produce good soldiers, because where nature fails, the lack can be supplied by ingenuity, which in this case is more important than nature. And choosing them in other places is not to be called selection, because selection means taking the best from a region and having power to choose those who are not willing as well as those who are willing to serve. It is not, however, possible to make this selection except in places subject to you, because you cannot get those you wish in lands that are not yours, but you must take those who are willing.

COSIMO. Yet it is possible, even among those willing to come, to choose some and to omit some; and therefore it can be called selection.

FABRIZIO. You speak the truth to a certain extent. But consider the defects that such selection has in itself, because many times we even discern that it is not selection. The first thing: those who are not your subjects and who serve willingly are not the best but rather the worst of a region; because if any there are of bad reputation, lazy, uncontrolled, without religion, fugitives from the authority of their fathers, swearers, gamblers, in every way badly brought up, they are the ones who are willing to serve as soldiers. Such habits are as contrary as possible to true and good soldiership. When so many such men offer themselves to you that they exceed the number you have designated, you can choose them, but when the material is bad, the selection cannot be good. Yet many times there are not enough to make up the number of which you have need, so that, since you are forced to take them all, it can no longer be called making a selection, but hiring infantry. With this bad method are formed today the armies in Italy and elsewhere, except in Germany, because nobody is hired by command of the prince but according to the desire of him who wishes to serve. Consider, then, what methods of these ancient armies can now be introduced into an army of men brought together in such a way.

COSIMO. What way can be used, then?

FABRIZIO. The one I mentioned: to select them from the prince's subjects and by his authority.

COSIMO. Among those thus selected can some ancient methods be introduced?

FABRIZIO. You well know there could, if he who commanded them were their prince or accustomed lord, in a principate, or if he were a citizen and for the time a general, in a republic. Otherwise it is difficult to do anything good.

COSIMO. Why?

FABRIZIO. I shall tell you in time. For the present I wish this to be enough for you: namely, that it is not possible to work well in any other way.

### [*The soldier's qualifications*]

COSIMO. Since, then, he must make this selection in his own lands, whence do you judge it would be better to draw them, from the city or from the country?

FABRIZIO. Those who have written on this all agree that it is better to draw them from the country, since they will be men used to hardships; brought up to labor; accustomed to being in the sun, to avoiding the shade; able to use tools, to dig a ditch, to carry a burden, and to be without guile and without malice. But in this matter my opinion would be that since those employed are of two sorts, foot and horse, those on foot should be chosen from the country, and those on horseback from the cities.

COSIMO. At what age would you take them?

FABRIZIO. I should take them, when I had to raise a new army, from seventeen to forty years; when it was established and I had to renew it, at seventeen always.

COSIMO. I do not well understand this distinction.

FABRIZIO. I shall tell you. If I had to set up an army where there was none, it would be necessary to choose all those men who were most apt, if only they were of military age, so that they could be trained, as I shall explain. But when I should have to make a selection in places where this army had been set up, as additional soldiers I should take those seventeen years old, because the older men would already be selected and enrolled.

### [*The efficiency of a citizen army*]

COSIMO. Then you would wish to set up a citizen army like that in our lands.

FABRIZIO. You are right. It is true that I should arm them, officer them, train them, and organize them in a way that I think may not be that in which you have organized them.

COSIMO. Then you praise the citizen army?

FABRIZIO. Why do you suppose I would condemn it?

COSIMO. Because many wise men have always found fault with it.

FABRIZIO. It is a contradiction to say that a wise man finds fault with the citizen army. He can indeed be thought wise and be misjudged.

COSIMO. The bad showing it has always made will make us hold to such an opinion.

FABRIZIO. Beware that the defect is not yours rather than its, as you will recognize before we finish this discussion.

COSIMO. You will do something most acceptable. Still I wish to tell you in what respect these men find fault with it, in order that you may be better able to provide its defense. This is what they say: either it will be useless, and to trust ourselves to it will make us lose our power; or it will be effective, and by means of it he who controls it can easily take away our power. They bring up the Romans, who, by means of these forces of their own, lost their liberty. They bring up the Venetians and the King of France, of whom the first, in order not to have to obey one of their citizens, made use of the forces of others; and the King has disarmed his people in order to be able more easily to command them. But they fear uselessness much more than this. For this uselessness they bring up two principal reasons. One is that the men are inexperienced; the other is that they are made to serve by force; because they say that things are not thoroughly learned, and that by force nothing is ever done well.

FABRIZIO. All these reasons you speak of are from men who understand only things that are not far off, as I shall plainly show you. And first, as to the uselessness, I tell you that no military force can be employed that is more useful than one's own, and that one cannot provide one's own army except in this way. And since this gives no possibility for debate, I do not intend to waste time on it, because all the examples of ancient history are with us. And because they bring up inexperience and force, I say it is true that inexperience produces lack of courage, and force produces discontent. But they can be made to gain courage and experience by means of the method of arming them, exercising them, and organizing them, as in the progress of this discourse you will see. But as to force, you must understand that when men are brought into military service on the command of the prince, they will come to it not altogether through force nor altogether voluntarily, because free will alone would cause all the difficulties I spoke of above: namely, that there would not be a selection and there would be few who would go; and likewise pure force would produce evil results. Therefore one ought to take a mid/dle course, in which there would not be force alone nor free will alone, but the men will be so influenced by respect for their prince that they will fear his anger more than immediate inconvenience. And it will always happen that this will be a force mixed with free will in such a way that from it will not arise such discontent as to produce bad effects. I do not at all mean by this that such an army cannot be beaten, because the Roman armies were beaten many times, and the army of Hannibal was beaten, so one can see that an army cannot be organized of which anybody can promise that it never will be defeated. Hence these wise men of yours ought not to measure the uselessness of this army by its having lost once but should believe that just as it loses, so it can conquer and remove the cause of the loss. And if they investigate this situation, they will find that it has not resulted from a defect in method, but from the organization's not having been made perfect. And as I have said, they ought to provide for it not by finding fault with the citizen army but by improving it. How this is to be done you will learn as we proceed.

### [*A citizen army not an instrument of tyranny*]

As to fearing that such an organization may take your state from you by means of one who will be made head of it, I answer that weapons borne by citizens or subjects, given by the laws and well regulated, never do damage; on the contrary they are always an advantage, and cities keep themselves uncorrupted longer by means of those weapons than without them. So Rome was free four hundred years and was armed; Sparta, eight hundred; many other cities have been unarmed and have been free less than forty years. Because cities have need of armies; when they do not have their own forces, they hire foreigners; and foreign forces sooner do injury to the public welfare than native ones, because they are easier to bribe, and a citizen who is trying to become powerful can sooner avail himself of them; and to some extent he has material easier to deal with, since he is to oppress men who are unarmed. Besides this, a city ought to fear two enemies more than one. A city that makes use of foreign armies fears at once the foreigner she hires and the citizen, and as to this fear being necessary, remember what I said a little earlier about Francesco Sforza. A city that uses its own forces, fears only its own citizen. But among all the reasons that can be given, I wish this to serve me: namely, that never did anybody establish a republic or a kingdom who did not suppose that the same persons who inhabited it would need with their weapons to defend it.

[*The mistake of the Venetians in abandoning a citizen army*]

And if the Venetians had been wise in this, as in all their other regulations, they would have made a new monarchy in the world. They deserve blame so much the more in that by their first lawgivers they were armed. But since they did not have territory on the land, they were armed on the sea, where they waged their wars effectively, and with arms in their hands they strengthened their native city. But when there came a time in which they had to make war on land to defend Vicenza, in a case where they should have sent a citizen of theirs to fight on land, they hired for their general the marquis of Mantua. This was that ill-fated decision that cut off from them their legs for climbing to the sky and becoming great. And if they made it because, although they knew how to make war on the sea, they believed they should not trust themselves to make it on land, it was lack of trust that was not wise, because it is easier for a sea captain, accustomed to fighting with the winds, with the waters and with men, to become a land captain, who needs to fight with men alone, than it is for a land captain to become a sea captain. And my Romans, knowing how to fight on the land and not on the sea, when they came to war with the Carthaginians, who were powerful on the sea, did not hire Greeks or Spaniards familiar with the sea but imposed that duty on the citizens whom they were in the habit of sending on land, and they won. If the Venetians did it in order that one of their citizens should not become a tyrant, their fear was unreasonable because, in addition to the arguments on this matter that I mentioned a little earlier, if a citizen with sea forces had never become tyrant of a city lying on the sea, so much the less could he do so with land forces. Therefore they should have realized that arms in the hands of citizens could not turn them into tyrants over the city, but that bad measure of government, fitting a city for tyranny, can do so. And since they had a good government, they did not need to fear their armies. They chose, therefore, an imprudent plan, which has caused them the loss of much glory and much prosperity. As to the error that the King of France makes in not keeping his people disciplined for war (which those men of yours bring up as an instance), no man who lays aside his personal feeling will judge that such a policy is not a defect in that kingdom, for failure to attend to this matter is the one thing that makes her weak.

But I have made much too long a digression and perhaps have gone beyond my subject. Yet I have done it to answer you and to show you that no one can use as a foundation forces other than one's own, and that one's own forces can be organized in no other way than in a citizen army, nor in other ways can regulations for armies be introduced into any place, nor is there any other method for establishing a military system. If you read the regulations that those first kings established in Rome, and especially Servius Tullius, you will find that the arrangement of the classes is nothing else than a regulation permitting the rapid putting together of an army for the defense of that city.

### [More on the soldier's qualifications]

But let us turn to our selection. I say again that if I had to add to an old organization, I should take those of seventeen years of age; if I had to make a new one, I should take them of every age from seventeen to forty, in order to be able quickly to make use of them.

COSIMO. Would you make any distinction in the occupations from which you select them?

FABRIZIO. The writers I have mentioned do it, because they advise against the choice of falconers, fishermen, cooks, pimps, and whoever makes a business of providing pleasure; but they hold that one should take, in addition to tillers of the soil, smiths, horseshoers, carpenters, butchers, hunters, and the like. But I should make little distinction between them, with respect to guessing from the occupation the goodness of the man, but I surely would with respect to being able to use him with most profit. And for this reason the countrymen who are used to tilling the soil are more valuable than any others, because of all occupations this is most used in armies. After these are the smiths, carpenters, horseshoers, masons, of whom it is useful to have plenty because their skills can be applied to many things, and it is a very good thing to have a soldier from whom you get double service.

COSIMO. What indicates those who are or are not fit for military service?

FABRIZIO. I intend to speak of the manner of choosing a new levy in order later to make an army of it, because partly it is the same thing as discussing the selection that is made at the renewal of an old organization. I say, then, that the goodness of one whom you have to choose as a soldier is known either through experience, by means of some gallant deed of his, or through conjecture. Evidence of fitness cannot be found in men who are selected for the first time and who have never before been selected, and few or none who have served before are found in citizen armies that are newly established. Yet in the lack of this experience, one must turn to conjecture, which is made from the men's age, their occupations, and their appearance. Of the first two I have spoken; it remains to speak of the third. And so I say that some have preferred that the soldier should be tall, among whom was Pyrrhus. Some others have chosen them only for their bodily strength, as Caesar did; such strength of body and of spirit can be conjectured from the make-up of the limbs and from the attractiveness of the expression. And therefore those who write about it say that it is well to have the eyes lively and bright, the neck sinewy, the chest broad, the arms muscular, the fingers long, the belly little, the hips round,[3] the calves and the feet lean; these qualities always make a man agile and strong, which are two things that in a soldier are desired above everything else. Above all there should be regard for the men's habits and their possession of honor and modesty; otherwise one who incites to discord and starts corruption may be chosen. No one believes that in miserable training and in a vile spirit can be found any quality in any way to be praised.

### [How the Romans selected soldiers]

It does not seem to me superfluous; on the contrary, I believe it is necessary, in order that you may understand better the importance of this selection, to tell you the method that the Roman consuls at the beginning of their magistracies observed in choosing the Roman legions; in their selection (since in those from whom they selected there was a mixture, caused by continual wars, of veterans and new men) they were able to proceed on the basis of experience among the old and conjecture among the new. And this should be noted: these men were selected either to be used at once, or to be trained at once and used in time of need. I have spoken and shall speak wholly of that which is levied to be used in time of need, because my intention is to show you that an army can be organized in countries where

---

3. *This renders Vegetius 1. 6:* exilior clunibus: *"rather lean in the hips."*

there is no military establishment; in these countries men cannot be chosen for immediate use. But in those where it is the custom to draft armies, and on the authority of the ruler, it is quite possible to have them for immediate service, as was to be seen at Rome and as can be seen today among the Swiss. Because among the chosen, if there are some new men, there are also so many of those accustomed to military organizations that, when the new and the old are mixed together, they make a body that is united and good. Notwith-standing, the emperors, when they began to keep the assignments of their soldiers permanent, put in charge of the new troops, whom they called *tirones*, a master to train them, as is seen in the life of Maxi-minus the Emperor. This business, while Rome was free, was carried on not in the armies but within the city. And since it was normal in the city to have military exercises in which the young men were trained, the result was that when later they were selected to go to war, they were so accustomed to sham military service that they easily could adapt themselves to the real. But when later the emperors abolished this training, they were obliged to use the methods I have explained to you.

So, coming to the Roman method of selection, I say that after the Roman consuls, on whom was laid the responsibility for war, had taken over the magistracy, in order to organize their armies (because it was the custom that each of them should have two legions of Romans, who were the might of their armies), they appointed twenty-four military tribunes, assigning six to each legion to carry on the duty today carried on by those we call constables. They then called an assembly of all the Roman men fit to bear arms and stationed the tribunes of each legion separate one from the other. Then by lot they drew the tribes from which the selection was first to be made, and from the tribe allotted they chose four of the best men, from whom was selected one by the tribunes of the first legion; from the other three, one was selected by the tribunes of the second legion; of the other two, one was chosen by the tribunes of the third; and the last one fell to the fourth legion. After these four, they chose four others, from which, first, one was selected by the tribunes of the second legion; the second by those of the third; the third by those of the fourth; the fourth man remained for the first. Then four more were chosen; the third legion chose the first; the fourth, the second; the first, the third; the fourth was left for the second; and so they varied in order this mode of selecting, so that the choice came out equal and the legions were uniform.

And as we said above, this levy could be made for immediate use, because it was made of men of whom a good part were tested in real military service and all of whom were trained in sham service; hence this choice could be made both by conjecture and by test. But where a military organization is to be set up anew, and therefore men must be chosen for a time of need, this selection can be made only by conjecture, derived from age and appearance.

### [The numbers and payment of citizen soldiers]

COSIMO. I fully believe that all you have said is true. But before you go on to further discussion, I wish to ask you about something you have made me remember, by saying that the levy that has to be made where men are not used to serving must be made by conjecture; therefore in many quarters I have heard our citizen army blamed, and especially as to the number, because many say that a smaller number should be taken; this would have the advantage that they would be better men and better chosen; so much annoyance would not be given to the men; it would be possible to give them some pay with which they would be more contented; and they could be better commanded. Hence I should like to learn your opinion in this matter, and whether you prefer the large number to the small one, and what methods you would take in selecting them in both numbers.

FABRIZIO. Without doubt the large number is better and more necessary than the small one; in fact, to put it better, where a large number cannot be organized, a perfect citizen army cannot be organized. I shall easily dispose of all the reasons given by those objectors. I say, then, first, that the smaller number, where there are plenty of people, as for example in Tuscany, does not secure better men or a more selective choice. Because if you wish, in selecting men, to judge them from experience, you find in that region very few whom experience has made probable choices, both because few of them have been in war, and because, of those few, very few have given a demonstration such that they deserve to be chosen rather than the others; he who has to select in such places must lay aside experience and take men by conjecture. Since one is brought, then, to such a necessity, I should like to find out, if there come before me twenty young men of good appearance, according to what rule I should take or leave anybody. Hence, without doubt, I believe that every man will admit that there will be a smaller error in taking them all to arm and train, since one cannot know which of them may be better, and in putting off the making of a more certain choice until later, when, by testing them in their training, those of more spirit and vitality will be recognized. So that, everything considered, in this case to choose a few of them in order to get better ones is all false.

As to making less inconvenience to the country and to the men, I say that the citizen army, whether large or small, makes no inconvenience, because this method does not take men from any of their affairs and does not tie them up so that they cannot carry on their business, since they are required to assemble for training on holidays only. This does no harm either to the country or to the men; on the contrary, it would please the young men, who on festival days now remain wretchedly idle in their usual resorts, because they would go with pleasure to these exercises, for since the managing of arms is a fine spectacle, young men enjoy it. As to ability to pay a smaller number, thereby keeping them more obedient and more contented, I answer that there cannot be an organization composed of so few men that they can be regularly paid in such a way that the payment will satisfy them. For instance if a military establishment of five thousand men is set up and they are paid to their satisfaction, they must receive at least ten thousand ducats a month. In the first place that number of infantry is not enough to make an army, and yet such expenditure is more than a state can bear. On the other hand, it is not enough to keep the men contented and under obligation so that they can be employed as the government wishes. Hence you would spend largely on such a policy and yet your forces would be small, insufficient either to defend you or to carry on any of your undertakings. If you give them more or take more of them, so much more difficult it will be for you to pay them. If you give them less or take a less number, so much less satisfied will they be, or so much less benefit will they bring you. Hence those who talk of organizing a citizen army and paying it while it is at home talk of things either impossible or useless. But of course it is necessary to pay them when they are raised in order to be led to war. Yet if such a levy should give to those who are enrolled in it some annoyances in times of peace (what they are I do not see), there are for recompense all the benefits that an ordered military force brings to a country, because without it nothing there is secure.

I conclude that he who wishes a small number in order to pay them, or because of any other of the reasons brought up by you, does not understand the matter. Another fact that supports my opinion is that always any number diminishes in your hands, because of the countless hindrances that men encounter, so that a small number will turn into nothing. Besides, if your citizen army is large, you can, as you choose, make use of the few or of the many. In addition to this, it has to serve you in reality and in reputation, and always you will get more reputation from a large number. Add to this that, since you organize citizen forces in order to keep the men trained, if you enlist a small number of men in many places, so distant are those enlisted from one another that you cannot without very great trouble to them assemble them for training. Without this training, the citizen army is useless, as will be explained in the proper place.

[*Does a citizen army cause disorder?*]

COSIMO. You have covered my question with what you have said. But I desire now that you clear up for me another doubt. These men say that such a multitude of armed men is likely to bring confusion, quarreling, and disorder to the country.

FABRIZIO. This is another worthless notion, for the reason I shall give you. Those chosen to bear arms can cause disorder in two ways: either among themselves or in opposition to others. These things can easily be prevented if the levy itself does not prevent it; this levy diminishes rather than encourages quarrels among the men, because when you conscript them you give them arms and leaders. If the region where you levy them is so unwarlike that its men have no arms and is so united that it has no leaders, this levy makes the people bolder against foreigners but does not make them in any way more disunited; men who are well trained fear the laws whether armed or unarmed, and they cannot rebel unless the leaders you give them cause rebellion; how this happens I shall soon tell. If the country where you levy them is warlike and disunited, this levy alone encourages union. In such a country men have their arms and leaders, yet their arms are useless for war and their leaders encourage quarrels; but this levy gives them arms useful for war and leaders who suppress quarrels. Otherwise, as soon as any man in that region is wronged, he runs to the head of his party, who, to keep up his own reputation, encourages the sufferer to vengeance, not to peace. The opposite course is taken by a leader who is a public officer, so that in this way you remove cause for dissensions, and furnish cause for union; thus provinces that are united and effeminate lose their cow-ardice and maintain their union. The disunited and quarrelsome ones unite and turn to the public benefit that energy which they are in the habit of using contrary to law.

### [*Transfer of leaders checks their ambition*]

As to making sure they shall not injure others, you should con-sider that they cannot do this except by means of the leaders who rule them. To make sure that the leaders do not cause disorders, you must take care that they do not gain too much authority over their men. You must consider also that this authority is gained either through nature or through circumstances. As to nature, you must provide that a man who is born in a place is not set over the men enrolled there, but is made leader in places where he has no natural connections. As to circumstances, the thing must be so arranged that each year the leaders are changed from district to district, because continuous authority over the same men produces among them such close union that it easily can be changed into something damaging to the prince.

### [*The Assyrians changed leaders; the Romans did not*]

As to such changes, how valuable they are to those who have used them and damaging to those who have not observed them can be learned from the example of the kingdom of the Assyrians and of the empire of the Romans, where we see that that kingdom lasted a thousand years without rebellion and without any civil war; this long life came from nothing else than the changes from place to place that every year were made in those officers who were put in charge of the armies. Neither in the Roman empire, after the family of Caesar failed, did so many civil wars spring up among the generals of the armies, and so many conspiracies among the aforementioned generals against the emperors, for any other reason than that those generals were kept continuously in the same commands. And if some of those first emperors and those who later ruled the empire creditably, as Hadrian, Marcus, Severus, and the like, had had insight enough to introduce this custom of transferring the generals in that empire, without doubt they would have made it quieter and more lasting.  Because the generals would have had less opportunity for rebellion, the emperors less cause to fear, and the Senate, when there was a break in the succession, would in the election of the emperor have had more authority, and as a consequence the choice would have been better.  But objectionable customs, through either men's ignorance or their lack of attention, cannot by means of either bad or good examples be got rid of.

COSIMO.  I do not know if with my questioning I have almost taken you out of your course, because from the selection we have got into another discussion, and if I had not a little while ago excused myself for it, I should believe that I deserve some rebuke.

### [*Cavalry in a citizen army*]

FABRIZIO.  Don't let that distress you, because all this discussion was necessary if we were going to discuss the citizen army, which, since many blame it, I had to vindicate, if we intended that this first part of the selection should be treated in this place.  And before I go on to other parts, I wish to speak of the selection of the cavalry.  This was made, among the ancients, from the richest, with consideration of age and the quality of the man.  And they chose three hundred of them for a legion, so that the Roman cavalry in each consular army did not exceed the number of six hundred.

COSIMO.  Would you form a citizen force of cavalry in order to train them at home and to make use of them in time of need?

FABRIZIO.  Yes indeed; it is necessary and cannot be done other' wise if one wishes to have arms that are one's own and does not wish to have to get them from those who make a business of war.

COSIMO.  How would you choose them?

FABRIZIO.  I would imitate the Romans: I would take the richest; I would give them leaders in the same way as today leaders are given to the others, and I would arm them and train them.

COSIMO.  To these would it be a good thing to give some pay?

FABRIZIO.  Certainly; but only so much as is necessary to feed a man's horse, because, if you bring expense on your subjects, it will be possible for them to complain of you.  Therefore it will be neces' sary to pay them for the horse and the expense of it.

COSIMO. What number of them will you provide, and how will you arm them?

FABRIZIO. You are passing into another discussion. I shall tell you about that in its place, which will be after I have told you how the infantry ought to be armed, and how they are to be prepared for fighting a battle.

## BOOK 2. [*ARMS, TRAINING, EVOLUTIONS*]

### [*Roman weapons*]

When the men have been found, they must be armed. And for this purpose, we need to examine the arms used by the ancients, and from them to select the best. The Romans divided their infantry into heavy and light armed. Those with light arms they called by the one name *velites*. By this were meant all who shot with the sling, with the bow and with darts; the greater part of them, for defense, had their heads covered and some sort of round shield on their arms. These fought outside the ranks and at a distance from the soldiers in heavy armor; the latter wore a helmet that came down to the shoul-ders, and a corselet with cuisses down to the knee; their legs and their arms were covered with greaves and arm plates; and they had on their arms shields almost four feet long and two feet wide, with a rim of iron above, strong enough to sustain a blow, and another below so that by striking on the ground they would not wear out. For offense the heavy-armed men had girded on their left sides swords almost three feet long, and on their right sides stilettos. Each man had a javelin in his hand, which was called a *pilum*; on joining battle he threw it at the enemy. These are the chief Roman arms, with which they overcame all the world. And though some ancient writers on the subject give them, in addition to the aforesaid arms, a spear in the hand like a boar spear, I do not know how a man holding a shield could use a heavy spear, because if he tries to manage it with both hands, the shield hinders him; with one hand, he cannot do much because of the spear's weight. Besides this, men crowded together and in ranks cannot fight with weapons on long shafts except in the very front where they have free space for extending the full length of the shaft; in the inside ranks they cannot do so because the nature of battalions, as I shall explain when I deal with their array, is con-

tinually to close up; even though this is inconvenient, it causes less
fear than does opening out, where the danger is very evident. Hence
all weapons that exceed four feet in length are useless at close quarters.
Therefore if you have a spear and attempt to use it with both hands,
not being impeded with a shield, you cannot damage with it an
enemy who is very near. If you take it with one hand, in order to
make use of your shield, you cannot grasp it except by the middle;
then so much of the spear extends to the rear that the men behind
impede you in managing it. To make sure that the Romans either
did not have spears, or that, if they had them, they made little use of
them, read about all the battles that Titus Livius describes in his
*History*, and you will see that he seldom mentions the spear; on the
contrary, he always says that having hurled their *pila*, they put their
hands to their swords. Therefore I omit these spears and assume that
the Romans used the sword for offense, and for defense, the shield
and the armor mentioned above.

### [*Greek weapons*]

The Greeks did not arm themselves as heavily for defense as did
the Romans; for offense they depended more on the spear than on the
sword, especially the Macedonian phalangites, who carried spears
they called sarissas, nineteen feet long, with which they opened the
hostile troops and kept the ranks in their own phalanxes. And
though some writers say that they also had shields, I do not see, for
the reasons given above, how the sarissas and these could go together.
Furthermore, in the battle that Paulus Emilius fought with Perseus
King of Macedonia, I do not recall any mention of shields, but only
of the sarissas and of the Roman army's difficulties in overcoming
them. Hence I conjecture that a Macedonian phalanx was not
different from today's brigade of Swiss, who in their pikes have all
their force and all their power. The Romans adorned their infantry
not merely with armor but with plumes, which make the appearance
of an army beautiful to its friends, terrible to its enemies.

### [*The arms of Roman cavalry*]

In the earliest times the Roman horsemen had for protection a
round shield, and their heads were covered; otherwise they were
unarmored; they had a sword, and a spear with iron only at the front
end, long and slender; as a result they could not give firmness to the

shield,[1] and the spear broke in use. The men, being unarmored, were exposed to blows. Then as time went on they were armored like the infantry, though their shields were shorter and square; their spears were stronger and with two irons, so that if one end broke off they could use the other. With these arms, on foot and on horseback, my Romans conquered the whole world. Since we see the result, we must believe that their forces were the best armed that ever existed. Titus Livius in his *Histories* confirms this many times when in making comparison with hostile armies he says: "The Romans in courage, in the type of their weapons and in discipline were superior." Therefore I have spoken more in detail of the victors' weapons than of those used by the vanquished.

### [Infantry weapons in Machiavelli's day]

I believe I need to discuss only the weapons now used. The infantry have for defense breastplates of steel and for offense lances seventeen feet long which they call pikes, with swords at their sides round at the point rather than sharp. This is the normal equipment of the infantry today, because few of them have their bodies and arms armored, none his head. As you know, the few who are armored carry not a pike but a halberd with a shaft nearly six feet long and with its iron curved back like an ax. They have among them harquebusiers who, with the violence of their fire, perform the duty anciently carried on by the slingers and archers. This method of arming was devised by the German peoples and especially by the Swiss, who, being poor and wishing to live in freedom, were and are obliged to resist the ambition of the princes of Germany, who, being rich, are able to keep horses, which these people cannot do because of their poverty. Hence being on foot and attempting to defend themselves from enemies on horseback, they had to adopt ancient methods and to discover arms that would defend them from the fury of the cavalry. This need has made them either retain or adopt ancient methods, without which, as every prudent man affirms, infantry is wholly useless. They took, therefore, as weapons these pikes, arms most useful not merely for resisting cavalry but for defeating them. And by means of these arms and these methods, the Germans

---

1. Not clear. Polybius 6. 4, which Machiavelli is here following, says they could not fix their spear-points in anything (or, strike them heavily against anything); that is, they could not do much damage with them.

have attained such boldness that fifteen or twenty thousand of them will assail any number, however large, of cavalry. And of this, during the past twenty-five years, we have seen many demonstrations. So convincing have been the examples of their effectiveness, founded on these arms and these methods, that since King Charles crossed into Italy every nation has imitated them, to such an extent that the Spanish armies have obtained a very high reputation.

### [*Roman and modern weapons compared*]

COSIMO. What method of arming do you praise more, this German method or the ancient Roman?

FABRIZIO. The Roman without doubt. And I shall tell you what is good and what is bad in both of them. The German infantry so armed can resist and defeat cavalry; they are more rapid on the march and in drawing themselves up because they are not laden with armor. On the other hand, they are exposed to all blows, both from a distance and near at hand, because they are unarmored. They are useless in attacks on cities and in every struggle where there is vigorous resistance. But the Romans resisted and overcame cavalry, as do these; they were safe from blows near at hand and from a distance because they were covered with armor; they could better attack and better resist attacks because they had shields; in crowded ranks they could make more effective use of the sword than the Germans can of the pike; and though the latter have the sword, since they are without the shield, the sword becomes in such a case useless. The Romans could safely attack cities, since their heads were protected and they could protect themselves better with their shields. Thus they had no other inconvenience than the weight of their armor and the trouble of having to carry it; this they overcame by accustoming their bodies to hardships and by toughening them to endure labor. And you know that from things to which they are accustomed, men do not suffer. You must understand this: It may be necessary for the infantry to fight with foot soldiers and with cavalry, and always those will be useless who cannot repel cavalry or, if they can repel them, must still be afraid of infantry who are better armed and better organized than themselves. Now if you consider the German infantry and the Roman, you will find the Germans provided for defeating cavalry, as we have said, but at a great disadvantage when they fight with infantry organized as well as they are and armed as were the Romans. So there will be this advantage of one over the other: the Romans could overcome infantry and cavalry; the Germans only cavalry.

COSIMO. I should like you to furnish examples more specific, so that we may understand better.

FABRIZIO. I put it thus: you will find in many places in our histories that Roman infantry overcame innumerable cavalry, and you will never find that they were overcome by men on foot, either through any defect in their armament or through any advantage the enemy had in their weapons. Because if their armament had shown any defect, one of two things must have resulted: either, on encountering men better armed than themselves, they would not have gone ahead with their conquests, or they would have adopted such foreign methods and abandoned their own. Because neither happened, one easily conjectures that they were better armed than any other people. It has not happened so with the German infantry, because they have come out badly in the test whenever they have had to fight with men on foot as well-drilled and stubborn as themselves. This has happened when they have met enemies having an advantage in weapons.

### [Carmignuola exposes the weakness of the Swiss]

Filippo Visconti, Duke of Milan, when assailed by eighteen thousand Swiss, sent against them the Count Carmignuola, who was then his general. With six thousand cavalry and a few infantry he moved against them and, coming to close quarters, was thrown back with great loss. Then Carmignuola, as a prudent man, at once realized the power of the hostile weapons, and their superiority against cavalry, and the weakness of cavalry against men on foot so drawn up. So after reorganizing his people he again moved against the Swiss, and when he was near them made his men-at-arms dismount from their horses; in that way fighting with the Swiss, he killed all of them except three thousand; they, seeing themselves destroyed without any way of escape, threw their arms to the ground and gave themselves up.

COSIMO. Whence came so great a disadvantage?

FABRIZIO. I told you a little while ago, but since you did not understand, I shall repeat it for you. The German infantry, as I said a little before, being almost without armor for defense, have, for offense, the pike and the sword. They come with these arms and in their kind of array to attack the enemy, who, being well armored to defend themselves, as were Carmignuola's dismounted men-at-arms, come to the attack with swords and in battle-array; they have no other difficulty except that of getting near enough to the Swiss to reach them with the sword, because when the attacker gets to them, he fights safely, since the Switzer cannot strike with his pike an enemy close to him, on account of the length of the shaft, but must take his sword, which is useless to him, since he is unarmored and is opposing an enemy who is fully armored. Hence he who considers the advantage and the disadvantage of both will see that the unarmored man has no way of escape; and to overcome the first push of the pikes and to pass their extended points is not very difficult, when those opposing them are well armored. For the battalions move (you will understand better when I show how they are drawn up), and when they move, of necessity they draw near one another in such a way that they clash breast to breast; and if the pikes kill some or throw them to the ground, those who remain on foot are so many that they are enough for the victory. For these reasons Carmignuola won with such great slaughter of the Swiss and so little loss of his own men.

COSIMO. Remember that Carmignuola's soldiers were men-at-arms, who, though they were afoot, were all covered with iron and therefore were able to stand the test that they did; hence I think it would be necessary to arm infantry like them, if it is to stand the same test.

### [Spanish swordsmen overcome German pikemen]

FABRIZIO. If you remember how I said the Romans were armored, you will not think so. An infantryman who has his head covered with steel, his breast protected by a corselet and by a shield, his legs and his arms armored, is much more fit to protect himself from the pikes and to get within them than is a man-at-arms on foot. I give briefly a modern example. Not long ago some Spanish infantry from Sicily arrived in the Kingdom of Naples to aid Gonsalvo, who was besieged in Barletta by the French. Against them moved Monsieur d'Aubigny with his men-at-arms and about four thousand German infantry. The Germans came to close quarters. With their pikes low they opened the Spanish infantry; yet the latter, aided by their shields and the agility of their bodies, mingled themselves with the Germans until they could reach them with the sword; from this resulted the death of almost all the Germans and victory for the Spaniards. Everybody knows how many German infantry died in the battle of Ravenna. This had the same cause, for the Spanish infantry came within sword-stroke of the German infantry and would have destroyed the Germans if the French cavalry had not rescued them. Nevertheless the Spanish, in close order, gained a safe place. I conclude, then, that not only can good infantry resist cavalry but also it need have no fear of infantry. This, as I have said many times, comes from their arms and from their manner of array.

### [Ideal equipment for infantry]

COSIMO. Tell us, then, how you would arm them.

FABRIZIO. I should choose from the Roman arms and from the German, and I should arm half of them like the Romans and the other half like the Germans. Because, if among six thousand infantrymen, as I shall tell you a little later, I had three thousand infantry with their shields in Roman fashion, and two thousand pikes and a thousand musketeers in the German fashion, they would be enough for me, because I should put the pikes either in the front of the battalions or wherever I most feared cavalry. And those with the shield and the sword I should use to support the pikes and to win the combat, as I shall show you. Hence I believe that infantry so organized would today conquer every other infantry.

### [Cavalry weapons]

COSIMO. What you have said satisfies us as to the infantry, but as to the cavalry we should like to know which you think the more effective armament, ours or the ancient one.

FABRIZIO. I believe that in these times, on account of our arched saddles and our stirrups, not used by the ancients, the soldier sits more firmly on his horse than then. I believe also that he is more safely armored, so that today a squadron of men-at-arms, because of its great weight, is harder to resist than were ancient cavalry. Granting all this, I nevertheless judge that we should not reckon more on cavalry than the ancients did. As I said above, many times in our days they have been put to shame by the infantry; and they will be whenever they encounter infantry armed and organized as I have indicated. Tigranes King of Armenia brought against the Roman army commanded by Lucullus a hundred and fifty thousand horse-men, among whom were many armored like our men-at-arms, called cataphracts; on the other side the Roman cavalry were not as many as six thousand, with twenty-five thousand infantry, so that Tigranes, seeing the army of the enemy, said: "These are cavalry enough for an embassy." Nevertheless, coming to blows, he was defeated. The historian of that combat belittles those cataphracts, showing that they were useless because, having their faces covered, they were little fitted to see and to harm the enemy, and being overweighted with armor, they could not, when they fell, get up again or in any way make use of their bodies.

### [*Infantry superior to cavalry*]

I say, therefore, that those peoples or kingdoms that esteem cavalry more than infantry are always weak and exposed to every kind of ruin, like Italy in our times, for she has been sacked, ruined and overrun by foreigners for no other sin than that she has given little attention to soldiers on foot and put all her soldiers on horseback. There ought nevertheless to be some cavalry—but as the second and not the first reliance of an army—because for scouting, for raiding and laying waste hostile country, for keeping an enemy harassed and worried and under arms all the time, for cutting off his provisions, they are necessary and very useful. But as to the battles and en-counters in the field that are the chief thing in war and the end for which armies are organized, cavalry are more useful for pursuing the enemy when he is routed than for any other service in battle; they are much less efficient than the foot soldiers.

### [*Conditions favorable for cavalry*]

COSIMO. Two problems occur to me: First, I know that the Parthians employed in war only cavalry, yet they divided the world with the Romans. Second, I wish you to tell me how infantry can resist cavalry, and why infantry are efficient and cavalry weak.

FABRIZIO. I told you or I intended to tell you that my discussion of military affairs does not cross the boundaries of Europe. Hence, I am not obliged to give you a reason for what is usual in Asia. Yet I have this to say: the military methods of the Parthians were entirely opposed to those of the Romans, because the Parthians all fought on horseback, and moved when fighting in confusion and disorder; this manner of fighting was unsound and full of uncertainty. The Romans, one can say, were almost all on foot and fought in union and with steadiness. At different times one defeated the other according as the battlefield was extensive or limited; on the limited the Romans were superior; on the extensive the Parthians, who were able to accomplish great feats with that soldiery, on account of the region they had to defend. This was very extensive: the sea is a thousand miles away, the rivers distant from one another two or three days' journey, the cities likewise, and the inhabitants scattered. Hence a Roman army, heavy and slow through its armor and its organization, could not move across it without receiving great damage, because its defenders were on horseback and very rapid, so that today they were in one place and tomorrow fifty miles away. The results were that the Parthians could win with cavalry alone, for they ruined Crassus' army and endangered Marc Antony's. But as I said, I do not intend in this discussion of mine to speak of soldiery outside Europe. Therefore I wish to stand on methods used by the Romans and the Greeks in the past, and the Germans today.

## [*Weaknesses of cavalry*]

But let us come to your other question, on the sort of organization and natural efficiency which enable infantry to overcome cavalry. I answer, first, that cavalry cannot, like infantry, go everywhere. They are slower than infantry in obeying when it is time to vary their order of battle, because if when they are going ahead they need to move back, or when they are moving back they need to go ahead, or to move when they are at a halt, or when they are advancing to halt, there is no doubt that in an instant the cavalry cannot do it as can the infantry. When disordered by some violent motion, cavalry return into order only with difficulty, even when that violent motion is over; yet infantry can do so very rapidly. It happens, besides this, that many times a spirited man will be on a cowardly horse and a cowardly man on a spirited horse; such disparities of spirit must cause disorder. Nor should anybody be astonished that a knot of infantrymen can resist any charge of cavalry, because the horse is a perceiving animal which recognizes dangers and is unwilling to enter them.

And if you will consider the forces making him go forward and those holding him back, you will see that without doubt those holding him back are greater than those urging him on, because the spur drives him forward, but on the other hand the sword and the pike keep him back. So we see, through ancient and modern tests, that a knot of infantrymen is secure against cavalry, indeed is unconquerable by it. And if you argue against this that the impetus with which a horse comes makes him more furious in striking anybody who tries to resist and makes him care less for the pike than for the spur, I say that if a horse at a distance sees that he is going to strike the points of the pikes, either of himself he slackens his course, and when he feels himself pricked stops entirely, or when he comes up to them he turns to the right or to the left. If you wish to experiment with this, attempt to run a horse against a wall; seldom will you find, no matter what his impetus, that he will run against it. Caesar, when he was to fight with the Swiss in France, dismounted and made everybody dismount and remove the horses from the troop, as more fit for flight than for combat.

### [*Precautions against cavalry*]

But in spite of those impediments natural to horses, a general who leads infantry ought to choose roads that impede horses as much as possible; seldom will a commander be unable to secure himself through the quality of the country. If you march through the hills, the site frees you from those cavalry charges you fear. If you go through the plains, few plains there are that with cultivated places and woods will not make you safe, because every copse, every bank even though slight, takes away the horses' impetus, and every cultivated place where there are vines and fruit trees impedes them. And if you come to a battle, the same things are true as in marching, because every little impediment that the horse meets lessens his impetus. One thing, nevertheless, I must not forget to say, namely, that the Romans set such high value on their tactics and had such trust in their weapons that if, to protect themselves from cavalry, they were forced to choose either a place so rough that they could not form order of battle, or one where they would have to fear cavalry more but where they could extend their array, they always took the smooth and gave up the rough.

[*Physical training for soldiers*]

But because it is time to pass to their training, having armed our infantry according to the ancient and the modern custom, we shall see what sort of exercises the Romans had them practice. Before the infantry are led into battle, even though they are well chosen and better armed, they should with the greatest zeal be trained, because without this training no soldier is ever good. Such training should be of three sorts: first, the soldier must toughen his body and make it fit for hardship and swifter and more agile; second, he must learn to use weapons; third, he must learn to keep his proper place in the army, both in marching and in fighting and encamping. These are the three principal activities of any army, because if an army marches, encamps and fights in order and in a practiced way, the general comes off with honor, even though the battle does not have a successful end. Hence all the ancient republics so provided for such training, by means of customs and laws, that no part of them was omitted. So they trained their young men to be swift in running, agile in leaping, strong in hurling the bar and in wrestling. And these three powers are almost essential in a soldier: speed makes him fit to seize places ahead of the enemy, to come upon them unexpected and unprepared for, and to follow them when they are defeated; agility enables him to avoid a blow, to leap a ditch, to get over a bank; strength makes him more easily carry his arms, attack the enemy, repel a charge. Above all, in order to make their bodies more fit for hardships, they accustomed themselves to carry great weights. This habituation is essential because on difficult expeditions the soldier must often carry rations for many days in addition to his arms; if he is not trained to this labor, he cannot perform it; he cannot therefore escape peril or gain fame from victory.

[*Roman training in the use of weapons*]

In teaching the use of weapons, the Romans used the following methods. They required the young men to wear armor weighing twice as much as real armor, and instead of a sword they gave them a club weighted with lead, which in comparison with the sword was very heavy. They had each one set a stake in the ground six feet high and so strong that blows would not break it or knock it down; against this stake the young man exercised himself with shield and sword as against an enemy; sometimes he stabbed at it as though he wished to wound the head or the face, sometimes as if he wished to thrust it through the side, sometimes through the legs, sometimes he drew back, sometimes he pressed forward. And in this exercise they had this purpose: to make them skilful in covering themselves and in wounding the enemy, and since their sham weapons were very heavy, their real ones then seemed light. Always the Romans required their soldiers to use the point and not the edge, because such attack is more deadly, there is less protection against it and it less uncovers him who assails and is easier to repeat than with the edge. Do not wonder that those ancients thought about the smallest things, because when it is a matter of men's coming to close combat, every slight advantage is of great importance, so I remind you of what the writers say about this, without giving you anything new.

### [*The wisdom of the ancient training*]

In the estimation of the ancients nothing was more valuable to a republic than to contain many men trained in arms, because not the splendor of gems and gold makes enemies submit to you, but only the fear of arms. Further, mistakes made in other things can sometimes be corrected; but mistakes made in war, since the penalty comes at once, cannot be corrected. Besides this, knowing how to fight makes men bolder, because nobody fears to do what he believes he knows how to do. Hence the ancients decreed that their citizens should be trained in every warlike activity and had them cast against that stake javelins heavier than the real ones. This exercise, besides making men expert in casting, also makes the arms more supple and stronger. They taught them also to shoot with the bow and with the sling. They had teachers in charge of all these matters. Thus when citizens were chosen to go to war, they already had the disposition and courage of soldiers. There was nothing left for them to learn except to move in the ranks and to keep in them, whether they were marching or fighting. This they learned easily by mingling with men who through long military service knew how to keep their ranks.

### [*Modern training to be similar to the Roman*]

COSIMO. What training would you require at the present time?
FABRIZIO. Many of those I have mentioned, such as to run and to wrestle, to leap, to endure exertion in armor heavier than the

common sort, and to shoot with the crossbow and with the bow, to which I would add the harquebus, a new weapon, as you know, and necessary. And to these exercises I would accustom all the young men of my state, but with greater effort and more care that part of them enrolled for service; and on every holiday they should be trained. I should also have them learn to swim; this is very useful because not always are there bridges across the rivers and boats are not always ready; hence if your army does not know how to swim, it will be deprived of many advantages and you will lose many opportunities for doing something useful. The Romans arranged that the young men should be trained in the Campus Martius for no other reason than that, since the Tiber was near, when they were tired by exercise on land, they could refresh themselves in the water and get part of their exercise by swimming.

### [*Cavalry exercises*]

I should also, like the ancients, have training for those who serve on horseback. This is very necessary because, in addition to knowing how to ride, they must be able to handle themselves on horseback. For this purpose wooden horses were provided, on which they gained skill, leaping on them when armed and when unarmed, without any help and on either side. They did this so that in an instant, at a signal from an officer, the cavalry were on foot, and similarly at a signal they remounted.

### [*Good training in modern times*]

As such exercises both on foot and on horseback were then easy, so now they would not be difficult for any republic or any prince attempting to put them in practice among his young men, as experience shows in some cities in the West where such methods are kept alive, with this arrangement: they divide all their inhabitants into various groups, and call every group after the type of weapon they use in war. And because they use pikes, halberds, bows and harquebuses, they call them pikemen, halberdiers, archers and harquebusiers. Every inhabitant, then, must declare in what group he wants to be listed. And since all, either because of age or other hindrances, are not suited for war, they make a selection from each group and call them the Oath-bound; these are obliged to practice on holidays with those arms for which they are named. Each man has his place assigned by the public, where such training is to be carried on. Those who belong to that group, but are not among the Oath-bound, assist with money in the expenses necessary in such training. So what they do we could do, but our imprudence does not let us adopt any good resolution. As a result of such training, the ancients had good infantry, and now those I mentioned in the West have better infantry than ours. For the ancients trained them either at home, as the old republics did, or in armies, as the Emperors did, for the reasons mentioned above. But to train them at home we are not willing; in the field we cannot because they are not our sub-jects,[2] and we cannot obligate them to training other than they decide on for themselves. That is the reason why first such training and next the laws have been neglected and why kingdoms and republics, especially those in Italy, are now so weak.

### [*Military discipline*]

But let us return to our subject. Continuing this matter of training, I say that it is not enough to make good armies for the men to be hardened and made strong, swift, and agile; they must also learn to remain in their ranks, to obey the signals, the musical calls and the voices of the officers, and must be able when standing still, drawing back, going forward, fighting and marching to keep their ranks. Because without this discipline, accurately and carefully planned and practiced, no army was ever good. Without doubt spirited but unorganized men are much weaker than the timid but well-organized, because organization expels men's fear; disorder les-sens their spirit.

### [*The brigade and its constitution*]

That you may understand better what will be said below, you must know that every nation, in organizing its men for war, has formed in its army or in its military forces a chief body which, though varying in name, has hardly varied in numbers; all nations have composed it of six to eight thousand men. This body the Romans called a legion, the Greeks a phalanx, the French a *caterva*. This same thing in our times the Swiss, who alone retain some shadow of the ancient military system, call in their language what in ours means *brigade*. I admit that each nation has then divided this

2. *The men in the mercenary armies of Machiavelli's time.*

brigade into various battalions and organized it to meet requirements. I believe, however, that we may base our discourse on this name as that best known, and then, according to ancient and modern methods, organize our brigade as well as we can. Because the Romans divided their legion, which was composed of five or six thousand men, into ten cohorts, I plan that we divide our brigade into ten battalions and compose it of six thousand men on foot. And we give every battalion four hundred and fifty men, four hundred armed with heavy equipment and fifty with light equipment. The heavy-armed consist of three hundred with shields and swords, called shield-men; and a hundred with pikes, called regular pikemen. The light-armed are fifty infantrymen armed with harquebuses, cross-bows, partisans and bucklers; they are called by the ancient name of regular *velites*. All the ten battalions therefore amount to three thousand shield-men, a thousand regular pikemen, and five hundred regular *velites*; all of these make up the number of four thousand five hundred infantrymen. Yet we say that we wish to make the brigade six thousand; hence we need to add fifteen hundred more infantrymen; of these a thousand, whom I shall call irregular pikemen, carry pikes, and five hundred, whom I shall call irregular *velites*, are lightly armed. Thus my infantry, according to what I said a little earlier, is made up half of shields and half of pikes and other weapons.

I put in charge of every battalion a constable, four centurions, and forty decurions, and in addition a head for the regular *velites*, with five decurions. I give to the thousand irregular pikemen three constables, ten centurions and a hundred decurions; to the irregular *velites*, two constables, five centurions and fifty decurions. I then appoint a general head of the whole brigade. I intend each constable to have his color-bearer and his musician. Therefore a brigade of ten battalions is composed of three thousand shield-men, a thousand regular and a thousand irregular pikemen, and five hundred regular and five hundred irregular *velites*. These amount to six thousand infantry, among whom are six hundred decurions,[3] and in addition fifteen constables with fifteen musicians and fifteen color-bearers, fifty-five centurions, ten heads of regular *velites* and one general of the whole brigade with his color-bearer and his musician. And I have deliberately repeated this organization several times, so that after-

3. *The texts by error give this as fifteen hundred.*

wards, when I show you the methods of arranging the battalions and the armies, you will not be confused.

### [Battalion training fundamental]

I say, then, that any king or any republic should organize with these arms and in these groups those of his subjects whom he or/ ganizes for service, and should form in his country as many brigades as it can support. After they are organized according to the aforesaid allotment, when training them in their tactics, it is enough to train them battalion by battalion. Even though the number of men in each of these cannot by itself give the effect of a proper army, never/ theless each man can learn to do what pertains to him individually. For in armies two kinds of duty must be carried out: one, that which must be done by the men in each battalion, and the other that which every battalion must do when it is with the others in an army. Men who do the first well, observe the second easily; without battalion discipline, army discipline can never be attained. As I have said, then, each of these battalions can by itself learn to keep the order of the files in every kind of movement and place, then can learn to array itself and to understand the music which directs it in battle. From that music the battalions, like galley oarsmen from the whistle, must be able to understand what they are to do, whether to remain in position, or to go ahead, or to move back, or where to turn their weapons and their faces. When they can keep their files so well that neither place nor motion disorders them, and understand fully the leader's commands by means of music, and can quickly return to their positions, these battalions, as I said, when many of them are brought together, can then easily learn to do what the whole body of a complete army, made up of many battalions, needs to do.

### [Brigade training]

Because such general training is also of no slight value, once or twice a year in time of peace, the whole brigade must be brought together, given the form of a complete army and trained for some days as if it had to fight a battle, putting the front, the flanks and the supports in their places. And since a general arranges his army for battle with regard both to the enemy he sees and to the one he fears though unseen, he trains his army in both methods, and teaches it to march and, when there is need, to fight, showing your[4] soldiers how, when assailed from one side or from the other, they are to conduct themselves. When he draws up his army to fight against an enemy they see, he shows them how they begin the engagement, where they are to retire if they are thrown back, who is to come up in their places, and what signals, what music, what words they must obey, and he trains them with sham battles and attacks in such a way that they wish for real ones. A brave army is not made so by having brave men in it, but by having its tactics well worked out. If I am one of the first to enter combat, and I know where I am to retreat if I am overpowered, and who will come up in my place, I always fight with courage, since I see aid close at hand. If I am in the second group of combatants, when the first is repelled and driven back I am not terrified, because I have reckoned that it could happen and have wished for it, in order that my group may give victory to my master, and not the other one.

Such training is very necessary when a new army is raised, and when the army is old they are necessary; though the Romans knew from boyhood the tactics of their armies, yet their commanders, before they came against the enemy, continually trained them in those tactics. Josephus in his *History* says that the continual training of the Roman armies made the entire crowd that follows the army for profit useful in battles, because they all could take their places in the ranks and maintain them as they fought. But with armies of new men—either those whom you have assembled for combat at once or those whom you are forming into a citizen army for combat in the future—lacking this training for both individual battalions and the whole army, you will accomplish nothing. Since tactics are essential, you must with double labor and effort demonstrate them to recruits who do not know them, as well as maintain them in men who know them, as we see that many excellent leaders have unsparingly devoted themselves to maintaining and teaching tactics.

## [Details of battalion training]

COSIMO. I infer that this discourse has rather carried you away, because you have not yet explained how the battalions are trained, though you have spoken of the whole army and of battles.

4. *Machiavelli uses the second person as though in direct address to the prince; there is no other instance in the immediate context.*

FABRIZIO. You are right. And truly the reason for it is the love I have for these methods and the sorrow I feel when they are not put into practice. All the same, do not fear that I shall not come back to the mark. As I have told you, the thing of first importance in the training of the battalions is to teach them how to keep their ranks. To this end, they must be trained in those formations that are called acting the snail. And because I said that one of these battalions includes four hundred infantrymen armed with heavy weapons, I shall base my account on this number. They are, then, to be drawn up in eighty ranks of five men per rank. Afterward, moving either rapidly or slowly, they can be brought close together and opened out; how to do this I can show better with deeds than with words. Moreover, description is hardly needed, because everyone who is accustomed to armies knows how this evolution proceeds, which is good for nothing else than to accustom the soldiers to keep their ranks. But let us come to forming one of these battalions.

[*Forms of the battalion; the solid double square*]

I say that it has three principal forms. The first, the most useful, is entirely solid, having the shape of two squares. The second is a square with the front horned. The third is to arrange it with a space in the middle called a piazza. The first of the three can be formed in two ways. One is to double the ranks; that is, the second rank enters into the first, the fourth into the third, the sixth into the fifth, and so on until, instead of eighty ranks with five in a rank, there are forty ranks with ten in a rank. Then double them a second time in the same way, joining one rank to the other, and so there will be twenty ranks with twenty men in a rank. This makes just about two squares because, though there are as many men in one direction as in the other, yet along the ranks they are so close together that one man's side touches the next one's, but in the other direction they are distant at least four feet from each other; hence the square is longer from the back to the front than from one side to the other. And because today we must speak many times of the parts in front, behind, and on the sides of these battalions and of the whole army together, you are to understand that when I say *head* or *front*, I mean the parts that are forward; when I say *backs*, I mean the parts behind; when I say *flanks*, the parts on the sides. The fifty regular *velites* of the battalion do not mingle with the other ranks, but when the battalion is formed, spread out along its flanks.

[*A second method for forming the solid double square*]

The second method for forming the battalion is the following. Because it is better than the first, I wish to put before your eyes how it ought to be carried out. I believe you remember the number of men and the officers who make it up and what weapons they carry. The first form normal for a battalion, as I said, is that of twenty ranks with twenty men to a rank; five ranks of pikemen are in front and fifteen ranks of shield-men behind. Two centurions are at the front and two at the back, to perform the duty of those whom the ancients called *tergiductores*; the constable with the color-bearer and the musician stand in the space between the five ranks of pikemen and the fifteen of shield-men; one of the decurions stands on either flank ot each rank, so that each one has his men at his side; those on the left hand have their men on their right; those on the right hand have their men on their left. The fifty *velites* are on the flanks and at the rear of the battalion. In order that this battalion may put itself into the form just described, when the soldiers are marching in the usual way, it must proceed as follows. Suppose the infantrymen back in eighty ranks of five in each rank, such as we mentioned a little while ago, leaving the *velites* either at the head or at the rear, since they are out-side this formation; the arrangement is such that every centurion has immediately behind him twenty ranks, five ranks of pikes and the remainder shields. The constable stands with the music and with the colors in the space between the pikes and the shields of the second centurion, and they occupy the places of three shield-bearers. Of the decurions, twenty are on the flanks of the first centurion's ranks on the left, and twenty are on the flanks of the last centurion's ranks on the right. You must understand that the decurions who command the pikes carry the pike; those who command the shields carry the same weapons as the men. When the ranks are, then, drawn up in this order and you wish as they march to form them into a battalion ready for combat, you make the first centurion halt with the first twenty ranks; then the second keeps on marching and, circling around to the right, goes along the flank of the twenty halted ranks until he is in the same rank as the other centurion, when he halts also; and the third centurion keeps on marching, also circling to the right, and marches along the flank of the ranks that have halted until he is in the same rank with the two other centurions, and when he halts the fourth centurion should continue with his ranks, yet bending to the right along the flanks of the halted ranks, until he comes to the rank of the other centurions, where he halts. And at once two only of the centurions leave the front and go to the rear of the battalion, which is then drawn up exactly in the way and order that we described above. The *velites* spread themselves out along its flanks, as they were disposed in the first manner. The first method for forming the double square is called doubling by right line; this method is called doubling by the flank. The first is easier; this second is more orderly and comes out more exactly, and you can better correct it at your will, because in the first you must follow the numbers, because five makes you ten; ten, twenty; twenty, forty; so that by direct doubling you cannot make a front of fifteen, twenty-five, thirty, or thirty-five, but must go where the doubled number leads you. Yet it happens every day, in special actions, that a leader must resist with six hundred or eight hundred infantry, in such a way that doubling by right line would disorder him. Hence the second method pleases me more; such greater difficulty as it offers must yield to practice and training.

### [*The importance of order*]

I tell you, then, that it is more important than anything else to have soldiers who know how to get into their ranks quickly. And it is necessary to keep them in these battalions, to train them and to make them move vigorously either forward or backward and pass through difficult places without disturbing their order, because the soldiers who can do this well are trained soldiers and, even though they have never looked the enemy in the face, can be called old soldiers. On the contrary, those who do not know how to keep their order, even if they have been in a thousand wars, should always be looked on as new soldiers. This is with respect to putting them into battle array when they are in short ranks, marching. But when they are in array and then get into disorder because of something unexpected in topography or enemy action, the important and difficult thing is to get them back into order at once. This requires much training and experience; on it the ancients put great effort.

## [*Insignia*]

Two things are therefore necessary: first, to provide this battalion with good individual markings; second, always to keep the same positions, so that the same infantrymen are always in the same ranks. For instance, if a man has begun by standing in the second, he should always thereafter remain in it, and not merely in the same rank but in the same place in it; to carry this out, as I have said, plenty of individual markings are needed. First, the banner must be marked in such a way that when several battalions join, each man can recognize his own. Second, the constable and the centurions should have plumes on their heads, distinct and recognizable, and—what is of more import—there must be an arrangement by which the decu- rions may be known. To this the ancients gave so much care that, besides other things, they had each decurion's number marked on his helmet, calling him first, second, third, fourth, etc. And they were not even content with this, because on each soldier's shield was marked the number of his rank and the number of the place in it that belonged to him. If, then, the men are so distinguished and are accustomed to keep in these places, they can easily and quickly be put into order again when they become disordered, because when the banner is in position, the centurions and the decurions can judge their places by eye. If, then, the left-hand ones take their stand on the left and the right-hand ones on the right at their usual distances, the infantry, guided by their rules and by the differences in the individual markings, can be in their proper places at once, just as, when you mix up the staves of a barrel that you have marked first, you can put it together again with the greatest ease, but if you have not marked them, you cannot put it together again.

## [*Battalion evolutions*]

With diligence and practice these things are taught quickly and quickly learned, and when learned they are with difficulty forgotten, because the new men are guided by the old ones, and in time a legion through these exercises becomes entirely practiced in war. The men must also be taught to turn about all together and, when necessary, to make the flanks and the rear into the front, and the front into flanks and rear. This is very easy, because every man needs only to turn his person in the direction ordered; and where they face, there the front comes to be. It is true that when they turn to either flank, the ranks get out of proportion, because there is little distance from the front to the rear, and from one flank to the other much distance, which is all contrary to the normal order of the battalions. Therefore practice and discretion must rearrange them. But this is a slight disorder, because they themselves can easily remedy it. But more important and requiring more practice is the turning of a battalion as though it were one solid body. For this much prudence and much practice is required. If, for instance, it is to turn to the left, the left flank must halt and the soldiers nearest to those standing still must move so slowly that those on the right do not have to run; otherwise the battalion will be in complete confusion.

### [*Order for special conditions*]

Moreover, it happens continually, when an army moves from place to place, that the battalions not posted in front have to fight not to the van but the flanks or to the rear, in such a way that the battalions have on a sudden to make their flanks or their rear into their front; if such battalions at a time like that are to bear their part, according to what has been said above, they must have the pikes on the side that is to be the front, and the decurions, centurions and constable must be in their places as the situation demands. Therefore, if they are to be so drawn up in battle array, the eighty ranks of five per rank must be managed as follows: Put all the pikes in the first twenty ranks, and of their decurions, put five in the first place and five in the last. The other sixty ranks that come behind are all shields and amount to three companies. The first and the last rank of each company must be decurions; the constable with his banner and with the music must be in the midst of the first company of shields; the centurions placed at the head of every company. When they are so arranged, if you wish the pikes to come on the left flank, you must redouble upon them company by company from the right flank; if you wish to have them come on the right flank, you have to redouble from the left. So this battalion comes out with pikes on one flank, with the decurions at the front and at the rear, with the centurions at the front and with the constable in the middle. This form it holds on the march; then on the coming of the enemy and of the time for making the flank into a front, there is nothing to do except have all the soldiers turn their faces toward the flank where the pikes are, and then the battalion turns with the ranks and the officers in the manner that is laid out above because, except the centurions, all are in their places and the centurions quickly and without difficulty get there. If when marching forward it needs to fight to the rear, the ranks must be arranged in such a manner that when it enters battle the pikes are at the rear; to get them there requires only a slight change in forma-tion: ordinarily in forming the battalion every company has five ranks of pikes ahead, but for this combat it has them behind; in all other ways it observes the formation I spoke of first.

### [*The leader must adapt his formation to circumstances*]

COSIMO. You said, if I remember well, that this method of training is such that you can bring these battalions together into an army and that this practice is intended to enable them to form them-selves in one. But if these four hundred and fifty infantrymen have to carry on an affair separately, how will you arrange them?

FABRIZIO. Their leader will then have to judge where he wants to place the pikes and put them there; this does not contradict in any way the order mentioned above. Because, though that method is to be followed in carrying on a battle in company with the other battalions, nevertheless there is no rule that fits all the ways in which you may need to manage. In showing the other two ways I suggest for arranging the battalions, I shall still more fully answer your question, because either these ways never are used, or they are used when a battalion is alone and not in the company of others.

### [*The formation with two horns*]

So to come to the method of arranging it with two horns, I say that you must arrange the eighty ranks of five per rank in this manner: station in the middle a centurion, and behind him twenty-five ranks made up of two pikes on the left and three shields on the right, and after the first five, put in the twenty ranks following twenty decurions, all between the pikes and the shields, except those who carry pikes, who stand with the pikes. After these twenty-five ranks so arranged, is placed another centurion, who has behind him fifteen ranks of shields; behind him, between the music and the banner, is the con-stable, who also has behind him fifteen ranks of shields. After these is placed the third centurion; behind him are twenty-five ranks, in every one of which three shields are on the left and two pikes on the right, and after the first five ranks there are twenty decurions, placed between the pikes and the shields. Behind these ranks is the fourth centurion. In order to make a battalion with two horns from these ranks so arranged, the first centurion with the twenty-five ranks behind him must halt. Then the second centurion with the fifteen ranks of shield-men behind him must move, swing to his right, go along the right flank of the twenty-five ranks until he comes to the fifteenth rank, and there halt. Then the constable moves with the fifteen ranks of shield-men behind him and, still swinging to the right, goes along the right flank of the fifteen ranks that moved first, until he reaches their head; there he halts. Then the third centurion moves with his twenty-five ranks and with the fourth centurion who was in their rear, and still swinging to the right, goes along the right flank of the last fifteen ranks of the shield-men; he does not halt when he is at their head but continues until the last ranks of the twenty-five are on a level with the rearmost ranks. And when this is done, the centurion who is head of the first fifteen ranks of shield-men leaves his place and goes to the rear, at the left corner. So there results a battalion of fifteen solid ranks with twenty infantrymen per rank, with two horns, one on each corner of the front; and each one has ten ranks with five to a rank, and a space remains between the two horns as wide as ten men occupy when they stand abreast. The leader is between the two horns, and at each point of the horn a centurion. There is also a centurion in the rear at each corner. There are two files of pikes and twenty decurions on each flank. These two horns serve to hold between them the artillery, when this bat-talion has any, and the baggage. The *velites* must stay along the flanks, close to the pikes.

### [*The formation with a clear space in the middle*]

But in order to change this horned battalion into one with a central open space, nothing need be done except from the fifteen ranks of twenty men per rank to take eight ranks and put them at the points of the two horns, which then instead of horns become sides of the open space. In this space the baggage is placed, and the leader and the banner are there, but not the artillery, which is put either in front or along the flanks. These are the methods to be used by a battalion when it needs to pass alone through suspected places. Nevertheless, the solid battalion, without horns and without an open middle, is better. Still, in order to give safety to the unarmed, that horned order is necessary.

### [*Other formations*]

The Swiss have many other forms for battalions. Among these is one in the shape of a cross, in order that in the spaces between its arms they may secure their harquebusiers from hostile attack. Because battalions so formed are adapted to fighting by themselves, but my intention is to show how several united battalions fight, I shall not try to demonstrate these forms.

### [*The irregular pikemen and* velites]

COSIMO. I believe I understand well enough the method to be used in training the men in these battalions. But if I remember well, you said also that, besides the ten battalions, you would add to the brigade a thousand irregular pikes and five hundred irregular *velites*. Would you plan to conscript and train these?

FABRIZIO. I should, and with very great pains. The pikes at least I should train band by band, in the methods of the battalions, like the others; because I should make more use of these than of the regular battalions in all special services, as in convoying, plundering and the like. But the *velites* I should train at home without bringing them together, because, since it is their duty to fight scattered, they do not need to join with the others in the general exercises; it is enough to train them well in their special activities.

### [*Repetition of the importance of training*]

I have already said—and it is no burden to repeat it—that the men must be trained in these battalions in such a way that they know how to keep their ranks, recognize their places, and return to them promptly when either enemy or site disorders them, because a battalion that knows how to do these things then easily learns the place it should hold and what its function is in armies. When a prince or a republic is willing to undergo toil and put effort into these methods and this training, always it is true that in his country there are good soldiers. Such princes are superior to their neighbors; they give laws and do not take them from other men. But as I have said to you, the disorder in which we live causes these things to be neglected and not esteemed; therefore our armies are not good, and even if there be heads or limbs naturally capable, they cannot show it.

### [*Baggage animals*]

COSIMO. What baggage animals do you plan for each of these battalions?

FABRIZIO. First, I do not permit either centurions or decurions to ride when on the march; if the constable wishes to ride, he may have a mule but not a horse. I do indeed allow him two baggage animals, and each centurion one and every three decurions two, because in our quarters we quarter that number of them together, as we shall tell in its place, so that every battalion has thirty-six baggage animals. These necessarily carry the tents, the dishes for cooking, axes and iron bars enough for making the camps, and anything more that they easily can.

### [*The function of the officers*]

COSIMO. I believe that the officers set up by you in each of these battalions are necessary; yet I fear that so many commanders will cause confusion.

FABRIZIO. This would be true if they were not responsible to one head, but when they are so responsible, they bring about order. Indeed, without them command is impossible, because a wall that leans at every point needs many and frequent supports, even though they are not strong, rather than a few, even though strong, because the strength of one will not hinder a fall at a distance. Hence it is needful in armies that among every ten men one should have more vigor, more courage or at least more authority; with his spirit, with his words, with his example, he holds the others firm and disposed to fight. And that these things I have mentioned, such as the officers, the banners, the musical instruments, are necessary in an army is evident from our having them all in our armies, but none of them does his duty. First, each decurion, if he is to do what he is ap-pointed for, must, as I have said, have certain men under his charge, and must lodge, carry out duties and stand in the lines with them, because the decurions are put in their places like measuring-stick and mortar to keep the ranks straight and solid; thus the ranks cannot get into disorder or, if disordered, can quickly be brought back into their positions. But we today do not find any use for them except to pay them more than the others and to have them carry on some special duties. The same happens about the banners, for they are kept rather to make a fine show than for any real military function. But the ancients employed them as guides and for restoring order, because when the banner halted, each man knew the place he should hold near it and always returned there. He also knew that when the banner moved or stood still he was to stand firm or to move. Therefore in an army there must be enough groups and every group must have its banner and its leader. If it has this, it is likely to have many souls and, consequently, much life. The infantrymen, then, should march according to the banner, and the banner should move according to the music.

### [*Military music*]

When well handled, this music regulates the army, which by moving in paces that correspond to its beats, easily keeps in rank. Thence it is that the ancients had whistles and fifes and musical instruments perfectly modulated; because, just as one who dances moves in time with music and keeping with it does not err, so an army moving in obedience to music does not get disordered. And therefore they varied the music according as they wished to vary the movement and according as they wished to stir up or to quiet or to make firm the spirits of the men. As the music was of various kinds, they gave it various names. Doric music produced firmness, Phrygian produced impetuosity. Hence they say that when Alexander was at table and someone played Phrygian music, it excited his spirit so much that he laid his hands on his weapons. It would be necessary to find all these modes again, and if that were difficult, we should at least not omit those that teach the soldiers to obey. Each commander can vary them at will, so long as with practice he accustoms the ears of his soldiers to recognize them. But today military music generally yields no other benefit than the making of a noise.

### [*Where free states are numerous, able men are numerous*]

COSIMO. I should like to learn from you, if ever you have meditated on it, whence comes so much cowardice and so much disorder, and in these times so much neglect of this training.

FABRIZIO. I shall gladly tell you what I think about it. You know that for excellence in war many have gained renown in Europe, few in Africa, and fewer in Asia. This comes about because these two last parts of the world have had one principality or two, and few republics; but Europe alone has had a number of kingdoms and countless republics. Men become excellent and show their ability only as they are employed and brought forward by their prince or republic or king as it may be. Hence it follows that where political powers are many, many able men appear; where such powers are few, few. In Asia there have been Ninus, Cyrus, Artaxerxes, Mithridates, and a very few others who match them. In Africa, omitting Egyptian antiquity, we can name Massinissa, Jugurtha, and the generals produced by the Carthaginian republic; yet when compared with the Europeans they are very few; in Europe excellent men are without number and we could list also many more if the malice of time had not destroyed their names. For the world has been wiser and braver whenever many states have esteemed wisdom and bravery through either necessity or some human quality. There rose in Asia then, few able men, because that region was all in one kingdom which, through its size being most of the time quiet, could not produce men excellent in their callings. In Africa it was the same, yet she produced some because of the Carthaginian republic. For excellent men come in larger numbers from republics than from kingdoms, since republics usually honor wisdom and bravery; kingdoms fear them. Hence the first cultivate wise and brave men; the second destroy them.

He who considers the continent of Europe, then, finds that it has been full of republics and princedoms forced, because one feared the other, to keep military organization alive and to honor those excelling in it. In Greece, besides the kingdom of the Macedonians, there were many republics, and in each of them rose very able men. In Italy there were the Romans, the Samnites, the Tuscans, the Cisalpine Gauls. France and Germany were full of republics and of princes; Spain the same. And even though in comparison with the Romans few others are named, that results from the malice of historians who follow Fortune; usually they are satisfied to honor the conquerors. It surely is reasonable that among the Samnites and the Tuscans, who fought a hundred and fifty years with the Roman people before they were conquered, a large number of excellent men did appear. The same in France and in Spain. At least that competence which the writers do not praise in individual men, they praise generally in the peoples when they exalt to the stars their stubbornness in defense of their liberty.

[*The effect of the Roman Empire; of Christianity*]

Since then it is true that where there are more states, more strong men rise up, of necessity when states are destroyed competence is destroyed along with them, since the cause disappears that makes men competent. Hence, when the Roman Empire later increased and did away with all the republics and the princedoms of Europe and of Africa and for the most part those of Asia, no road to com- petence was left except in Rome. The result was that competent men became as few in Europe as in Asia. Competence then reached its final decline, because when all competence was brought to Rome, as she was corrupt, soon there was corruption in almost all the world; and the peoples of Scythia could prey upon that Empire, which had destroyed the competence of others but could not maintain her own. Though afterward that Empire, through the inundation of barbar- ians, was divided into several parts, this competence was not reborn there. One reason why is that to resume customs after they have been destroyed takes time; another is that our way of living today, as a result of the Christian religion, does not impose the same necessity for defending ourselves as antiquity did. Then men overcome in war either were killed or kept in perpetual slavery, so that they passed their lives wretchedly; conquered cities were either laid waste or the inhabitants driven out, their goods taken from them and they them- selves sent wandering through the world. Hence those conquered in war suffered the utmost of every misery. Terrorized by this dread, men kept military training alive and honored those who were ex- cellent in it. Today this fear has for the most part disappeared; of the conquered, few are killed; no one is long held a prisoner because captives are easily freed. Cities, even though they have rebelled many times, are not destroyed; men are allowed to keep their property, so that the greatest evil they fear is a tax. Hence men do not wish to submit to military regulations and to endure steady hardships under them in order to escape dangers they fear little. Moreover, these countries of Europe are under very few heads, in comparison with their earlier condition, because all France obeys one king, all Spain another, Italy is in few parts; hence weak cities defend themselves by uniting with whoever conquers, and strong states, for the reasons given, do not fear complete ruin.

### [Modern cities and princes rely on Fortune, not on Vigor]

COSIMO. Yet, during the last twenty-five years we have seen many towns sacked, and some kingdoms have been lost. Their examples ought to teach the others to show some life and to take up again some of the old laws.

FABRIZIO. It is as you say. But if you observe what sort of cities have been sacked, you find that they are not the heads of a state but its members; you see that Tortona was sacked but not Milan, Capua but not Naples, Brescia but not Venice, Ravenna but not Rome. These instances do not make the ruling city change its opinion but rather make its people stand firmer in their belief that they can buy themselves off with taxes. Hence they are unwilling to submit to the vexations of military training, since they regard it as partly unnecessary, partly a complex thing they do not understand. The subject peoples, who need to be frightened by such disasters, have no power to remedy matters. Princes who have lost their states are too late for action; those who still hold them do not know how to use any remedy and have no wish to, because they hope without any trouble to keep going through Fortune and not through their own strength; they see, since there is little vigor here, that Fortune rules everything, and they are willing to have her rule them and do not hope to rule her. To realize that I have spoken the truth, look at Germany, where there are many princedoms and republics and much vigor. All that is good in present military methods comes from the example of the Germans, who are all jealous for their states and fear servitude (which is not feared elsewhere); hence they all keep themselves masters and in honor. I am sure I have said enough to show the causes of the present cowardice, according to my opinion. I do not know whether you agree or whether as a result of our discussion you feel some uncertainty.

### [Cavalry weapons: cross-bow and harquebus]

COSIMO. None; on the contrary, I completely understand it. I wish merely, turning to our principal matter, to learn how you would attach the cavalry to these battalions, and in what numbers and how commanded and how armed.

FABRIZIO. Perhaps you think I have forgotten them, but do not wonder; there are two reasons for my saying little of them. The first is that infantry is the might and substance of an army; the second is that cavalry practice is less corrupt than infantry practice, for if our cavalry are not stronger than those of ancient times, they are as strong. Moreover, I spoke a little while ago of the method of training them. As for arming them, I would arm them as we do at present, both the light cavalry and the men-at-arms. But I prefer that the light cavalry all be crossbowmen, with a few harquebusiers among them; the latter, though in other affairs of war they are of little use, are very useful for one thing: they terrorize peasants and get them away from a pass they are guarding, because one harquebusier will frighten them more than twenty other armed men.

### [*Numbers and impedimenta of cavalry*]

Coming to the number of cavalry, I say that having chosen to imitate the Roman military system, I do not consider more than three hundred cavalry useful for each brigade; of these I plan that a hundred and fifty be men-at-arms and a hundred and fifty light cavalry. I give each of these groups a leader, appointing also fifteen decurions for each group, and giving each one a musical instrument and a banner. I plan that every ten men-at-arms shall have five pack animals and every ten light horsemen shall have two; like those of the infantry, these are to carry tents, cooking vessels, axes, stakes and other equipment, if space is left. Nor should you think this contrary to good practice, since now each man-at-arms has four horsemen in his service; but to allow it is an abuse, for in Germany the man-at-arms is alone with his one horse;' every twenty men-at-arms have merely one cart carrying their necessaries behind them. The Roman horsemen were quite alone, yet it is true that the *triarii* camped near the cavalry and were required to aid them in the care of their horses; this we can easily imitate, as will appear in assigning their camping places. What the Romans did, then, and what the Germans do today, we too can do; indeed if we do not do it, we err. These cavalrymen, organized and enrolled along with the brigade, can sometimes be assembled when the battalions are united and can

---

5. *The French or Italian man-at-arms had four or more attendants, acting as servants or as soldiers or in both capacities, and might have a horse other than his charger. The German man-at-arms had no attendants and but one horse.*

act so as to give some appearance of attack; this would be more for getting them acquainted with one another than for other necessity.

But let this be enough on this subject now; and let us go on to give form to an army, so that we can offer battle to the enemy and hope to win. For that end military power is organized and so much effort spent on it.

## BOOK 3. [*THE IDEAL ARMY IN ACTION*]

Cosimo. Since we are changing the discussion, I should like to have the questioner changed, because I do not like to be thought presumptuous—something I have always blamed in others. Therefore I lay aside the dictatorship and give this authority to whoever wishes it among these friends of mine.

Zanobi. It would be very pleasant for us to have you continue; yet if you are unwilling to, at least tell us who is to step into your place.

Cosimo. I wish to give this responsibility to Signor Fabrizio.

Fabrizio. I am willing to take it, and I should like to have us follow the Venetian custom, namely, that the youngest speak first, because, since this is business for young men, I am persuaded that young men will be more fit to discuss it, as they are quicker to carry it out.

Cosimo. Then it falls to you, Luigi. And as I am pleased with such a successor, so you will be pleased with such a questioner. Hence I beg that we may return to the subject and not lose any more time.

### [*Tactics, combat, training*]

Fabrizio. I know that if I am going to explain clearly how an army is drawn up for battle, I need to tell how the Greeks and the Romans arranged the various bodies in their armies. Nevertheless, since you yourselves can read and consider these things with the help of the ancient authors, I shall omit many particulars and shall bring up merely what I think we should imitate from them, if in our times we hope to give our military organization some measure of perfection. This will require me at one and the same time to show you how an army should be drawn up for battle, how it should fight true combats, and how it is to be trained in sham combats.

## [*Reserves necessary; the Roman method*]

The greatest mistake made by those who draw up an army for battle is to give it just one front and make it depend on one charge and one fortune. This comes from their having lost the method used by the ancients of receiving one body within another; yet without this method, soldiers in reserve cannot support those first engaged or defend them or enter into the fight in their place—something that the Romans managed excellently. In order, then, to explain this meth-od, I say that the Romans divided each legion into three parts: *hastati, principes, triarii*; of these, the *hastati* were put in the very front of the army with their units close together and solid; behind them were the *principes*, but arranged with their units farther apart; after these were stationed the *triarii*, with their units so far apart that when it was necessary they could receive among them the *principes* and the *hastati*. They had, besides these, slingers and bowmen and other lightly armed men who were not stationed in these ranks but were placed at the front of the army between the cavalry and the infantry. These light-armed men, then, began the combat; if they were victorious, which seldom happened, they followed up their victory; if they were driven back, they retired along the flanks of the army or through the intervals left for such a purpose and came among the unarmed. After they withdrew, the *hastati* came to blows with the enemy; if they were overcome, they retired little by little into the spaces left between the units of the *principes* and, together with them, renewed the fight. If these too were overpowered, they all retired into the spaces between the units of the *triarii*; then the three groups, forming one mass, recommenced the combat; if they were defeated, they had no remedy because no further way for reinforcement was left. The cavalry were placed on the flanks of the army, posted as though they were the two wings of one body, and sometimes fought against the hostile cavalry, sometimes supported the infantry, as need required. This method of re-forming three times can hardly be surpassed, because Fortune must abandon you three times, and your enemy must have strength enough to defeat you three times.

## [*The Greek method of supporting a front line*]

The Greeks with their phalanxes did not have this method of re-forming; though in them there were many officers and many units, nevertheless they made up only one body, or rather one front. The method they used in supporting one another was not to draw back one group into another, like the Romans, but for one man to go into the place of another. They did it in this way: their phalanx was made up of ranks; and if we assume that they put in one rank fifty men and then confronted the enemy, only the first six ranks could fight, because their spears, which they called sarissas, were so long that the sixth rank extended the points of their spears in front of the first rank. When they fought, then, if any of the first rank fell, either through death or through wounds, at once there went into his place the one who was behind him in the second rank, and into the place that remained vacant in the second, came the one that was behind in the third, and so successively in an instant the ranks behind made up for the failure of those in front. Hence the ranks always were complete and no place was empty of fighters except the last rank, which kept being used up because it had no one in its rear who could restore it; thus the losses suffered by the first ranks used up the last ones, and the first ones remained always complete. So these phalanxes, because of their organization, were used up sooner than broken, because their great size made them rather slow in movement. At the beginning, the Romans used phalanxes and drew up their legions in the likeness of the Greek ones. Later this organization did not please them and they divided their legions into several bodies, that is, into cohorts and maniples, because they decided, as I said just above, that a body would have more life that had more souls, and that was composed of more parts in such a way that each one would direct itself.

[*The Swiss squares support one another*]

The Swiss brigades in our day use all the methods of the phalanx, both in being drawn up large and solid and in one's supporting the other. In fighting a battle, they put the brigades one on the flank of the other, for if they should put one behind the other, they would have no way in which the first, on drawing back, could be received by the other. In order that one may support the other, they use this arrangement: they put one brigade in front and a second behind it on its right, so that if the first needs aid, the second can move forward and assist it. They put the third phalanx behind these, but distant a harquebus shot. They do this because, if the first two are driven back, the third will be able to move forward, and they will have room enough—both those thrown back and the one that moves ahead—to avoid collision with one another. So great a multitude cannot be received like a small unit, but the small distinct units in a Roman legion could be placed so that they were received by those in the rear, and easily supported by them. That this arrangement of the Swiss is not so good as the ancient Roman one is shown by many examples of the Roman legions when they fought with the Greek phalanxes; the latter were always destroyed by the former because of the nature of their weapons, as I said above. Hence the Roman method of support was more effective than the solidity of the phalanxes.

### [The ideal army uses both Greek and Roman weapons]

Having then, with these examples, to organize an army, it has seemed good to me to keep the weapons and the methods partly of the Greek phalanxes and partly of the Roman legions. Therefore I have said that I want in a brigade two thousand pikes, the weapons of the Macedonian phalanxes, and three thousand shields with swords, the weapons of the Romans. I have divided the brigade into ten battalions, as the Romans did the legion into ten cohorts. I have ordered the *velites* (the light-armed men) to begin the combat as the Romans did. As the weapons are mixed and have shares from both nations, so there should be shares from both also in the organ-ization. Hence I have decided that every battalion should have five ranks of pikes at the front and the rest should be shields, in order with the front to repel the cavalry and to enter easily into the bat-talions of the hostile infantry, since in the first encounter they would have pikes like the enemy, which I believe will be enough to repel them; then the shields will overcome the enemy. If you note the efficacy of this plan, you will see that all these weapons completely carry out their functions, because the pikes are useful against cavalry and against infantry excellently carry out their function before the combat is pressed close; when it is crowded they are useless. Hence the Swiss, to escape this inconvenience, place in their files behind every three pikes a halberd in order to give space to the pikes, which otherwise would not have enough. If then our pikes are put in front and our shields behind, the pikes resist the cavalry and in beginning the combat open up and harm the infantry, but when the combat gets crowded and pikes become useless, their places are taken by the shields and the swords, which in the thickest crowding can be managed.

LUIGI. We now wait eagerly to learn how you would draw up the army for a battle with these arms and these methods.

### [*The organization of the Roman army*]

FABRIZIO. And I do not intend now to show you anything else than this. You must understand that in an ordinary Roman army, called a consular army, there were not more than two legions of Roman citizens, amounting to six hundred cavalry and about eleven thousand infantry. They had in addition an equal number of in/ fantry and cavalry sent to them by their allies and confederates; these they divided into two parts, calling one the right wing and the other the left wing. Never did they allow the auxiliary infantry to out/ number the legionary infantry, though they were glad to have a larger number of auxiliary cavalry. With this army, made up of twenty/two thousand infantry and about two thousand serviceable cavalry,[1] one Consul carried out every duty and went on every expedition. Yet when they needed to oppose larger forces, they combined two Consuls with two armies. You should also note that, ordinarily, in all the principal actions that armies carry on, namely, marching, encamping and fighting, they put the legions in the middle, because they intended to give most cohesion to the force on which they most relied, as I shall show you in my discussion of all three actions. The auxiliary infantry, because of the practice they had with the legionary infantry, were as good as the legionaries, being disciplined as they were, and therefore were similarly drawn up for battle. He then who knows how the Ro/ mans drew up one legion for battle knows how they drew up a whole army. Therefore, having told how they divided a legion into three parts and how one part received the other, I have told in full how a whole army was drawn up for battle.

### [*The battle array of the ideal army*]

Since I wish next to lay out a battle in Roman fashion, as they had two legions, I shall take two brigades, and when I have arranged these, the disposition of an entire army can be understood, because

---

1. *According to the figures given, this should be one thousand two hundred. Otherwise, the additional auxiliary cavalry are eight hundred.*

in adding more people there is nothing to do except make the dis-
positions larger. I do not believe I need to remind you how many
infantry a brigade has, and that it has ten battalions, and what officers
there are for each battalion and what weapons they have, and what
the pikes are and the regular and the irregular *velites*, for a little while
ago I told you this distinctly and admonished you to commit it to
memory as necessary to the understanding of all the other arrangements; therefore I shall come to the exposition of battle order without
repeating anything. According to my plan, the ten battalions of one
brigade are put on the left flank and the ten of the other on the right.
Those on the left are arranged as follows; five battalions are placed
one beside the other in front, in such a way that between each one
and the next is a space of eight feet,[2] so that they occupy in breadth
two hundred and eighty-two feet of space and in depth eighty.
Behind these five battalions three others are placed, distant eighty feet
in a straight line from the first; two of these come directly behind the
two outermost of the five, and the other is in the middle. And so
these three occupy the same space in breadth and depth as the five,
but where the latter have between them spaces of eight feet, these
have spaces of sixty-six. After these I put the last two battalions
directly behind the three and distant eighty feet in a straight line from
those three, and I put each one behind the outermost of the three, so
that the space between the two would be about one hundred and
eighty-two feet. All these battalions when so arranged, then, occupy
in breadth two hundred and eighty feet and in depth four hundred.
The irregular pikes I draw up along the flanks of these battalions on
the left side, forty feet away from them, making a hundred and forty-
three ranks with seven in a rank, in such a way that with their length
they protect the entire left side of the ten battalions when drawn up
as I have described, and I still have forty ranks to guard the baggage
animals and the unarmed remaining at the rear of the army. The
decurions and the centurions are in their assigned places, and of the
three constables I put one at the head, one in the middle, and the
third in the last rank; the third has the office of leader of the rear, for
so the ancients called the officer in charge of the army's rear. But
returning to the front of the army, I put next to the irregular pikes the

2. *Machiavelli's unit of measure is the Florentine* braccio, *22.835 inches. I have used it as
equivalent to two feet; my distances therefore are more than Machiavelli intended by slightly more
than half an inch per foot.*

irregular *velites*, of whom as you know there are five hundred; I give them a space of eighty feet. Beside these, and still on the left, I put the men-at-arms, to whom I allow a space of three hundred feet. After these are the light cavalry, to whom I give the same space as to the men-at-arms. The regular *velites* I leave around their battalions. They stand in spaces that I leave between the battalions, so they can be like servants to them, if indeed I do not prefer to put the *velites* next to the irregular pikes, which I shall do or not as I think best. The general officer of the brigade I put in the space between the first and the second line of battalions, or in front and in the space between the outer battalion of the first five and the irregular pikes, as I think more advisable. He has thirty or forty selected men around him, prudent enough to carry out a mission and able through their strength to resist an attack. He is also between the music and the banner. This is the order in which I dispose a brigade on the left; it is the disposition of half the army. It occupies one thousand and twenty-two feet in breadth, and in depth what I indicated above, not counting the space held by that part of the irregular pikes who form a shield for the unarmed, two hundred feet.

## [The second brigade]

I arrange the other brigade on the right exactly as I have arranged that on the left, leaving between the two brigades a space of sixty feet. At the front of this space I put some pieces of artillery. Behind them stands the general in command of the entire army. Around him, with the music and the chief banner, he has at least two hundred selected men, for the most part on foot, among whom are ten or more fit for carrying out any order. He is so mounted and armed that he can be on horseback or on foot as may be necessary.

## [The artillery of the ideal army]

As to the army's artillery, ten cannon are enough for the siege of towns, not exceeding fifty pounds weight; these I use in the field rather for the protection of the encampment than for carrying on battle. The other cannon are all rather of ten pounds weight than of fifteen. I put these in front of the entire army, except when the country lies in such a way that I can put them on the flank in a secure place where the enemy cannot attack them.

### [*This army combines Greek and Roman advantages*]

An army of this type, when so drawn up, keeps in battle the order of the phalanx and the order of the Roman legion: in front are pikes, and the infantry are all arranged in files, so that when they make contact with the enemy and hold him, in the manner of the phalanx they restore the front ranks with those behind. On the other hand, if they are charged in such a way that they are compelled to break their ranks and draw back, they enter into the intervals between the second battalions behind them and unite with them; having formed a body, they resist the enemy and fight with them. And if this is not enough, in the same way they retire again and for the third time fight; hence in this order, as to fighting, there are reinforcements both according to the Greek manner and according to the Roman.

### [*The army's strength*]

As to the strength of the army, it cannot be more strongly arranged, because each flank is very well provided both with officers and with weapons, and no part of it is weak except the part behind the unarmed, and even that has its flanks guarded by the irregular pikes. The enemy cannot attack it on any side where it will not find it in order; and the part in the rear cannot be assailed, because there cannot be an enemy strong enough to attack you equally on all sides; if he is so strong, you are not going to put yourself in the field against him. Even if he is one-third larger than you and is as well organized as you are, if he weakens himself by assailing you in several places and you defeat one part of him, all goes badly for him. From cavalry, even though they are more numerous than yours, you are entirely secure, because the array of pikes that guards you defends you from every charge they make, even if your own cavalry are driven back. The officers, besides, are in places such that they easily give orders and obey. The spaces between one battalion and another and between one body and another not merely enable one to receive another but also give room for the messengers who go and come by order of the general.

### [*The form of the brigade determines that of the army*]

And as I said before that the Romans had about twenty-four thousand men in an army, so this one has; and as their other soldiers took their method of fighting and the form of the army from the legions, so these soldiers that you join to your two brigades take their form and method from them. If they have an example, it is easy for them to imitate, because, on adding either two further brigades to the army, or as many soldiers from others as come to the same number, there is nothing to do except double the order, if earlier you put ten battalions on the left side, now you put twenty there, or you contract or expand the order as the site or the enemy compels you.

### [*The army in battle*]

LUIGI. Truly, Sir, I imagine this army in such a way that I actually see it and I burn with desire to behold it in action. I should not, for anything in the world, like you to become a Fabius Maximus, planning to keep your enemy idle and to put off the battle, for I should speak worse of you than the Roman people did of him.

### [*The artillery begins the action*]

FABRIZIO. Do not fear. Do you not hear the artillery? Ours have already fired but have done little damage to the enemy, and our irregular *velites* leave their places at the same time as the light cavalry, and in open order and with as much speed and as much noise as possible attack the enemy, whose artillery has discharged once, firing over the heads of our infantry without doing them any harm. To keep it from firing a second time, you see that our *velites* and cavalry have already taken it and that the enemy, in order to defend it, has moved forward, so that the artillery of both friends and enemies can no longer do its duty.

### [*General combat*]

You see with what valor our men fight and with what discipline, as a result of the training that has made it their habit and of the confidence they have in the army; you see how at its own pace and with the men-at-arms on its flanks, it moves on regularly to come to close quarters with the adversary. You see our artillery, which, to give them room and leave the space free for them, has retired through the space left open by the *velites*. You see the general who encourages them and shows them that victory is certain. You see that the *velites* and the light cavalry have spread themselves out and returned to the flanks of the army to see if they can harm their adversaries by a flank attack. Now the armies have come together. Observe with how much vigor they resist the charge of the enemy and with how much silence, and how the general commands the men-at-arms to resist and not to charge and not to separate from the array of the infantry. See how our light horse charge a band of hostile harquebusiers who are attempting a flank attack and how the hostile cavalry rescue them. Hence, trapped between the two bodies of cavalry and unable to shoot, they retreat to their battalions. See with what speed our pikes make their attack and how the infantrymen are already so close to one another that the pikes can no longer be managed, so that, according to the discipline we have taught, our pikemen little by little retire among the shields. Observe how meanwhile a great band of hostile men-at-arms drives away our men-at-arms from our left flank and how ours, according to their discipline, retire to the shelter of the irregular pikes and, re-forming with their aid, drive back the enemy and kill a good part of them. Meanwhile all the regular pikes of the first battalions withdraw into the array of the shields and leave the fight to the shield-men; observe them killing the enemy with great vigor, safety and ease. Do you not see, as they fight, their array so crowded that they scarcely can use their swords? Observe how the enemy are dying. Armed only with the pike and with their type of sword (the pike useless through being too long, the sword through their finding the enemy too well armored), part of them fall wounded or dead, part flee. See them flee on the right flank; they flee also on the left; behold, the victory is ours. Have we not won a battle most successfully? But with still greater success we would win if I were permitted to put it into action. And you see we have not needed to use either the second or the third line of battle; our first front has been enough to overcome them. In this matter I have nothing else to say except to explain any doubt that occurs to you.

LUIGI. You have won this battle with so much speed that I am completely astonished and so bewildered that I do not believe I could explain it well if any doubt did remain in my mind. Yet, trusting myself to your prudence, I will take courage to say what I think.

### [*The small part taken by artillery*]

Tell me first: why did you not have your artillery shoot more than once? And why did you have it quickly retire into the army and afterward did not make mention of it? It seems to me also that you put the guns of the enemy high and arranged them at your will, which can very well be. Yet, when it happens—and I believe it will often happen—that they hit the troops, what recourse have you?

And since I have begun with the artillery, I should like to finish this whole question, in order not to have to discuss it further. I have heard many speak with contempt of the arms and the array of the ancient armies, arguing that today they could do little, rather would be wholly useless through the artillery's violence, because this breaks ranks and pierces armor in such a way that it seems to them madness to form ranks that cannot be kept and to suffer fatigue in wearing armor that cannot protect you.

*[Rapid attack a protection against artillery]*

FABRIZIO. This question of yours, because it has several heads, needs a long answer. It is true that I did not make the artillery shoot more than once, and even of this once, I was in doubt. The reason is that it is more important for anyone to keep himself from being hit than to hit the enemy. You must understand that if artillery is not to damage you, of necessity it is where it cannot reach you, or you put yourself behind a wall or behind a bank. Nothing else can hold it off; moreover, such walls must be very strong. Yet generals who go out to fight a battle cannot remain behind walls or banks or where they cannot be reached. They must, then, since they cannot find a means for protecting themselves, find a means by which they will be least damaged. They can find no other way than quickly to seize the artillery beforehand. The method of seizing it beforehand is to go to attack it rapidly and in loose order, not slowly and in a mass, because when speed is used, the discharge cannot be repeated, and when the order is loose, it harms a smaller number of men. A band of men in close order cannot do this; if it moves rapidly, it loses its order; if it goes in loose formation, the enemy does not have much trouble in breaking it; indeed it has broken itself. Therefore I arranged the army in such a way that it could do both one thing and the other, because when I put on its flanks a thousand *velites*, I arranged that after our artillery had fired, these *velites* go out with the light cavalry to take the hostile artillery. Therefore I did not have my artillery shoot again, in order not to give time to that of the enemy, because I could not both give myself time and take it from others. For the very reason why

I did not have it fire a second time, I considered not having it fire the first time, so that the enemy could not shoot even once. For in order to make the hostile artillery useless, there is no other means than to attack it; if the enemy abandon it, you take it; if they decide to defend it, they have to leave it in their rear; hence, taken by enemies or by friends, it cannot fire.

### [Classical parallels]

I should think that without examples these reasons would satisfy you; yet, since I can give some from the ancients, I wish to do so. Ventidius, coming to a battle with the Parthians, whose strength consisted for the most part in bows and in arrows, let them come almost up to his tents before he led his army out; this he did only that he could engage them quickly and not give them time to shoot. Caesar relates that in a battle in France, the enemy attacked him with such speed that his men did not have time to throw their javelins according to the Roman custom. Hence you see that if you wish anything shooting from a distance not to harm you when you are in the field, you have no other remedy than the utmost speed in taking it.

### [Artillery smoke obstructs the vision]

Another cause also moved me to omit firing the artillery; perhaps you will laugh at it but I think it not to be despised. There is nothing that makes greater confusion in an army than to obstruct its view; many strong armies have been routed when their vision has been obstructed by the dust or the sun. There is nothing that more obstructs the view than the smoke artillery makes in firing; hence I believe it more prudent to let the enemy blind himself than for you, when blind, to attack him. Therefore either I would not fire or (because that would not be approved because of the artillery's reputation) I would put the artillery on the wings of the army; then when it fired its smoke would not blind the army's front; this is the important thing for my soldiers. That to obstruct the enemy's view is useful can be shown by Epaminondas' example: to blind a hostile army about to fight a battle with him, he had his light cavalry gallop before the front of the enemy to raise the dust high and obstruct their view; this gave him victory in that battle.

*[The limitations of artillery; devices against it]*

As to your saying that I directed the shots of the artillery according to my own will by making them pass over the heads of the infantry, I reply to you that there are many more times, beyond comparison, when the heavy guns do not strike the infantry than when they do strike them. For the infantry is so low and the guns are so hard to manage that, if you raise them a little, they fire over the heads of the infantry, and if you lower them, they hit the earth and the shot does not reach the troops. The infantry are protected also by the unevenness of the land, because every little thicket or bank between them and the guns is a protection. The horses, and especially those of the menatarms, because they have to stand closer together than the light horses and, being taller, are more easily hit, can be kept in the rear until the artillery has fired. It is true that much more harm is done by the harquebuses and the light artillery than by the heavy, against which the chief protection is to come to close quarters quickly; if in the first attack they kill somebody, in such conditions somebody always is killed. A good general and a good army do not fear an individual harm but a universal one; they imitate the Swiss, who never avoid a battle because they are dismayed by the artillery; on the contrary, they inflict capital punishment on those who for fear of it either leave their rank or with their bodies give any sign of fear. I had the artillery, as soon as it had fired, retire into the army that it might give free passage to the battalions. I made no further mention of it because it is useless in combat at close quarters.

*[Notwithstanding the fury of artillery, ancient methods are still used]*

You have also said that because of the fury of this instrument, many consider the ancient arms and methods useless; this speech of yours suggests that the moderns have found methods and weapons that against artillery are effective. If you know any, I should be glad to have you explain them to me, because up to now I have never seen any of them nor do I believe any can be found. Indeed I should like to ask for what reasons the foot soldiers in our times wear the breastplate and the corselet of steel, and men on horseback are completely covered with armor, because those who condemn the ancient wearing of armor as useless against artillery, ought to give up modern armor too. I should like to know for what reason the Swiss, imi tating ancient methods, form a close-packed brigade of six or eight thousand infantrymen and for what reason all other infantry imitates them, since this order is exposed to the same danger, with respect to artillery, to which are exposed all others that might be imitated from antiquity. I believe a champion of artillery would not know what to answer; but if you should ask soldiers who have some judgment, they would answer, first, that they go armored because, though that armor does not protect them from artillery, it does protect them from arrows, from pikes, from swords, from stones and from every other injurious thing that comes from the enemy. They would also answer that they go drawn up in close order like the Swiss so as to be able more easily to charge infantry, to resist cavalry better, and to give the enemy more difficulty in breaking them. Evidently soldiers need to fear many things besides artillery; from these they protect themselves with armor and with good order. From this it follows that the better armored an army is and the more its ranks are locked together and strong, the more secure it is. Hence any who think artillery all-important must be either of little prudence or must have thought very little on these things. If we see that a very small part of the ancient method of arming that is used today, namely, the pike, and a very small part of their organization, namely, the brigades of the Swiss, do us so much good and give our armies so much strength, why are we not to believe that other arms and other customs that have been given up are useful? Besides, if we do not consider the artillery in putting ourselves in close formation like the Swiss, what other methods can make us fear it more? For evidently no arrangement can make us fear it so much as those that crowd men together. In addition, the artillery of the enemy does not frighten me off from putting myself with my army near a city where it can harm me with full security, since I cannot take it because it is protected by walls which permit it to repeat its shots at pleasure; indeed I can only hinder it, in time, with my artillery. Why, then, am I to fear it in the field where I can quickly take it? Hence I conclude with this: artillery, in my opinion, does not make it impossible to use ancient methods and show ancient vigor. If I had not spoken with you another time of this instrument, I should here be more lengthy; but I wish to rest on what I then said about it.[3]

3. DISCOURSES 2. 17.

[*Can artillery be protected?*]

LUIGI. We understand very well everything you have said about artillery; and indeed you prove that to take it quickly is the best device that can be used against it, when you are in the field and an army is confronting you. About this one doubt occurs to me, be' cause it seems to me that an enemy might station his guns in such a place within his army that they would harm you and yet be so well guarded by his infantry that you could not take them. You have, if I remember well, in drawing up your army for battle, made intervals of eight feet between the battalions and intervals of forty between the battalions and the irregular pikes. If the enemy should arrange his army just like yours, and thereupon put the artillery pieces right in those intervals, I believe that from that position they could injure you with complete security for themselves, because you could not enter into the forces of the enemy to take them.

FABRIZIO. You raise difficulties very prudently, and I shall make an effort either to settle your difficulties or to show how to deal with them. I have told you that continually these battalions, whether because of marching or because of fighting, are in motion, and always by nature they keep closing up; hence, if you make the intervals where you put the artillery of small size, in a short time they close up so much that the artillery cannot function; if to avoid this danger you make them large, you run into a greater one, for by means of these intervals you furnish the enemy an opportunity not merely for taking the artillery but for defeating you. But you must know that the cannon, especially those on carriages, cannot be kept within the troops, because cannon face in one direction when they move and in another when they fire; hence if they are to move and to fire, they must turn before they fire, and for turning they need so much space that fifty gun carriages would disorder any army. Therefore they must be kept outside the array, where you can attack them by the method explained just above. But let us grant that they can be kept within the ranks and that we can find a middle course by which troops when in close order do not hinder the artillery and when in open order do not offer a path to the enemy. I say that this can easily be countered by making intervals in your array opposite the guns to offer a free way to their shots; thus their fury is made useless. You can easily do so because the enemy, wishing his artillery to be secure, must put it back in the intervals; hence its shots, if they are not to harm his own men, must pass along a straight line and always by the same one. Therefore by giving them room you easily escape them. For this is a general rule: to things that cannot be resisted, way must be given. So the ancients did for elephants and scythed chariots.

[*The superiority of the army described*]

I believe, rather I am more than certain, that you think I have planned and won a battle to suit myself. Nevertheless, I answer you this (if what I have said up to now is not enough), namely, that it is impossible for an army so drawn up and armed not at the first encounter to overcome any army drawn up as modern armies are. These most of the time offer but one front, do not have shields and are to such an extent without armor that they cannot defend themselves from an enemy near at hand. And they are drawn up in such a way that if they put their battalions side by side they make the army thin; if they put them one behind the other, since one does not have any way to receive the other, they make it confused and apt to be easily upset. And though they give three names to their armies and divide them into three sections, vanguard, main battle, and rear guard, nevertheless they use these distinctions only for marching and for distinguishing their camping places. In battles they all depend on one first rush and one first chance.

[*How pikemen repel cavalry*]

LUIGI. I noted also, in the course of your battle, that your cavalry was driven back by the hostile cavalry, so that it retired behind the irregular pikes. The result of this was that with their aid it resisted the enemy and drove them back. I believe the pikes able to resist the cavalry, as you say, but in a large and solid square such as is formed by the Swiss. Yet you in your army have in front five ranks of pikes and on the flank seven, so I do not see how you can resist cavalry.

FABRIZIO. Though I have told you that in the Macedonian phalanx six ranks could use their weapons at the same time, you must nevertheless understand that a Swiss battalion, even if it has a thousand ranks, can engage only four or at most five of them, because of the length of the pikes. These are seventeen feet long; three feet are taken up by the hands; hence the first rank has fourteen feet of pike left free; the second rank, besides what is needed for the hands, uses three feet in the space between the first rank and itself; hence it has eleven feet of usable pike. In the same way, the third rank has eight; the fourth rank has five; the fifth rank has two. The other ranks are useless for thrusting but serve to renew these five ranks, as we have said, and to make them a sort of barbican. If then five of their ranks can master cavalry, why cannot five of ours master it, for ours too do not lack ranks in their rear to back them up and give them the same support, though they do not have pikes like those in front? And if the ranks of irregular pikes posted on the flanks seem thin, I can form them into squares and station them on the flanks of the two battalions that I put in the last line of the army. From that place all of them together can at the same time easily assist the front and the rear of the army and give aid to the cavalry, as need requires them.

### [*Battlearray to be varied according to circumstances*]

LUIGI. Would you always use this same form of array when you plan to carry on a battle?

FABRIZIO. No, by no means, because you have to vary the form of the army according to the nature of the site and the nature and number of the enemy, as we shall show by example before ending this discussion. But we give you this form not so much because it is stronger than the others, though in fact it is very strong, as because it gives you a rule and a method for understanding the ways for arranging the others; for every science has its general rules, on which to a great extent it is based. One thing only I emphasize: never draw up an army in such a way that those who fight in front cannot be relieved by those posted in the rear; he who commits this error makes the greater part of his army useless, and if it encounters men of any vigor it cannot win.

### [*Why the brigade is strongest in front*]

LUIGI. A doubt has arisen in my mind about this matter. I have seen that, in the disposition of the battalions, you make the front of five to a line, the middle of three, and the rear of two. But I should believe it better to arrange them in the opposite way, because I imagine that an army would be harder to break if those attacking it, as they penetrated deeper, found it always more solid; but your arrangement seems to me to bring about that as they enter deeper into it, they find it always weaker.

FABRIZIO. If you will recall that to the *triarii*, who formed the third line of the Roman legion, not more than six hundred men were assigned, you will fear less when you see that I put two battalions in the rear group, because, though following Roman example, I put in the rear group nine hundred infantrymen; hence, since I am following the Roman method, I fall into error by taking too many rather than too few. Though this example should suffice, I shall tell you the reason. It is this: the extreme front of an army is made solid and compact because it has to resist the rush of the enemy and does not have to receive into itself any of its friends; for this reason it must abound in men, because too few would make it weak either through loose order or through small numbers. But the second group, because it has to receive friends before resisting enemies, has large intervals; therefore it is smaller in number than the first, because if it is of greater or equal number, of necessity intervals are not left in it (which would be opposed to good practice) or if they are left, it must extend beyond the flanks of the front line, thus making the form of the army imperfect. And what you say is not true: namely, that the enemy, as he penetrates deeper into the brigade, finds it always weaker, because the enemy never can fight with the second line unless the first is joined with it; hence they find the middle of the brigade stronger and not weaker, since they have to fight with the first and the second lines together. The same thing happens when the enemy get to the third line, because there they have to fight not only with the two fresh battalions they find there, but with the entire brigade. And because this last part has to receive more men, the spaces must be greater and those who receive must be fewer in number.

### [There is room for the retirement of the front lines]

LUIGI. What you have said satisfies me, but give me an answer also about this: if the first five battalions retire among the three second and then the eight among the third two, it does not seem possible, when the eight are brought together, and finally the ten, that either when they are eight or when they are ten they can be contained in the same space as contained the five.

FABRIZIO. I first reply that it is not the same space, because the five have between them four spaces which they can occupy when they retire among the three and the two; there is also the space between the two brigades and that between the battalions and the irregular pikes; these spaces all give room. Furthermore the battalions do not occupy the same amount of space when they are undisturbed in their ranks as they do when they are disturbed, because in disturb- ance they either crowd together or they loosen their ranks. They loosen them when they are so afraid that they take to flight; they crowd them together when they fear in such a way that they try to make themselves safe not with flight but with defense; hence in this case they would be crowding together and not loosening out. Add to this that the five ranks of pikes in front, after they have begun the combat, get into the midst of their battalions in order to retire to the rear of the army, so as to give place to the shield-men, who are able to fight; these pikemen, going to the rear of the army, can be em- ployed in whatever the general thinks good for them to do, whereas in front, after the combat is well started, they are wholly useless. Thus for the rest of the men the spaces provided turn out to be entirely adequate. Moreover, if these spaces are not enough, the flanks at the side are men and not walls; hence by yielding and making room they can give the space capacity enough to take them in.

LUIGI. As to the ranks of irregular pikes that you put on the flanks of the army—when the first battalions retire into the second, do you intend that they stand firm and remain as two horns for the army, or do you intend that with the battalions they too retire? If they have to do this, I do not see how they can move, because they do not have behind them battalions with open spaces that can receive them.

FABRIZIO. If the enemy does not attack them when he forces the battalions to draw back, they can stand firm in their ranks and strike the enemy on the flank, when the first battalions have retired; but if the enemy attacks them too, as seems reasonable, since he is strong enough to overcome the others, these also will have to retire. This they can do very well, even though they have no one behind to receive them, because from the middle to the front they can double on the right, one rank entering into another in the way we explained when we spoke of the method of doubling. It is true that when in doubling they wish to draw back, they must use another method than I showed you, for I said that the second rank had to enter into the first, the fourth into the third, and so on; in this case they would need to begin not in front but at the rear, in order that in doubling the ranks they would succeed in drawing back, not in going ahead.

### [*Practice in formations; insignia*]

But to reply to everything you can object to about this battle I have demonstrated, I say again that I have drawn up this army and shown this battle for two reasons: one, to show how it is drawn up; the second, to show you how it is trained. Its arrangement I believe you understand fully. And as to the exercise, I tell you that it is necessary as often as you can to put them together in these forms, because the officers must learn how to keep their battalions in these positions, because it is the duty of the individual soldiers to keep their proper positions in each battalion, and because it is the duty of the battalion officers to keep their battalions under control in any position of the army, and ready to obey the orders of the general. They must know, then, how to unite one battalion with another and how to take their places in an instant. And therefore the banner of each battalion must have written on it, in a conspicuous place, its number, both so that orders can be given to that battalion and so that the general and the soldiers by that number can more easily recognize it. The brigades should also be numbered and have the number on their principal banner. All the soldiers must, then, know the number of the brigade put on the left or on the right wing, the numbers of the battalions put in the front or in the middle, and so the others in the same way.

### [*The ranks of the officers*]

It should also be arranged that these numbers show the scale of rank in the army. For instance, the lowest in rank should be the decurion, the next the head of the fifty regular *velites*, the third the centurion, the fourth the head of the first battalion, the fifth of the second, the sixth of the third, and so on, up to the tenth battalion, the leader of which would be honored in the place just below the commander of a brigade; nor should anyone be able to attain that leadership if he had not risen through all these grades. And because, in addition to these officers, there are three constables of irregular pikes and two of irregular *velites*, I should plan to have them of the same rank as the constable of the first battalion, and I should not care if there were six men of equal rank, because each one of them would strive to be promoted to the second battalion.

When each of these leaders, then, knows the station of his battalion, it follows of necessity that at the sound of the trumpet, when the chief banner is raised, every man in the army is in his place. This is the first exercise to which an army should be trained, that is, to get itself quickly together. To this end, every day and many times a day it must be put into order and got out of order.

### [*Flags*]

LUIGI. What insignia would you like the banners of all the army to have, besides the number?

FABRIZIO. That of the general should have the insignia of the army's prince; all the others can have the same insignia but varied in the fields or varied in the insignia, as the master of the army wishes, for this is of little importance, if only they can tell one banner from another.

### [*Drill in marching and in battle tactics*]

But let us pass to the second exercise in which an army is to be drilled. That is to make it move and march at a suitable pace and to see that as it moves it keeps its formation. The third exercise teaches it to maneuver just as it must in battle. The guns are to fire and be taken to the rear; the irregular *velites* are to go out and after an appearance of attack to draw back again; the first battalions are to retire as if forced back into the spaces between the second ones, and then all are to retire into the third, and from there each is to return to his place. They must be so accustomed to this exercise that to each man everything will be known and familiar, as with practice and familiarity quickly comes about. The fourth exercise is to learn to recognize by means of the music and the banners the orders of the general, because what is told them in words the soldiers will understand without other means for giving orders.

### [*Signals by music*]

Because the success of this method of giving orders depends upon the music, I shall tell what music the ancients used. The Lacedaemonians, as Thucydides says, in their armies used flutes, judging that harmony most apt to make their armies march with firmness and not with excitement. Moved by the same reason, the Carthaginians in their first attack used the lyre. Halyattes King of Lydia used in war the lyre and the flute. But Alexander the Great and the Romans used horns and bugles, thinking that by means of such instruments they enkindled the spirits of their soldiers and made them fight more vigorously. So as in giving weapons to the army we have followed the Greek and Roman manner, in distributing the instruments of music we keep to the habits of the two nations. Therefore near the general I place the trumpets, as better fitted than any other music to be heard in the midst of noise of every kind. All the other instruments near the constables and the officers of battalions I wish to be little drums and flutes, played not as they now are in armies but as they are usually played at banquets. The general, then, indicates with the trumpets when the soldiers are to stop or to go forward or to go backward, when the artillery is to fire, when the irregular *velites* are to move and, with the variety of such music, he makes plain to the army all the movements that in ordinary course can be made plain. These trumpets then are followed by the drums. In this exercise, because it is very important, the general thoroughly trains his army. The cavalry use trumpets in the same way, but of less power and different tone from those of the general.

This is all that occurs to me on the formations of the army and on its training.

### [Shouting in battle]

LUIGI. I pray you will not think it troublesome to explain one thing: why do you have the light cavalry and the irregular *velites* move with yells and shouts and tumult when they attack, but then, in pushing forward the rest of the army, you show the affair going on with the utmost silence? Because I do not understand the cause of this variation, I should like you to explain it.

FABRIZIO. Ancient generals hold varied opinions about coming to close quarters: whether the army should with shouts hurry its pace or in silence go slowly. This last method serves to hold the ranks firmer and to make the general's orders better understood. The first serves to excite the spirits of the men. Because I believe we should consider both of these, I had some move with shouting and the others in silence. I hold that continual shouting is not at all advisable, because it hinders the giving of orders; and that is very pernicious.

Nor does it stand to reason that the Romans continued to shout after the first attack, because we read in their histories that many times a general's words and exhortations halted soldiers who were fleeing, and in various ways in accord with his orders they varied their ranks. This would not have happened if their shouts had overpowered his voice.

## BOOK 4. [*SUGGESTIONS TO GENERALS*]

LUIGI. Since under my command a battle has been won so honorably, I think it wise no longer to tempt Fortune, knowing how variable and unstable she is. Therefore I wish to lay aside the dictatorship and to have Zanobi now carry on this office of questioner, if we are to follow the plan that it shall belong to the youngest. And I know that he will not refuse this honor or, to put it better, this labor, both to please me and also because he is naturally more spirited than I am; nor will he fear to enter these struggles where he can be conquered as well as conquer.

ZANOBI. I am ready for any duty you give me, though I should prefer to listen, because up to now, as I have listened to your discussions, your questions have satisfied me better than those occurring to me. But I do hope, Sir, that you can spare time and will have patience if we annoy you with these formalities of ours.

FABRIZIO. Rather you give me pleasure, because this variation in questioners reveals your various abilities and various desires. But is there anything further that you think should be added to the material we have discussed?

ZANOBI. I wish you would explain two matters before we pass to another topic. One is whether any other method for drawing up armies occurs to you. The other is what a general should consider before entering battle and what expedients he should use in any unexpected event.

### [*The army must be drawn up as conditions require*]

FABRIZIO. I shall make an effort to satisfy you. I shall not indeed answer your questions individually, because, while I answer one, many times it happens that I answer the other. I have told you that I have set before you a type of army such that, by means of that type, I can give my army all the forms that the enemy or the site requires, because in this case one proceeds according to both the site and the enemy. But note this: there is no more dangerous form than to extend the front of your army greatly if you do not clearly have a very effective and a very large army; on the contrary, you ought to make it deep and not very wide rather than very wide and thin. Because when you have few men in comparison with the enemy, you ought to search for other expedients, such as drawing up your army in a place where you will be protected by a river or a swamp, in such a way that you cannot be surrounded, or guarding yourself on the flanks with ditches, as Caesar did in France. And in this case you must consider a general principle: namely, that of extending or contracting your front according to your numbers and those of the enemy. If your enemy is smaller in number, you should seek for open places, especially if your men are disciplined, so that you can not merely surround the enemy but can extend your order of battle, because in places rough and difficult, since you cannot employ your units, you will really have no advantage. For this reason the Romans almost always sought open fields and avoided difficult ones. If your soldiers are few or badly disciplined, you should do the opposite, looking for places where either a small number can save you or where lack of experience will not injure you.

## [*Choice of a position*]

You should also choose an elevated position, from which you can more easily charge the enemy. Nevertheless you ought to be careful not to draw up your army near the base of a slope, where the hostile army can take position above you; because then, in regard to artillery, the enemy's higher position would cause you disadvantage, because you could always and easily be harmed by his artillery without being able to shelter yourself against it and, impeded by your own men, you could not easily damage it. It is also good when arranging an army for battle to consider the sun and the wind, that neither one may strike you in front, for both obstruct your vision, one with its rays, the other with dust. And besides, the wind is unfavorable to weapons discharged against the enemy and makes their blows weaker. As to the sun, you should not merely be careful that it does not for the moment strike your face, but you must plan so that as the day goes on it still will not trouble you. And for this you must, when you draw up your men, have the sun directly behind you, so that it will take a long time to get in your face. This method was observed by Hannibal at Cannae and by Marius against the Cimbri.

### [*Choice of ground for cavalry*]

If you are much inferior in cavalry, draw up your army among vines and trees and similar obstacles, as the Spaniards did in our time when they defeated the French at Cirignuola in the Kingdom. And frequently with the same soldiers, by varying only disposition and place, a loser becomes a victor. So it was with the Cartha-ginians, who, after many defeats by Marcus Regulus, were at last victorious through the advice of Xantippus, the Lacedaemonian; he had them descend into the plain, where, by virtue of their cavalry and elephants, they overcame the Romans.

### [*Application of superior force at one point*]

Ancient examples, I believe, also show that almost all excellent generals, when they knew the enemy had made one part of his line of battle strong, did not oppose that part with their strongest portion but with their weakest, and opposed their strongest to the enemy's weakest. Then on joining battle, they commanded their most power-ful part merely to resist the enemy and not to push him, and their weakest part they ordered to let itself be overcome and to draw back as far as the rearmost section of the army. This causes an enemy great confusion in two ways: first, he finds his strongest part surrounded; second, since he supposes he has gained the victory quickly, he seldom escapes being thrown into confusion; the result is his speedy defeat. Cornelius Scipio, when in Spain against Hasdrubal, the Carthaginian, learned that Hasdrubal knew that Scipio always drew up his army with the legions in the center, which thus was the strongest part of his army; Hasdrubal was therefore going to use a similar arrangement. Hence when Scipio came to battle, he changed his order, putting the legions on the wings of his army, and in the center putting all his weakest men. Then as the combat began he suddenly had the men posted in the center move slowly, while the wings of the army drove forward with speed; thus merely the wings of the two armies fought, but the sections in the center, being distant from each other, did not come together. As the result, Scipio's most powerful part fought with Hasdrubal's weakest part and overcame it.

This method was useful at that time, but today artillery prohibits it, because to leave space in the middle, between the two armies, would give time for firing; as we said above, such fire is very damaging. Hence we are forced to reject this method and, as we said a little while ago, to have the entire army join battle and the weaker part yield.

### [*Devices useful in battle*]

When a general finds his army larger than his enemy's and wishes to surround him unforeseen, he can arrange his army with a front equal to that of his adversary; then when the battle is joined he can have the front retire little by little and the flanks extend themselves. It will happen every time that the enemy will find themselves sur-rounded before they realize it. If a general wishes to fight with almost a certainty that he cannot be beaten, he should draw up his army in a place where he has a refuge near at hand and secure, either among swamps or among mountains or in a powerful city, because in this case he cannot be pursued by the enemy and the enemy can be pursued by him. This plan was used by Hannibal when Fortune began to be adverse to him and he feared the courage of Marcus Marcellus. Some, to confuse the ranks of the enemy, have com-manded those who are lightly armed to begin the battle, and when they have begun, to retire into the array; and later, when the armies have struck together and the front of each one is occupied in fighting, they have had them come out on the flanks of the battalions; thus they disordered and defeated the enemy. If a general is inferior in cavalry, he can, in addition to the methods spoken of, put a bat-talion of pikes behind the cavalry and, in the combat, order them to give way to the pikes; he will always come out ahead. Many have been in the habit of selecting some lightly armed infantry to fight among the cavalry; this has been a great aid to the cavalry.

### [*The tactics of Hannibal and Scipio*]

Of all those who have drawn up armies for battle, the most praised have been Hannibal and Scipio when they fought in Africa. Because Hannibal's army was made up of Carthaginians and of auxiliaries of various sorts, he put in the very front eighty elephants; behind them he stationed the auxiliaries; after them he put his Carthaginians; in the last place he put the Italians, in whom he had

little confidence. He arranged matters in this way so that the auxiliaries, having the enemy in front, and being shut in behind by his
own men, would not be able to flee; hence, being obliged to fight,
they would conquer or tire out the Romans. He thought that then
his fresh and vigorous Carthaginians would easily overcome the
tired Romans. Over against this arrangement, Scipio put the *hastati*,
the *principes*, and the *triarii* in the usual manner so that one could
receive the other and support the other. He made the front of the
army full of intervals; and in order that this should not be apparent
but that rather the line should appear solid, he filled these intervals
with *velites*. To them he gave orders that as soon as the elephants
came they should yield and, entering among the legions by the usual
spaces, should leave the passage free to the elephants. Thus he succeeded in rendering their charge vain, so that on coming to close
quarters he was superior.

### [*Scipio's innovation*]

ZANOBI. By bringing up this battle, you have made me recall
that in the course of the fight Scipio did not have the *hastati* retire into
the ranks of the *principes*, but divided them and had them retire to the
wings of the army in order to make room when he wished to push
the *principes* forward. So I hope you will tell me what influenced
him not to follow the usual arrangement.

FABRIZIO. I shall tell you. Hannibal had put all the excellence
of his army into the second line. Therefore Scipio, in order to oppose to it equal excellence, crowded the *principes* and the *triarii* together
in such a way that, since the intervals in the *principes* were occupied
by the *triarii*, there was no space where the *hastati* could be received.
So he had the *hastati* divide and go to the wings of the army instead
of drawing them back among the *principes*. But note that this manner of opening the first line to give place to the second cannot be used
except when a general is stronger, because then he can easily do so,
as Scipio did. But being inferior and pushed back, you cannot
do it except with your obvious ruin; therefore you must have
ranks to the rear that can receive you.

### [*Scythe-bearing chariots*]

But let us return to our discussion. The ancient Asiatics, among
other things they devised to damage the enemy, used chariots with

scythes at their sides; these served not merely to open the lines with their rush but also to kill their opponents with the scythes. Against their charge provision was made in three ways: either the density of the ranks repelled them; or spaces between the groups received them like Hannibal's elephants; or by contrivance some powerful resist‐ ance was made, such as Sulla the Roman made against Archelaus, who had many of these scythe‐bearing chariots. To resist them, Sulla fixed plenty of stakes in the ground in front of his first line, so that the chariots, being held up, lost their momentum. Worth ob‐ serving is the new method Sulla used against Archelaus in drawing up his army; he put the *velites* and the cavalry in the rear, and all the heavy‐armed in front, leaving in their line sufficient intervals through which he could send forward the soldiers in the rear when necessity required it; thus, after the battle had joined, with the aid of the cavalry to whom he had left the way open, he gained the victory.

### [*Confusing the enemy*]

In order in the midst of battle to confuse the hostile army, it is necessary to make something happen that will bewilder them, either by announcing some reinforcement that is coming or by showing something that appears like it, so that the enemy, deceived by that appearance, are frightened, and when frightened can easily be over‐ come. These methods were used by Minucius Rufus and Acilius Glabrio, Roman consuls. Caius Sulpitius also put a large number of camp followers on mules and other animals useless in war, but drawn up in such a way that they represented men‐at‐arms, and ordered that they should appear on a hill while he was closely en‐ gaged with the French; from this came his victory. The same thing was done by Marius when he fought against the Germans.

### [*Surprise and similar devices*]

Since, then, pretended attacks are of great value while the fight is going on, it must be that true ones will be much more useful, especially if unexpectedly, in the midst of the combat you can attack the enemy's rear or flank. This is hard to do if the country does not aid you, because when it is open, you cannot conceal part of your men, as you must in such undertakings; but in places that are wooded and mountainous and therefore suitable for ambushes, you can conceal part of your men, so that suddenly and contrary to the enemy's expectation, you can attack them—which will always cause you to gain the victory. It has sometimes been very effective, while the fight was going on, to scatter reports announcing that the general of the enemy was dead, or that the other flank of the army has been victorious. Many times this device has given its user the victory. The hostile cavalry is easily thrown into confusion by shapes or noises strange to it; hence Croesus opposed camels to the horses of his adversaries, and Pyrrhus opposed the Roman cavalry with elephants, whose appearance upset and confused it. In our times the Turk defeated the Sophy in Persia and the Soldan in Syria with nothing else than the noise of the harquebuses, which with their unwonted noise so frightened the cavalry that the Turk easily overcame it. The Spanish, to conquer Hamilcar's army, put in their van oxcarts full of dry brush which, on coming to close quarters, they set on fire. Hence the oxen, trying to escape the fire, plunged into Hamilcar's army and opened it. Generals are wont, as we have said, to deceive the enemy in fighting by drawing them into ambushes where the country is suitable, but when it is open and roomy, many make ditches and cover them lightly with brush and earth but leave some spaces firm so that they can withdraw among them. Then, when the battle is joined, they retire among them, but when the enemy follows, he is ruined in them.

### [Devices for keeping up the spirits of one's soldiers]

If in the battle some accident occurs to dismay your soldiers, it is a very prudent thing to find a way to dissimulate it and change it into good, as did Tullus Hostilius and Lucius Sulla, who, seeing that while they were fighting part of their men had gone over to the hostile side and that the affair had greatly dismayed their soldiers, at once made it known through the whole army that everything was going according to plan; this not merely did not upset the army but increased its courage so much that it was victorious. It happened also to Sulla that when he had sent certain soldiers to carry out something and they were killed, he said, in order that his army should not be dismayed, that he had sent them deliberately into the hands of the enemy because he had found them unreliable. Sertorius, fighting a battle in Spain, killed one who reported the death of one of his officers, for fear that if he said the same thing to the others, he would dismay them.

### [*Devices for checking flight*]

It is very difficult when an army has already started to flee to halt it and bring it back to the combat. And you must make this distinc- tion: either it has all started, and then it is impossible to re-form it; or part of it has started, and then something can be done. Many Ro- man generals by getting in front of those who were running away have halted them, making them ashamed of their flight, as Lucius Sulla did, for when part of his legions actually were running away, chased by Mithridates' soldiers, he put himself in front of them with his sword in his hand, shouting: "If anybody asks you where you have left your general, say: 'We left him in Boeotia where he was fighting.'" Attilius the Consul opposed to soldiers who were running away others who were not running and gave them to understand that if they did not turn around they would be killed by their friends and by their enemies. Philip of Macedonia, understanding that his men feared the Scythian soldiers, put behind his army some of his most faithful cavalry and ordered them to kill whoever ran; hence his men, preferring to die fighting rather than running, conquered. Many Romans, not so much to stop a flight as to give their men a reason for making greater effort, have, while they were fighting, taken a banner from the hands of their men and thrown it among the enemy and offered rewards to any one who would regain it.

### [*Improving victory and minimizing defeat*]

I think the subject permits me to add some things that happen after the battle, especially since they are short and such as not to be omitted, and much suited to this discussion. I say, then, that battles are lost or won. When a general wins, he ought with all speed to follow up his victory, imitating in this matter Caesar and not Han- nibal, who, by standing still after he had defeated the Romans at Cannae, lost thereby the mastery of Rome. The other after a victory never rested, but in pursuing his defeated enemies showed greater vigor and dash than in attacking them when they were unshaken. When he loses, a general should try to get some benefit from the loss, especially if some remnant of his army is left. Such opportunity can come from the negligence of an enemy, who after a victory often grows careless and gives you a chance to defeat him, as the Roman Martius defeated the Carthaginian armies. These, having killed the two Scipios and vanquished their armies, disregarded the remnant of the soldiers left alive with Martius, who then assailed and van/ quished them. His example teaches that nothing is so likely to succeed as what your enemy thinks you unable to attempt, because usually men are injured most where they fear least. Therefore when a general cannot do this, he should at least give the most intense effort to making his failure less damaging. To do so, you must take measures to keep your enemy from following you easily[1] or must give him good cause for hesitation. In the first instance some generals, when they knew they were losing, have ordered their officers to flee in different directions and by different roads, after giving orders where they were later to regather. They did this in order that the enemy, fearing to divide his army, would allow the safe escape of all or the greater part of the defeated army. In the second case, many have openly abandoned their most precious things, so that the enemy, delayed by the spoil, would give them more time for flight. Titus Didius used no little cleverness in concealing the damage he had received in combat, for after fighting until night with the loss of many of his men, in the night he had the greater part of them buried, so that in the morning, when the enemy saw so many of their men dead and so few of the Romans, they thought they had the disad/ vantage and fled.

### [Confusing hostile plans by adapting oneself to them]

I hope that thus I have, though confusedly, as I said, replied for the most part to your inquiry. It is true that with respect to the form of armies, it remains for me to tell you that sometimes generals have adopted the custom of drawing them up with the front in the shape of a wedge, judging that in this way they would more easily be able to open the hostile army. In opposition to this form some have used a form in the shape of scissors, in order to receive that wedge in the space left vacant and to surround it and assail it from every side. On these things I wish you to take this general rule: the best remedy that can be used against a design of the enemy is to do willingly what he intends you shall do by force; by doing it willingly, you do it in order and to your advantage and his disadvantage. If you do it when you are forced to, it is your ruin. To strengthen this, I shall not hesitate to repeat something already said. Does your adversary make

---

1. *Note the characteristic shift to* you, *as often in* THE PRINCE.

a wedge to open your ranks? If you go with these open, you disorder him and he does not disorder you. Thus Hannibal put elephants in the front of his army in order to open with them the army of Scipio; so Scipio went with his army open, and it was the cause both of his victory and of the ruin of the other. Hasdrubal put his more valiant men in the center of the front of his army, to drive back Scipio's men; so Scipio ordered that of themselves they should retire, and defeated him. So plans of this sort, when they are foreseen, are the cause of victory for him against whom they have been devised.

## [*When to engage in battle*]

It still remains for me, if I remember correctly, to tell you what a general ought to consider before he undertakes a battle. On which I have to say, first, that a general is never to fight a battle if he does not have the advantage, or if he is not compelled by necessity. Advantage comes from site, from organization, from having either more or better men. Necessity comes when you see that if you do not fight you must surely lose, that, for instance, you lack money and therefore your army is certain to go to pieces; or that hunger is going to attack you; or that your enemy is expecting to increase his army with new men. In these instances you should always fight, even if you are at a disadvantage, because it is much better to tempt Fortune when she possibly will favor you than, not tempting her, to face certain ruin. And it is as serious a fault for a general not to fight, in this case, as it is to have a chance to win and not to recognize it through ignorance or to let it slip through cowardice.

## [*Seizing an advantage*]

Sometimes your enemy gives you advantages and sometimes your own prudence. Many in crossing rivers have been defeated by an alert enemy who has waited until they are half on each side; then he has assailed them as Caesar did the Swiss, when he destroyed a fourth of them because they were divided by a river. Sometimes your enemy is tired because he has followed you too thoughtlessly, so that, if you are fresh and rested, you ought not to let such an opportunity pass. Besides this, if your enemy offers you battle early in the morning, you can put off coming out of your encampment for many hours; and when he has been a long time under arms and has lost the first eagerness with which he came, then you can fight with him.

This method was used by Scipio and Metellus in Spain, one against Hasdrubal, the other against Sertorius. If your enemy has reduced his forces, either through having separated his armies, as did the Scipios in Spain, or for some other reason, you should try your luck. The majority of prudent generals receive the rush of the enemy rather than go with a rush to assail him, because vehemence is easily repelled by men who are firm and solid, and vehemence repelled is easily changed into cowardice. So Fabius did against the Samnites and against the Gauls, and was victorious, and Decius his colleague was left dead there. Some who have feared the ability of their enemy have begun the battle at an hour near night, in order that if they were defeated, their own men, protected by the darkness, could save themselves. Some, knowing that the hostile army is kept by some superstition from fighting at a certain time, have chosen that time for the combat and have conquered. Caesar acted on this plan in France against Ariovistus, and Vespasian in Syria against the Jews.

*[The general's advisers and what he should discuss with them]*

The greatest and most important matter that a general should attend to is to have near him faithful men, very skilful in war and prudent, with whom he continually advises, with whom he discusses his own soldiers and those of the enemy: Which are in greater numbers? Which better armed, or better on horseback, or better trained? Which are more suited to endure hardship? In which can he put more confidence, the infantry or the cavalry? Then they should consider the place where they are, if it is more suited for the enemy or for their own army; which of them more easily gets supplies; if it is well to put off the battle or to engage in it; what advantage time can give him or take away from him, because many times the soldiers, seeing the war stretch out, get sick of it and, worn out by fatigue and monotony, abandon you. It is above all important to know the commander of the enemy and whom he has around him: whether he is rash or cautious, timid or bold; and to see how far you can trust the auxiliary soldiers. Above all you ought to guard against leading into battle an army that is afraid or in any way is uncertain of victory; because the surest sign of losing is not to believe you can win. Therefore in this case you should avoid battle, either by doing as did

Fabius Maximus, who, by encamping in strong places, deprived Hannibal of courage to attack him; or if you believe your enemy will attack you even in a strong place, you should leave the field and divide your soldiers among your cities, in order that the tedium of beseiging them may wear him out.

ZANOBI. Can such a general not avoid battle in some other way than by dividing his men and putting them in various cities?

## [*Avoiding battle*]

FABRIZIO. I believe that earlier I told some of you that a general who remains in the field cannot avoid battle if his enemy intends to fight in any circumstances;[2] he has but one remedy: that is to put himself with his army at least fifty miles distant from his adversary, in order to have time to get out of the way when the other comes to attack him. Even Fabius Maximus never refused battle with Hannibal; on the contrary, he planned to fight when he had the advantage, and Hannibal did not feel sure that he would defeat Fabius by attacking him in the places where he was encamped; if Hannibal had decided that he could defeat him, Fabius would have been forced to fight no matter what, or to flee. Philip King of Macedonia, the father of Perseus, when at war with the Romans, put his encampment on a very high mountain in order not to have to fight a battle with them; but the Romans attacked him on the mountain and defeated him. Vercingetorix, the French general, in order not to fight with Caesar, who contrary to his expectations had crossed a river, went many miles away with his soldiers. In our times, if the Venetians were unwilling to come to battle with the King of France, they should not have waited until the French army had crossed the Adda,[3] but should have removed far from it, like Vercingetorix. In this instance, after waiting, they were not wise enough to find in the crossing of the soldiers their opportunity to fight, nor wise enough to avoid battle, for the French, being near when the Venetians left their camp, attacked and defeated them. At any rate, battle cannot be avoided when your enemy in whatever case intends to fight. Nor should anybody bring up Fabius, because however much he avoided battle, Hannibal avoided it just as much.

2. DISCOURSES *3. 10. Here Fabrizio is Machiavelli himself.*
3. *The battle of Vailà; see the Index.*

*[Soldiers overconfident and underconfident]*

Often your soldiers are eager to fight when you know that in numbers or site or something else you are at a disadvantage, and you would like to rid them of their eagerness. On the other hand, necessity or occasion may force you to battle when your soldiers are not confident but are indisposed to fight. Hence in one case you need to dismay them and in the other to rouse them. If dismay is needed, when persuasions are not enough, there is no better way than to give part of them as prey to the enemy, in order that both those who have fought and those who have not may believe you. You also may find it possible to do by plan what Fabius Maximus did by chance. In Fabius' army, as you know, there was a desire to fight with Hannibal's army; his master of horse shared this desire; Fabius thought combat unwise; hence, because of this disagreement, he divided his army. Fabius kept his part in camp; the other leader fought and, getting into great danger, would have been defeated if Fabius had not rescued him. Through this experience the master of the horse and the whole army learned how wise they were in obeying Fabius. As to stirring soldiers up to fight, it is a good plan for the general to make them indignant by showing that the enemy are making insulting speeches about them; he can pretend that he is in communication with the enemy and has bribed part of them; he can camp in a place where his men can see the enemy and have some slight combats with them, because things seen daily are more easily despised; he can act as though he were angry and, with a suitable oration, reprove his soldiers for their sluggishness and, to make them ashamed, say that he intends to fight alone, if they will not bear him company. And above all he ought to take pains about the following, if he wishes the soldiers to be obstinate in battle: not to permit them to send home any of their property or deposit it anywhere until the war ends, so that they realize that though flight may save their lives, it will not save their property, the love of which, not less than that of life, makes men obstinate in defense.

*[The general as orator]*

ZANOBI. You have said that the soldiers can be made eager for battle by speaking to them. Do you mean, by this, that it is necessary to speak to the entire army or to the officers?

FABRIZIO. To persuade or dissuade a few about a thing is very easy, because, if words are not enough, you can use authority and force; but the difficulty is to remove from a multitude a belief that is unfavorable and contrary either to the common good or to your belief, when you can use only words proper to be heard by all, since you are trying to persuade them all. Therefore an excellent general is usually an orator because, unless he knows how to speak to the whole army, he will have difficulty in doing anything good; but anything of the sort is in these times of ours completely obsolete. Read the life of Alexander the Great and see how many times it was necessary for him to assemble the army and speak publicly to it; otherwise, when it had become rich and laden with booty, he would never have led it with so much hardship and distress through the deserts of Arabia and into India. For there are countless times when things come up by which an army would be ruined if the general either could not or was not accustomed to speak to it; this speaking lightens fear, sets courage afire, increases determination, uncovers deceptions, promises rewards, shows perils and the way to escape them, reproaches, begs, threatens, fills with hope, praises, berates and does everything through which human passions are extinguished or excited. Hence any prince or republic intending to set up a new military establishment and bring reputation to such an army must accustom its soldiers to hearing their generals speak, and must accustom its generals to speak skilfully.

## [Religion]

Also very powerful in keeping the ancient soldiers well disposed were religion and the oath sworn when they were taken into service, because in all their transgressions they were threatened not alone with the ills they could fear from men but with those they could expect from God. This condition, mingled with other religious customs, many times made every sort of undertaking easy for the ancient generals, and always will make them so, where religion is feared and observed. Sertorius availed himself of this, pretending that he spoke with a deer which, on the part of God, promised him victory. Sulla said that he spoke with an image that he had taken from the temple of Apollo. Many have said that in a dream they have seen God, exhorting them to fight. In the time of our fathers, Charles VII, King of France, in the war that he made against the English, said that he took counsel with a girl sent by God, who was called everywhere the Maid of France; and this was the cause of his victory.

### [*Other ways to make soldiers determined*]

It is possible also to use methods that will make your men feel slight respect for the enemy. For example, Agesilaus the Spartan set before his soldiers some Persians stripped naked, so that seeing their delicate limbs, they would not fear them. Some have forced their men to fight through necessity, taking from them every hope of saving themselves except by winning. This is the most spirited device and the best that can be used, if the soldier is to be made determined. His determination is increased by confidence in his general and his native land, and love for them. Confidence is caused by arms, discipline, recent victories, and the general's reputation. Love for a man's native land is caused by nature; that for his general, more by ability than by any kindness. Necessities may be many, but strongest is that which forces you to conquer or to die.

## BOOK 5. [*MARCHING IN HOSTILE TERRITORY; SUPPLIES; BOOTY*]

### [*The Roman order of march*]

FABRIZIO. I have shown you how an army is arrayed to fight a battle with another army drawn up against it, and have told you how the other is beaten and, after that, many details related to the various accidents that can happen in battle. So it is now time to show you how an army is prepared against an enemy whom no one sees but from whom you continually fear attack. This is your condition when you march through a hostile or suspected region. And first you must understand that a Roman army, as a matter of course, always sent ahead some platoons of cavalry to reconnoiter the road. Then followed the right wing. After that came all the baggage belonging to it. After these came a legion followed by its baggage. Then another legion and next to it, its baggage. After them came the left wing with its baggage behind it, and last of all, the remainder of the cavalry followed. This is in brief the manner in which they ordinarily marched. And if on the march the army was assailed in front or in the rear, at once they made the baggage train retire to the right or to the left, according as it happened or as best fitted the terrain; and all the soldiers together, free from their impediments, faced in the direction from which the enemy came. If they were assailed on the flank, the baggage was drawn back in the direction that was secure, and the soldiers faced in the other. This method, since it is good and wisely planned, I think should be imitated by sending the light cavalry ahead to reconnoiter the country; then, if there are four brigades, they should march in line, each with its baggage behind it. And because there is baggage of two kinds, that of individual soldiers and that for the general use of the whole army, I should divide the general baggage into four parts and to every brigade I should give its own part, also dividing into four parts the artillery and all the unarmed persons, in order that each group of armed men will have equal impediments.

### [Marching in constant expectation of attack]

But because sometimes you march through a region not merely suspected but so far hostile that every hour you fear to be attacked, you must change the form of your march and go in a regulated fashion in order to move securely, so that neither the countrymen nor an army can harm you through finding you unprepared at any point. In such cases the ancient generals were in the habit of marching with the army in a square (for so they called this form, not because it was perfectly square, but because it was fitted for fighting in four direc-tions), and they said they were continually ready for both marching and battle. From this method I do not intend to depart, and I intend to arrange my two brigades, which I have taken as the model of an army, in the following manner. Since I wish, then, to march through a hostile region and to be able to react on any side if I were unexpectedly attacked, and since I wish, according to the ancients, to form it into a square, I shall attempt to make a square of which the vacant part measures on every side four hundred and twenty-four feet,[1] in this way: I first arrange the flanks, one flank distant from the other four hundred and twenty-four feet, and I put on each flank five battalions, one behind another from front to back and with spaces between them of six feet; these with their spaces, since each

---

1. *In the measurements, except those of weapons, in this and the following books, the Floren-tine braccio, slightly more than 1.9 feet, has for simplicity been taken as two feet; hence measure-ments in feet are too large by almost one-twentieth.*

battalion occupies eighty feet, occupy four hundred and twenty-four feet.  Between the fronts, then, and the rears of these two flanks, I put the other ten battalions, in each place five, arranging them in such a way that four of them are close to the front of the right flank, and four to the rear of the left flank, leaving between them intervals of six feet; then one is close to the front of the left flank, and one to the rear of the right flank.  And because the open space between one flank and the other is four hundred and twenty-four feet and these battalions, which are put side by side from left to right and not from front to back, occupy with their intervals two hundred and sixty-eight feet, there remains between the four battalions placed in the front on the right flank and the one placed on the left flank a space of one hundred and fifty-six feet; and this same space is left between the battalions posted in the rear; nor is there any difference except that one space, in the rear, is nearer the right wing, and the other, in front, is nearer the left wing.  In the space of one hundred and fifty-six feet in front I put all the regular *velites*; in that at the rear the irregular ones, so that there are a thousand of them for each space.  And since the space within the army is to be in every direction four hundred and twenty-four feet, the five battalions put at the head of the formation and those that are put at its tail must not occupy any part of the space that the flanks cover; and therefore the five battalions that are behind must touch with their front the tail of the flanks, and those in front with their tail must touch the head of the flanks; hence at every corner of this army there is a space for receiving another battalion. And because there are four spaces, I take four bands of the irregular pikes and in every corner I put one of them; and the two bands of the said pikes that are left over I put in the middle of the open space of this army in a square of battalions,[2] at the head of which is the general with his men about him.

### [*Preparation for combat*]

And because these battalions, so drawn up, all march in one direction, but do not all fight in one direction, it is necessary, in putting them together, to arrange for combat those sides that are not guarded by the other battalions.  And therefore it must be considered

---

2. *In Book 2 we learn that there were for each battalion three constables of irregular pikemen; yet there are ten centurions. Presumably, then, one constable has charge of four hundred men, the others of three hundred. Three hundred would not fill up one of the corners of the army square.*

that the five battalions in front are protected on all sides except their front; and therefore these are to be drawn up in the usual way with the pikes ahead. The five battalions that are in the rear are protected on all sides except their rear; and therefore they are drawn up in such a way that the pikes come at their rear, as we shall show in its place. The five battalions that are on the right flank are protected on all sides except their right flank. The five that are on the left flank are protected on all sides except their left flank; and therefore in arranging the battalions, the pikes are put on the flank that remains uncovered. And because the decurions must come at the front and at the rear, in order that in combat all the arms and all the members may be in their places, the method of doing this will be told when we deal with the methods of arranging the battalions.

### [*Management of artillery and cavalry*]

The artillery I divide; I put one part of it outside on the right flank and the other on the left flank. The light cavalry I send in front to reconnoiter the country. Of the men-at-arms I put part in the rear on the right flank and part on the left, distant eighty feet from the battalions. And in whatever way you draw up an army, you have to accept, as to the cavalry, this general rule: that they always must be put in the rear or on the flanks. He who puts them forward, directly in front of the army, has to do one of two things: either he must put them so far ahead that if they are driven back, they have space enough to give them time for turning aside from your infantry and not plunging into it; or the infantry must be arranged in such a way, with so many intervals, that the cavalry by means of them may enter among the infantry without disordering them. No one should disregard this reminder, because many through not attending to it have been ruined and by their own men have been thrown into disorder and defeated. The baggage and the unarmed men are put in the open space within the army, and are divided off in such a way that they easily give passage to anybody who needs to go from one side to the other or from front to rear of the army.

### [*The two brigades divided*]

So then, these battalions, without the artillery and the cavalry, occupy on the outside in every direction five hundred and sixty-four feet of space.[3] And because this square is made up of two brigades, it is necessary to divide the part that is made up of one brigade from the part made up of the other. And because the brigades are known by number and each of them has, as you know, ten battalions and a general, I put the first five battalions of the first brigade in front, the other five on the left flank, and the general himself in the left angle of the front. The second brigade then puts its first five battalions on the right flank and the other five at the rear, and the general himself in the right angle; he then holds the position of commander of the rear.

### [*Attack by irregular and regular forces*]

When the army is drawn up in this way it is to march, and in moving forward it is to keep exactly the order I have described. Beyond question it is safe from all throngs of countrymen. Nor does the general need to make any other provision against attacks by mobs than sometimes to assign to some cavalry or band of *velites* the task of driving them back. Nor do these mobs of people ever come within reach of sword or pike to attack you, because unorganized people fear those who are organized; with shouts and noise they always make a great show of attack without actually closing with you, like curs around a mastiff. Hannibal, when he came to Italy to attack the Romans, passed through all France and always paid little attention to mobs of the French. When you march, you must have ahead of you pioneers and ditch-diggers to prepare the road; they can be guarded by the horsemen who are sent ahead to scout. An army in this array marches ten miles a day, and enough sun is left for it to encamp and get supper, because ordinarily an army marches twenty miles. If it is attacked by a regular army, this attack cannot come suddenly, because a regular army comes at your pace; hence you have time to rearrange your troops for battle and quickly to bring them into the form of army, or one similar to it, that I showed you above.

### [*Preparation for attack in front*]

If you are assailed in front, you need do nothing except have the artillery on the flanks and the cavalry at the rear come ahead and put

3. *As Machiavelli has explained in Books 2 and 3, a battalion is almost a double square requiring for its front 50 feet and for its depth 80 feet. Hence the battalions at the back and at the front of the army square extend farther from the open space than do those on the flanks. Therefore*

themselves in the places and at the distances mentioned above. The thousand *velites* in front leave that position, divide into five hundred in a group, and go to a position between the cavalry and the wing of the army. Then, into the opening they have left, enter the two bands of irregular pikes that I put in the middle of the open space within the army. The thousand *velites* whom I put in the rear leave that place and scatter themselves along the flanks of the battalions for their support; and through the opening they leave, all the baggage and the unarmed men pass out, to station themselves in the rear of the battalions. When the open space is vacant and everybody has gone to his place, the five battalions that I put at the rear of the army go forward through the open place between the two wings and go toward the battalions in front; and three of them pause eighty feet behind those in front, with equal intervals between themselves; and the other two remain behind, at a distance of eighty feet more. This form can be arranged quickly and is almost like that first disposition of the army earlier explained, and if it is narrower in front, it is thicker in the flanks, which does not give it less strength. But be-cause the five battalions at the rear have their pikes at the rear, for the reasons we gave before, they must come to the front, if they are to support the van of the army; therefore they either turn battalion by battalion as a solid body, or the pikes quickly enter among the ranks of the shields and go to the front—a method that is quicker and causes less disorder than to have them turn. And so those at the rear act in every sort of attack, as I shall show you.

### [Attack on rear or flanks]

If the enemy comes against the rear, immediately each man turns his face where he had his back; and at once the army has changed its front into its rear and its rear into its front. Then it uses all those methods for disposing that front that I spoke of above. If the enemy attack the right flank, the whole army turn their faces to that side; and then do all the things for the strengthening of the right which were spoken of above; so that the cavalry, the *velites*, and the artillery are in their proper places on that front to the right. There is this difference alone that, in varying the fronts, some of those who change move a

---

*adding double these numbers to the 424 feet of the open inner space, the outer dimensions are 524 by 584 feet. Machiavelli's 564 is unaccountable.*

shorter distance and others a longer. It is evident that when the right flank becomes the front, the *velites* who enter into the interval between the wing of the army and the cavalry are those nearest the left wing, and into their place go the two bands of irregular pikes posted in the middle. But before they enter there, the baggage and the unarmed must through the opening vacate the space within the army and retire behind the left wing, which then becomes the rear of the army. The other *velites* posted in the rear, according to the original arrange- ment, in this case do not move, so that their place is not left open; for it would be changed from rear to flank. All other things must be done as for a frontal attack. What has just been said about making the right flank into a front is to be understood as applying when the left flank becomes a front; the same methods are to be observed.

### [*Attack on two or more sides*]

If an enemy comes in numbers and good order to attack you on two sides, the two sides attacked must be strengthened from the two not attacked; each front must duplicate the other in arrangement, and between the two fronts, the artillery, the *velites*, and the cavalry must be divided. If the enemy attacks on three or four sides, either you or he is clearly lacking in prudence; if you are wise, you never put yourself in a place where the enemy can assail you on three or four sides with soldiers numerous and well disciplined, be- cause in order to attack with safety he must have such numbers that on every side he can assail you with almost as many men as make up your whole army. If you are so imprudent as to put yourself among the lands and forces of an enemy who has more than three times as many disciplined soldiers as you have, if you come off badly you can complain only of yourself. If it happens not through your fault but through some accident, you lose without shame, and your results are like those of the Scipios in Spain and of Hasdrubal in Italy. But if the enemy does not have many more men than you and attempts, in order to disorganize you, to attack you from many sides, it will be folly for him and good luck for you; because if he does this he is very foolish, for you can easily charge one group and resist another, and in a short time ruin him.

## [*Practice necessary*]

This way of drawing up an army against an enemy who is not seen but is feared is necessary; and it is very useful to accustom your soldiers to take formation and to march in such an order and, in marching, to draw up for combat according to the first method, and then to return into the formation in which they were marching; when in that, to make a front of the rear, then of the flank, and from that formation to return to their first one. Such exercise and familiarizing are necessary, if you expect to have an army that is disciplined and usable. In such matters the generals and the officers must busy them selves; for military discipline is nothing else than to be well able to command and carry out these matters; nor is a disciplined army anything other than one well trained in these movements; nor would it be possible that he who in the present time made good use of such discipline would ever be defeated. And if this square form that I have shown you is somewhat difficult, it is necessary that such a difficulty be dealt with in training; because any army that once learns to draw up and to remain in the formation described will then more easily keep in those formations that do not offer so much difficulty.

ZANOBI. I believe, as you say, that these formations are very necessary; and I for my part cannot add to them or take away. It is true that I am eager to learn from you two things: one, if when you intend to make the rear or the flank into the front and you try to make the battalions turn, whether this is ordered by the voice or by music; the second, if those whom you send ahead to work on the roads in order to make a way for the army are the soldiers of your bat talions themselves or other humble people assigned to that duty.

## [*How orders should be given*]

FABRIZIO. Your first question is of much importance, because many times imperfect understanding or bad interpreting of the generals' orders has caused confusion in their armies; therefore the words in which orders are given in time of peril should be clear and distinct. And if you give orders with music, you must make sure that there be such difference between one kind and the other that one cannot be mistaken for the other; and if you give orders with words, you ought to take care to avoid general words and use special ones, and of the special ones, avoid those that can be wrongly interpreted. Many

times the words *Back! back!* have made an army go to pieces. Therefore this word should be avoided and in its place should be used
*Retire.* If you wish to make the men turn to change front either to
one flank or to the rear, you should never use *Turn around*, but say
*To the left! To the right! To the rear! To the front!* So all the other
words should be simple and distinct, as *Charge! Stand firm! Forward! As you were!* And everything that can be done with words
should be so done; the others should be done with music.

### [*Pioneers*]

As to the pioneers, which is your second question, I would have
that duty done by my own soldiers, both because it was so done in
ancient armies, and also that there might be in the army fewer unarmed people and less baggage; and I should choose from every
battalion the number I needed and have them take pioneering tools
and give their arms to the nearest files, who would carry them; then
if the enemy came the pioneers would need only to take their weapons
again and return to their ranks.

ZANOBI. These pioneering tools—who would carry them?

FABRIZIO. The wagons for carrying such things, as assigned.

ZANOBI. I fear that you will never bring these soldiers of yours
to digging.

FABRIZIO. Everything will be discussed in its place.

### [*Provisions in Roman armies*]

Just now I wish to let this matter rest and talk of the army's way
of living, because I believe that after it has toiled so much, the time
has come to let it rest and to refresh it with food. You must understand that a prince should labor to make his army as mobile as
possible and rid it of all the things that burden it and make its
expeditions difficult. Among those that give most difficulty is keeping an army supplied with wine and with baked bread. To wine,
the ancients gave no heed, because if they did not have it they drank
water mixed with a little vinegar to give it flavor. Hence among the
supplies of food for the army was vinegar and not wine. They did
not bake their bread in ovens, as is done in cities, but provided flour;
and with that every soldier satisfied himself in his own way, having
for condiments lard and fat, which gave flavor to the bread they made
and kept the men strong. Hence the supplies of food for the army

were flour, vinegar, lard, and fat, and for the horses barley. They had, ordinarily, herds of animals, large and small, that followed the army; these, since they did not need to be carried, did not give much trouble. The result of this method was that an ancient army would march sometimes many days through solitary and difficult places without enduring any hardship about victuals, because it lived on things it easily could take along behind it.

### [*Provisions in degenerate modern armies*]

The contrary is true of modern armies: they are not willing to do without wine, and expect to eat bread baked in the same way as at home, of which they cannot have a supply that will last a long time; hence they are often hungry, or are supplied, if at all, with difficulty and at very great expense.[4] Therefore I would bring my soldiers back to the Roman way of living, and I should plan that they ate no bread except what they themselves baked. As to wine, I should not prohibit drinking it or bringing it into the army, but I should go to no effort or trouble to get it; and as to other provisions, I should conduct myself in every way as did the ancients. If you will consider this matter well, you will see how many difficulties I have removed, and of how many troubles and hardships I have relieved an army and a general, and how easy I have made any undertaking they may wish to carry on.

### [*The disposition of booty*]

ZANOBI. We have defeated the enemy in the field, then marched through his country; it is reasonable that booty should have been taken, towns obliged to pay ransom, prisoners made. Therefore I should like to know how the ancients conducted themselves in these matters.

FABRIZIO. Now I am going to satisfy you. I believe you realize, because at other times I have talked with some of you about it, how the present wars make poorer both those rulers who win and those who lose, for if one loses his state, the other loses his money and his goods; in ancient times that did not happen, because the victory in war gained riches. In our day war brings poverty because we do not

---

4. *One of Machiavelli's letters written during the Pisan war is concerned with the difficulties of providing the army with bread (*COMMISSION TO THE ARMY BEFORE PISA, *letter of 18 May 1509).*

now manage the booty as the ancients did but we leave it all in the power of the soldiers. This method produces two very great abuses: one I have mentioned; the other is that the soldier becomes more eager for plunder and less observant of the regulations; and many times eagerness for booty has made an army lose after it has won a victory.

### [*How the Romans dealt with booty*]

The Romans, therefore, who were masters in this business, provided for both of these difficulties by ordering that all the booty should belong to the public and that the public should then distribute it as seemed best. And therefore they had in their armies quaestors, who were, as we should say, finance officers, with whom all the ransoms and the booty were deposited. This was used by the consul for giving the soldiers their regular pay, for caring for the wounded and the sick, and for the other needs of the army. It was, however, possible for the consul (and he did it often) to turn over booty to the soldiers; but such a concession caused no lack of discipline, because, when a hostile army had been defeated, all the booty was put in a central place and then distributed to one Roman after another according to the rank of each man. This method caused the soldiers to attend to winning and not to robbing. The Roman legions overcame the enemy but did not pursue him, because they never left their ranks; only the cavalry pursued him, along with the light-armed and (if there were any) such soldiers as did not belong to the legions. Yet if the booty had belonged to any man who took it, the legions could not possibly or reasonably have been kept in formation; yet disorder among them would have caused many dangers. As a result of its policy the Roman state grew rich, and every consul at his triumph brought into the treasury much wealth coming from ransoms and booty.

### [*How to handle pay*]

The ancients had another well-considered policy: when each soldier was paid, he was obliged to deposit one-third with the standard-bearer of his battalion, who never gave it back to him until the war was over. This they did for two reasons: first, in order that the soldier should save his pay, because, the greater part of them being young and heedless, the more they have, the more without necessity they spend; second, in order that, knowing that their property was with the standard, they would take better care of that standard and defend it with more stubbornness; and so this device made them economical and valorous. We must observe all these things if we are to bring armies back within proper bounds.

ZANOBI. I believe an army marching from place to place can by no possibility avoid dangerous accidents, requiring ingenuity from the general and efficiency from the soldiers, if they are to escape; therefore I shall be glad to have you tell me about any you recall.

### [*Ambushes*]

FABRIZIO. I shall satisfy you with pleasure, since it is altogether necessary if I am to give full information on military training. Above everything else, when marching with an army, a general must take precaution against ambushes, into which you get in two ways: either you move into them when on the march, or the enemy's craft draws you in without your having any warning.

If the first case is to be prevented, you must send ahead double guards to examine the country; they must use so much the more diligence as the country is the more suited to ambushes, as are countries that are forested and hilly, because invariably ambushes are placed in a forest or behind a hill. And as the ambush ruins you if you do not foresee it, so if you do foresee it you are not troubled. Birds and dust have many times revealed the enemy, because when-ever he comes to attack you he will raise a great deal of dust that will indicate his approach. Similarly, in places where he was to pass, a general has often seen the rising of doves or other birds that fly in numbers, and their circling around and not lighting. These mani-festations have shown him where the ambush of the enemy lies; so sending soldiers ahead to discover it, he has saved himself and damaged his enemy.

As to the second case, that of being drawn into one, which our men call being drawn into a net, you must be shrewd about not believing easily things not in accord with reason. For example, if the enemy puts some booty before you, you ought to believe that within it there is a hook and that it conceals some trick. If many of the enemy are put to flight by your few, if a few of the enemy assail your many, if the enemy turn in sudden flight, and one not reason-able—invariably in such cases you ought to fear a trick. And you should never believe that the enemy does not know how to carry on his affairs; rather, if you hope to be less deceived and hope to run less risk, in proportion as your enemy is weaker, in proportion as he is less cautious, you should the more respect him. And in this you have to use two different methods, because you need to be affected by him in both your thought and your conduct. Yet by words and other outward signs you must make it appear that you despise him, because this last method makes your soldiers more hopeful that they will gain the victory; the first makes you yourself more cautious and less likely to be tricked.

## [*Scouting*]

You must understand that when you march through hostile country, there is more and greater peril than in fighting a battle; therefore the general when marching ought to redouble his diligence. The first thing he should do is to have all the country through which he marches described and mapped in such a way that he will know the places, their population, the distances, the roads, the mountains, the rivers, the swamps, and all their characteristics. To make sure that he knows this, he must in various ways get hold of those who know the places, and question them with care and compare their words and, according to the comparisons, make note. He ought to send ahead cavalry with prudent officers, not so much to look for the enemy as to observe the country, to see if it agrees with the map and with his information about it. He ought also to send under guard guides who hope for reward and fear punishment. Above all he ought to act so that the army will not know to what duty he guides it; because there is nothing in war more useful than to keep silent about the things that are to be done.

## [*Methods for safe marching*]

To prevent a sudden attack from disordering your soldiers, you must remind them to be ready with their arms; because things that are foreseen do less damage. Many, in order to escape the confusions of the road, have put under the ensigns the baggage and the unarmed men, and ordered them to follow those banners, so that if when on the march they should have to halt or to retreat, they can do it more easily; since this is a useful device, I approve fully. Precautions should also be taken that one part of the army when marching does not separate itself from another, or that, because one part goes rapidly and the other slowly, the army is not thinned out; such things cause disorder. Therefore it is necessary to place officers on the flanks who will keep the pace uniform, holding back those too eager and urging on the slow; such a pace cannot be regulated better than with music. The roads should be widened to permit at least one battalion always to move in full array. You must consider the habits and the qualities of the enemy, and whether he is in the habit of attacking in the morning or in the middle of the day or in the evening, whether he is more powerful in infantry or in cavalry, and according as you learn, you must arrange and provide.

### [*Devices for escaping a pursuing army*]

But let us come to some particular cases. It happens sometimes that you draw back from the enemy because you judge yourself weaker, and for that reason do not wish to fight a battle with him; yet as he follows at your heels, you reach the bank of a river that will take time in the crossing; hence the enemy is on the point of over‑taking you and attacking you. Some who have found themselves in such danger have encircled the rear of their army with a ditch and filled it with brush and set fire to it, and then have crossed with their army without the possibility of hindrance by the enemy, who was kept back by the fire between them.

ZANOBI. It seems to me hard to believe that such a fire could hold them back, especially since I remember that I have heard that Hanno the Carthaginian, when besieged by his enemies, surrounded himself on that side where he wished to make his exit with piles of wood and set fire to them; then, since the enemy did not watch him carefully on that side, he had his army pass through the flames, making each man hold his shield to his face to protect himself from the fire and the smoke.

FABRIZIO. You speak well. But consider what I have said and what Hanno did, for I said that they made a ditch and filled it with brush, so that anybody who wished to pass had to contend with the ditch and with the fire. Hanno made the fire without the ditch; and because he was intending to go through it, he could not have made it fierce, because even without the ditch it would have hindered him. Do you not know that Nabis the Spartan, when besieged in Sparta by the Romans, set fire to part of his city to hinder the passage of the

Romans, who had already entered it? And by means of these flames he not merely hindered their passage but drove them out.

### [How Quintus Lutatius crossed a river]

But let us return to our subject. Quintus Lutatius, a Roman, when he reached a river with the Cimbri pursuing him, made it appear that he was giving the enemy time to fight him, so they would give him time to cross; to do so, he feigned that he was camping there, had ditches dug and tents set up and sent cavalry through the fields for plunder. The Cimbri, thereupon believing that he was encamping, encamped and divided into several parts in order to provide food. Learning this, Lutatius crossed the river without giving them any chance to hinder him. Some, in order to cross a river having no bridge, have diverted it and led one stream behind them, and then have easily crossed the other stream which had become lower. When rivers are swift, a general enables his infantry to cross more securely by putting the strongest cavalrymen just above the ford to resist the water, and others below to assist the infantry if the river overpowers any of them as they cross. Soldiers also can cross unfordable rivers with bridges, with boats, and with wineskins; therefore it is good to have in armies facilities for making all these things.

### [How Caesar crossed a river]

Sometimes when you wish to cross a river, the enemy drawn up on the opposite bank hinders you. To overcome this difficulty, I do not know a better example to imitate than that of Caesar. Having his army on the shore of a river in France, where his crossing was blocked by Vercingetorix the Frenchman, whose soldiers were on the other side, Caesar marched several days along the river. The enemy did the same. Then, encamping in a forested place, fit for concealing soldiers, Caesar took from every legion three cohorts, commanding them to remain quiet there until he had gone; then they were to throw a bridge across the river and fortify it. He with the rest of his men continued his march. Vercingetorix, seeing the number of the legions and believing that none of them had remained behind, also continued his march. When Caesar thought the bridge was finished, he turned back and, finding everything in order, crossed the river without difficulty.

[*Fording rivers*]

ZANOBI. Have you any rule for recognizing fords?

FABRIZIO. Yes, we have. Always in the place between still water and running water which appears like a line to anyone looking at it, the river is less deep and can be forded more easily than else/ where, because always the river has deposited more at that spot and is more blocked by such matter as it carries with it through the deeper part. This has been tested many times, so it is quite true.

ZANOBI. If the river has deepened the ford, so that horses go under there, what remedy do you offer?

FABRIZIO. To make gratings of timber, put them in the bottom of the river, and cross on them.

[*The escape of an army hemmed in by mountains and enemies*]

But let us continue our discussion. If a general takes his army between two mountains, where there are only two roads by which to reach safety, that leading ahead and that leading back, and both are occupied by the enemy, he can escape by the means others have used before him. It is this: to dig in his rear a ditch large and difficult to cross, making it appear to the enemy that he intends to protect him/ self with that, in order with all his forces, without fearing for his rear, to go by force through the road in front of him which remains open. When the enemy believe this, they strengthen themselves on the open side and abandon the closed one. The general then throws across the ditch a timber bridge constructed for the purpose and leaves the place without hindrance, freeing himself from the power of the enemy. When Lucius Minutius, a Roman Consul, was in Liguria with his army, the enemy shut him up between certain mountains where he could not get out. Thereupon he sent some Numidian cavalry he had in his army, who were badly equipped and rode horses that were little and scrawny, toward the places guarded by the enemy. The first appearance of the Numidians caused the enemy to assemble to defend the pass. But when the enemy saw the Numidi/ ans in disorder and—as it seemed—badly mounted, they thought them of no importance and relaxed the ranks of the guard. When the Numidians observed this, setting spurs to their horses and rushing upon their opponents, they passed through without the enemy being able to take any measures. After their passage, they wasted and spoiled the country until they forced the enemy to leave the pass open to Lucius' army.

### [*Marc Antony's device against the Parthians*]

Some generals who have been attacked by a great multitude of enemies have drawn close together and given the enemy a chance to surround them entirely, and then, at the place where they have seen the enemy weakest they have attacked, and thus they have made room and saved themselves. Marc Antony, when he was retreating before the Parthian army, observed that every day when he moved at sunrise the enemy assailed him, and they annoyed him throughout the day's march. As a result, he decided not to move before noon. Hence the Parthians, believing that on that day he did not plan to break camp, returned to their quarters, and Marc Antony then marched all the rest of the day without any annoyance. This same general, to escape the arrow flights of the Parthians, ordered his soldiers to kneel when the Parthians came toward them; then the second file of the battalions put their shields over the heads of the first, the third over the second, the fourth over the third, and so on; thus the whole army was as though under a roof and defended from the hostile archery.

This is all I think of to tell you about what can happen to a marching army. Therefore if nothing else occurs to you, I shall pass on to another subject.

## BOOK 6. [*ENCAMPING A MODEL ARMY; STRATAGEM AND PSYCHOLOGICAL WARFARE; WINTER CAMPAIGNS*]

ZANOBI. I believe it will be well, since we are going to change our theme, for Batista to take up his duty and for me to lay mine aside. In this matter we shall be imitating good generals, according to what I have just heard here from His Lordship; for they put their best soldiers in the front and the rear of the army, since they believe they must have in front those who will vigorously begin the fight, and in the rear those who will vigorously support it. Cosimo, then, began this discourse prudently, and Batista prudently will end it. Luigi and I in these middle portions have kept it going. And as each of us has taken his part willingly, I think Batista will not be inclined to refuse his.

BATISTA. I have allowed myself to be directed up to now; so I am going to allow myself to be in the future. Therefore, *signore*, be so good as to go on with your discourse, and if we interrupt you with these matters, excuse us.

FABRIZIO. You are doing, as I have already told you, something that much pleases me, because your interrupting does not impede my imagination but rather refreshes it.

But to continue our subject, I say that now it is time for us to encamp this army of ours, for you know that everything needs rest, and safe rest, because to rest but not to rest safely is not perfect rest. I fear indeed that you have been wishing that I should first have encamped it, then had it march, and at last fight; and we have done the opposite. To this we were brought by necessity, because, in order to show how an army when marching shifts marching order to that for fighting, we first had to show how it was drawn up for battle.

### [*Greek and Roman encampments*]

But returning to our subject, I say that if the encampment is to be secure it must be strong and orderly. The general's care makes it orderly; situation or art makes it strong. The Greeks sought for strong sites, and would never put themselves where there was not either a steep place or the bank of a river or many trees or some other natural barrier to protect them. But the Romans camped in security not so much through situation as through art; nor would they ever camp in places where they could not, according to their method, furnish space to all their people. From this it came that the Romans kept one form of camp, because they intended that the site should obey them, not they the site. The Greeks could not observe this custom, because, since they obeyed the site and sites vary in form, they had to vary their mode of encamping and the form of their encampments. The Romans, then, where a site lacked strength, supplied it with art and industry. And because in this discourse of mine I have determined to imitate the Romans, I shall not in my method of encamping depart from them; not, however, observing all their methods, but taking only such of them as at the present time seem applicable.

*[The composition of a model army]*

I have many times said to you that the Romans had in their consular armies two legions of Romans, who amounted to about eleven thousand infantry and six hundred cavalry; in addition they had eleven thousand more infantry composed of men sent by their friends to aid them; in their armies never did they have more foreign soldiers than Romans, except of cavalry, about which they did not care if they exceeded the number in their legions; and in all their actions they put the legions in the center and the auxiliaries on the flanks. This custom they also observed in encamping, as you have read for yourself in those who write of their affairs, and therefore I am not going to tell you exactly how they camped, but am only going to tell you with what method I at present would encamp my army, and then you will recognize what I have taken from Roman methods. You know that, corresponding to the two Roman legions, I have two brigades of infantry, of six thousand infantry and three hundred serviceable cavalry to a brigade, and you know into what battalions, according to what arms, and under what names I have divided them. You know that in the drawing up of the army to march and to fight, I have not made mention of other soldiers but have shown only that when the soldiers are doubled in number nothing else is needed than to double the formation I have described.

But since at present I wish to show you the method of camping, I think I should not stop merely with two brigades but bring together a proper army, composed, in imitation of the Romans, of two brigades and an equal number of auxiliaries. I do this that the form of the camp may be more perfect, since I shall explain the encamp⁄ment of a perfect army—something that in my other demonstrations has not seemed to me necessary. So wishing to encamp a proper army of twenty⁄four thousand infantry and twelve hundred service⁄able cavalry,[1] divided into four brigades, two composed of my own people and two of foreigners, I adopt the method to be explained.

*[Main outline of encampment: general's quarters]*

Having found the site where I wish to encamp, I set up the general's banner and around it I lay out a square of which every face is distant from it one hundred feet; of these faces, each one looks

1. *In the original* two thousand.

toward one of the four quarters of the heavens, namely, east, west, south, and north. In this space I plan to have the quarters of the general. And because I desire to be prudent, and because so for the most part the Romans did, I divide the armed men from the un-armed and separate those with baggage from those without it. I place all or the greater part of the armed men in the eastward part of the camp, and the unarmed and those with baggage in the western part, making the east the front and the west the rear of the encamp-ment; the south and the north are the flanks. And to distinguish the quarters of the armed men, I use this method: I start a line at the general's banner and carry it eastward for a distance of thirteen hundred and sixty feet. I then make two parallel lines having that one between them and equal to it in length, and each of them distant from it thirty feet. At the end of these I place the East Gate, and the space between the two outer lines makes a street, extending from the gate to the quarters of the general; this street is sixty feet broad and twelve hundred and sixty feet long (because one hundred feet are occupied by the quarters of the general); it is called General Street. I then run another street from the South Gate to the North Gate, and it passes through the head of General Street and skirts the general's quarters on the east; it is twenty-five hundred feet long (because it extends through the entire breadth of the encampment) and is sixty feet broad ;it is called Cross Street.

## [*Quarters for the native brigades*]

Having laid out, then, the general's quarters and these two streets, I lay out quarters for the two native brigades; I quarter one of them on the right side of General Street and one on the left. And so, crossing the space occupied by the breadth of Cross Street, I put thirty-two camping spaces on the left side of General Street and thirty-two on the right side, leaving between the sixteenth and seven-teenth camping spaces a space of sixty feet; this serves for a Transverse Street crossing all the quarters of the brigades, as will appear when they are assigned. In the spaces at the front of these two rows of camping spaces, that is, in those bordering on Cross Street, I lodge the officers of the men-at-arms. In the fifteen succeeding spaces on each side are the men-at-arms themselves; since each battalion has a hundred and fifty men, each camping space accommodates ten men. The total camping space for the officers of the men-at-arms is eighty feet broad and twenty feet deep. (Note that when I say breadth, I mean the space from south to north, and when I say depth, I mean that from west to east.) The spaces of the men-at-arms are thirty feet deep and sixty feet broad. In the other fifteen spaces in each row (beginning when Transverse Street is passed and having the same dimensions as the spaces for the men-at-arms) I quarter the light cavalry; since they amount to a hundred and fifty, ten horsemen occupy each space. In the sixteenth space, which is left over, I quarter their commander, giving him the same room as the com-mander of the men-at-arms. Thus the quarters of the cavalry of the two brigades have General Street between them and bound the quarters of the infantry, as I shall tell.

You note that I quarter the three hundred cavalry of each brigade, with their officers, in thirty-two spaces laid out on General Street and beginning at Cross Street and that between the sixteenth and the seventeenth there remains a space of sixty feet to make Transverse Street. In order therefore to quarter the twenty battalions of the two regular brigades, I place the camping spaces of every two battalions behind the spaces for the cavalry; each space is thirty feet deep and sixty feet broad like those of the cavalry, and they are joined in the rear, so that one touches the other. In all the first spaces on each side, bordering on Cross Street, I quarter the constable of a battalion, so that such a space corresponds to the camping space of the com-mander of the men-at-arms; the breadth of these spaces is only forty feet and their depth only twenty.

In the other fifteen spaces which on each side succeed this as far as Transverse Street, I quarter on each side a battalion of infantry, which, amounting to four hundred and fifty, provides thirty for each space. The other fifteen spaces I make contiguous on each side to those of the light cavalry, with the same dimensions, where I quarter on each side another battalion of infantry. In the last space I put on each side a constable of battalion; this space, next to that of the com-mander of the light cavalry, is twenty feet deep and forty feet broad. So these first two rows of quarters are half for cavalry and half for infantry. Because, as I have said, I plan that all the cavalry be useful, they do not have servants to assist them in attending to their horses and other necessary things; hence I plan that the infantry quartered behind the cavalry shall assist in providing for and attending to the

horses, and therefore shall be exempt from other duties of the camp—
a custom that was observed by the Romans.

Behind these spaces on each side I leave a space of sixty feet for a
street; one of these two is called First Street Right, the other, First
Street Left. I then put on each side another row of thirty-two double
spaces, which are back to back to one another, with the same dimensions as those I have mentioned, and divided after the sixteenth in
the same way, to make the Transverse Street. There I quarter on each
side four battalions of infantry with their constables on the ends at the
foot and at the head. Having left, then, on each side another space
of sixty feet for a street, which is to be called on one side Second
Street Right, and on the other side Second Street Left, I place on
each side another row of thirty-two double spaces, with the same
distances and divisions. There I quarter on either side four more
battalions with their constables. And so are quartered, in three rows
of quarters on a side, the cavalry and the battalions of the two regular
brigades; between them they have General Street.

### [*Quarters for auxiliary battalions*]

The two brigades of auxiliaries, because I have them made up of
the same number of men as the regular brigades, I quarter on each
side of the two regular brigades, with the same arrangement of
spaces, putting first a row of double spaces, half of them quarters for
cavalry and half for infantry, distant sixty feet from the others, in
order to make streets called Third Street Right and Third Street
Left. Then I make on each side two other rows of spaces, laid out
and arranged in the same way as those of the regular brigades,
which will make two other streets; all of them will be named from
the number and the side where they are put. Hence this part of the
army will be completely quartered in twelve rows of double spaces,
and in thirteen streets, counting General Street and Cross Street.

### [*Officers' quarters and market place*]

I plan to have a space left, between the quarters and the ditch, of
two hundred feet all around. If you reckon all these spaces, you see
that from the center of the general's quarters to the East Gate is
thirteen hundred and sixty feet. There remain, then, two spaces, one
of which extends from the general's quarters to the South Gate, the
other from the same quarters to the North Gate; measured from the

point in the middle, each one contains twelve hundred and fifty feet. Taking, then, from each of these spaces one hundred feet, occupied by the general's quarters, and ninety feet of open space which I wish to give it on both sides, and sixty feet of street which divides each of the spaces mentioned in the middle, and two hundred feet that are left on every side between the quarters and the ditch, we have left for quarters on each side a space eight hundred feet in breadth and two hundred feet in depth, if we give the depth the same measurement as the general's quarters. Dividing, then, the said depth in the middle, we have, on each side of the general, forty spaces one hundred feet deep and forty broad, which make in all eighty spaces. In these we quarter the generals of brigades, the chamberlains, the masters of camp, and all those who hold offices in the army, leaving some of them vacant for foreign volunteers and for those who serve by favor of the general.[2] Behind the general's quarters, I lay out a street from the south to the north, sixty feet wide, called Front Street. It passes beside the eighty spaces aforesaid, so that this street and Cross Street have between them the quarters of the general and the eighty spaces on its flanks. At this Front Street and opposite the general's quarters, I begin another street that goes from Front Street to the West Gate, also with a width of sixty feet, and it corresponds in position and length with General Street and is called Market Street. When these two streets are laid out, I arrange the square where the market will be held, which I put at the head of Market Street, opposite the quarters of the general and touching Front Street; I plan this market place to be square, and assign it a hundred and ninety-two feet on each side.[3] On the right and on the left of the said market place, I put two rows of camping spaces, of which every row has eight double spaces twenty-four feet deep and sixty feet broad. Thus I have sixteen camping spaces on either side of the market place, which lies between the two rows, or thirty-two in all. In these I quarter the cavalry left over from the auxiliary brigades; if these quarters are not enough, I assign to them some of those that have the general's quarters in their midst, especially those nearer the ditches.

2. *Gentleman volunteers.*

3. *Here and for the twenty-four just below I translate the numbers given in unamended texts. The usual depths of lodgings, however, are either 30 feet or 40 feet. The latter numbers would give the lodgings at the sides of the marketplace 240 feet or 320 feet and the market-place would be 240 or 320 feet square.*

*[Quarters for irregular pikes and* velites; *artillery stations]*

We must also quarter the irregular pikes and *velites* of each brigade, because you remember that in addition to ten battalions we allow a thousand irregular pikes and five hundred *velites* to each brigade. Thus the two native brigades have two thousand irregular pikes and a thousand irregular *velites*, and the auxiliaries as many more. Hence we still have six thousand infantry to quarter; all of these I put in the western section and along the ditches. From the end of Front Street on the north, then, leaving two hundred feet vacant between them and the ditch, I put a row of five double camping spaces, which altogether occupy a hundred and fifty feet in depth and a hundred and twenty in width; hence on dividing the breadth, I give each space thirty feet in depth and sixty in breadth. Since there are ten spaces, they quarter three hundred infantry, if to each space I assign thirty infantrymen. Then, leaving an interval of sixty-two feet, I put in like fashion and with like dimensions another row of five double spaces and then another, until there are five sets of five double spaces each, which amount to fifty spaces placed in a straight line on the northern side, all distant from the ditches two hundred feet, which quarter fifteen hundred infantrymen. Turning then to the left toward the West Gate, I put in that entire tract between them and the said gate five other sets of double quarters, with the same dimensions and the same arrangement (it is true that between one set and the next the interval is not more than thirty feet), in which I quarter fifteen hundred more infantry; and so from the North Gate to the West Gate, following the ditches, in a hundred spaces, laid out in ten sets of five double spaces each, according to my plan, all the irregular pikes and *velites* of the native brigades are quartered. From the West Gate to the South Gate, following the ditches, in just the same way in ten other sets of ten spaces each, according to plan, I quarter the irregular pikes and *velites* of the auxiliary brigades. Their commanders or constables can take those quarters that seem to them most suitable on the side toward the ditches.

The artillery I dispose along the whole length of the banks of the ditches.

*[Quarters for non-combatants and other impedimenta]*

In all the rest of the space that remains toward the west, I quarter all the unarmed and all the impedimenta of the army. And it is to be understood that under this name of impedimenta, as you know, the ancients understood all that train and all those things that are necessary to an army, except the soldiers, namely: carpenters, smiths, horseshoers, cobblers, engineers, cannoneers (though these can be put among the number of the armed men), herdsmen with their herds of sheep and cattle that are needed for the provisions of the army, and workers in every trade, along with the public wagons of public munitions necessary to life and equipment. I do not assign their quarters individually; I merely lay out streets that must not be occupied by them. Then the other spaces that remain between the streets, which will be four, I assign according to their kind to all the said impedimenta, that is, one to the herdsmen, the next to the artificers and skilled workers, the next to public wagons of supplies, the fourth to those of arms. The streets, which I intend to be left without being occupied, are Market Street, Front Street, and, besides, a street called Middle Street, which begins at the north and goes toward the south and passes through the middle point of Market Street, and on the west side gives the same service as does Transverse Street on the east side. There also is a street that passes, on the inner side, along the quarters of the irregular pikes and *velites*. All these streets are sixty feet wide.

The artillery I place along the ditches of the camp on their inner sides.

*[Importance of wide streets and open spaces in a camp]*

BATISTA. I confess that I do not understand it, and moreover I do not believe that to say so will be disgraceful for me, since this is not my business. Nevertheless this arrangement pleases me much. I wish only that you would satisfy these doubts: one, why you make the streets and the surrounding spaces so wide; the second, which gives me more trouble, is how these spaces that you designate for quarters are to be used.

FABRIZIO. Understand that I make the streets all sixty feet wide to enable a battalion of infantry to go along them in formation, for, if you remember, I said that each one occupies fifty or sixty feet in width. That the space between the ditch and the quarters be two hundred feet is essential, to enable you to handle the battalions and the artillery, to take the booty along it, and when necessary to have space for drawing back with new ditches and new embankments. It is also better for the quarters to be well removed from the ditches, in order to be more removed from fires and other things that the enemy can throw to damage them.

[*The plan of the camp invariable. Ditches and embankments*]

As to your second question, my intention is not that every space I have laid out be covered with one tent alone but that it be used as is convenient for those who are quartered there, and with more or fewer tents, so long as they do not get beyond its bounds. For laying out these quarters, experienced and excellent architects are needed, who, as soon as the general has chosen the place, shape and divide it, marking out the streets, and dividing the spaces with cords and with stakes in such a way that in practice they are quickly arranged and divided. To provide that no confusion arises, the camp must always be made in the same way, so that each man knows in what street and in what space he is quartered. This must be observed every time, in every place, and in such a way that the camp seems a movable city, which, wherever it goes, carries with it the same streets, the same houses, and the same appearance. This cannot be observed by those who, seeking for strong sites, have to change form according to variations of the site. But the Romans made the place strong with ditches, with a wall and with embankments, because they made a stockade around the camp, and in front of that the ditch, ordinarily twelve feet wide and six deep; these dimensions they increased according as they intended to remain in a place and according as they feared the enemy. I for myself at present do not put up the stockade, unless indeed I intend to spend the winter in a place. I do, however, make the ditch and the embankment not less than the aforesaid, but greater according to necessity. I prepare also, for the sake of the artillery, at every corner of the encampment a half circle of ditch, from which the artillery can strike on the flank whoever attacks the ditches.

[*Setting up the camp*]

In this exercise of knowing how to arrange a camp we must also train the soldiers, and in addition make the officers ready to lay it out and the soldiers quick to know their places. Nor is either difficult, as in its place I explain more fully. Hence I now wish to pass to the guards of the camp, because unless guards are placed all the other labors are useless.

BATISTA. Before you go on to the guards, I wish you would tell me this: When anybody wishes to put his quarters near an enemy, what method shall he use, for I do not see how there would be time for arranging them without danger.

FABRIZIO. You must know this: No general encamps near his enemy except one who is disposed to fight whenever his enemy wishes; and when one is so disposed, there is no peril except the ordinary one, because two-thirds of the army are drawn up to fight the battle and the other third prepares the quarters. The Romans in such a case gave this work of fortifying the quarters to the *triarii*, and the *principes* and the *hastati* remained under arms. They did this because, since the *triarii* were the last to fight, they would have time, if the enemy came, to leave their work and take arms and go to their places. You, in imitation of the Romans, can have the camp prepared by those battalions whom you intend to put in the last section of the army in place of the *triarii*.

[*Guards for the encampments*]

Let us take up discussion of the guards. It does not appear to me that I have learned that the ancients, in order to guard the camp at night, placed outside the ditches at a distance guards called pickets, as is done today. I believe they acted thus because they thought the army could easily be deceived, on account of the difficulty there is in inspecting the pickets and since they can be bribed or overpowered by the enemy; so that to trust themselves to them partly or wholly they thought dangerous. And therefore the full number of the guard was within the ditches. They watched with great diligence and according to a very careful system, punishing with death anybody who deviated from that system. In order not to tire you I shall not tell further how it was arranged by them, since you can read it for yourself if up to now you have not read it. I shall merely tell what I shall do. I shall ordinarily have one-third of the army armed at night, and the fourth part of that always afoot, which will be distributed along all the embankments and throughout the army, with double guards posted at every corner, of whom part will keep their stations, part will constantly move from one corner of the encampment to the other. This arrangement I speak of I shall also observe in the daytime when the enemy are near. As to the giving of the word and changing that every evening and doing the other things that are usual in such guards, because they are known, I need not speak further of them.

### [*Nightly checks of the men in camp*]

I bring up just one thing, because it is very important and when it is observed produces much good and when it is not observed, much ill. This is that great pains be taken about anyone who is not quartered in the camp in the evening and anyone who comes there for the first time. This is a thing easily inspected by one who encamps with such order as we have designated, because, since every space has the number of its men fixed, it is easy to see if there are too few or too many men, and when men are absent without leave to punish them as fugitives, and if there are too many, to learn who they are, what they are doing, and other facts about them. Such care makes the enemy unable, except with difficulty, to carry on negotiations with your officers and to become acquainted with your plans. If the Romans had not observed this with diligence, Claudius Nero, when Hannibal was near him, could not have left his encampment in Lucania and gone to the Marches and returned without Hannibal's foreknowledge of it.

### [*Necessity for harsh laws harshly administered*]

To make these good rules is not enough if you do not with great severity compel them to be observed, for there is nothing else in an army that requires such careful observance as this demands. Therefore the laws in support of it must be harsh and hard and their executor very harsh. The Romans punished with capital punishment anybody who failed on guard, who abandoned the place that was given to him for fighting, who carried anything secretly outside the encampment, anybody who said he had done some striking thing in the combat and had not done it, anybody who fought contrary to the orders of the general, and anybody who in fear threw away his arms. If a cohort or an entire legion was guilty of such a fault, in order not to kill them all, they put all their names in a bag and drew out the tenth part of them and killed them. This penalty was so handled that if everybody did not feel it, everybody nevertheless feared it. Yet because where the punishments are heavy, there should also be rewards, in order that men may at once fear and hope, they fixed rewards for every excellent deed: for him who in battle saved the life of a citizen, for him who first climbed over the wall of a hostile city, for him who first entered the camp of the enemy, for him who in combat wounded or killed an enemy, and for him who knocked an enemy off his horse. Thus any sort of brave act was by the Consuls recognized and rewarded, and by everybody publicly praised. Those who obtained gifts for any of these things, in addition to the glory and the fame they gained from them among the soldiers, after they had returned to their native city, with solemn ceremony and great display among their friends and relatives exhibited them. It is no wonder, then, if that people gained so great an empire, since it paid so much attention to penalty and reward for those who by their good or their evil works deserved either praise or blame; of these things we ought to practice the greater part.

## [The guilty men punished by their comrades]

I believe I should not be silent about one of their methods of punishment, which was that when the guilty man was convicted before the tribune or the Consul, the officer with a rod lightly struck him. After this stroke, the guilty man had the right to flee and all the soldiers to kill him, so that at once everybody threw at him either stones or darts or hit him with other weapons, so that he lived but a short time and very seldom escaped; such as escaped did not have the right to return home, except with so many restrictions and ignominies that it was much better to die. At present this method is almost carried out by the Swiss, who have the condemned men put to death by the mass of the other soldiers. This is well considered and excellently done, because to bring about that a person will not be a guilty man's defender, the best remedy that can be found is to make him his punisher; because with a different regard he favors him, and with a different desire he wishes his punishment when he himself is the executioner than when the execution is the duty of another. To keep the people, then, from favoring a man in his errors, the great remedy is to manage that the people judge him. In support of this I bring forward the example of Manlius Capitolinus, who, when he was accused by the Senate, was defended by the people as long as it was not his judge, but on becoming arbiter in his case, it condemned him to death. This is, then, a method of punishing that gets rid of uproar and causes the fulfilment of justice.

### [*Religion an aid to discipline*]

Because to control armed men the fear neither of the laws nor of men is enough, the ancients added to them the authority of God; and therefore with very great ceremonies they had their soldiers swear to observe military discipline, in order that if they acted against it, they would have to fear not merely the laws and men but God; and they used every device to give them strong religious feeling.

BATISTA. Did the Romans permit women in their armies, and did men play there the idle games they do today?

FABRIZIO. They prohibited both of them. This prohibition was not very difficult because so many were the exercises in which the soldiers every day—now individually, now generally—were employed, that no time was left them for thinking of either Venus or games or any of the other things that make soldiers rebellious and useless.

BATISTA. That satisfies me. But tell me, when the army had to break camp, what method did they follow?

### [*Breaking camp*]

FABRIZIO. Orders were sounded on the general's trumpet three times. At the first sounding they struck the tents and made up the packs; at the second they loaded the beasts of burden; at the third they moved in the manner described above, with the impedimenta after each section of armed men, putting the legions in the middle. Therefore you are first to move an auxiliary brigade, and then its individual impedimenta, and with them a fourth part of the public impedimenta, which are all of those quartered in one of the large spaces explained a little while ago. Therefore each of these must be assigned to one brigade, in order that when the army moves everybody may know his place in marching. Thus every brigade is to go away with its own impedimenta, and with the fourth part of the public impedimenta behind it, just as we showed that the Roman army marched.

BATISTA. In determining the camp site did they have other considerations than those you have mentioned?

[*Considerations of health and supply in choosing a camp site*]

FABRIZIO. I tell you again that the Romans planned, in encamping, to be able to keep the form their method had accustomed them to; for the sake of observing it, they made no exceptions.

But as to the other considerations, two are principal: one, to put the camp in a healthy place; the other, to put it where the enemy will be unable to besiege it and cut off the road to water and provisions. To avoid sickness, then, they avoided swampy places and those exposed to injurious winds. These they recognized not so much from the qualities of the site as from the faces of the inhabitants, and when they saw them badly colored or consumptive or seriously infected with some other disease, they did not camp there. As to not being besieged, you must consider the nature of the place and where friends are stationed and where enemies; then you conjecture whether you can be besieged or not. And therefore the general must be very well informed on the topography of the regions where he encamps, and must have around him plenty who have the same knowledge. Sickness and hunger are also escaped by not getting the army into confusion, because if it is to be kept healthy, the soldiers must sleep under tents, must camp where there are trees to give them shade, where there is firewood so that they can cook their food, and must not march in the heat. For this reason, they must get out of camp before daylight in the summer, and in the winter must not march through the snow and the ice without having means for making fire, and must not lack necessary clothing and must not be allowed to drink bad water. If any get sick, have them looked after by physicians, because a general has no way of escape when he has to fight with disease and with the enemy. Nothing is so useful for keeping the army healthy as exercise; therefore the ancients every day had them exercise. From that we learn how much exercise is worth; in camps it makes you healthy and in battles victorious.

As to hunger, you must see not merely that the enemy does not cut off your food supplies, but must provide places from which you can get food, and must see that what you have is not wasted. Therefore it behooves you always to have food in store with the army for a month, and then to lay a quota on your neighboring friends to provide you with it daily, and to prepare a store of it in some strong place and, above all, to issue it with care, giving every day to each man a reasonable amount. You must attend to this matter in such a way that it will not cause you difficulty, because every other thing in war finally can be overcome; this only finally overcomes you. Nor will you ever have an enemy who can defeat you with hunger who will seek to overcome you with steel, because, though such a victory is not so honorable, it is safer and more certain. It is not possible, then, for any army to escape hunger that does not observe justice and that extravagantly uses up whatever it pleases; because through one of these abuses, no supplies come to you, through the other, those that come are uselessly exhausted. Therefore the ancients made the rule that what was given out must be used up and at the time when the commander directed; so that no soldier ate except when the general did. How far this is observed by modern armies, everybody knows, and truly they cannot be called disciplined and sober like the ancients, but dissolute and drunken.

BATISTA. You said when you began to treat the organization of the camp that you did not intend to keep merely to two brigades but that you intended to take four of them, in order to show how a proper army encamps. For this reason I wish you to tell me two things: one, when I have more or fewer people, how I am to encamp them; the other, what number of soldiers would be enough for you in fighting against any enemy whatever.

FABRIZIO. To the first question I answer that if the army is larger or smaller by as many as four or six thousand infantry, one takes away or adds spaces for quarters as is necessary; and in this way it is possible to go up or down indefinitely. Nevertheless, the Romans, when they joined together two consular armies, made two encampments and turned the places for the unarmed toward one another.

[*Discipline more important than numbers. The optimum number of troops*]

As to the second question, I answer that the ordinary Roman army was of about twenty-four thousand soldiers; when a larger force was opposed to them, the most they brought together were fifty thousand. With this number they met two hundred thousand French, who attacked them after their first war with the Carthaginians. With this same number they opposed Hannibal. You should observe that the Romans and the Greeks carried on war with few men, made strong with discipline and art. The Westerners and the Easterners have made it with a multitude; but one of these peoples, namely the Westerners, makes use of natural spirit, the other of the great submissiveness those men show to their king. But in Greece and in Italy, since there was neither natural spirit nor natural submissiveness to their king, it has been necessary to turn to discipline, which is of such great power that it has enabled the few to overcome the spirit and the natural persistence of the many. Hence I say to you that if you are to imitate the Romans and the Greeks, do not exceed the number of fifty thousand soldiers, or even take still fewer, because more cause confusion and do not allow the use of discipline and of the methods that have been learned. So Pyrrhus used to say that with fifteen thousand men he was willing to assail the world.

## [*The value of stratagems*]

But let us pass to another subject. We have made this army of ours win a battle, and shown the difficulties that occur in combat; we have made it march, and told to what hindrances it is subject when marching; and at the end we have encamped it where it can not merely get a little repose from its past labors but also can plan how it is going to finish the war. In camps we have to deal with many things, especially if some enemies remain in the field and there are some suspected towns, about which it is well to be safe; and those that are hostile we must capture. Hence we need to deal with these things and to pass through these difficulties with that same glory with which up to now we have fought.

Therefore, descending to particulars, I say that if you are to succeed in getting many men or many people to do things that are useful to you and very harmful to them (such as tearing down the walls of their cities, or sending into exile many of their citizens) you must choose one of two courses. Either so deceive them that each one thinks he is not concerned, so that as a result, since they do not aid one another, you completely defeat them all; or give them all an order which they are required to carry out on the same day, so that, since each one believes himself the only one to whom the order is given, they think about obedience and not about opposition; thus everybody carries out your order without rebellion. If you suspect the loyalty of any district and wish to make yourself sure of it and to take possession of it unexpectedly, you cannot more easily disguise your plan than by sharing with that district some design of yours, asking it for aid, and indicating that you intend to carry on some other undertaking, but that any thought of that district is far from your mind. This causes it not to think about defending itself, since it does not believe you think of harming it, and gives you opportunity for easy satisfaction of your desire. When you suspect that there is in your army someone who keeps your enemy informed of your plans, you cannot do better, if you wish to profit from his evil intention, than to inform him about things you do not intend to do, but about things that you do intend to do, you will keep silent, and you will say that you fear things that you do not fear, and those that you do fear you will conceal. This will lead the enemy, in the belief that he knows your plans, to undertake various actions in which you can easily deceive and defeat him.

## [Secrecy]

If you intend, as did Claudius Nero, to diminish your army by sending aid to some friend, and the enemy is not to know of it, do not diminish your quarters, but keep your ensigns and your array intact, putting the same fires and the same guards everywhere. So if to your army you add new people and wish the enemy not to know that you have been reinforced, do not increase your quarters. To keep your actions and your plans secret always has been a very good thing. For that reason Metellus, when he was with the armies in Spain, replied to one who asked him what he was going to do the next day, that if his shirt knew he would burn it. Marcus Crassus said to one who asked him when he was going to move the army: "Do you believe that you will be the only one not to hear the trumpet?" To learn the secrets of an enemy and to know his methods, some have tried the scheme of sending ambassadors, and with them, in the clothing of servants, men very skilful in war, who, taking occasion to see the hostile army and to observe its strong and its weak points, have furnished a possibility for defeating it. Some have sent into exile one of their intimates, and through his efforts have learned the plans of their adversary. It is possible also to learn such secrets from enemies when for that purpose one takes prisoners. Marius, in the war that he fought with the Cimbri, in order to learn about the fidelity of those French who then inhabited Lombardy and were allied with the Roman people, sent them letters some open and some sealed, and in the open ones he wrote that they should not open the sealed ones except on a certain date; but before that date asking them back and finding them open, he knew that their fidelity was not perfect.

### [*How to distract the enemy and divide his forces*]

Further, some generals, being attacked, have decided not to fight the enemy, but have gone to assail his country and forced him to return to defend his home. Many times this plan turns out well, because your soldiers begin to win, and to fill themselves with spoil and with confidence; those of the enemy grow timid, since it seems to them that from victors they have changed into losers. Hence for him who has made this diversion it has often come out well. But it can be done only by one whose own country is stronger than that of the enemy, because if it is otherwise, he loses. A general besieged in his camp by his enemy often profits from setting on foot negotiations for an agreement and making a truce with him for some days; this procedure frequently makes enemies more negligent in every act, so that, profiting by their negligence, you easily get a chance to escape from their hands. In this way Sulla freed himself twice from his enemies, and with this same trick Hasdrubal in Spain got away from the forces of Claudius Nero, who had besieged him. It is useful also, in order to free yourself from the forces of the enemy, to do something in addition to what has been mentioned to keep him uncertain. This is done in two ways: either by attacking him with part of your forces, in order that, intent on that fight, he may give the rest of your people an opportunity to save themselves; or by causing some new and strange event that by its novelty makes him wonder, and for that reason remain in doubt and stationary; you know Hannibal did so when, being shut up by Fabius Maximus, in the night he put lighted torches between the horns of many cattle, so that Fabius, puzzled by this novelty, did not attempt in any way to impede his passage.

Among his other actions, a general ought to strive with all his skill to divide the forces of the enemy, either by making him suspi-cious of men in whom he trusts, or by giving him some cause for dividing his forces and in that way becoming weaker. The first method is applied by caring for things that belong to one of the men the enemy has around him, as in war by preserving his people and his possessions, and by restoring to him his sons or some necessaries of his without ransom. You know that Hannibal, having burned the fields around Rome, left uninjured only those of Fabius Maxi-mus. You know how Coriolanus, coming with an army to Rome, preserved the property of the nobles and that of the people he burned and plundered. Metellus, when commanding the army against Ju-gurtha, asked all the ambassadors the King sent him to turn Jugurtha over to him as a prisoner; then writing to these same men letters about the matter, he so managed that in a short time Jugurtha was suspi-cious of all his councillors and in various ways got rid of them. When Hannibal was at Antiochus' court, the Roman ambassadors dealt with him so intimately that Antiochus, suspicious of him, did not afterward put any faith in his advice.

There is no more certain way to divide hostile soldiers than to have the country of part of them attacked, so that they abandon the war to go to defend it. This method was used by Fabius when his army was opposed to the forces of the French, the Tuscans, the Umbrians, and the Samnites. Titus Didius, having few soldiers in comparison with the number of the enemy and expecting a legion from Rome, which the enemy expected to attack on the road, kept them from doing so: he spread through his army a report that the next day he intended to fight a battle, and then managed that some prisoners he held got chances to escape; by reporting the Consul's orders for fighting the next day, they kept the enemy from going to attack that legion, in order not to diminish their forces. In that way it came in safety. This method served not to divide the enemy's forces but to double his own. Some other generals, in order to divide the enemy's army, have used the method of letting him enter their coun-try and take at will many towns, so that by putting garrisons in them he diminished his forces. Having in this way made him weak, they have attacked and overcome him. Some others, wishing to go into one province, have pretended that they were about to attack another, and have been so skilful that, suddenly entering the one where their invasion was not feared, they have conquered it before the enemy had time to defend it. Because your enemy, not being certain that you are not going to turn back to the place you first threatened, is forced not to abandon one place and to aid the other; so often he defends neither.

### [Maintaining order and loyalty]

In addition to the things mentioned, it is important for a general, if sedition or discord appears among his soldiers, to know how to suppress it with skill. The best method is to punish the leaders of the trouble, but to do it in such a way that they are overcome before they realize it. The way is this: if they are at a distance, summon not only the guilty but also all the others; not supposing that the summons is for the sake of punishing them, the guilty will not disobey but will give opportunity for their punishment. When they have come, you make yourself strong with those not at fault, and with their aid punish the others. When there is discord among soldiers, the best procedure is to get them into danger, for fear invariably brings them back into union. But what above everything else keeps the army united is the reputation of the general; this comes only from his ability, because neither blood nor rank ever gives it without ability. And the first thing a general is expected to do is to keep his soldiers punished and paid. Whenever there is little pay, there must be little punishment, because you cannot punish a soldier who robs, if you do not pay him, and since he must live, he cannot abstain from robbing. But if you pay him and do not punish him, he becomes altogether insolent; because you become of little esteem, whenever he who leads cannot maintain the authority belonging to his rank.[4] When it is not maintained, of necessity there follow tumult and quarrels which ruin an army.

### [How the Romans profited from unfavorable auguries]

Moreover, the ancient generals had one worry from which the present ones are almost free, which was the interpreting to their

4. *A characteristic shift in person.*

advantage of unfavorable auguries: if a bolt of lightning fell in the army, if there was an eclipse of the sun or the moon, if there was an earthquake, if in mounting or dismounting from his horse the general fell, the soldiers interpreted it as an unlucky sign and became so fearful that if they entered battle they easily lost. And for this reason the ancient generals, as soon as such an accident happened, either showed that it resulted from some natural cause or interpreted it to their advantage. Caesar, falling in Africa as he left his ship, said: "Africa, I seize you." And many have explained the cause of an eclipse of the moon and of earthquakes. Such things cannot happen in our times, both because our men are not so superstitious and because our religion keeps itself far from such opinions. Nevertheless whenever they do come up, we must imitate the methods of the ancients.

[*Tactics against a desperate enemy. Expedients for outwitting the enemy*]

When either hunger or other natural necessity or human passion has brought your enemy to complete desperation and, driven by that, he comes to fight with you, you ought to remain in your encampment and to avoid battle so far as is in your power. So the Lacedaemonians did against the Messenians; so Caesar did against Afranius and Petreius. When Fulvius was Consul against the Cimbri, for many successive days he had his cavalry assail the enemy, and observed how the Cimbri left their camp to follow his men. Then he put an ambush behind the camp of the Cimbri and, when he had the cavalry attack and the Cimbri came out of their camp to follow them, Fulvius captured and sacked it. It has been very useful to some generals, having their armies near hostile armies, to send their people with the enemy's insignia to rob and burn their own country. As a result of this the enemy have thought they were people who came to their aid and they as well have run to aid them in getting booty, and thus have fallen into disorder and given their opponent a chance to overcome them. This plan was used by Alexander of Epirus in fighting against the Illyrians, and by Leptines of Syracuse against the Carthaginians; and for both of them their plan easily succeeded. Many have overcome the enemy by giving them a chance to eat and drink without limit, by pretending to be afraid and leaving their camp full of wine and of herds. Then, when the enemy were full beyond all normal habit, they have attacked them and ruinously defeated them. So Tomyris did against Cyrus, and Tiberius Gracchus against the Spaniards. Some have poisoned the wine and other things to be eaten, in order the more easily to defeat them.

### [*Dangers in the use of pickets and scouts. Ruses*]

I said a little earlier that I have not learned that at night the ancients kept pickets outside. I judge they acted thus in order to avoid the trouble pickets can cause: sometimes even scouts sent out in the daytime to scout for the enemy have caused the ruin of their sender; many times when they have been captured they have been forced to reveal the signal for calling their friends, who, coming at the signal, have been killed or captured. To deceive the enemy, it sometimes is enough to vary one of your habits, so that an enemy who depends on it is ruined. For example, a general who was in the habit of giving his soldiers the signal of the enemy's approach at night by fire and in daytime by smoke, commanded that his soldiers should without stopping raise smoke and fire, and that after a time, on the enemy's approach, they should cease. Their enemies, believing they came without being observed and not seeing anybody give a signal that they were discovered, made their adversary's victory easier by moving in disorder. Memnon of Rhodes, wishing to get a hostile army away from strong positions, sent a pretended deserter who declared that his army was in dissension and the larger part of it had gone; and to give the thing credibility, Memnon had as proof certain commotions made in the camp, as a result of which the enemy, thinking they would be able to defeat him, attacked him and were overthrown.

### [*The folly of making an enemy desperate*]

It is necessary, above everything that has been mentioned, to be careful not to bring the enemy into utter despair. About this Caesar was careful when fighting the Germans; he opened a road for them, seeing that since they could not run away necessity was making them bold; he preferred labor in pursuing them when they were fleeing to danger in defeating them when they were defending themselves. Lucullus, seeing that some Macedonian cavalry who were with him were going over to the enemy's side, at once had the trumpet sound for battle and ordered his other people to follow them. Hence the enemy, believing that Lucullus wanted to join battle, went to charge the Macedonians with such speed that they were obliged to defend themselves; so they became against their will not fugitives but com-batants.

### [*Protection against treachery*]

It is important also to know how to make yourself sure of a city, when you doubt its fidelity, after you have won a battle or before. This you can learn from various cases in antiquity. Pompey, fearing the Catinensians, prayed them to be so kind as to receive some sick men from his army, and sending in the disguise of sick men some who were very strong, he took the city. Publius Valerius, distrusting the loyalty of the Epidaurians, had an indulgence come to a church outside the city, as we should put it, and when all the people had gone there to be pardoned, locked the gates and received inside only those whom he trusted. Alexander the Great, wishing to go into Asia and to make himself certain of Thrace, took with him all the princes of that province, giving them pensions, and over the people of Thrace he set men of low rank. And thus he made the rulers content, by paying them, and the people quiet, since they did not have leaders to disquiet them.

### [*A conqueror's reputation for justice his most powerful weapon*]

But chief among the things through which generals gain the people's favor are instances of continence and of justice, like that of Scipio in Spain when he restored that beautiful young woman to her husband and her father. By this he did more to get possession of Spain than he did with weapons. Caesar, by having pay given for the wood he used to make the stockade around his army in France, gained for himself such a name for justice that he made easy the conquest of that province. I do not know that anything is left for me to say on these events; and no part of this subject remains that we have not discussed. The only thing we have failed to speak of is the manner of besieging and defending towns, which I shall be glad to do, if indeed it will not bore you.

BATISTA. Your great kindness makes us follow our desires with-out fear of being thought presumptuous, since you freely offer us what we should be ashamed to ask. Therefore we say this only: that you cannot bestow on us a greater or more acceptable favor than to finish your discourse. But before you go to this other matter, settle one doubt for us: Is it better to continue war also in the winter as is done today, or to make it merely in the summer and go into quarters in the winter, like the ancients?

*[Dangers of a winter campaign. Battle the supreme test]*

FABRIZIO. Well now, except for the prudence of the questioner, we would have omitted a subject that deserves consideration. I tell you once more that the ancients did everything better and with greater prudence than we do; and if in other affairs we make some errors, in affairs of war we make them all. There is nothing more imprudent or more dangerous to a general than to make war in the winter; and he who pushes it on is in more danger than he who awaits it. The reason is this: all the effort of military discipline is directed to preparation for battle with your enemy; this is the end toward which a general has to move, because battle gives you a war won or lost. He, then, who knows best how to prepare, he who has the best disciplined army, has most advantage in battle and most hope of winning. On the other side, there is nothing more opposed to organization than rough ground or cold, wet weather, because a rough site does not let you draw up your forces according to discipline; cold, wet weather does not let you keep your people together; hence you cannot with united forces present yourself to the enemy, but must of necessity camp disunited and without order, since you are controlled by the towns, the villages and the farmhouses that take you in; thus all the effort used by you in disciplining your army is in vain. Do not wonder that today they carry on war in the winter, because, since the armies are without discipline, they do not realize the damage that is done them by their failure to camp in a body, because it does not trouble them that they cannot keep such organization and observe such discipline as they do not have. But they ought to see how many troubles have been caused by campaigning in the winter, and remember that the French, in the year 1503,[5] were defeated on the Garigliano by the winter and not by the Spaniards. As I have told you, he who attacks suffers still greater disadvantage, because the bad weather does more harm, since he is in country familiar to his opponent and is trying to make war; hence,

5. *Machiavelli, in Rome at the time, reported in his letters to the Florentine government the news from the seat of the war.*

in order to keep together, you must bear the inconveniences of the rain and the cold or, in order to avoid them, must divide your people. But he who waits is able to choose his place as he wishes and to await his enemy with his people fresh. He can unite them quickly and attack a band of the enemy, who cannot resist their onset. So the French were defeated, and so generals will always be defeated who in the winter assail an enemy who possesses prudence. A general, therefore, who intends that his force, his organization, his discipline, and his ability should in no way avail him, should make war in the field in the winter. Because the Romans planned that all these things into which they put so much effort should be of value to them, they avoided winter not otherwise than they did rough moun-tains and difficult places and whatever else might deprive them of power to show their art and their ability.

So this is enough for your question, and we may come to deal with the defense and attack of cities and of their sites and of their construction.

## BOOK 7. [BESIEGING AND DEFENDING CITIES; PRECEPTS FOR WARFARE; THE IDEAL GEN-ERAL; HOPE FOR ITALY]

You must realize that cities and castles can be strong either by nature or by artificial fortification. By nature places are strong that are surrounded by rivers or by swamps, like Mantua and Ferrara, or that are placed on a rock or a steep mountain, like Monaco and San Leo; because of artillery and mines those situated on mountains not very difficult to climb are today very weak. Therefore most of the time men when building seek today for a plain, in order to make a fortress artificially strong.

### [The best city wall]

The first ingenious device is to make the wall twisting and full of turns and recesses. This method makes it impossible for the enemy to come close to it, since he can easily be hit not only in front but on the flank. If the walls are made high, they are too much exposed to the fire of the artillery; if they are too low, they are easy to scale. When you make ditches in front of them offering difficulty for ladders, if the enemy fills these ditches (as a large army easily can) the wall is in the possession of the enemy. Therefore, always deferring to a better judgment, I believe that if you are to provide against both inconveniences, the wall should be made high and should have ditches inside and not outside. This is the strongest method of building that can be used, because it defends you from the artillery and from the ladders, and does not make the filling of the ditch easy for the enemy. It is good, then, for the wall to be as high as your means permit and not less than six feet thick, to make its destruction more difficult. It should have towers placed at intervals of four hundred feet; the ditch inside should be at least sixty feet wide and twenty-four deep, and all the earth dug out to make the ditch should be thrown toward the city and held up by a wall that starts at the bottom of the ditch and goes high enough above the ground to shelter a man behind it; this makes the depth of the ditch greater. In the bottom of the ditch casemates should be built every four hundred feet to destroy with cannon fire anyone who descends into it.[1] The heavy artillery defending the city must be placed behind the wall enclosed by the ditch, because in the defense of the exterior wall, since it is high, only guns of small or medium size can conveniently be used.

If the enemy attacks by scaling, the height of the first wall fully protects you. If he attacks with artillery, he must first batter the outer wall. Yet when it is battered, since the nature of all battering is to make a wall fall toward the side battered, the ruin of the wall, since a ditch does not receive it and bury it, much increases the depth of the ditch. Hence an assailant cannot go farther, because he finds a ruin that keeps him back, a ditch that hinders him, and hostile artillery that from the wall of the ditch safely kills him. A single method must be his remedy: to fill the ditch. This is very difficult because its capacity is great and because of the difficulty in getting up to it, since the wall is winding and concave; between the irregularities, for the reasons given above, assailants cannot easily enter, and then, carrying material for filling the ditch, they would have to climb over a difficult ruin. Therefore I hold a city so planned wholly impregnable.

1. *This device of a ditch inside the city wall and other suggestions on contemporary siege warfare in* THE ART OF WAR, *especially this seventh book, suggest Machiavelli's knowledge of the siege of Padua in 1509, mentioned in 2* DECENNALE *211. Cf.* DISCOURSES *2. 17. See also Ariosto,* ORLANDO FURIOSO *14. 106.*

BATISTA. If in addition to the ditch inside the outer wall, one were also dug outside, would the defenses not be stronger?

FABRIZIO. Without doubt; but my idea is that if you dig one ditch only, it is better inside than outside the outer wall.

BATISTA. Would you advise having water in the ditches, or do you prefer to have them dry?

### [*Moats* vs. *dry ditches*]

FABRIZIO. Opinions differ, because ditches full of water protect you from mines underground, while ditches without water are harder to fill. But considering everything, I would make them without water, as safer, for in the winter the ditches freeze over and make the capture of a city easy, as happened at Mirandola when Pope Julius besieged the town. To guard myself from mines, I should make the ditches so deep that he who tried to go under them would find water. On the same plan I should build the walls and ditches of castles; then they will be equally difficult to take.

### [*No detached forts for cities*]

One thing I especially wish to urge on him who is to defend a city, namely that he should not build small forts outside the city wall and detached from it. To him who builds castles I suggest that he make no refuges within them, into which the defenders can retire when the first wall is lost. I am led to give the first advice because you should not make a thing by means of which, without remedy, you start losing your earlier reputation, and which by its loss makes your other arrangements less esteemed, and terrifies those who have under-taken your defense. And what I say will always come to pass if you make detached forts outside the city you are to defend;[2] for invariably you will lose them, since today it is not possible to defend little things when they are exposed to the fury of artillery; so, since you will lose them, they may be the beginning and cause of your ruin. Genoa, when she rebelled against King Louis of France, made some small forts on those hills that surround her; these, when they were lost (and they were lost quickly) caused the loss of the city.

2. *This passage has led to the mistaken idea that Machiavelli opposed the use of bastions, then coming into use, and later highly developed. The word* bastione *in this passage does not mean* bastion *but, as I have rendered it,* detached fort. *The Machiavellian word for bastion was* baluardo, *as appears in his Familiar Letter of 17 May 1526, and in* THE ACCOUNT OF A VISIT MADE TO FORTIFY FLORENCE. *Cf. his* DISCOURSE ON PISAN AFFAIRS.

[*Castles not to be subdivided*]

As to the second piece of advice, I affirm that nothing is more dangerous to a castle than to have within it refuges to which defenders can retire, because the hope of safety that men feel as they abandon a place causes its loss,[3] and that loss causes the loss of the whole castle. An instance is the recent loss of the castle of Forlì, when the Countess Caterina defended it against Cesare Borgia, son of Pope Alexander VI, who had led there the army of the King of France. That whole fortress was full of places to which the garrison could retire: first there was the citadel[4] separated from the castle by a ditch crossed by means of a drawbridge. The castle itself was divided into three parts and each part was separated from the preceding part by ditches and water; bridges led from one part to the next. As a result, when the Duke battered with artillery one part of the castle and made an opening in the wall, Messer Giovanni da Casale, who was in charge of the garrison, did not consider defending the opening but abandoned it and retired into another place. But when the soldiers of the Duke entered without opposition into the first part, in a moment they took the entire castle by becoming masters of the bridges leading from each part to the next. This castle, then, that was thought impregnable, was lost because of two defects: first, it had too many refuges; second, each refuge was not master of its own bridge. So the badly planned fortress and the incapacity of its commander brought shame upon the Countess' bold undertaking. She would have had spirit to await an army, as neither the King of Naples nor the Duke of Milan had done. But though her efforts did not turn out well, nonetheless she carried off such esteem as her valor deserved. This was testified to by many epigrams made in her honor at the time. Therefore if I had to construct fortresses, I should build them with strong walls and with ditches in the way we have discussed, and I should build nothing inside them except houses to live in, and these should be so slight and low as not to obstruct the general's view of all the walls, as he stands in the midst of the court; thus he can see with his own eyes where he needs to give help, and everybody understands that if the walls and the ditch are lost, the

3. *Men easily give up one place when they hope to find safety in retirement to another.*
4. citadel. *The name given to a walled area, perhaps even including a normally inhabited part of a city, lying beyond the fortifications of the castle itself.*

castle is completely lost. If I did make any refuges there, I should construct their bridges in such a way that each refuge would be master of its bridges, which would be so made as to come down on pillars in the middle of the ditch.

## [*The fury of artillery. Gates*]

BATISTA. You say that today little things cannot be defended, yet I have heard the opposite said, that the smaller a thing is, the better it can be defended.

FABRIZIO. You are mistaken, because you cannot today call a place strong if the defenders do not have space for making new ditches and new embankments behind which to retire, because so great is the fury of the artillery that to rely on the protection of one ditch[5] and one embankment alone is to deceive yourself; hence it detached works—granted that they do not surpass their usual size, because then they would be cities and castles—are not made in such a way that the defenders can retire behind new defenses, they are quickly lost. It is then wise to abandon such detached works and to fortify the entrances of cities and to cover their gates with ravelins, so that no one can go in or go out of the gate in a straight line, and between the ravelin and the gate there should be a ditch with a bridge. The gates should also be defended with portcullises, in order to enable you to get your men back inside after they have gone outside to fight, and if the enemy pursues them, to prevent him in the confusion from coming in with your own men. For this reason the devices the ancients called *cataractae* have been invented; these by falling shut out the enemy and save your friends, because in such a case you cannot avail yourself either of the bridges or of the gate, since both of them are occupied by the throng.

BATISTA. I have seen these portcullises that you speak of, made in Germany of wooden bars in the form of an iron grating, and those of ours are made of planks tightly fitted together. I should like to know how this difference arises and which are more effective.

## [*French methods superior*]

FABRIZIO. I tell you again that the methods and habits of war in all the world, in comparison with those of the ancients, have

5. *The texts give wall (muro) but the earlier part of the sentence indicates* ditch.

declined, but in Italy they have completely disappeared; if anything here is a little more effective, it comes from the example of the northerners. You must have heard, and these others can remember, with what weakness we built before King Charles of France came into Italy in 1494. The merlons were made as narrow as one foot, the arrow-slits and embrasures were made with a small opening outside and a large one inside, and with many other defects which, in order not to be tiresome, I shall omit; because if merlons are narrow, the protection they give is easily removed, and embrasures of that sort are easily broken open. Now from the French we have learned to make merlons large and thick, and that embrasures should be large at the inner side and grow smaller until they reach the middle of the wall and then once more grow large toward the outside surface. This makes it difficult for artillery to remove their defensive qualities. Moreover, the French have many other arrangements like these, which our men, since they have not seen them, have not considered.

Among them is this device of the portcullis made in the form of a grating, which is a far better method than yours, because, if you have for the protection of a gate a portcullis that is solid like yours, when you let it down you close yourself inside and cannot damage the enemy through it, so that with axes and fire he can attack it in safety. But if it is made in the fashion of a grating, when it is let down you can defend it through those interstices and openings with spears, with cross-bows and with every other sort of arms.

### [*Gun carriages: French* vs. *Italian construction*]

BATISTA. I have seen in Italy another northern fashion, namely that gun carriages are made with the spokes of the wheels inclined toward the tip of the axle. I should like to know why they are so made, since to me they seem stronger when straight, like those of our wheels.

FABRIZIO. Never suppose that things departing from the usual forms do so by chance; if you believe that they do so to be more beautiful, you err, because where the first necessity is strength, no account is taken of beauty. The whole reason is that those spokes are much securer and stronger than yours. The fact is this: the carriage either sits level or slants to the right or to the left. When it is level, the wheels support equally the weight of the load; being divided equally between them, the weight does not burden them much.

When the carriage slants, its entire weight rests on the wheel toward which it slants. If its spokes are straight, they can easily be broken because as the wheel slants its spokes also slant; hence they do not bear the weight in a direct line. So when the carriage is level and they bear least weight, they are at their strongest; when the carriage is uneven and they have to bear more weight, they are weaker. Exactly the opposite happens to the inclined spokes of the French carriage: when the carriage, slanting to one side, presses on them from above, the spokes then become erect, since they normally slope; then with the utmost ease they support the whole weight, but when the carriage is level and they slope, they support only half of it.

### [The fortification of bridges by the French]

But let us return to our cities and castles. In addition to what I have mentioned, the French, for greater security to their city gates and so that in sieges they can more easily bring soldiers inside and get them out, use another arrangement, of which I have not yet seen in Italy any instance. That is, they erect at the outer end of a movable bridge two pillars, and on the top of each of them they balance a beam, in such a way that half of it comes over the bridge, the other half outside. Then the parts that are outside they join together throughout with small beams, which fill the space between one beam and the other in the fashion of a grating, and on the inside they fix to the end of each beam a chain. Then when they wish to close the bridge at the outer end, they loose the chains and let fall all that grating-like part, which, by going down, closes the bridge, and when they wish to open it, they pull the chains and the grating begins to rise. It can be raised so much that a man and not a horse can pass beneath it, and so much that a horse and a man can pass, and it can be fully closed because it is let down and raised up like a screen between merlons. This arrangement is more secure than the portcullis, because the enemy cannot so easily impede it that it will not fall, since it does not fall in a straight line like the portcullis, which can easily be propped up.

### [A zone of scorched earth around the city]

It is the duty, then, of those who set out to build a city to attend to the arrangement of all the things mentioned, and they should also decree that for at least a mile around the walls no one is allowed to carry on farming or to put up walls, but the land must be all plain, without a bush or a bank or trees or houses to obstruct the view and give shelter to an enemy who pitches his camp. And note that a city which has ditches outside with banks higher than the level of the land is very weak; because those give shelter to the enemy who assails you and do not impede him in attacking you, because they can easily be opened and give room for his artillery.

### [*Internal arrangements for defense*]

But let us go inside the city. I do not wish to lose much time in showing you that besides the things mentioned you must have stores of food and munitions, because they are things everybody knows, and without them every other provision is useless. And generally it is necessary to do two things: to provide for yourself and to take from the enemy opportunity to avail himself of the things of your country. Therefore the fodder, the animals, the grain that you cannot store in the city must be destroyed. Another thing necessary in defending a city is to arrange that nothing be done in confusion and disorder, and to provide that in every emergency each man may know what he should do. The method is this: the women, the old men, the children and the weak must stay in their houses and leave the city free to the young and strong. The latter with their weapons are distributed for defense, part of them on the walls, part at the gates, part in the principal places of the city, to deal with those troubles that can spring up within it; another part is not restricted to any one place, but is to aid all, when summoned by necessity. And if things are so arranged, it is difficult for tumults to arise that can throw you into confusion. Still I want you to note this in the attack and the defense of cities: nothing gives an enemy so much hope of capturing a city as to know that it is not accustomed to seeing an enemy, because many times without any trial of strength cities are lost through terror alone. Therefore a wise general who attacks such a city will make all his demonstrations fear-inspiring. On the other hand, he who is attacked should put on the side of the city assailed by the enemy valiant soldiers not to be terrified by imagination but affected only by actual attack, because if a first assault is fruitless, the courage of the besieged increases and then the enemy is forced to conquer the city by might and not by reputation.

## [*Ancient artillery*]

The mechanical devices with which the ancients defended cities were many, as catapults, onagers, scorpions, cross-bows, sling-staves and slings. There were also many with which they attacked, as rams, towers, mice, mantlets, penthouses, hooks, and tortoises. In their place we have today cannon, which serve both those who attack and those who defend. Therefore I shall not speak further of ancient weapons.

## [*Starvation in a besieged city*]

But let us return to our subject and come to individual attacks. You must see to it that your city cannot be taken through starvation and cannot be forced by assaults. As to starvation, I have said that to be well provided with food before the siege begins is essential. When food is lacking because a siege is long, extraordinary means have sometimes been used to supply you by friends attempting to aid you, especially if a river runs through the midst of the besieged city. When Hannibal besieged the town of Casalino, and the Romans could not send anything else by the river, they threw into it a great quantity of nuts, which, carried by the stream without any possibility of being stopped, fed the Casalinensians for some time. Some when besieged, in order to show the enemy that they have grain left and to make them despair of taking the city through hunger, have either thrown bread outside the walls or have fed grain to a steer and then let him be captured, so that when he is killed and found full of grain, he will show what plenty they have. On the other hand, excellent generals have used various means for starving their enemy. Fabius allowed the Campanians to sow that they might lack the grain they sowed. Dionysius, when besieging Reggio, pretended that he wished to make a treaty with them, and during the negotiations provided himself with food; when by this method he had emptied Reggio of food, he shut the city up again and starved her into surrender. Alexander the Great, intending to capture Leucadia, captured all the towns around it and let their people take refuge in it; after the arrival of that unexpected multitude, he starved it out.

## [*Assaults*]

As to assaults, one ought to guard against the first onset, with which the Romans many times took cities, assailing them at once and on every side; they called it attacking the city with a circle, as Scipio did when he took New Carthage in Spain. If you can repel such an onset, you cannot afterward be easily overcome. Even if an enemy enters the city by gaining the walls, the inhabitants still have a resource, if they do not give up, because many armies, even after they have entered a town, have been either driven out or killed. The resource is that the inhabitants hold out in high places and fight from the houses and the towers. This situation the city's invaders strive to master in two ways: one, by opening the city gates and giving the inhabitants a road by which they safely can flee; the other, by sending out a proclamation saying that nobody will be injured except those who are armed, and that all who throw down their arms will be pardoned. This method has made victory easy in many cities. Besides this, you take cities easily if you come upon them by surprise. You can do so when you are so far distant with your army that no one believes either that you intend to attack or that you can do it without its being known beforehand, because of the distance. Then if you attack secretly and carefully, almost always you succeed in gaining the victory. I do not like to speak of things that have happened in our times, because it is hard for me to talk of myself and of my doings; of others I should not know what to say. Nevertheless in this connection I cannot but bring up the example of Cesare Borgia, called Duke Valentino. When he was at Nocera with his army, under the pretense of marching to attack Camerino, he turned toward Urbino and captured in one day and without any trouble a state that any other general would hardly have captured with much time and expense.

## [*Taking a city by deception; defense against deception*]

Those who are besieged must also be on guard against the deceptions and tricks of the enemy. Therefore the besieged should not rely on anything they see the enemy do continually but should invariably believe that such habitual actions hide some deception and that the habit can to their injury be changed. Domitius Calvinus when besieging a city formed the custom of marching every day around her

walls with a large part of his soldiers. Hence the inhabitants, believing he did it for exercise, slackened their guard. When Domitius
learned this, he assaulted the town and took her. Some generals,
learning that aid was coming to the besieged, have furnished their
soldiers with the insignia of the army that was coming; thus these
soldiers have got inside and taken the city. Cimon the Athenian set
fire one night to a temple outside the city he was besieging; as a result
the citizens, going to save the temple, left their city in Cimon's
power. Some generals have killed men coming from the besieged
town to find plunder and clothed some of their own soldiers with the
plunderers' clothing; then they have sent them into the city. Still
further, ancient generals used various methods for stripping of their
garrisons cities they wished to take. Scipio, wishing to take some
African towns in which the Carthaginians had put garrisons, many
times pretended that he was about to assail them but that then through
fear he not merely refrained but moved away from them. Believing
this fear genuine, Hannibal removed all the garrisons from those
towns in order to follow Scipio with larger forces and defeat him
more easily. When Scipio knew this, he sent Massinissa his general
to capture them. Pyrrhus, when operating in Slavonia against the
capital of that country, in which many soldiers had assembled as a
garrison, pretended that he despaired of taking her; by moving against
other places he caused her to diminish her own garrison to aid the
others; then he easily captured her. Many generals have poisoned
waters and turned rivers aside in order to take cities, even though in
the end they might not succeed. The besieged are also likely to
surrender when frightened with news of a victory won or of new
reinforcements coming to their disadvantage. Efforts have been made
by ancient generals to capture cities by betrayal, bribing somebody
inside, but they have used various methods. Some have sent one of
their own men who, under the name of a fugitive, would get among
the enemy esteem and trust, which then he would use for his
general's benefit. Some in this way have learned the habits of sentinels and through that knowledge taken the city. Some have found
a pretext for blocking the gate with a wagon or with beams so that it
could not be closed, and in this way have given the enemy easy
entrance. Hannibal persuaded a man to deliver to him a town
belonging to the Romans. This man was to pretend to go hunting
at night, explaining that he could not go in the daytime for fear of

the enemy; when he returned with his hunting party, he was to take inside with him some of Hannibal's men and, killing the guard, put the gate in Hannibal's hands. You can also deceive the besieged by drawing them outside the city and away from it by giving the appearance of running away when they attack you. Many, among them Hannibal, have even let their own camps be taken in order to get an opportunity to enter a city and take it.[6] Besiegers have also deceived the garrisons of cities by pretending to go away, as did Phormio the Athenian. Having plundered the country of the Calcedonians, he received their ambassadors and with fine promises made the city feel secure; under cover of these promises the unsuspicious citizens were soon subjugated by Phormio. The besieged should guard themselves against any men in the city whom they suspect; sometimes such a man can be made harmless with reward rather than with severity. Marcellus, knowing that Lucius Bantius of Nola was inclined to favor Hannibal, used toward him such great kindness and liberality that he changed him from an enemy into a good friend.

### [*Guarding the walls*]

Moreover, the besieged ought to use more diligence about their sentinels when the enemy is at a distance than when he is near, and ought to guard best those places that they suppose least likely to be attacked; because many cities have been lost when the enemy assailed them on a side where they did not think they would be assailed. And this false opinion comes from two causes: either the place is strong and believed to be inaccessible, or stratagem is used by the enemy in assailing it on one side with deceptive uproar and on the other silently and with a real attack. Hence the besieged ought to be very careful about this; above everything, at all times and especially at night they should put good sentinels on the walls, and not only men but dogs, and select fierce and ready ones, which by smelling will find out the enemy early and with their barking reveal them. And not merely dogs, but we learn that geese also have saved a city, as happened to the Romans when the French besieged the Capitol. Alcibiades, to see if the guards kept alert when Athens was besieged

6. *By abandoning his camp to soldiers who sallied out from the besieged city, Hannibal put his whole army between his camp and the city, which then, since it was weakened by the absence of the soldiers who had sallied out, he could take.*

by the Spartans, ordered that when at night he raised a light all the guards should raise one, establishing a penalty for him who did not obey. Iphicrates the Athenian killed a guard who was sleeping, saying he left him as he found him.

### [How to send messages out of a besieged city]

Those who are besieged have taken various methods for sending messages to their friends, and in order not to send information by word of mouth, they write letters in cipher and conceal them in various ways. The ciphers are according to the choice of him who arranges them; the manner of concealing them is varied. One man has written inside the scabbard of a sword; others have put letters in unbaked bread and then baked it and given it as though it were his food to him who carries them. Some have put them in the most secret places of the body. Some have put them in a collar of a dog accompanying him who carries them. Some have put trivial matters in a letter and afterward, between the lines, written with fluids which when wet and heated reveal letters. This method has been most cleverly practiced in our times in an instance when a certain man, wishing to make known some secrets to his friends who lived in a city and not wishing to trust anybody, sent communications written in the usual way, and then interlined as I explained above, and had them put up at the doors of the churches; these, being observed by some who recognized certain secret marks, were taken down and read. This method is very subtle, because he who carries the letters can be deceived in the matter and does not run any risk. There are countless other methods that each one for himself is able to invent and learn about. But with greater ease one can write to the besieged than the besieged can to their friends outside, because their letters can be sent only by one who comes out of the city under the mask of a fugitive, which is a thing doubtful and dangerous when the enemy is at all alert. But as to those that are sent in, he who is sent can find many excuses for going into the besieging army, and from there, taking a suitable opportunity, can jump into the city.

### [The emergency ditch inside the wall]

But let us come to speaking of sieges at the present time. I say that if you are attacked in your city, and she is not provided with a ditch inside the wall, such as I explained a little while ago, you must make sure that the enemy does not enter through the breaches in the wall made by the artillery (because there is no preventive against the making of a breach). For this purpose, while the artillery is battering, you must run inside the wall that is being pounded a ditch at least sixty feet wide, and throw all the earth dug out toward the city, to make a bank and deepen the ditch, and it behooves you to hasten this work so much that when the wall is ruined the ditch is dug at least ten or twelve feet deep. While the ditch is being dug, you must shut it in at each end with a casemate. When the wall is so strong that it gives you time to make the ditch and the casemate, the part that is battered is stronger than the rest of the city, because such a reinforcement assumes the form we gave to a ditch inside the wall. But when the wall is weak and does not give you time, then it is that you need to show your valor and to resist with armed men and with all your forces. This method of adding to their defenses was used by the Pisans, when you besieged them, and they could use it because their wall was strong; its strength gave them time, and the soil was cohesive and very suitable for raising embankments and making defenses, but if they had lacked that advantage, they would have been lost. Therefore it is always prudent to provide ahead of time, by making a ditch within the wall entirely around the city, as we explained a little earlier, because then the citizens with ease and security await the enemy, since they have already prepared their defenses.

### [*Taking cities by mining*]

We find that the ancients many times took cities by digging underground in two ways: either they secretly made an underground passage that opened in the city and entered through it (in that way the Romans took the city of the Veientians) or by digging they took away the footing of a wall and made it fall. This last method is today more effective and makes cities placed on heights weaker, because they can more easily be mined. If then there is put in the holes some of that powder that in an instant takes fire, not merely is the wall ruined but mountains are laid open and entire fortresses shattered into many pieces. The remedy against this is to build in the plain and make the ditch that circles your city so deep that the enemy cannot dig beneath it without finding water, which is the only enemy of these mines. Indeed if you are defending a city on a hill, you cannot provide against them with any other means than by making inside your walls many deep pits, which serve you as safety vents for the enemy's mines. Another remedy is to make a counter mine, when you learn where your enemy is digging. This method easily impedes him, but if you are besieged by a prudent enemy you will have difficulty in learning his intentions early enough.

### [*The conduct of the besieged*]

Above all, the besieged must take care not to be surprised during times of rest, as after a battle has been fought, and after the sentinels have been relieved—in the morning at daybreak and in the evening at twilight—and above all when the soldiers are eating. At such times many cities have been captured, and those inside cities have destroyed many armies. Hence always on every side you must watch diligently and be in good part armed. I will not omit saying that the defense of a city or a camp is difficult because you have to divide your forces; since the enemy can at will attack you from any side with united forces, you must guard every place. Thus he attacks you with all his forces and you with only part of yours defend yourself. Further, the besieged can be wholly conquered; the besiegers can only be driven back. For this reason many who have been besieged in a camp or a city, though they were inferior in strength, have of a sudden gone outside with all their soldiers and overcome the enemy. Marcellus did this at Nola. Caesar did this in France. When his camp was assailed by a very large number of French, he saw that he could not defend it because he had to divide his force into many parts, and that if he remained within his stockade he could not strike the enemy with vigor. Therefore, opening his camp on one side and shifting all his forces there, he attacked with such valor that he overcame and conquered the enemy.

The firmness also of the besieged many times causes the besiegers despair and loss of courage. When Pompey was facing Caesar and the Caesarian army was suffering greatly from hunger, some of their bread was carried to Pompey, who, seeing that it was made of grass, ordered that it should not be shown to his army in order not to discourage his men by letting them know what sort of enemies they had. Nothing did the Romans so much honor in the war with Hannibal as their firmness, because in every sort of the most hostile and adverse fortune they never asked peace or made any sign of fear.

On the contrary, when Hannibal was close to Rome, they sold the fields where he was encamped at a higher price than in ordinary times such fields would normally have brought. Moreover the Romans remained so determined in their undertakings that they did not, in order to defend Rome, abandon their offensive against Capua, which, at the very time when Rome was besieged, the Romans were besieging.

I know I have told you many things you have learned and reflected on for yourself. Nevertheless I have done so, as I said only today, in order through them to show you better the quality of this army, and also to satisfy those, if there are any such, who have not had so good an opportunity to learn them as you have.

### [General rules for warfare]

In fact I believe nothing is now left to give you except some general rules, which will seem very familiar to you. They are the following:

What helps your enemy hurts you, and what helps you hurts your enemy.

The leader who is most watchful in observing the intentions of his enemy and undergoes most fatigue in training his own army runs into fewer dangers and can better hope for victory.

Never lead your soldiers to battle if you have not first made yourself sure of their courage and established that they are without fear and in order. Never make a trial of them except when you see that they expect to win.

It is better to overcome the enemy with hunger than with steel, for in victory with the latter Fortune is much more powerful than ability.

No plan is better than one hidden from the enemy until you have carried it out.

In war the power to recognize your chance and take it is of more use than anything else.

Nature brings forth few valiant men; effort and training make plenty of them.

Discipline does more in war than enthusiasm.

When people leave the enemy's side to come into your service, if they are faithful they are always great acquisitions to you; your adversary's forces are more reduced by the loss of men who flee than of men who are killed, even though so-called deserters are suspected by their new friends and hateful to their old ones.

In drawing up for battle, you do better when you place many reserves behind the front line than when you thin out your soldiers to make your front wider.

With difficulty he is beaten who can estimate his own forces and those of his enemy.

More important is the valor of soldiers than their numbers; more benefit comes at times from topography than from valor.

Things new and sudden dismay armies; things familiar and slow are little esteemed by them. Therefore make your army deal with and learn a new enemy in minor combats before you come to a battle with him.

He who pursues in disorder an enemy that has been defeated does not attempt anything else than to become a loser rather than a victor.

He who does not provide the supplies necessary for living is beaten without steel.

He who relies more on cavalry than on infantry, or on infantry than on cavalry, should choose suitable ground.

If in the daytime you wish to see whether any spy has come into the camp, have every man go to his quarters.

Change your plan when you find out that the enemy has foreseen it.

Get advice on the things you ought to do from many; what you then decide to do, discuss with few.

Soldiers, when they live in barracks, are kept in order through fear and punishment; when they are led to war, through hope and reward.

Good generals never fight battles unless necessity forces them or opportunity calls them.

Do not let your enemies know how you plan to draw your army up for combat. And in whatever way you arrange it, be sure that the first squadrons can be received by the second and the third.

In battle never employ a battalion for anything except the duty you have assigned it, if you do not wish to cause disorder.

Against unexpected events, it is hard to provide a remedy; against those that are foreseen, easy.

Men, steel, money, and bread are the sinews of war; but of these four the most necessary are the first two, because men and steel find money and bread, but bread and money do not find men and steel.

An unarmed rich man is the booty of a poor soldier.

Train your soldiers to despise dainty food and costly dress.

### [*Matters omitted in this discussion and why*]

This is all I think of to suggest to you by way of general rules, though I know I could have said many other things throughout this discussion, for instance, how and in how many ways the ancients drew up their troops; how they clothed them and how in various ways they trained them. I could add many details that I have omitted as unnecessary, both because you can read them for yourself and because I have not been attempting to show you exactly what an ancient army was but rather how in these times an army can be organized that will be more effective than ours are. Hence I preferred not to talk of ancient matters further than I thought necessary for expounding modern ones.

I know also that I could have enlarged on mounted soldiers and then spoken of naval war, because those who analyze warfare say that there is an army for the sea and one for the land, one on foot and one on horseback. Of that for the sea I would not presume to speak, because I have had no experience of it; I leave its discussion to the Genoese and the Venetians, who in the past have done great things in such pursuits.

### [*Supplying cavalry horses*]

Of cavalry I shall say nothing further; as I said earlier, these soldiers are now less degenerate than the infantry. Besides, if the infantry, who form the backbone of any army, are well organized, they necessarily produce good cavalry. I would merely remind a ruler organizing a military force in his state that for the sake of a large supply of horses, he should make two provisions. First, he should distribute mares of good blood throughout his rural districts and accustom his subjects to deal in colts as in this country you do in calves and mules. Second, that the dealers may find purchasers, I would deny the right to keep a mule to anybody who did not also keep a horse; thus a man wishing to have one riding animal only would be forced to keep a horse; still more, I would not allow a man who did not keep a horse to dress in silk. Such rules I understand have been made by certain princes in our times, and in a very short time their countries have produced excellent cavalry. About all the other things relating to cavalry, I rely on what I have said today and on what is customary.

## [*The good general*]

Would you like also, perhaps, to know what qualities a general needs? On that I shall inform you very briefly, because I could not choose any man except one able to do all the things we have today discussed; yet they would not suffice if he could not find out things for himself, because no man without inventiveness was ever great in his profession; and if in other pursuits inventiveness brings honor, in warfare especially it brings honor. We see that everything invented, even though slight, is praised by historians; for example, you know that they praise Alexander the Great because, in order to leave camp less conspicuously, he did not give the signal with a trumpet but with a hat on a lance. He is also praised because he trained his soldiers on coming to close quarters with their enemies, to kneel on the left knee in order more vigorously to withstand a charge. This innovation having given him victory, gave him also such renown that all the statues erected in his honor were posed in that attitude.

But because it is time to finish this discussion, I return to my subject; thus I shall partly escape the penalty incurred by those in this city who do not return to it. Perhaps you remember, Cosimo, saying to me that since on one hand I exalted antiquity and blamed those who in important matters did not imitate it, and on the other hand did not myself imitate it in the affairs of war in which I have been concerned, you could see no reason for my conduct. To this I answered that men who wish to do a thing should first prepare themselves to do it, so that they can carry it out when occasion permits. Whether or not I know how to bring military affairs back to the ancient customs, I wish you to judge who have heard me discuss this matter at length. From that you can realize how much time I have spent in these reflections, and also I believe can imagine how great is my desire to put them into effect. If I have been permitted to do so, or if ever I had an opportunity, you can easily conjecture. Yet to make you surer and for my fuller justification, I wish to bring forward the causes. In part I shall observe my promise to you: to show what at present is hard and what is easy in such imitation of the ancients. I say, therefore, that no activity today carried on by men can more easily be brought back to ancient methods than warfare, but it can be so brought only by men who are princes of such great states that they can assemble from their subjects at least fifteen or twenty thousand young men. On the other hand, for rulers not having such states nothing is more difficult than military reformation.

### [*The glory of forming a new army*]

In order that you may better understand this matter, you must recall that two types of general have become famous. The first type includes those who have done great things with an army prepared by its normal discipline, as were the larger part of the Roman citizens and others who have directed armies. These generals had no other trouble than to keep them good and to make an effort to lead them safely. The second type includes those who not merely had to beat the enemy but, before they came to that, had to make their own army good and well disciplined. These without doubt deserve much more praise than generals who worked effectively with good and experienced armies. Of the second type are Pelopidas and Epaminondas, Tullus Hostilius, Philip of Macedon (Alexander's father), Cyrus King of the Persians, and Gracchus the Roman. All these first had to make an army good and then had to fight with it. All of them did it, through their prudence and through having subjects whom they could subject to such training. Yet in an alien region full of corrupt men unaccustomed to any honorable obedience, none of them, though possessing every excellent quality, could have done any work deserving praise.

### [*Licentious modern armies*]

In Italy, then, to know how to manage an army already formed is not enough; a general must first know how to form it and then know how to command it. Yet for this there must be princes who, having much territory and many subjects, have opportunity to do so. Among these I cannot be—I who have never commanded and can by no possibility command other than foreign armies and men obligated to others and not to myself. Whether among such men I could introduce any of these things that I have discussed today, I leave to your judgment. When can I make one of the soldiers that serve today wear more armor than is usual, and besides armor, carry food for two or three days, and a shovel? When can I make him dig or keep him every day many hours under arms in practice maneuvers, so that later I can make use of him in real ones? When will they abstain from gaming, from whoring, from cursing, from the outrages they daily commit? When can they be brought back to such discipline and such obedience and respect that a tree full of apples can stand in the middle of the camp and be left untouched, as we read many times happened in ancient armies? What can I promise them to make them respect me with love or fear, if after the war is finished, they no longer will have any connection with me? What can I do to make them modest, who are born and brought up without modesty? Why should they respect me when they do not know me? By what God or by what saints can I have them take oath? By those they worship or those they blaspheme? What one they worship I do not know, but I know well that they blaspheme them all. How can I believe they will observe their promises to those for whom every hour they show contempt? How can those who feel contempt for God respect men? What sort of good form, then, can be stamped upon this matter?

### [*The Swiss and the Spanish*]

And if you bring up against me that the Swiss and Spaniards are good, I confess to you that they are far better than the Italians. But if you have observed my discourse and the way in which both act, you will see that they lack many things necessary for reaching the perfection of the ancients. The Swiss are made good by a custom normal to them caused by what I mentioned to you today; the others by a kind of necessity; serving in a foreign land and realizing that, having no place of refuge, they must die or conquer, they have become good. But it is a goodness in many parts defective, because in it there is nothing else good except that they are accustomed to meet the enemy at the point of the pike and the sword. Moreover what they lack nobody is in a position to teach, and so much the less one who does not speak their language.

### [*Italian soldiers. Echoes of* THE PRINCE, *chap. 26*]

But let us return to the Italians. Not having wise princes, they have not adopted any good customs and, not being under such force of necessity as the Spaniards, do not adopt any for themselves. Hence they are still the scorn of the world. Yet the people are not to blame for it, but certainly their princes are to blame, who have been punished, and for their ignorance have received the fitting penalty of losing their states ignominiously, and without their doing any courageous deed. Do you wish to see if what I say is true? Consider how many wars there have been in Italy from King Charles' coming until now; and though wars usually make men warlike and give them reputations, these wars, in proportion as they have been greater and fiercer, so much the more have caused loss of reputation to the limbs and the heads.[7] This had to be, because the traditional methods have not been and are not good; and as to new methods, there is no one among us who knows how to adopt any. And do not ever believe that reputation will come to Italian arms except through the means I have shown and by the work of those who have great states in Italy, because this form can be impressed on simple men, rough and native, not on the malicious, the badly governed, and the foreign. A good sculptor will never think he can make an excellent statue from a piece of marble badly blocked out, but he can from one still in the rough.

[*The incapacity of Italian princes, an echo of* THE PRINCE, *chap. 24*]

The common belief of our Italian princes, before they felt the blows of Transalpine war, was that a prince needed only to think of a sharp reply in his study, to write a fine letter, to show quickness and cleverness in quotable sayings and replies, to know how to spin a fraud, to be adorned with gems and with gold, to sleep and eat with greater splendor than others, to be surrounded with wanton pleasures, to deal with subjects avariciously and proudly, to decay in laziness, to give positions in the army by favor, to despise anybody who showed them any praiseworthy course, and to expect their words to be taken as the responses of oracles. It did not enter the minds of these wretches that they were preparing themselves to be the prey of whoever attacked them. From that came in 1494 great terrors, sudden flights, and astonishing losses; and thus three of the most powerful states in Italy have been many times spoiled and plundered. But what is worse is that those who are left continue in the same error and

7. *The subjects and the rulers.*

live by the same bad system, and do not consider that those who in antiquity wished to keep their states did and caused to be done all those things that I have discussed, and that their effort was to prepare the body for hardships and the mind not to fear perils. Thence it came that Caesar, Alexander, and all those excellent men and princes were in the front rank of the combatants and went on foot in armor, and if ever they lost their high positions, expected to lose their lives. Thus they lived and died gallantly. And if in them or in some of them we can condemn too much ambition for rule, we shall never find any softness to condemn, or anything that makes men delicate or unwarlike. These things, if Italian princes read and be-lieved them, are such that those princes could not do other than change their form of living. Their provinces would then change their fortunes.

### [*Attempts at a citizen army by Venice and Ferrara*]

And because in the beginning of our discussion you complained of your citizen army, I tell you that if you have organized it as I have explained above and it has failed when tested, you can with reason complain of it. But if it is not so organized and trained as I have said, it can complain of you that you have produced an abortion, not a figure that is perfect. The Venetians also and the Duke of Ferrara began it and did not carry it out—which happened through their incompetence, not that of their people.[8] And I assert to you that, of these who today have states in Italy, he, rather than anyone else, will be lord of this country who first sets out on this road. And it will happen to his state as to the kingdom of the Macedonians when ruled by Philip, who learned the method of organizing his army from Epaminondas the Theban. While the rest of Greece sat idle or busied herself in the acting of comedies, Philip by means of this organization and these exercises became so powerful that in a few years he could entirely conquer her, and could leave his son such a foundation that he made himself ruler of all the world.

8. *Machiavelli usually represents the Venetians as using the normal mercenary system and as therefore failing (especially* THE PRINCE 12*). The brief reference here shows that he knew of Venetian and Ferrarese attempts to find soldiers among their subjects (Piero Pieri,* LA CRISI MILITARE ITALIANA NEL RINASCIMENTO, *Napoli, 1934, pp. 226–228). Machiavelli shows some inclination to forget that Florence showed the evils of the mercenary system more clearly than any other state in Italy, and to assign Florentine conditions to all of them.*

*[Italy capable of new things]*

He then who despises these ideas, if he is a prince, despises his princedom; if he is a citizen, his city. And I repine at Nature, who either should have made me such that I could not see this or should have given me the possibility for putting it into effect. Since I am an old man, I do not imagine today that I can have opportunity for it. Therefore I have been liberal of it with you who, being young and gifted, can at the right time, if the things I have said please you, aid and advise your princes to their advantage. By Italy's condition I do not wish you to be dismayed or terrified, because this land seems born to raise up dead things, as she has in poetry, in painting, and in sculpture. But so far as I am concerned, since I am advanced in years, I have no hope. Yet assuredly if Fortune had in the past granted me a state large enough to permit such an attempt, I believe that in a short time I could have shown the world how much ancient customs are worth. Without doubt I would have made my state greater with glory or lost it without shame.

*The diagrams which follow on the next seven pages are reproduced from a copy, in the translator's library, of the Aldine edition (Venice, 1540) of the* ART OF WAR. *A translation of the text is given below. Following these are two diagrams, based on* FIGURA QUINTA *and* FIGURA SETTIMA, *taken from* L. Arthur Burd, Le Fonti Letterarie di Machiavelli nell' Arte della Guerra (Rome, 1897).

## Nicolò Machiavelli, Florentine citizen and secretary, to the reader.

I believe it necessary, in order that you readers may be able without difficulty to understand the arrangement of the battalions and of the armies and of the encampments, as they are presented in the description, to give you a diagram for each of them. But first I must tell with what symbols or characters the infantry, the cavalry and every other individual component are indicated. Observe then that this symbol

| | | | |
|---|---|---|---|
| O | means Infantry with shields | φ | means Head of the battalion |
| ð | Infantry with pikes | ʊ | Capitan general |
| X | Leaders of ten | S | The music |
| ꝛ | Regular lightarmed men | Z | The standard |
| ſ | Irregular lightarmed men | φ' | Men at arms |
| c | Centurions | Υ | Light cavalry |
| ꜿ | Constables of battalions | θ | Cannon |

The first figure [FIGURA PRIMA] shows the form of a normal battalion, and the way in which it is made double by way of the flank, according to the description. [BOOK 2, *pages 612614*]

The same figure shows how in the same way the 80 files (merely with the change that the five files of pikes in the van are at the rear) are so handled in the doubling that all the pikes take the rear. This is done when the battalion is moving ahead and the enemy are feared at the rear. [BOOK 2, *pp. 616, 617*]

The second figure [FIGURA SECUNDA] shows how a battalion, which is moving forward and has to fight on one flank, is drawn up, as is explained in the text. [BOOK 2, *page 616*]

The third figure [FIGURA TERZA] shows how a battalion is drawn up with two horns, and then with an unoccupied space in the middle, as is explained in the text. [BOOK 2, *pages 617, 618*]

The fourth figure [FIGURA QUARTA] shows the form of an army drawn up to fight a battle with the enemy, as the text describes it. [BOOK 3, *pages 630633*]

The fifth figure [FIGURA QUINTA] shows the form of an army drawn up in a square, as is explained in the text. [BOOK 5, *pages 663666*]

The sixth figure [FIGURA SESTA] shows the form of an army shifted from the hollow square to the usual form for fighting a battle, as is explained in the text. [BOOK 5, *pages 666669*]

The seventh figure [FIGURA SETTIMA] shows the form of the encampment, as it is presented above. [BOOK 6, *pages 680687*]

Nicolò Machiavegli, cittadino, et secretario Fiorentino, à chi legge.

O credo, che sia necessario, à volere che voi lettori possiate senza difficultà intendere l'ordine delle battaglie, et de gli esserciti, et de gli alloggiamenti, secondo che nella narratione si dispone, mostrarvi le figure di qualunque di loro: donde conviene prima dichiarirvi sotto quali segni, ò caratteri i fanti, i cavagli, et ogni altro particolare membro si dimostra.

Sapiate adunque che questa littera

significa

Fanti con lo scudo
Fanti con la picca
Capidieci
Veliti ordinarij
Veliti straordinarij
Centurioni
Connestaboli delle battaglie
Capo del battaglione
Capitano generale
il suono
La bandiera
Huomini d'arme
Cavagli leggieri
Artegliarie.

Nella prima figura si descrive la forma d'una battaglia ordinaria, et in che modo si raddoppia per fianco, secondo che nell'ordine suo è descritto.

Nella medesima figura si dimostra come con quel medesimo ordine delle L X X X. file, mutando solamente che le cinque file di picche, che sono dinanzi alle centurie, sieno dietro, si fa nel raddoppiarle, che tutte le picche tornano di dietro il che si fa, quando si camina per testa, et si torna il nemico à spalle.

Nella seconda figura si dimostra come una battaglia, che camina per testa, et ha à combattere per fianco, si ordina, secondo che nel trattato si contiene.

Nella terza figura si dimostra, come s'ordina una battaglia con due corna, et dipoi cò la piazza in mezzo, secondo che nel trattato si dispone.

Nella quarta figura si dimostra la forma d'uno essercito ordinato per far la giornata col nemico, secondo che nel trattato si dispone.

Nella quinta figura si dimostra la forma d'uno essercito quadrato, secondo che nel trattato si contiene.

Nella sesta figura si dimostra la forma d'uno essercito ridotto ad uno essercito quadrato alla forma dello ordinario per fare giornata, secondo che nel testo si contiene.

Nella settima figura si dimostra la forma dello alloggiamento, secondo che di sopra si ragiona.

FIGVRA

PRIMA

SECVNDA

FIGVRA

TERZA

z c s

FIGVRA

z d s

FIGVRA QVARTA

552

CARIAGGI, ET DISARMATI.

552

FIGVRA QVINTA.

SESTA

FIGVRA

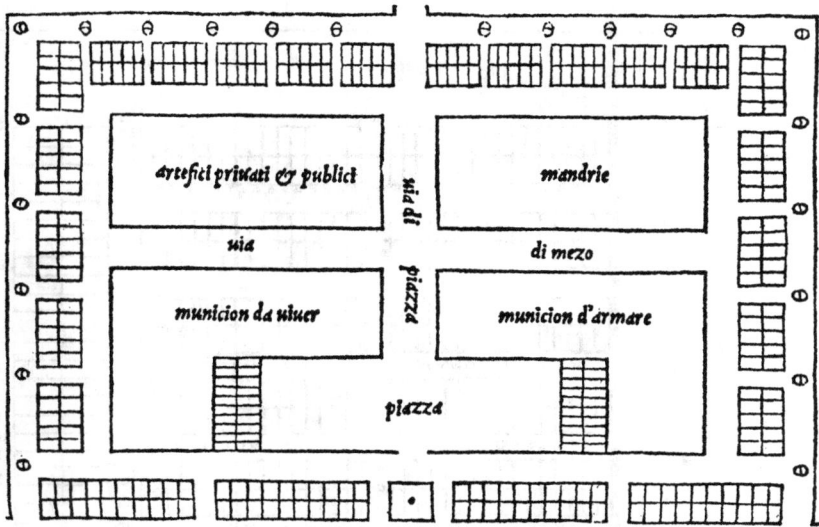

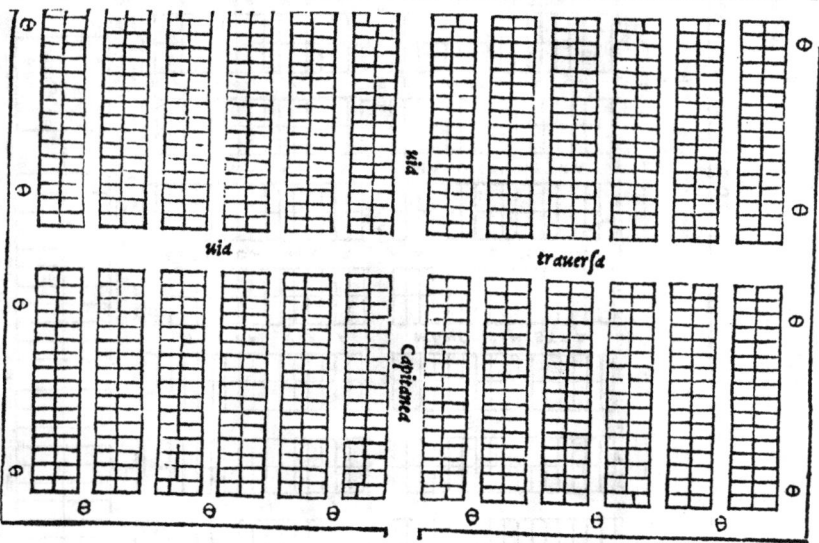

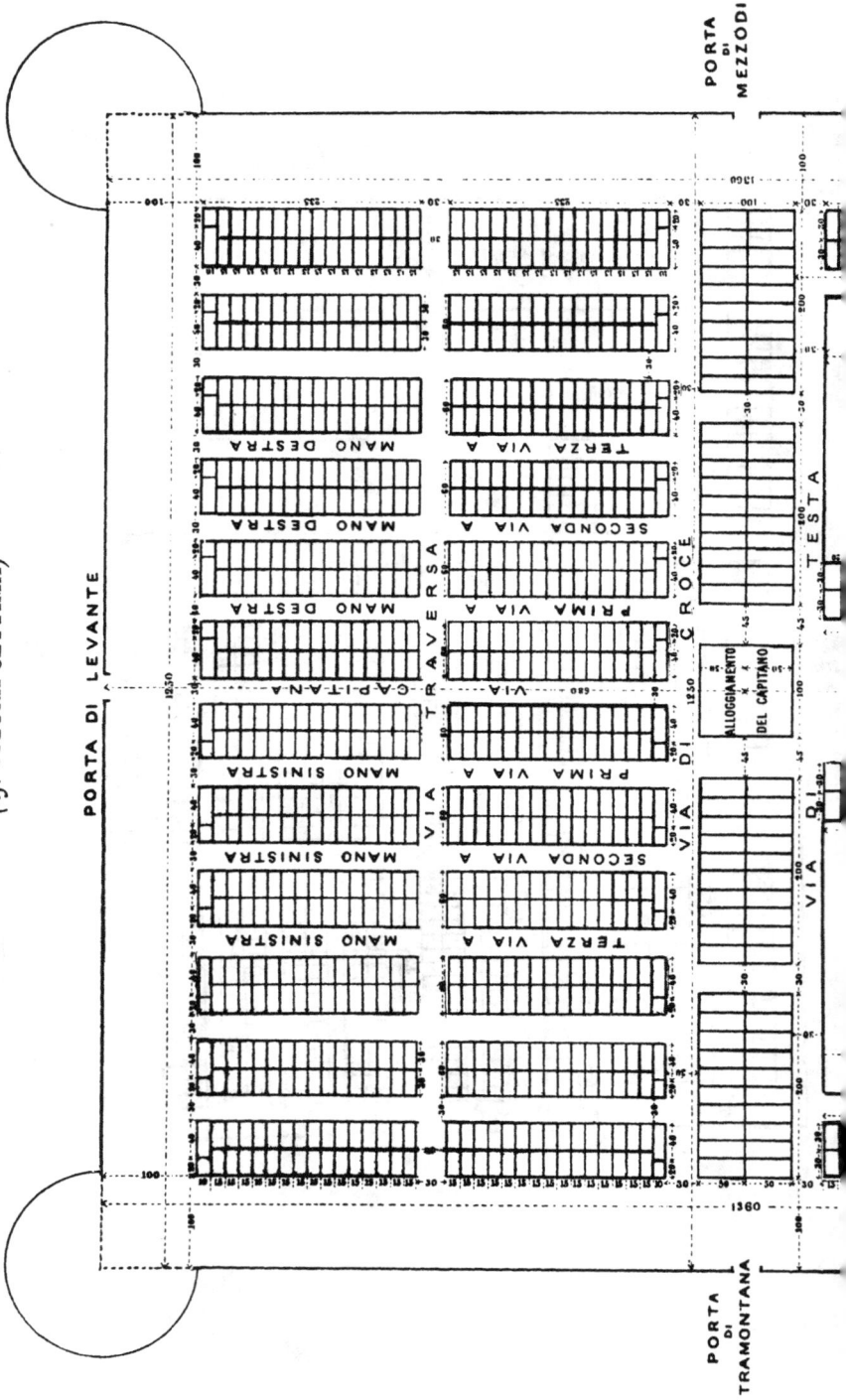

*The method of encamping an army*
(*cf.* FIGURA SETTIMA)

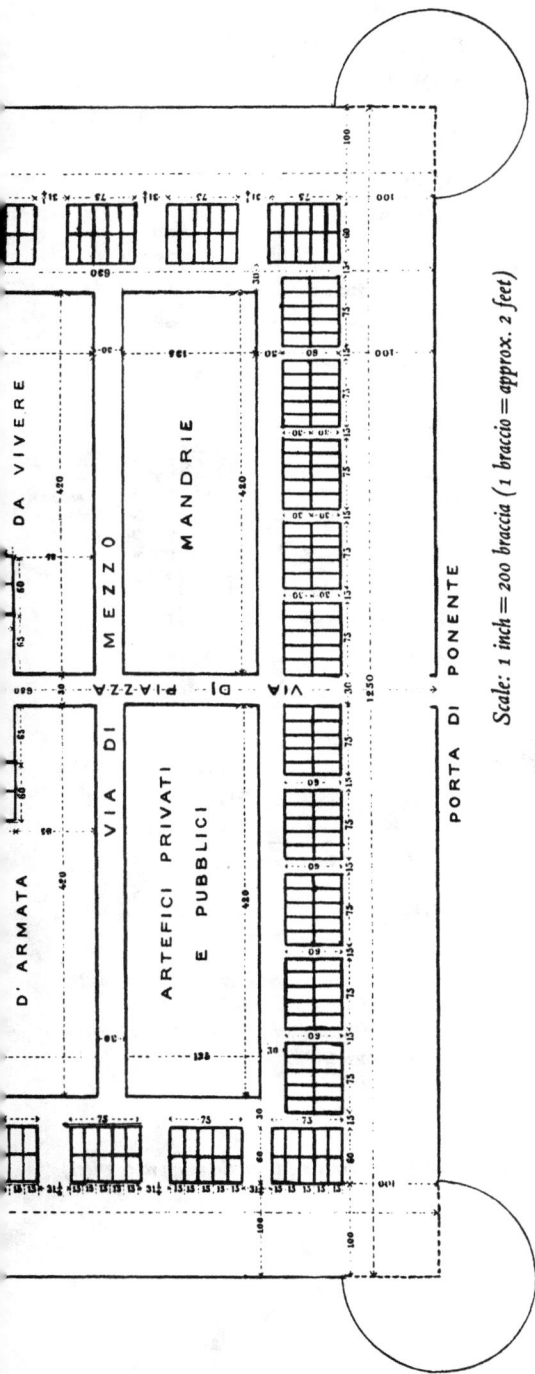

*Scale: 1 inch = 200 braccia (1 braccio = approx. 2 feet)*

Two battalions in marching order, so drawn up that they can resist an
unforeseen attack by the enemy from every side
(cf. FIGURA QUINTA)

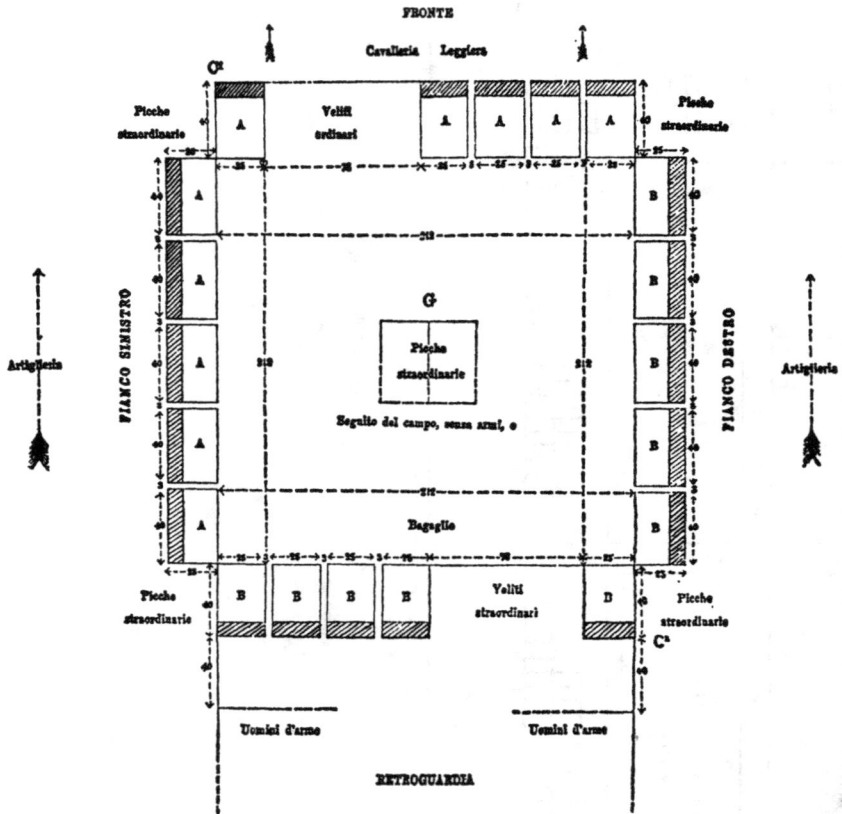

NOTE: *The rectangles marked with the letter* A *represent the subdivisions (battalions) of the
first brigade; those marked with the letter* B *the subdivisions of the second brigade.*

*The measurements of the space occupied by the pikes in the center are not given by Machiavelli.
The shaded spaces indicate the position of the pikes in each troop.*

C¹: *Commander of the first brigade*
C²: *Commander of the second brigade*
G : *General in chief*

*Scale: 1 inch = 100 braccia (1 braccio = approx. 2 feet)*

# THE ACCOUNT OF A VISIT MADE TO FORTIFY FLORENCE: A LETTER TO THE AMBASSADOR OF THE REPUB-LIC IN ROME

[*This visit was made on 4 April 1526. Pope Clement VII, fearing the Imperial army, which in the following year was to sack Rome, wished to improve the fortifications of Florence. In the execution of this design, Machia-velli was given an important part, being Overseer of the Walls and Secretary of the Commission in charge of them. Thus under the Medici he at last secured a position in Florentine government comparable to the one he lost when the Medici returned. His letters to Guicciardini from 4 April to 2 June 1526 supplement this report.*

*In* THE ART OF WAR, *book 7, Machiavelli treats the defense of cities. The present report shows him profiting from a lecture and demonstration by Pietro Navarro, one of the important generals and military experts of the day. More interesting than the subject matter itself is the suggestion of Machiavelli listening intently and adding to his own knowledge. Had he been able to revise* THE ART OF WAR, *he would have improved the part on fortified cities. It is appropriate that his last important piece of official writing should combine his eagerness for knowledge and his devotion to Florence.*]

WE INVESTIGATED FIRST, BEGINNING AT MOUNT Uliveto, the entire project that has been discussed of putting inside[1] the walls those hills that rise up on the other side of Arno, and we considered it all, as far as Ricorboli.[2] The General thought this a great undertaking and one that would have many good results. Yet he said that to carry it out there must be neither haste nor pressure and that many soldiers would be needed to guard it but that it would have this good result: an entire army could assemble there without giving trouble to the inhabited part of the city.

1. *Inside the new walls proposed.*
2. *Mount Uliveto is on the south side of Arno, beyond the western end of the city wall; it is the standpoint of the maker of the map of Florence given on the end-papers. Ricorboli is beyond the eastern extremity of the walls.*

Having considered the above, we decided to limit ourselves to the walls, especially to those that protect the part across Arno, in order to understand from the General how those parts, if they were not walled,[3] could be made strong. And first, we set out from the Gate of San Niccolò,[4] and it seemed to the General that that gate, with all the district as far as the San Miniato Gate (since that locality is all situated under the mountain) cannot be held or defended in any way and—what is worse—cannot be made strong. Hence he judges that we must shut it out of the city, and not merely abandon it but destroy it.[5] And therefore he thinks it necessary to run a wall from the first tower above the San Miniato Gate, and thence to carry it obliquely toward Arno until it touches Arno just below the mills of San Niccolò, and at the angle between the new wall and the old to make a bastion which will command the face of the old wall and of the new, and in the middle of the new wall to put a gate with its bastions and ravelins, according to the custom of making them strong today.

When this is done, as has been said, you would need to level all the houses that remain outside the walls in that district. After this project, we continued our walk, and having gone along the wall on the outside about four hundred feet,[6] when we had come to the summit of the hill where there is a high tower, he decided that a strong bastion should be made there, by lowering that tower, and carrying the bastion out about one hundred and twenty feet, so that it would include certain small houses now in front of the tower. This bastion makes a great fortress in that place because it commands all the hills around, defends the weakness of those walls that both below and above are joined to it as far as San Giorgio, and terrifies whoever from that side may plan to beseige us.

We came after that to the Gate of San Giorgio, which he thought should be lowered and a round bastion made there, with an exit on the flank, as is customary. Having passed this gate, still outside, about three hundred feet, we came to a certain sharp corner of the wall where the wall changes its direction and goes to the right. He

3. If the more inclusive new wall was not built.

4. The most eastern gate on the south side of Arno. For this and other places, see the endpapers.

5. See FAMILIAR LETTERS, 4 April 1526, No. 206. A city expecting attack would destroy everything near the walls that could give shelter to the enemy.

6. I have taken the Florentine braccio as two feet; actually it is but 22.835 inches.

thinks that there either a casemate should be made or a round bastion that would command the flank. And you must understand that he takes for granted that in every place where there are walls, ditches should be made, because he says that these are the chief defenses of cities. Having gone farther, about another three hundred feet, where there were certain barbicans, he advised the making of another bastion, which, if it were made strong and brought well forward, could be done without making the bastion at the corner aforesaid. Having passed this place, we came to a tower, which he thinks should be widened and lowered and treated in such a way that on it could be placed two pieces of heavy artillery; and so it should be done to all the other towers we visited. And he says that being arranged one close to another, they make a great fortress, not merely for striking to their flanks but also to their front. Because he says that according to reason cities must have more artillery than it is possible to haul behind an army; and whenever you can plant more against the enemy than the enemy can plant against you, it is impossible for him to attack you, because many guns overcome few, so that if you can put heavy guns on all your towers, and the towers are numerous, it follows of necessity that the enemy can with difficulty attack you.

Following our course, we came where one begins to descend toward the Gate of San Piero Gattolino.[7] The General paused there, and in order to consider better all that site from the San Giorgio Gate to there, we entered the farm of Bartolommeo Bartolini, and having seen everything, he thought of a new method of fortifying all that side from the said San Giorgio Gate to where we were without having to make those bastions of which we have spoken above. This new way is to run a wall from the very beginning of the slope that goes toward San Piero Gattolino, turning to the left toward the San Giorgio Gate, going according to the slopes of those little valleys, and joining the old wall at the San Giorgio Gate, and the old wall that would be left inside is to be destroyed.

This new wall from where it begins to where it ends, going by a straight line, would be about one thousand feet, and its greatest distance from the old wall would not be four hundred feet. It would do these good things: it would protect that section better,

7. *Porta Romana.*

because that old wall is useless and this would be new and useful; the old wall, because it has a deep hollow behind it, cannot speedily be reinforced,[8] and this, which would have the plain behind it, can be reinforced. It would come farther forward to command the hills around,[9] so that the enemy with difficulty could command it, and the old wall is easily commanded; it would save the expense of ditches because the slopes would take the place of ditches; it would save the cost of all those bastions which would have to be made on the old wall because it would suffice to make on the new wall certain offensive positions toward the flanks that would not cost much; so altogether it appears that it almost would be less costly to bring forward this part of the wall than to strengthen the old wall with ditches and bastions.

Having considered this site, we returned to the wall and descended toward San Piero Gattolino, and he decided that at the next to the last tower a bastion should be made that would extend beyond the tower sixty feet; and all the other towers, as has been said, should be widened and lowered. He thinks that the Gate of San Piero Gattolino should be lowered, and that a bastion should be made there that would include the entire gate in such a way as to command the wall toward San Giorgio and toward San Friano. Considering then how near the hill of San Donato a Scopeto is to the walls that extend from the Gate of San Piero Gattolino to a walled-up gate that leads toward Camaldoli, he advises that all the wall that is between these two gates, namely, between San Piero Gattolino and the walled-up one, should be destroyed and another new one should be made between the one gate and the other, which should be distant from the old one at the most four hundred feet, in order to be farther distant from that hill; in that region, since inside there are many little gardens, no other damage would be done than having to destroy a monastery of the monks of San Niccolò. We then followed our course toward San Friano; he thinks it wise to make at the next to the last tower, toward San Friano, a bastion that would extend thirty feet beyond the tower; the gate at San Friano should be made strong with a bastion; the towers up to Arno should be widened and lowered. At the corner of the wall that looks into

8. By digging behind it an emergency ditch and throwing up an embankment. See ART OF WAR, bk. 7.

9. To dominate them with cannon fire.

Arno, where there is a mill, he would make a bastion that would include the mill and command everything.

We descended from there into Arno,[10] and going along the wall toward the Bridge alla Carraia, he indicated that that wall should be well provided with embrasures, which would allow fire at a low level across Arno, and where that little storehouse stands,[11] to make a little tower which, more for fine appearance than anything else, should project at the flank. And having in the way aforesaid ob-served all the walls beyond Arno, and the hills that are near them, we asked him about those walls toward the Prato, which are visible from the hill of Uliveto, and those of San Giorgio from San Donato a Scopeto, and those of the Giustizia[12] visible from San Miniato, all of which can be observed from those hills.[13] He said that it was of no moment because, partly through their being distant, partly through the possibility of protecting them with transverse embankments, it was not easy for the enemy to annoy you from that direction.

Having seen all the section on the other side of Arno, we came to this side of the river, and began at the Little Gate of the Mills of the Prato, and first we had him observe Via Gora,[14] how those houses touch the wall that runs in the same direction as Arno. Then we passed through the gate and entered into the Millrace of the Medici and walked along to its end, and went up on that platform or terrace which is at the head of the Millrace.[15] He indicated that that place could be made very strong if a bastion were made that would include all the mills (its wall on the inside looking toward the garden of the Millrace could be made thin, because it cannot be battered) and that there should be made at the low point of the garden of the Millrace, where I say that terrace is, another bastion, which on the side would extend along the terrace, and on the front would command Arno transversely. He says that if this is done the enemy never would be able to approach, since the Millrace is there, which makes a ditch,

10. *Into the channel, close to the water.*

11. *On the map referred to in n. 2 appears a small building at the end of the Bridge alla Carraia which would seem to be the little storehouse.*

12. *The eastern part of Florence, north of Arno.*

13. *These hills are all so situated as to permit a raking fire along parts of the wall that they overlook.*

14. *Via Gora degli Ognisanti, now Via Montebello.*

15. *That is, having gone through the Little Gate of the Mills, they turned to the east and went to the point where the wall touches Arno.*

and since they could be attacked in front and on the flanks from bastions, and from behind by the guns that would be on the other side of the river. And so the houses of the Via Gora cause no weak ness to that part. He advises tearing down the buildings on the covering of the channel from the dam,[16] which is near that bastion of the terrace, in order that above it two pieces of artillery could be planted. Besides this, because the houses that extend from the terrace to the Bridge alla Carraia are masters of the river, he would like to take from them this mastery by making a wall that would cover them,[17] because he says that, for fear of treachery, it is not well that private persons should be masters of that part. He says that the Little Gate of the Mills would be protected by the bastion.

Having observed and decided on this section, we left the Little Gate of the Mills and went along the walls outside as far as the corner that reaches the Mugnone,[18] where the wall then turns to the right toward the Prato Gate. He advises making a very strong bastion at that corner,[19] which would give security both in the direction of the mills and in that of the Prato Gate. He would like the Mugnone, both there and wherever it flows, to be brought into use as a ditch, and in that place, from the corner to the Prato Gate he would like a wall built along the Mugnone, which would retain the earth on the left side, and then, near the bastion on the corner, there should be made across the Mugnone a dam for the water, which could be opened and closed according to need, and along the wall from the bastion to the Little Gate a ditch should be dug, and into it should be led part of the Mugnone, and then when the ditch comes to the mills, it should twist toward Arno, and the mouth should be walled on each side. He wants all the points higher than that wall, which are certain crests that rise above the merlons, to be brought down to a level with the merlons. He advises that the Prato Gate should be

16. *The dam below the Bridge alla Carraia. The race had been walled over as a building spot.*

17. *There would be a new wall between them and Arno, extending the existing wall eastward as far as the Bridge alla Carraia.*

18. *They moved west to the farthest corner of the city. The course of the Mugnone has been changed, so that it no longer appears at this place.*

19. *In an official letter of 8 June 1526, also to the Florentine ambassador in Rome, Machia velli reports that Navarro recommended here a round bastion. Other engineers spoke for an angular bastion. On the advantages of the latter Machiavelli speaks briefly. His knowledge had grown greatly since he wrote Art of War, chap. 7.*

lowered and constructed with a bastion, as has been said of those across Arno.

We then went to the Faenza Gate, and all the little towers on the way he would like to have lowered and brought to a level with the merlons, and they should be widened or made more roomy, farther on especially. Since there is a long distance from the Faenza Gate to the Prato Gate, he wishes to cut down one of those towers between them for use as a bastion, enlarging it so much that cannon can be put there on a low level.

Then we went to the San Gallo Gate, which should be strength' ened like the others, and at one of those towers should be made something of a bastion. And because here the Mugnone begins to run along the walls, he indicates that, if it is to be used as a ditch, high up the stream, where it would go best, there should be made a slight obstruction, in order that the water may be clearer when it flows into the part used as a ditch.[20]

The General wished to see the hill that is opposite the San Gallo Gate, and when he had got there he said that the enemy would have at that point a strong and fine lodgment, but that it could not do other harm to the city than in that place to keep the enemy safe. We then went on to the Pinti Gate, which should be made strong like the others by making, between that and San Gallo, out of one of those towers in the middle something of a bastion like that we mentioned for the other two gates. Leaving the Pinti Gate and going along the wall about twelve hundred feet, we came to an angle where there is a tower with three angles and the wall bends strongly to the right, toward the Gate alla Croce, and from the angle to the Gate alla Croce is about eight hundred feet. And therefore he thinks that there on the angle should be made a great bastion, which would extend beyond the tower sixty feet or more and would guard well those two strips of wall and powerfully assail the country in front.

We came then to the Gate alla Croce, which ought to be strength' ened like the others, and going from there along the wall, we visited a tower that is opposite the Angel Raphael,[21] which he would like to enlarge considerably, in order to give more defense to the place near Arno. We came to the Giustizia Gate,[22] where he advised the

20. *To prevent the ditches from being filled with sediment.*
21. *A church in the eastern part of the city.*
22. *The last gate in the northeastern wall, close to Arno. The Temple was outside the gate.*

destruction of the Temple and all those shanties that are around that place, and the building there of a very large bastion, in order that it may defend powerfully that entrance of Arno.[23] He would like also to have the Tower della Munizione,[24] near the gate, lowered and made larger, in order that this section may be still stronger.[25]

23. *The place where the river enters the city.*
24. *This tower was down the river from its entrance into the city.*
25. *Sixteenth-century maps of Florence show that the general plan of this report was put into practice.*

# TERCETS ON AMBITION

[*The similarity of idea and even word to some of Machiavelli's reports to the Florentine government from Verona in 1509 (26 November; 7 December) puts the dramatic date, and probably the real date, of this poem at the end of that year.*

*In direct contact with reality, depth of emotion, and* saeva indignatio, *this* capitolo *surpasses any of Machiavelli's other compositions in* terza rima. *As to idea, more clearly than any of his other works it shows his sympathy for innocent people subjected by conquerors to the violence of war.*]

## To Luigi Guicciardini

1 LUIGI, SINCE YOU ARE SO AMAZED BY THIS DIRE event that has come about in Siena, it does not seem to me that you take the world as it really is.

4 And if this report seems strange to you, as you have assured me in your letter, meditate a little deeper on mortal craving;

7 because from the sun of Scythia to that of Egypt, from Gibraltar to the opposite shore, we see the sprouting of this transgression.

10 What province or what city escapes it? What village, what hovel? Everywhere Ambition and Avarice penetrate.

13 When man was born into the world, they were born too; and if they had no existence, happy enough would be our condition.

16 Hardly had God made the stars, the heavens, the light, the elements, and man—master over so many things of beauty—

19 and had quelled the pride of the angels, and from Paradise had banished Adam with his wife for their tasting of the apple,

22 when (after the birth of Cain and Abel, as with their father and by their labor they were living happy in their poor dwelling)

25 a hidden power which sustains itself in the heaven, among the

*l. 1 Luigi Guicciardini, brother of the historian Francesco. The Capitolo is an epistle written, actually or dramatically, from Verona in 1509, during the war of Pope Julius II and his allies against Venice.*

*l. 2 A quarrel within the Petrucci family.*

*l. 8 Instead of Gibraltar, some texts read England. The meaning is from the extreme west to the farthest east, that is, the whole world, as viewed in classical times.*

stars which heaven as it whirls encloses—to man's being by no means friendly—

28  to deprive us of peace and to set us at war, to take away from us all quiet and all good, sent two Furies to dwell on the earth.

31  Naked they are, and both of them come with such grace that, to the eyes of many, in grace and in happiness they abound.

34  Each one of them has four faces along with eight hands; and these allow them to grip you and to see in whatever direction they turn.

37  Envy, Sloth, and Hatred are their companions, and with their pestilence they fill the world, and with them go Cruelty, Pride, and Deceit.

40  These drive Concord to the depths. To show their limitless desire, they bear in their hands a bottomless urn.

43  Through them the quiet and happy life always lived in Adam's dwelling with Peace and Charity took flight.

46  With their pestilential venom they armed Cain against his good brother, filling with it his vitals, his heart, and his bosom.

49  And they revealed their mighty power, since in primitive times they could make a heart ambitious, a heart covetous,

52  when men were living naked and destitute of all riches, and when as yet there were no examples of poverty and of wealth.

55  Oh human spirit insatiable, arrogant, crafty, and shifting, and above all else malignant, iniquitous, violent, and savage,

58  because through your longing so ambitious, the first violent death was seen in the world, and the first grass red with blood!

61  Since this evil seed is now mature, since evil's cause is multiplied, there is no reason for men to repent of doing evil.

64  From this it results that one goes down and another goes up; on this depends, without law or agreement, the shifting of every mortal condition.

67  From France this many times has brought the king; this vice has broken up the states of King Alfonso and Lodovico and San Marco.

70  Not merely whatever good his enemy has, but what he seems to have—and so always the world has been, modern and ancient—

l. 30  *Avarice and Ambition.*
l. 60  *An image soon to be used by Ariosto in* ORLANDO FURIOSO, *e.g.* 31. 89.
l. 67  *The French through avarice and ambition have invaded Italy.*

73 every man values. Every man hopes to climb higher by crushing now one, now another, rather than through his own wisdom and goodness.

76 To each of us, another's success is always vexatious; and therefore always, with effort and trouble, for another's ill we are watchful and alert.

79 To this our natural instinct draws us, by our own motion and our own feeling, if laws or greater forces do not restrain us.

82 But if you wish to know the reason why one people commands and the other weeps, while everywhere the sovereign is Ambition;

85 why France continues as victor; on the other hand why all Italy is shattered by a stormy sea of troubles;

88 and why upon these lands has come the affliction of that wicked seed which Ambition and Avarice bring to fruit,

91 I say that if with Ambition are joined a valiant heart, a well-armed vigor, then for himself a man seldom fears evil.

94 When through her own nature a country lives unbridled, and then, by accident, is organized and established under good laws,

97 Ambition uses against foreign peoples that violence which neither the law nor the king permits her to use at home

100 (wherefore home-born trouble almost always ceases); yet she is sure to keep disturbing the sheepfolds of others, wherever that violence of hers has planted its banner.

103 In an opposite way, that land is servile, exposed to every harm, to every injury, in which the people are ambitious and cowardly.

106 If Cowardice and Bad Government sit side by side with this Ambition, every sort of distress, every kind of ruin, every other ill comes quickly.

109 And when someone blames Nature if in Italy, so much afflicted and worn, men are not born so vigorous and hardy,

112 I say that this does not excuse and justify our lack of worth, for discipline can make up where Nature is lacking.

115 This in times gone by made Italy flourish, and for conquering the world from end to end, stern discipline gave her daring.

118 Now she lives, if it is life to live in tears, beneath the havoc and the fate which this great Sloth of hers deserves.

121 Such Sloth amounts to Cowardice with her companion vices.

l. 121 *The text of this tercet is uncertain.*

From Ambition come those wounds that have killed the Italian provinces.

124 Pass over Siena's fraternal contests; turn your eyes, Luigi, to this region, upon these people thunderstruck and bewildered,

127 you will see how Ambition results in two kinds of action: one party robs and the other weeps for its wealth ravaged and scattered.

130 Let him turn his eyes here who wishes to behold the sorrows of others, and let him consider if ever before now the sun has looked upon such savagery.

133 A man is weeping for his father dead and a woman for her husband; another man, beaten and naked, you see driven in sadness from his own dwelling.

136 Oh how many times, when the father has held his son tight in his arms, a single thrust has pierced the breasts of them both!

139 Another is abandoning his ancestral home, as he accuses cruel and ungrateful gods, with his brood overcome with sorrow.

142 Oh, strange events such as never have happened before in the world! Every day many children are born through sword cuts in the womb.

145 To her daughter, overcome with sorrow, the mother says: "For what an unhappy marriage, for what a cruel husband have I kept you!"

148 Foul with blood are the ditches and streams, full of heads, of legs, of arms, and other members gashed and severed.

151 Birds of prey, wild beasts, dogs are now their family tombs— Oh tombs repulsive, horrible and unnatural!

154 Always their faces are gloomy and dark, like those of a man terrified and numbed by new injuries or sudden fears.

157 Wherever you turn your eyes, you see the earth wet with tears and blood, and the air full of screams, of sobs, and sighs.

*l. 125 to this region: to Verona and the surrounding region, the seat of war.*

*l. 127 The ambitious French, for the time successful, plunder Lombardy: the ambitious but unsuccessful Venetians lament their losses.*

*l. 159 "The invading soldiers have set to robbing and plundering the country, and I hear and see terrible things such as I have never known of before, so bad that into the minds of these country people there has entered a desire to die and to revenge themselves, for they have become more determined and furious against the enemies of the Venetians than the Jews were against the Romans. It happens every day that one of them who is made prisoner lets himself be killed rather than abandon the Venetian side. Just yesterday one of them was brought before this Bishop, and he said he was of the Venetian party, and as such he intended to die, and he did not want to live as anything else, so that the Bishop had him hanged. And neither a promise to let him off nor any*

160  If from others a man will deign to learn the ways of Ambition, the sad example of these wretches can teach him.

163  Since no man has power to drive her out of himself, needful it is that Judgment and Sound Intellect, with Method and Vigor, be her companions.

166  San Marco, to his cost, and perhaps in vain, discovers late that he needs to hold the sword and not the book in his hand.

169  Yet in a different way man struggles to rule, for the most part; and according as he gains more, he loses it sooner and with greater reproach.

172  So, if often something comes into being that is rapid and insis-tent, which troubles and makes sad the heart of each man,

175  let no one be astonished at that, because in the world most men let themselves be mastered by Fortune.

178  Alas! For while with another's affliction I am keeping my thought engaged and my speech, I am weighed down with greater fear.

181  I see Ambition, with that swarm which Heaven at the world's beginning allotted her, flying over the Tuscan mountains;

184  and already she has scattered so many sparks among those people swollen with envy that she will burn their towns and their farmsteads if grace or better government does not bring her to nought.

---

*other favor was able to pull him away from this belief"* (LEGATION TO MANTUA, *letter of 26 Nov. 1509, from Verona*).

l. 166 *St. Mark, patron of Venice, is often represented holding a book. In a letter from Verona (7 Dec. 1509), Machiavelli says: "We hear that the Venetians in all those places over which they have authority are having painted a Saint Mark who instead of a book has a sword in his hand; from which it appears that they have found out to their cost that, for holding states, studies and books are not enough."*

l. 169 *Both Venice and Florence attempted to gain empires without developing the necessary military spirit.*

# TERCETS ON INGRATITUDE
## OR ENVY

[*The reference to Gonsalvo di Cordova (1453-1515) as living in disgrace (line 164) indicates composition in 1507-1515.*

*This subject was close to Machiavelli's heart, as appears in his emphasis on public ingratitude to Michele di Lando, in the* HISTORY OF FLORENCE. *Envy, also important in the poem, was one of the causes of destructive divisions in cities.*]

### To Giovanni Folchi

1 GIOVANNI FOLCHI, TO LIVE AS A MALCONTENT, bitten by Envy's tooth, would give me more sorrow and more vexation,

4 if it were not that still the sweet strings of my harp, giving forth soft airs, make the Muses not deaf to my singing;

7 not that I hope to get any wreath for it, not that I hope to add a droplet of water to Helicon.

10 I know well how long the road is; I know I have not breath enough to reach the top of that longed-for hill.

13 Yet such desire all the time drives me that I believe I can pluck as I go, perhaps, some of the tiny plants that cover the slope.

16 By singing, then, I strive to take from my heart and to bridle that sorrow for my afflictions that madly pursues my soul;

19 and how the years of serving may be lost, how we may sow in sand and in water, will now be the theme of my verses.

22 When the stars, when the heavens were indignant at human pride, for man's abasement Ingratitude then was born in the world.

25 Of Avarice she was the daughter and of Suspicion; she was nursed in the arms of Envy; in the breasts of princes and kings she lives.

28 There as in her chief abode she makes her nest; from thence she

l. 1 *Giovanni Folchi: historically unimportant.*

anoints the hearts of all other men with the poison of her treachery.

31 Thus in all places this evil is felt, because everything is pierced and bitten by her nurse's envenomed tooth.

34 And if any man early enrolls himself among the fortunate, through Heaven's good wishes and her joyous aid, in no long time afterward he unsays his words,

37 when, wearied out, he sees his blood and his sweat and his life of good service repaid with injury and calumny.

40 This pestilent creature holds (and never are they fewer, because one after the other she puts them back into the quiver she has by her side)

43 three cruel arrows anointed with poison with which she never ceases to wound now this one now that at whom she directs her aim.

46 The first of the three that comes from her quiver makes a man merely bear witness that he has received a benefit; without according any return he confesses it.

49 And the second, which next she takes out, makes a man forget the favor he receives; yet doing the giver no injury, he merely denies it.

52 The last makes a man never remember or return a favor, and to the extent of his power he rends and bites his benefactor.

55 This stroke cuts through to the bone; this third wound is more deadly; this arrow comes with greater force.

58 Never does Ingratitude perish; never is she destroyed; a thousand times she rises up, if once she dies, because her father and her mother are immortal.

61 As I said, she triumphs in the heart of every ruler, but takes more delight in the heart of the populace when it is master.

64 The populace by her three arrows is wounded more severely, because always where little is known, more is suspected,

67 and its various persons, full of all manner of envy, keep Suspicion ever awake, and he keeps his ears open for slanders.

70 From this it comes that often we see a good citizen reaping grain unlike the seed he sowed in the field.

l. 32 *nurse: Envy (line 26, above).*

l. 64 *The populace is more suspicious than the ruler because less able to get good information.*

73 Bereft of peace and quiet was Italy at the time when the Punic sword was glutting its barbarous thirst,

76 yet already had been born in a Roman house, or rather sent from Heaven, a man divine, such that there never has been and never will be another like him.

79 When still a youth, on the Tesino this man with his own breast sheltered his father—the first foreshadowing of his happy destiny.

82 And after Cannae wiped out so many Romans, vigorous and alone with a sword in his hand he did not suffer Italy to be abandoned.

85 Then a little later, the Senate ordered him to Spanish soil, to take revenge for public injury and private suffering.

88 When in Africa also he raised his standards, first Syphax, and next Hannibal's fortune and native land he ruined.

91 Then the great barbarian turned his back; then he revenged the Roman blood shed by that enemy through the Italian valleys.

94 Afterward to Asia he went with his brother, and thereupon, through his prudence and goodness, from Asia he brought triumph back to Rome.

97 And in all the provinces and cities where he went he wrought countless noble deeds of piety, of fortitude and chastity.

100 What tongue can recount all his praises? What eye can look on such great light? O happy Romans! Happy times!

103 This unconquered and splendid leader has shown everyone that road which leads man to the highest glory.

106 Never in human hearts has been seen or will be seen—however worthy, splendid, and godlike—so much bravery and so much courtesy;

109 and among those who are dead and those who live, and among all peoples ancient or modern, there is not a man who equals Scipio.

112 But not for all that did Envy fear to show him the teeth of her madness, and to look on him with the pupils of her eyes aflame.

115 She had him accused in the midst of the people, and decreed that boundless benefit with boundless harm should be joined.

118 But when he saw this universal vice in arms against him, he decided of his own will to leave that ungrateful dwelling;

l. 77 *man divine: Scipio Africanus.*

121  and he gave place to the evil desire of others as soon as he saw
  that Rome must needs lose either freedom or himself.

124  He did not arm his soul with other revenge; merely he was not
  willing to leave to his native city those bones she did not deserve
  to keep.

127  And so the circle of his life he ended outside his family's nest.
  And so a harvest contrary to his sowing he gathered.

130  By no means was Rome the only city ungrateful to the utmost;
  look at Athens, where Ingratitude made her nest fouler than
  elsewhere;

133  and it was of no use to take up the shield against her, though
  against her many laws were made, to restrain a vice so terrible
  and cruel.

136  That city we think more foolish as we see that clearly she knew
  what was good and chose not to follow it.

139  Miltiades, Aristides and Phocion and the hard lot of Themisto-
  cles to her conduct were good witnesses.

142  For their illustrious and mighty works these were the glories they
  received from her: prison, exile, slander and death;

145  because in the eyes of the crowd towns that are captured, blood
  that is shed and honored wounds are wiped from the record by
  the slightest censure for a tiny fault.

148  But wicked slanders, and very bold ones, against a good citizen
  sometimes render tyrannical a nature once mild and humane.

151  Often a citizen becomes a tyrant and goes beyond the bounds of
  his country's law in order not to suffer Ingratitude's injury.

154  This made Caesar snatch the throne; and what Ingratitude did
  not bestow, rightful anger and rightful resentment gave him.

157  But let us pass over the people's self-interest. I turn to princes
  and moderns in whom likewise Nature put ungrateful hearts.

160  Ahmed Pasha, not long after he gave the throne to Bajazet, died
  with the cord twisted about his neck.

163  The Apulian lands Gonsalvo has left forsaken and he lives
  under his king's suspicion as recompense for overthrowing
  the Gauls.

166  Seek through all the world's wide spaces; you will find few
  grateful princes, if you read what is written of them;

l. 163 *Gonsalvo: Gonsalvo di Cordova, "The Great Captain," a Spanish general who
defeated the French in southern Italy, especially at the River Garigliano in 1503.*

*169*   and you will see shifters of governments and givers of kingdoms with death or exile always repaid,

*172*   because when you cause a government to shift, the prince you have made then fears your taking what you have bestowed

*175*   and does not keep faith or compact with you, because more powerful is his dread of you than the obligation incurred,

*178*   and for just so long this terror lasts as he requires to see your family destroyed, and the sepulchre of you and yours.

*181*   Hence often you labor in serving and then for your good service receive in return a wretched life and violent death.

*184*   So then, Ingratitude not being dead, let everyone flee from courts and governments, for there is no road that takes a man faster to weeping over what he longed for, when once he has gained it.

# TERCETS ON FORTUNE

[*Of unknown date.*

*Fortune has often been celebrated in poetry, even by Dante. In dealing with this idea that meant so much to him, as is evidenced by the twenty-fifth chapter of* THE PRINCE, *Machiavelli shows unusual command over figurative language.*]

## To Giovan Battista Soderini*

*1* WITH WHAT RIMES AND WHAT VERSES SHALL I sing of the kingdom of Fortune and of her chances favorable and adverse?

*4* Shall I sing how, demanding and injurious, as here we judge her, at the foot of her throne she brings all the world together?

*7* For fear, Giovan Battista, you have no reason, nor should you in any way dread other wounds than her blows,

*10* because this shifting creature often and by habit resists with the greatest might where she sees that nature is strongest.

*13* Her natural power for all men is too strong and her reign is always violent if prowess still greater than hers does not vanquish her.

*16* Hence I pray that you will consent to look somewhat at these verses of mine, to see if they hold anything worth your notice.

*19* Meanwhile the cruel goddess may turn on me her fierce eyes and read what now I sing of her kingdom.

*22* Though she sits on high above all and gives commands and rules with fury, she yet may look on him who has courage to sing of her dominion.

*25* By many this goddess is called omnipotent, because whoever comes into this life either late or early feels her power.

*28* She often keeps the good beneath her feet; the wicked she raises up; and if ever she promises you anything, never does she keep her promise.

* *This dedication is the recipient's only claim to distinction.*

31  She turns states and kingdoms upside down as she pleases; she deprives the just of the good that she freely gives to the unjust.

34  This unstable goddess and fickle deity often sets the undeserving on a throne to which the deserving never attains.

37  She times events as suits her; she raises us up, she puts us down without pity, without law or right.

40  Always her choice is not to favor one man in every season; she does not always keep afflicting a man at the very bottom of her wheel.

43  Whose daughter she is or from what family she sprang we know not; we do know of a certain that even by Jove her power is feared.

46  Over a palace open on every side she reigns, and she deprives no one of entering, but the getting out is not sure.

49  All the world there gathers around her, eager to see strange things, and full of ambition and full of hopes.

52  She stands on the highest point, where the sight of her is not denied to any man; but a little time turns her about and moves her.

55  And this aged witch has two faces, one of them fierce and the other mild; and as she turns, now she does not see you, now she beseeches, now she menaces you.

58  Whoever tries to enter, she receives benignly, but at him who later tries to go out she rages, and often his road for departing is taken from him.

61  Within her palace, as many wheels are turning as there are varied ways of climbing to those things which every living man strives to attain.

64  Sighs, blasphemies, and outrageous words are everywhere heard uttered by those whom Fortune conceals within her bounds.

67  By as much as they are richer and more powerful, by so much more they show discourtesy; by so much more they are less grateful for her favors.

70  Hence all the evil that comes upon mankind is charged to her; but any good that befalls a man he believes he gets through his own worth.

73  Among the strange and varied crowd of fellow servants whom that building holds, Audacity and Youth make highest showing.

76 We see Anxiety prostrate on the floor, so full of fears that he does nothing; then Penitence and Envy make war on him.

79 Here Opportunity alone finds sport, and always frisking about among the wheels is that tousel-haired and simple maiden.

82 And those wheels are ever turning, day and night, because Heaven commands (and she is not to be resisted) that Laziness and Necessity whirl them around.

85 The latter puts the world in order again, and the first lays it waste. We see in all seasons and at every hour the strength of Patience and how much she can accomplish.

88 Usury and Fraud enjoy themselves with their crew, powerful and rich; and among these companions Liberality stands, ragged and torn.

91 Above the gates that never, they say, are locked, sit Luck and Chance, without eyes and without ears.

94 Power, honor, riches, and health are ready as rewards; as punishment and affliction there are servitude, infamy, sickness, and poverty.

97 Fortune displays her mad fury with these distresses; the gifts she offers to those she loves.

100 That man most luckily forms his plan, among all the persons in Fortune's palace, who chooses a wheel befitting her wish,

103 since the inclinations that make you act, so far as they conform with her doings, are the causes of your good and your ill.

106 Yet you cannot therefore trust yourself to her nor hope to escape her hard bite, her hard blows, violent and cruel,

109 because while you are whirled about by the rim of a wheel that for the moment is lucky and good, she is wont to reverse its course in midcircle.

112 And since you cannot change your character nor give up the disposition that Heaven endows you with, in the midst of your journey she abandons you.

115 Therefore, if this he understood and fixed in his mind, a man who could leap from wheel to wheel would always be happy and fortunate,

118 but because to attain this is denied by the occult force that rules us, our condition changes with her course.

*l. 78 Penitence is the companion of Occasion or Fortune in Machiavelli's poem,* ON OCCA-SION, *a free rendering of Ausonius'* EPIGRAM ON THE STATUE OF OCCASION.

*121* Not a thing in the world is eternal; Fortune wills it so and makes herself splendid by it, so that her power may be more clearly seen.

*124* Therefore a man should take her for his star and, as far as he can, should every hour adjust himself to her variation.

*127* All that realm of hers, within and without, is adorned with narrative paintings of those triumphs from which she gets most honor.

*130* In the first space, painted in vigorous colors, we see that long ago under Egypt's king the world stood subjugated and conquered,

*133* and that for long years he held it subject in continuing peace, and that then the beauties of nature were expressed in writing.

*136* Next we see the Assyrians climbing up to the lofty scepter, when Fortune did not permit the king of Egypt to wield authority longer.

*139* Thereafter we see her happy to turn to the Medes; from the Medes to the Persians; and the hair of the Greeks she crowned with the diadem she took away from the Persians.

*142* Here we see Thebes and Memphis subdued, Babylon, Troy, and Carthage too, Jerusalem, Athens, Sparta, and Rome.

*145* Here is represented how splendid they were, noble, rich, and powerful, and how at the end Fortune made them their enemies' booty.

*148* Here we see the noble and god-like deeds of the Roman Empire; then how all the world went to pieces at her fall.

*151* As a rapid torrent, swollen to the utmost, destroys whatever its current anywhere reaches,

*154* and adds to one place and lowers another, shifts its banks, shifts its bed and its bottom, and makes the earth tremble where it passes,

*157* so Fortune in her furious onrush many times, now here now there, shifts and reshifts the world's affairs.

*160* If then your eyes light on what is beyond, in one panel Caesar and Alexander you see among those who prospered while alive.

*163* From their example we well realize how much he pleases For-

l. 127 *realm: palace.*

l. 128 *In this use of wall paintings to present history, Machiavelli precedes Ariosto,* ORLANDO FURIOSO *33. 1–58.*

tune and how acceptable he is who pushes her, who shoves her, who jostles her.

166 Yet nevertheless the coveted harbor one of the two failed to reach, and the other, covered with wounds, in his enemy's shadow was slain.

169 After this appear countless men who, that they might fall to earth with a heavier crash, with this goddess have climbed to excessive heights.

172 Among these, captive, dead, and mangled, lie Cyrus and Pompey, though Fortune carried both of them up to the heavens.

175 Have you ever seen anywhere how a raging eagle moves, driven by hunger and fasting?

178 And how he carries a tortoise on high, that the force of its fall may break it, and he can feed on the dead flesh?

181 So Fortune not that a man may remain on high carries him up, but that as he plunges down she may delight, and he as he falls may weep.

184 As we look at those who come next, we see how from the humblest rank men rise to high position and how uncertain life is.

187 There we see how she afflicts both Tullius and Marius, and the splendid horns of their fame many times now she exalts, now she cuts off.

190 We see at last that in days gone by few have been successful, and they have died before their wheel reversed itself or in turning carried them down to the bottom.

*l. 168 shadow: obviously Pompey's statue, near the base of which Caesar fell (Shakespeare* JULIUS CAESAR *3. 1. 132; 2. 198). Machiavelli's exceptional use of* ombra *is like that possible for the Latin* simulacrum, *which runs from shadow to statue.*

*l. 188 Such a figurative use of the horn Machiavelli could have taken from the Psalms, e.g.,* "My horn thou shalt exalt like the horn of an unicorn" *(92. 10); or from Ovid:* "venerunt capiti cornua sera mero" (AMORES *1. 11. 6), rendered very freely:* "Courage has entered my heart."

# THE [GOLDEN] ASS

[*In a letter of 17 December 1517, Machiavelli says that he plans to include in this poem the name of Lodovico Ariosto, who is not mentioned in the work as it stands. Evidently Machiavelli had intentions not to be inferred from the fragment he left.*]

## FIRST CHAPTER

1 The various chances, the suffering and the grief that under an ass's form I endured, I shall sing, if only Fortune consents.

4 I do not beg that Helicon send forth more water or that Phoebus lay down his bow and his quiver and with his lyre accompany my verses,

7 both because such favor is not in these times to be had by asking and because I am certain that for the music of an ass's bray there is no need for the lyre.

10 I am not seeking to get from my singing any pay, reward, or recompense, and moreover I do not mind a slanderer's bite, whether open or concealed,

13 because I am well aware how dull of hearing Gratitude is to every man's requests, and I am well aware how many of her benefits an ass remembers.

16 Bites and blows I do not regard as once I did, for I have grown to have the same nature as he whom I sing.

19 If I should, too, by my effort be held longer than is my wont, so I am commanded by that ass under whose form I have lived.

22 Long ago quite all of Siena tried to make one of them drink from the fountain of Branda, and they got into his mouth a droplet of water with the greatest ado.

25 But if the heavens do not hurl down fresh angers against me, a bray will make itself heard in all places; let it light on whom it list!

28 But before I begin to tell my ass's diverse adventures, I hope you won't be annoyed at hearing a tale.

31 Once there lived—and not yet has his family wholly vanished—

a certain young fellow right here in Florence among the people of old.

34 He suffered from an ailment that kept increasing, namely, that in every place he went running through the street, and at every time, without any heed.

37 And so much the more his father sorrowed over this condition, as the causes of his affliction were less understood;

40 and he secured many opinions from many wise men, and in the course of time applied to his son a thousand remedies of a thousand sorts.

43 Besides this he also made vows for him, perhaps; but the remedies all were useless, for always and in every place he ran.

46 At last a certain quack doctor—for many such can every day be seen here—promised his father to make him well.

49 And since those who promise benefit are always believed (from which it comes that men put such faith in doctors;

52 and often, by believing them, a man deprives himself of his property; it seems that this alone among the occupations feeds and lives on the ills of others),

55 so that father was in no doubt and put the case in that fellow's hands, since in that doctor's words he had faith.

58 And he put a hundred perfumes to his nose; he took blood from his head. Then he seemed to have convinced him he shouldn't run.

61 And when he had used his other remedies, he turned over the son to his father as cured, with these conditions that now we shall tell you:

64 that for four months never should he let him go outdoors by himself, but that someone should be with him who, if perchance he should set to flying,

67 in some good way or other would hold him back, partly by showing him his error and beseeching him to have regard for his honor.

70 So for more than a month he went out, decorous and sensible, between two of his brothers, full of respect and of regard;

73 but coming one day into the Via de' Martelli, from which he could see the Via Larga, his hair began to stand on end.

76 Nor could this youth restrain himself, when he saw this street so straight and wide, from turning again to his old pleasure;

79 and everything else abandoned, there came back to him the fancy for running, which goes on working and never is quiet;

82 so when he came to the head of the street, he dropped his cloak on the ground and said: "Christ can't keep me here," and off he ran.

85 And after that he always ran, as long as he lived. So his father lost what he had spent, and the doctor his effort in the case.

88 Because the mind of man, ever intent on what is natural to it, grants no protection against either habit or nature.

91 So I, having early turned my thought to nipping this and that, at one time stood quite still, kind and patient,

94 no more observing others' defects, but seeking in some other way to get ahead, so that I believed I was cured.

97 But the present age so grudging and evil, without a man's having the eyes of Argus, makes him always see bad more quickly than good.

100 Hence, if now I scatter a bit of poison, even though I am out of practice in speaking ill, the age compels me with its matter so abundant.

103 And our ass, which up and down so many stairs in this our world has taken his course, in order to see the nature of every mortal,

106 even though everywhere his long wanderings through its streets are observed, the heavens could not keep from braying.

109 So there will not be a person who will come close to this rude and stubborn herd, in order not to suffer its asinine tricks,

112 for everybody is well aware, who studies its nature, that one of the cleverest antics it knows is to give a couple of kicks and two farts.

115 And everybody to suit himself may gossip and tattle and have as much as he wants of smoke and pride, for it must always be that this ass will hit us;

118 and everyone may learn how the world has grown bad, because as quite the same I hope to paint it for you before bit and pack-saddle are eaten.

l. 110 *herd. Apparently this word refers only to the one ass.*

l. 116 *smoke: vanity.*

l. 120 *Machiavelli here modifies and combines two proverbial sayings. To "gnaw the bit" indicates anger and "to gnaw the pack-saddle" means to speak ill of those who have spoken against one.*

*121* And he who wishes to take it ill can loosen his belt.

l. 121 *he can loosen his belt: he can lump it.*

## SECOND CHAPTER

*1* When the sunny season returns, when spring—an enemy to the ice, to the cold, to the snow—drives winter away,

*4* the sky shows a very pleasant face, and Diana with her nymphs begins again to go hunting through the woods;

*7* and day shows itself brighter, especially if the sun is flaming between one horn and the other of the celestial Bull.

*10* Little asses, as they move around, are heard making a noise together sometimes in the evening as they go back home,

*13* so that whoever speaks is scarcely heard; hence from ancient times it has been the custom to say a thing the second time;

*16* because with a sharp and thundering voice one of them often brays or laughs, if he sees something that pleases him or smells it.

*19* In this season, at the hour when the day divides itself from the night, I found myself in as rough a place as ever I saw.

*22* I cannot tell you at all how I got there nor do I know at all the cause why I fell in that place where I wholly lost my liberty.

*25* I could not continue my steps by reason of my great fear and the darkness of night, for I could not see in the least where I was going.

*28* But much more was my fear increased by a blast on a horn so savage and strong that still my mind feels no assurance about it.

*31* And I seemed to see Death nearby with his scythe, and colored with that hue with which all his companions are colored.

*34* The air dark with clouds huge and thick, the path overspread with rocks, broken trees, and snags had laid low and vanquished my vigor.

*37* Against a big trunk I had scarcely supported myself, when suddenly a brightness appeared to me, not different from lightning flashes;

*40* but as the flashing did not then disappear (instead, increasing

l. 22 *Quoted, with slight change, from Dante,* INFERNO 1. 10. *Other Dantesque reminiscences also appear.*

and coming near me, it seemed always greater and clearer),

43 I had fixed my eye steadily upon it, and around it heard a murmur of moving boughs that was coming with it.

46 I was deprived of almost all my sense, and, terror-stricken by that strange thing, I kept my face turned toward what I was hearing,

49 when a woman of the utmost beauty, but breezy and brash, appeared to me with her locks blonde and disheveled.

52 With her left hand she carried through the forest a great light, and with her right she held a horn with which she made music.

55 With her in the midst of the uninhabited plain were numberless animals, following after her in order.

58 Bears, wolves and lions fierce and cruel, and stags and badgers and, with many other beasts of prey, a countless number of boars.

61 This made me much more fearful and I would have fled, pale and ghastly, if to will had been joined power.

64 But what star would have shown me port? And where, in my misery, would I have gone; or who would have led me to my path?

67 Uncertain continued all my thoughts, whether I ought to wait until she came to me, or whether with reverence I should go to meet her,

70 so much so that before I moved away from the tree-trunk she came up, and with an alert and smiling manner said: "Good evening."

73 And her greeting was as familiar, as full of grace as it could have been if she had seen me a thousand times.

76 I was completely reassured by that action, and so much the more because she called me by name in the greeting she gave me at the very first.

79 And then, with a smile, she said: "And how, do tell me, did you fall into these valleys which not one inhabitant tills or masters?"

82 My cheeks, which were pallid and wan, changed color and became like fire, and in silence I shrugged my shoulders.

85 I should have liked to say: "My little wit, vain hope and vain opinion have made me fall into this place."

88 But I was not able to form this speech in any way—such shame and such compassion for myself seized me.

91 And she laughing: "You do not need to be afraid to speak among these trees; just speak and tell what troubles your heart;

94 for though in this broken and solitary land I guide this flock, yet for many months past the entire course of your life has been known to me.

97 But because you cannot have learned our condition, I shall tell you into what place you have fallen and into what lands.

100 When in times gone by Circe had to abandon her ancient nest, before Jove seized dominion,

103 since she found no trustworthy refuge and no people who would receive her—so great was the rumor of her infamy—

106 in this dark forest, shady and dense, fleeing all human society and law, she fixed her dwelling and her seat.

109 So among these solitary rocks she lives as an enemy to men, fed by the sighs of these herds.

112 And because never does one who has come here get away, therefore never has news of her been heard, and still it is unheard.

115 In her service are many damsels, with whom alone she rules her kingdom, and I am one of their number.

118 To me is given as an eternal duty that this flock shall come with me to pasture among these woods and all their caves.

121 Hence it is fitting I should hold this light and this horn; both of them are good if it happens that when I am still out of doors the day is spent.

124 One reveals to me the road; with the other I make music, so if in the dense forest any animal is lost, he will know where I am.

127 And if you should ask me, I answer you: "You must know that in the world these animals you see were men like yourself."

130 And if you do not trust my words, observe a little how they stand around you and which one looks at you and which licks your feet.

133 And the cause of their looking at you is that each mourns for your fall and your suffering and your loss.

136 Each one, like you, was a wanderer in these forests, and then was transformed by my Queen into these shapes.

139 This special virtue is given her by heaven, that she can make a man change to a different shape, as soon as she looks fixedly on his face.

142 Therefore you must come with me and follow the steps of this
herd of mine if you do not wish to die in these woods.

145 And in order that Circe may not see the contour of your face,
and that you may come secretly, you will come on all fours in
the midst of this troop."

148 Then she moved on with a pleasant face; and I, not seeing there
any way of escape, went on all fours with the animals behind her.

151 side by side with a stag and with a bear.


## THIRD CHAPTER

1 Following the footsteps of my guide as I went on, with my back
turned toward the sky, in the midst of that dense crowd of
animals,

4 I was seized now by heat and now by chill; then with trembling
I examined my arms, lest they might have changed their hide
or hair.

7 My hands and my knees I ruined. Oh, you who sometimes go
on all fours can imagine without my telling in what state I was.

10 I had been going perhaps an hour on my knees among those
animals, when we came into a ditch between two great walls

13 (see ahead of us we could not, because the lamp dazzled us all,
carried by that woman we followed),

16 and then we heard a voice that whistled, with the sound of a
portal opened, both doors of which were squeaking.

19 When the prospect allowed our gaze, before our eyes a huge
edifice of wondrous height presented itself.

22 Magnificent and extensive was the place; but in order to reach it,
we needed to pass through the water of that ditch by fording.

25 A beam made a narrow little bridge on which our leader only
crossed, but the animals could not go upon it.

28 As soon as we reached the threshold of that high gate, in I went
full of distress and anxiety, in the midst of that crowd which is
worse than death.

31 And I felt much less terror because my lady, in order that I
might not fear, had on her entering there put out the light.

34 And that was the reason why I did not see from whence the
whistling had come, or who had opened to us when we entered.

*37* So, unnoticed among those animals, I found myself in a spacious courtyard, all bewildered, without being seen.

*40* And my lady, beautiful, tall and kindly, busied herself for an hour or more in settling the animals in their stable.

*43* Then, with the utmost grace she took me by the hand and led me into her chamber, where with her own hands she kindled a great fire,

*46* with which courteously she dried me, because the water had completely soaked me when I was forced to cross the ditch.

*49* When I was dried and somewhat rested from the distress and vexation with which that night had wearied me,

*52* I began: "My lady, I am keeping silent not at all because I do not realize exactly how much good you have done me, how much kindness.

*55* I had come to the end of my life, in a dark, cloudy and sunless place, when I was overtaken by the night.

*58* You led me with you, to save me; so to you I owe my life and everything related to it that I possess.

*61* But my memory of the dark wood and your fair face have made me keep silent (since in the latter I see and recognize all that to me is good)

*64* for they have made me now sad, now happy; sad because of the ill that came first, cheerful because of the good that came after;

*67* so I have not been able to clear my voice for speech until now when I am somewhat rested from that long road.

*70* But you, into whose power I surrender myself, and who with such courtesy have treated me that you cannot be paid with any gift,

*73* in this matter too will be courteous, so that it will not burden you to tell me the course of my life as you know it."

*76* "Among modern peoples and among ancient," she answered, "never has anyone borne more ingratitude or greater toil.

*79* Through your own fault this did not overtake you, as it happens to some, but because Chance was opposed to your good conduct.

*82* Chance closed upon you the gates of pity above all when she led you into this place so savage and strong.

*85* But because weeping has always been shameful to a man, he should turn to the blows of Fortune a face unstained with tears.

*88* You see the stars and the sky, you see the moon, you see the other planets go wandering, now high, now low, without any rest;

91 sometimes you see the sky cloudy, sometimes shining and clear, and likewise nothing on earth remains in the same condition always.

94 From this result peace and war; on this depend the hatreds among those whom one wall and one moat shut up together.

97 From this came your first suffering; this was altogether the cause of your toils without reward.

100 Not yet has Heaven altered its opinion, nor will alter it, while the Fates keep toward you their hard purpose.

103 And those feelings which you have found so hostile and so adverse not yet, not yet are purged;

106 but when their roots are dry, and the Heavens show themselves gracious, times happier than ever before will return;

109 and so pleasant and delightful they will be that you will get joy from the memory of both past and future affliction.

112 Perhaps you will yet take pride in retelling to various peoples the long account of your sufferings.

115 But before these stars show themselves propitious toward you, you will have to travel to explore the world, covered with a different skin,

118 because that Providence which supports the human species intends you to bear this affliction for your greater good.

121 Hence you must altogether lose your human semblance, and without it come with me to feed among the other beasts.

124 There can be no change in this harsh star; by putting you in this place, the ill is deferred, not canceled.

127 You are permitted to remain with me some time, that you may gain experience of the place and of those who inhabit it.

130 Then try not to become disheartened, but boldly take this weight on your shoulders, firm and strong,

133 for sometime it will be to your advantage that you have taken it."

## FOURTH CHAPTER

1 When the lady ceased speaking, I rose to my feet, disturbed by the words she had uttered.

4 Still I said: "I do not accuse the Heavens or any other, nor do I

intend to lament so ill a lot, because to evil more than to good I am wonted,

7 but if I must pass through the gates of Hell to that good you have spoken of, I am willing—much more through those ways by which you have taken me.

10 Fortune, then, may make of my life all that she must and all that she chooses, for well I know that for me she never will grieve."

13 Then my lady opened her arms and graciously, with the utmost gladness, ten times and more she kissed my face.

16 Next she said rejoicing: "Prudent soul, this journey of yours, this suffering of yours, will be sung by poet or historian.

19 But because I see the evening passing away, I wish us to take some refreshment and to make a change in our conversation.

22 And first we shall find some supper, for I know you need it, more than a little perhaps, if your constitution is not of iron;

25 and together we shall enjoy it in this place." And so saying, she arranged a little cloth on a table near the fire.

28 Then from a cupboard she took a little box, in which were bread, glasses and knives, a fowl, a salad well mixed and good,

31 and all the things that go with them. Then, turning to me, she said: "This supper every evening a girl prepares for me.

34 Also she brings this bottle full of wine, which will seem to you, if you try it, such as Val di Greve and Poppi produce.

37 Let us be joyful, then, and, as wise men do, think that good yet can come and that he who is standing at last must fall.

40 And when evil comes—for it always does come—take it down like a medicine, for he is crazy who tastes it and gets its flavor.

43 Now let us be happy, until in the morning it is time to go out with my flock, to obey my exalted queen."

46 So, forgetting troubles and sorrows, we happily supped together, and talked of a thousand little songs and a thousand loves.

49 Then, when we had supped, she undressed and had me get into her bed with her, as though I were her lover or her husband.

52 Now I must burden the Muses in order to tell of her beauty, for without their aid useless would be my description.

55 Her locks were yellow as gold, curled and waved, such that they seemed rays from a star or from the celestial choir.

58 Each eye appeared a little flame, so shining, so clear and so lively that all vision however acute was lost in it.

61 Her head had such an attractive grace that I do not know to what I can best compare it, because the eye was dazzled in looking at it.

64 Narrow arched and black were her brows, because at the shaping of them were all the gods, all the high and heavenly councils.

67 Of that which slopes down from these I should like to say something that would partly correspond to the truth, but I am silent about it because I could not describe it.

70 I do not know at all who made her mouth if Jove did not do it with his own hand; I do not believe any other hand could have made it.

73 Her teeth were more beautiful than ivory, and her tongue moved like a serpent between them and her lips,

76 from whence came out a voice that could still the winds and make the trees follow the speaker—so pleasing and sweet its harmony was.

79 Her neck and her chin were also visible, and other beauties enough to make happy every gloomy and unsuccessful lover.

82 I do not know whether what followed is unsuited for telling, for the reason that the truth often makes war on him who tells it.

85 Yet I will tell it, leaving reflection about it to him who wishes to blame me, because when silence is kept about a great pleasure, that pleasure is not complete.

88 I continued to pass my eyes over all her various parts as low as her breast, at the splendor of which I still kindle,

91 but seeing farther was refused me by a rich and shining coverlet with which that little bed was covered.

94 My mind was dull and uncertain, cold sad timid and doubtful, not knowing how far the path was open.

97 And as on the first evening, timid and bashful and wrapped in the counterpane near her husband, the new wife lies,

100 so round timid me the cover of the bed was wrapped, as though in my strength I had no trust.

103 But after the lady had looked at me for a time, smiling she said: "Do you think I am armed with nettles or thorns?

106 You are permitted to have that for which others, in order to get it, more than once have lamented with sighs and have caused a thousand disputes and a thousand quarrels.

*109* Surely, in order to be with me you would enter any hostile place or like Leander swim between Abydos and Sestos.

*112* Then why do you have so little vigor that these clothes between us make war on you and keep you so far from me?"

*115* Like an offender locked in prison, doubtful of life, who stands with his eyes fixed on the earth,

*118* but then, if he wins grace from his lord, he abandons every harsh thought and gains great ardor and valor,

*121* such was I, and such I became through her kind speaking; and I moved near her, extending my cold hand between the sheets.

*124* And when I touched her body, a sweetness came to my heart so pleasing that I do not believe I shall ever taste greater.

*125* Not in one place did my hand remain, and as it ran all over her body, my lost vigor quickly returned,

*128* and now being timid no longer, after sighing sweetly, I spoke and said: "Blessed be your beauties!

*133* Happy the hour when I set foot in the forest, and happy am I that things I have done or written have touched your heart."

*136* And with many amorous gestures and words, enfolded in those angelic beauties that made me forgetful of human things,

*139* I felt at my heart so many joys with such sweetness that I swooned in tasting the utmost of all sweets,

*142* all prostrate on her sweet bosom.

## FIFTH CHAPTER

*1* Now the cold night was coming to an end; the stars were fleeing one by one and on every side the sky was growing light;

*4* to the sun the light of the moon was yielding; when my lady said: "It is necessary, for such is the will of Fortune,

*7* if I do not wish to incur disgrace, to return to my herd and lead it to the place where it longs to take its accustomed food.

*10* You will remain alone in this cell, and this evening, on my return, I shall lead you where you will be able to see my herd at your ease.

*13* Do not go outside; this warning I give you to be remembered; do not answer if someone calls, because such an error has brought many others to grief."

*16* Then she left. And I, who had turned all my thoughts to that loving countenance, which shone more than all other faces,

19 being alone in the chamber, rose from the bed to lessen the great fire that was consuming my heart.

22 As soon as I parted from her, the arrow of reflection again filled that wound which by her means I had cured;

25 I was as one who has doubts of various things and grows bewildered, desiring the good he does not expect.

28 And because one thought follows another, my mind ran to bygone things that time as yet does not conceal from us;

31 it wandered here and there thinking again how Fortune often now caressed and now nipped the ancient peoples, noble and famous.

34 So wonderful I thought it that I wished to meditate on the cause of variations in earthly things.

37 That which more than anything else throws kingdoms down from the highest hills is this: that the powerful with their power are never sated.

40 From this it results that they are discontented who have lost, and hatred is stirred up to ruin the conquerors;

43 whence it comes about that one rises and the other dies; and the one who has risen is ever tortured with new ambition and with fear.

46 This appetite destroys our states; and the greater wonder is that all recognize this transgression, but not one flees from it.

49 Saint Mark, impetuous and importunate, believing he would always have the wind astern, did not care if he ruined all the rest;

52 nor did he see that too much power was damaging, and that it would be better to keep under water his tail and his croup.

55 Often a man has complained about the territory he ruled, and after the fact has then understood that to his own ruin and his own damage he has increased it.

58 Athens and Sparta, of which once there was such great renown in the world, fell in ruin only after they had conquered the powers round about them.

61 But in Germany at the present day each city lives secure through having less than six miles round about.

*l. 49 Venice, the City of St. Mark.*
*l. 56 Complained of small size and after expansion felt regret.*
*l. 63 A city should not possess territory farther than six miles from her walls.*

64 To our city Henry in his time caused no fear with all his might when he had seized her territories up to the walls;

67 but now that she has extended her power to the lands round about and become great and vast, she dreads everything, not merely huge armies,

70 because strength which is enough to support one body only is not sufficient to sustain a greater weight.

73 He who tries to touch both poles falls in ruin on the earth, as long ago did Icarus after his foolish flight.

76 It is true that a power is wont to exist long or but briefly according as its laws and methods are more or less good.

79 That kingdom which is pushed on to action by energy or by necessity will always go upward.

82 And on the contrary that city will be full of thickets and thorn bushes—changing her officials from winter to summer,

85 until at the end she will of necessity be destroyed and will in her aim be always mistaken—that city which has good laws and bad customs.

88 He who reads past events knows that empires begin with Ninus and end at last with Sardanapalus.

91 The first was held a man divine; that other was found among the serving maids like a woman who distributes flax.

94 Ability makes countries tranquil, and from Tranquillity, Laziness next emerges, and Laziness burns the towns and villages.

97 Then, after a country has for a time been subject to lawlessness, Ability often returns to live there once again.

100 Such a course she who governs us permits and requires, so that nothing beneath the sun ever will or can be firm.

103 And it is and always has been and always will be, that evil follows after good, good after evil.

106 One man, it is true, believes that a deadly thing for kingdoms— what brings about their destruction—is usury or some sin of the flesh,

109 and that the causes of their greatness, which keep them lofty and powerful, are fastings, alms and prayers.

*l. 65 In 1312 the Emperor Henry VII besieged Florence. The last circuit of walls was not then finished; temporary fortifications followed the course shown by the map on the end-papers. l. 100 she: Fortune.*

112 Another, more discreet and wise, holds that to ruin them such evil is not enough, and not enough to preserve them is such good.

115 To believe that without effort on your part God fights for you, while you are idle and on your knees, has ruined many king'doms and many states.

118 There is assuredly need for prayers; and altogether mad is he who forbids people their ceremonies and their devotions;

121 because in fact it seems that from them may be reaped union and good order; and on them in turn rests good and happy fortune.

124 But there should be no one with so small a brain that he will believe, if his house is falling, that God will save it without any other prop,

127 because he will die beneath that ruin.

## SIXTH CHAPTER

1 While I stood in doubt, with my troubled mind wrapped up in that thought, the sun had turned his half circle,

4 the half, I say, of our hemisphere, so that day was departing from us and the east was growing black,

7 when I knew from the sounding of a horn and from the bel'lowing of the unhappy herd that my lady was making her return.

10 And though I was intent on that thought which all day had pulled me to itself and from my breast had driven every other care,

13 when I heard my lady, of a truth I thought that every other thing was vain except her whose servant I had been made.

16 She, having come to me, most kindly encircled my neck with one of her arms; with the other she took my more distant hand.

19 Shame somewhat colored my face, nor was I able to say a thing to her; so great was the sweetness that conquered me.

22 Still, after some time, she and I talked together of many things, as one friend speaks with another.

25 But when her wearied limbs were rested and refreshed with her accustomed food, the lady, thus speaking, suggested:

28 "Earlier I promised to take you to a place where you could find out completely the nature of our condition;

31 so, if you please, get ready, and you will see people with whom
in the past you were well acquainted and had many dealings."

34 Then she rose and I went behind her as she directed, and not
without fear; yet I did not seem either sad or joyous.

37 Night had already come on in shadow and darkness, so that she
took in her hand a lantern whose light she could uncover or
hide as she wished.

40 When we had moved on, but not very far, I thought we entered
a big dormitory, such as we see used in convents.

43 There was an entrance just like theirs, and on each of the sides
were doors made somehow with poor workmanship.

46 Then the lady turned toward me and said that within these
doors her great herd was lying ready for me,

49 and because their kind was varied, their dwelling places were
various, and each one was with his consort.

52 "On the right hand, at the first entrance, are the lions," she said,
taking up her discourse, "with sharp teeth and with hooked
claws.

55 Whoever has a heart magnanimous and noble is changed by
Circe into that wild beast, but few of them are from your city.

58 Your hills indeed are made desert and deprived of every splendid
bough that made them less rocky and less rough.

61 If anyone is excessive in fury and rage, leading a rude and
violent life, he is among the bears in the second house;

64 and in the third, if I remember well, are wolves so voracious and
starved that no food contents them.

67 In the fourth is the dwelling of buffalos and cattle; and if with
that crowd any of yours is found, so much the worse for him.

70 He who delights in having good cheer and sleeps when he
watches by the fire is among the goats in the fifth troop.

73 I do not wish to tell you of every place, because if I tried to speak
of all there are, my speaking would be long and my time short.

76 Let this be enough, that before and behind us are stags, pan-
thers, and leopards, and beasts larger by far than elephants.

79 But try for a little to look directly at that large door opposite, into
which we shall enter, though it is late."

82 And before I made any answer, she moved on and said: "One
should always take pleasure when it costs nothing.

85 But to enable you, when you are inside, to recognize the place's
every quality and better to consider what you see,

88 you must know that under every roof of these buildings, there is
just one kind of brute animal, as I have already told you.

91 This one alone does not follow such a custom, and just as in
your Mallevato every prisoner goes there to pass away his time,

94 so to the place that I am showing you, each animal in the
cells of this cloister can go for recreation;

97 so by seeing this place you can accomplish your task without
looking over the others one by one, in which too many steps
would be expended.

100 Also in this section are brought together animals of higher intellect, higher rank and higher fortune,

103 and if they seem to you animals in appearance, still you can
partly recognize some of them by their ways, by their gestures,
by their eyes, by their bearing."

106 While she was speaking, we came to a place where the entire
door appeared to us with its details one by one.

109 A figure that seemed alive stood sculptured in marble above the
great arch that sheltered the entrance,

112 and like Hannibal seemed to ride on an elephant in triumph; his
clothing was that of a dignified man, renowned and eminent.

115 A garland of laurel he had on his head; his face was very
pleasant and happy; around him were people who showed him
honor.

118 "He is the famous Abbot of Gaeta," said the lady, "as I am sure
you know, who once was crowned as a poet.

121 By the gods of Heaven, as you see, his image was put in this
place along with the others now at his feet,

124 in order that each one who comes near him, without knowing
further, can judge what sort of people are shut up in there.

127 But now let us try not to lose so much time in looking at this
man that the hour of returning may overtake us.

*l. 92 A place near the prison of the Stinche in Florence where prisoners were allowed to*
*walk for exercise.*

*l. 118 In a mock ceremony at Rome in 1515 he went in procession, broken up by the fright of*
*the elephant he rode, to receive the poet's crown.*

130 Come with me, then, and if ever I was courteous, I shall seem
so to you this time in showing you these dark places,

133 if so much favor is not taken from me by Heaven."

## SEVENTH CHAPTER

1 We were setting foot already on the threshold of that door, and
the lady had given me a wish to go inside;

4 and in that wish of mine I was satisfied, because suddenly the
door opened and revealed to us the assembly within.

7 And so that it better could be seen, on our entering there she
wholly uncovered the light she had hidden beneath her garment.

10 At that light so shining and so sudden, as happens at the sight of
something new, more than two thousand animals raised up
their heads.

13 "Now if the sight pleases you," said the lady, "observe well the
enormous throng assembled in this place.

16 The sight should not seem tedious to you; they are not all land
animals; indeed among so many beasts there are some birds."

19 I raised my eyes and saw so many and such sorts of dumb
animals that I do not believe I ever could tell how many there
were and of what kinds.

22 And because I should bore you if I named them all, I shall
speak of a few, whose presence was most astonishing to my eyes.

25 I saw a cat through too much patience lose her prey and get
mocked for it, even though prudent and of good breed.

28 Then I saw a dragon, wholly wearied, turning himself over now
on his right side, then on his left, without ever resting.

31 I saw a fox, malicious and annoying, that still did not find a net
that could catch him; and a dog from Corsica baying at the
moon.

34 I saw a lion that had cut his own claws and pulled his teeth too
through his own counsels, not good and not sagacious.

37 A little farther on some injured animals—one having no tail,
another no ears—I saw standing blockish in utter quiet.

40 I looked them over and knew quite a number; and if I recall
correctly, for the most part they were a mixture of rabbits and
goats.

*ll. 25 ff. The animals may represent individual men; none has been identified.*

43 Beyond these, just a little to one side, I saw another animal, not like them, but by Nature made with more art.

46 Fine and delicate were his fleeces; he seemed proud of face and so spirited that I was eager to win his favor.

49 He was not showing his noble heart, for his claws were chained and his teeth; therefore he was eager to escape and angry.

52 One . . . . . .

55 I saw . . . . . .

58 Then I saw a giraffe, which was bending its neck to everybody; and to one side there was a tired bear that was snoring.

61 I saw a peacock with his graceful vestment moving about in peacock's pride, and he was not afraid that the world would go turning around completely.

64 There was an animal I did not recognize—so variegated was its skin and its hide—and on its croup was a raven.

67 A horrid beast I saw with red hair, which was an ox without horns; and at a distance he deceived me, because I thought he was a horse of great size.

70 Then I saw an ass in such poor condition that he could not carry his packsaddle, much less anything more; and he appeared a right August cucumber.

73 I saw a bloodhound whose sight was destroyed; and Circe would have made use of him if he had not like a blind man moved by touch.

76 I saw a tiny mouse that grieved at being so small and kept nibbling now at one animal, now at another.

79 Then I saw a hound that kept sniffing at this one's muzzle and that one's shoulder as though he were trying to find his master.

82 Since that time is remote and my memory fails, I cannot properly tell you what in one day I saw in that stable.

85 I wish to mention seeing a buffalo that made my hair stand erect with fright at his gaze and his bellowing so mighty.

88 A stag I saw that was in great terror, turning his course now here now there, such fear of death he had!

91 I saw on a beam an ermine unwilling to be looked at or touched. He was near a lark.

94 In many holes more than a hundred owls I saw, and a goose as

l. 52 *This and the next tercets are not extant.*
l. 72 *August cucumber: misshapen.*

white as snow, and a monkey acting as though he were going
to eat it.

97 I saw so many animals that it would be as difficult and weari-
some to tell their conditions as the time for looking at them
was short.

100 How many whom I had once considered Fabiuses and Catos
turned out to be sheep and rams when I learned of their natures
there!

103 How many feed upon those cruel slopes who sit high up in the
highest seats! How many eagles turn out hawks!

106 Though I was embarrassed by a thousand distresses, yet I should
have liked to speak with some of those animals if I had found
any interpreters there.

109 But my lady—who had observed my wish and my longing—
said: "Do not hesitate, your desire will be fulfilled."

112 Look for a little there where I am pointing my finger, without
moving a pace farther on along the wall, in the direction you
have been taking."

115 Then I saw in a low place, when I had turned my eyes toward
it, a big fat porker covered with mud.

118 I shall by no means tell whom he resembled; let it be enough for
you that he would come to three hundred pounds, yes more, if
he were hung on the hook.

121 And my guide said: "Let us go down there close to that hog, if
you really are eager to hear his desires and his words.

124 Because if you should try to draw him out of that puddle,
making him turn into a man, he would not desire it, like a fish
that lives in a river or a lake.

127 And because this seems incredible, in order that you may con-
vince yourself, you may ask him if he will come out."

130 Thereupon my lady stepped along; and in order not to be parted
from her at all, I took her by the hand she offered me.

133 Thus I came close to that hog.

## EIGHTH CHAPTER

1 As we came near, that hog raised his snout all smeared with
turd and mud, such that to look at him made me sick.

4 And because long before I had been known to him, he turned

toward me with a show of teeth, remaining otherwise quiet and without motion.

7 So I said to him, in the most gracious tones: "May God give you a better fate if it seems to you good; may God support you if you desire support.

10 If you are willing to talk with me, I shall be pleased; and in order that you may know for certain, if you really wish to, you can satisfy yourself.

13 To speak to you freely and openly, I say it to you with the permission of this lady, who has showed me this desert path.

16 The gods have granted me such great grace that she has thought it no burden to rescue me and take me from the afflictions you still suffer.

19 On her part she also wants me to tell you that she will free you from such great evil, if you wish to return to your early shape."

22 Erect the boar stood on his feet when he heard that, and in great excitement the muddy beast made this reply:

25 "I know not whence you come or from what region, but if you have come for nothing else than to get me away from here, go off about your business.

28 I have no wish to live with you; I refuse. I see clearly that you suffer from the error which for a long time bound me too.

31 So much your self love deceives you that you do not believe there is any good apart from human existence and its worth.

34 But if on me you direct your imagination, before you leave my presence I shall see to it that in such an error you no longer remain.

37 I shall begin with prudence, an excellent virtue, through which men magnify their excellence.

40 They know best how to apply this virtue who, without instruc⁄ tion, for themselves see how to pursue their own well⁄being and to avoid distress.

43 Without the least doubt I assert and affirm that superior to yours is our condition, and even you will not deny it soon.

46 Who is that preceptor who explains to us what any plant is, whether harmless or injurious? Not any research, not your ignorance.

l. *43 our condition: that of the animals.*

49 We change abode from shore to shore, and to leave one dwelling gives us no pain, if only we are happy and prosperous.

52 One avoids the ice and another avoids the sun, seeking the climate friendly to our way of life, as Nature who teaches us commands.

55 You, much more hapless than I can tell, go exploring one country and another, not to find a climate either cool or sunny,

58 but because your shameful greed for gain does not confirm your spirit in a life sparing, law-abiding and humble.

61 Often into an atmosphere rotten and sickly, leaving a healthful climate, you shift yourselves—and not that you may protect your livelihood.

64 We flee from the climate alone, you from poverty; in dangers you seek wealth; this has blocked against you the path of well-doing.

67 And if we wish to speak of strength, how much our condition surpasses yours is as plain as the sun in its brightness.

70 The bull, the wild lion, the elephant and others of us in countless numbers are found in the world whom a man cannot confront.

73 If reflection about the spirit is good, you will see that we have received a richer gift of hearts invincible, noble and strong.

76 Among us are done bold deeds and exploits without hope of a triumph or other fame, as once among those Romans who were famous.

79 In the lion you see great pride in a noble deed, and at a shameful act a wish to blot out its memory.

82 Still among us some beasts live who to escape from prison and chains, by dying gain both glory and liberty;

85 such valor they preserve in their breasts that after they lose their liberty their hearts cannot endure the life of slaves.

88 If on temperance you turn your gaze, you will plainly see that in this game we have surpassed your side.

91 On Venus we spend but short and little time, but you without measure follow her in every time and place.

94 Our species does not care for other food than the product of the heavens without art; you wish that which Nature cannot supply.

97 You are not content with one food only, as we are, but better to fulfil your greedy desires, you journey for such things to the kingdoms of the East.

100  That does not suffice which you can gather on land, for you
     enter into the Ocean's bosom to glut yourselves with his riches.

103  My talk would never come to an end if I should try to show how
     hapless you are above all other earthly creatures.

106  We are closer friends to Nature; to us she more freely dispenses
     her vigor, making you only beggars for all her good things.

109  If you wish to see this, make use of your senses; easily you will
     be convinced of a truth opposed to what perhaps you now
     believe.

112  In the eagle's eye, in the dog's ear and nose and taste as well we
     can show something better than you, though touch is left as
     more your own;

115  yet it is given not to do you honor but only that Venus' appetite
     can bring you greater affliction and trouble.

118  Every animal among us is born fully clad; this protects him from
     weather cold and harsh under every sky and on every shore.

121  Only man is born devoid of all protection; he has neither hide
     nor spine nor feather nor fleece nor bristles nor scales to make
     him a shield.

124  In weeping he begins his life, with the sound of a cry painful
     and choked, so that he is distressing to look at.

127  Then as he grows up, his life is verily short when compared
     with that of a stag, a raven, a goose.

130  Nature gave you hands and speech, and with them she gave you
     also ambition and avarice, with which her bounty is cancelled.

133  To how many ills Nature subjects you at starting! and after-
     wards Fortune—how much good she promises you without
     fulfilment!

136  Yours are ambition, licentiousness, lamentation and avarice,
     which bring on mange in the life you reckon so high.

139  No animal can be found that has a frailer life, and has for living
     a stronger desire, more disordered fear or greater madness.

142  One hog to another hog causes no pain, one stag to another;
     man by another man is slain, crucified and plundered.

145  Consider now how you ask that I again become man, being
     exempt from all miseries that I endured as long as I was a man.

148  And if any among men seems to you a god, happy and rejoicing,
     do not believe him such, because in this mud I live more happily;

151  here without anxiety I bathe and roll myself."

# MACHIAVELLI'S COMEDIES:
## *MANDRAGOLA* AND *CLIZIA*

[*The dates of composition are uncertain. Twelve years after the expedi-tion of Charles VIII of France into Italy, in 1494, the events of* CLIZIA *took place (Act I, scene 1). According to the Prolog, the play was acted a few years later, or not earlier than 1509. The events of* MANDRAGOLA *are ten years after the same expedition (Act I, scene 1), or somewhat earlier than those of* CLIZIA. *If the Prolog of* MANDRAGOLA *is of the same date as the play, it indicates composition in or after 1513, when Machiavelli was not prosperous. The first mention of the comedy is in a letter to Machia-velli by Battista della Palla, written 26 April 1520. Though the characters of* MANDRAGOLA *are mentioned in* CLIZIA *(Act II, scene 3), the story as there given is so unlike that of Nicia and Lucrezia that it can hardly refer to the play as we now have it. If it does not,* CLIZIA *is the earlier. The only fixed date for it is that of first performance, 1525. Under the conditions of the Italian stage, a long interval between writing and presentation is not remarkable.*

*In* CLIZIA, *Machiavelli is under the restraint of Plautus, but the defects of the Roman plot localized in Florence are skilfully minimized, and the additions are such that the result is funnier, more full-bodied in its characters, and more substantial in background than the* CASINA, *on which it is modeled. However absurd in his infatuation, Nicomaco comes out of a life of good sense and returns to it when cured. The comedy is genuinely one of Italian life, surpassing its Latin original.*

*For an estimate of Machiavelli's nature and genius, no work is at present, after centuries of concentration on* THE PRINCE, *so important as the* MAN-DRAGOLA, *one of the greatest, perhaps the very greatest, of Italian comedies. With this work before him, no one can assert that Niccolò is a scientist by subject and method and temperament, or that he is the founder of modern history, or that he is to be set among the researchers. From Ariosto or Molière or Ben Jonson or the creator of Falstaff we do not expect works of cold and merciless analysis. Neither are we to look for them from the creator of Messer Nicia or Father Timoteo. Is not the author of* THE PRINCE *also the comic dramatist?* THE PRINCE *is unrivaled of its kind; the* MAN-DRAGOLA *enables its maker to stand with Aristophanes and his company, as Dante with Homer and his school. Such great men are not likely to appear as Dr. Jekyll and Mr. Hyde. If the Dante of* ON MONARCHY *is still the*

Dante of his COMEDY, the Machiavelli of THE PRINCE, the DIS-
COURSES, and the HISTORY OF FLORENCE *is still the Machiavelli of
his comedy. Nor do we need to forget that these two men are not unlike in
their hopes for Italy.* THE PRINCE *is the work of a great comic poet, albeit
one who could sign one of his letters as also* tragico.

What is the nature of this comedy? A central figure, Dr. Nicia, is a
stupid character, if we are to borrow from the preface of CLIZIA Niccolò's
classification of comic characters. Stupidity is one of the main ills of man in
politics. There are the Florentines, wise in their own conceit, who repeated in
grave folly that Pistoia was to be held by divisions, Pisa by fortresses; even
Machiavelli's Cesare Borgia indulged in the folly of thinking he could con-
ciliate Pope Julius II. The hero of the play, Callimaco, at a loss in the
conduct of his affairs, trusts Ligurio to bring him to triumph, certain that his
agent is well selected. So the prince, wise in choosing men, can find a minister
who is both loyal and able. Lucretia, caught in the current she cannot resist,
adapts herself to it and then can enjoy it. Our Niccolò himself, with all his
theories favoring republics, could yet, in a similar fashion, when Fortune was
against him, accept with some content the Medici tyranny. The avaricious
cleric, Timoteo, is a type, written small, of the Roman curia that contributed
to the servitude of Italy. But above any specific correspondence is the comic
poet's observation, "remorseless," if one likes the word, beyond that of the
scientist, as the work of an intellect impartial yet constructive, and with the
warmth of human contact. Not to know MANDRAGOLA is not to know
THE PRINCE.]

# MANDRAGOLA

## Dramatis Personae

CALLIMACO, a young merchant
SIRO, his servant
MESSER NICIA, an old judge, husband of LUCRETIA
LIGURIO, a parasite
SOSTRATA, LUCRETIA'S mother
FRATE TIMOTEO, a wicked cleric
A WOMAN
LUCRETIA, wife of MESSER NICIA, loved by CALLIMACO


## CANZONE

*[to be spoken before the comedy, sung by nymphs and shepherds together]*

Because life is short
and many are the pains
that every man bears who lives and stints himself,
let us go on spending and wasting the years as we will,
for he who deprives himself of pleasure
only to live with labor and toil
does not understand the world's deceits,
and what ills and what strange events
crush almost all mortals.

To avoid such discontent
we have chosen secluded life,
and always in merry-making and gladness
we live as gallant young men and happy nymphs.
Now we have come here with our harmony
only to honor this merry festival
and this sweet company.

We are brought here besides
by the name of him who rules you,[1]

---

1. *Francesco Guicciardini. In 1526, when he was papal governor of Romagna, a performance of* MANDRAGOLA *before him at Faenza or Modena was planned but not carried out. The intermezzi were written for it.*

in whom may be seen all virtues
that unite in the Countenance Eternal.
For such sovereign grace,
for so fortunate a condition,
you can feel happy and rejoice,
and thank him who gives it to you.

## PROLOG

God bless you, well-wishing hearers, since it appears that these good wishes depend on our pleasing you. If you continue to make no noise, we shall tell you of a strange event that happened in this city. Look at the scenery that now is put before you: this is your Florence; another time it will be Rome or Pisa—a thing to make you laugh till you crack your cheeks.

This door here on my right opens into the house of a judge who learned in Buethius a great deal of law.[1] That street which is fitted into that corner there is the Street of Love,[2] where he who tumbles never gets up again. Then you can learn from his friar's dress what sort of prior or abbot lives at the church on the opposite side, if you don't leave this place too soon.

Callimaco Guadagni, a young man just arrived from Paris, lives there at that door on the left. He, above all the other smart young fellows, shows the marks and signs of carrying off the honors and the prize for courtesy. He greatly loved a prudent young woman and tricked her, as you will learn, and I hope you'll be tricked as she was.

The story is called *Mandragola*. You will see the reason when it is acted, I foretell. The writer is not very famous, yet if you do not laugh,[3] he will be ready to pay for your wine. A doleful lover, a judge by no means shrewd, a friar living wickedly, a parasite the darling of Malice will be sport for you today.

And if this material—since really it is slight—does not befit a

1. *I have rendered* Doctor *(of law) by* Judge, *to distinguish* Nicia *from the (pretended) physician, who is called* Messer.

Buetio *(not Boetio, Boethius), beginning with the word* bue, *meaning* ox, *a symbol of stupidity, presents Messer Nicia as stupid. As a student of law, Nicia would have read Boethius.*

2. *Street of Love: The Via dell'Amore, now included in Via Sant' Antonio, extended from the present Piazza dell'Unita Italiana to Via Faenza. But it seems unlikely that Machiavelli intends the name to be taken literally.*

3. *If he fails to make you laugh.*

man who likes to seem wise and dignified, make this excuse for him, that he is striving with these trifling thoughts to make his wretched life more pleasant, for otherwise he doesn't know where to turn his face, since he has been cut off from showing other powers with other deeds, there being no pay for his labors.

The pay he expects is that every man will stand aside and sneer, speaking ill of whatever he sees or hears. This is the reason, beyond all doubt, why from ancient worth the present age in every way is degenerate; for, seeing that everybody censures, men do not labor and strain to turn out with a thousand hardships a work that the wind will spoil and the fog conceal.

Yet if anyone supposes that by finding fault he can get the author by the hair and scare him or make him draw back a bit, I give any such man warning and tell him that the author, too, knows how to find fault, and that it was his earliest art; and in no part of the world where *si*[4] is heard does he stand in awe of anybody, even though he plays the servant to such as can wear a better cloak than he can.

But let all those find fault who care to. We must get back to our theme, so we won't run over our time too far. We can't pay attention to words or respect some freak who doesn't know, perhaps, whether he's still alive. Callimaco is coming out, and with him he has his servant, Siro, and he will tell the situation in full. Pay attention, all of you, and for the present don't expect any other summary.

    4. *si: Indicating the Italian language.*

## I.1

### CALLIMACO, SIRO

CALLIMACO. Siro, don't go away; I want you for a bit.
SIRO. Yes, sir.
CAL. I suppose you were puzzled when I left Paris in such a hurry and you're still puzzled, since I've been here a month already without doing a thing.
SIRO. It's true that I am.
CAL. If up to this time I haven't told you what I'm going to tell you now, it hasn't been because I don't trust you, but because it's my opinion that if a man doesn't want things known, he'd better not tell

them, unless he has to. But since I've decided I need your help, I want to tell you all about it.

SIRO. I'm your servant, and servants ought never to ask their masters questions about anything or pry into their business, but when the masters themselves tell them, they ought to serve them faithfully; and so I've done and so I'm going to do.

CAL. I'm sure of it. I believe you've heard me say a thousand times, but there's no harm in your hearing it a thousand and one, that when I was ten years old my guardians, since my father and my mother were dead, sent me to Paris, where I've lived twenty years. And because, at the end of ten years, the expedition of King Charles set going in Italy the wars that ruined this country, I decided to spend my life in Paris and never go back home, judging I'd be safer in that city than here,

SIRO. So you would be.

CAL. and arranging here to sell all my property, except my house, I committed myself to staying there, and there I have lived for the last ten years in complete happiness,

SIRO. Yes, I know you have.

CAL. laying out my time, partly in studies, partly in amusement, partly in business; and I employed myself in each of these in such fashion that one didn't keep me away from the other. And the result, as you know, was that I lived in the greatest peace, getting on well with everybody and trying not to make any enemies, so that I seemed to be in favor with the middle class, the gentlemen, the foreigner, the native, the poor, the rich.

SIRO. That's so.

CAL. But since Fortune decided that I was having too much good weather, she brought a certain Cammillo Calfucci to Paris.

SIRO. I'm beginning to guess your trouble.

CAL. Like the other Florentines, he often dined with me; and in the course of our talks, it happened one day that we got to arguing where the women were more beautiful, in Italy or in France. And because I couldn't discuss Italian women, having been so little when I went away, another Florentine who was there took the French side, and Cammillo the Italian. Then, after many arguments had been brought up on both sides, Cammillo, almost as though he were angry, said that even if all other Italian women were frights, a single one, a relative of his, was enough to get back their reputation.

SIRO. Now I'm clear about what you're going to say.

CAL. And he named Madam Lucretia, the wife of Messer Nicia Calfucci, and gave her such praise for beauty and manners that we were all spellbound, and in me he roused such eagerness to see her that, letting every other plan go, and paying no more attention to the wars or to the peace of Italy, I set out for this place. Now that I'm here, I've found Madam Lucretia's reputation much less than the truth—something that very seldom happens—and I'm on fire with such longing to be with her that I never have any peace.

SIRO. If you'd mentioned it to me in Paris, I should have known how to advise you, but now I don't know what to tell you.

CAL. I've not told you this to get your advice but partly to express my feelings, and so you can get yourself ready to help me when I need you.

SIRO. I'm quite ready for that, but what hopes do you have?

CAL. Hopes! None or very few. I'll explain. First, the nature of the woman fights against me, because she's very chaste and a complete stranger to love dealings. Her husband is very rich and lets her rule him entirely, and if he isn't young, he isn't altogether an old man, as I guess. She has no relatives or neighbors that she meets at parties or entertainments or any of the other amusements that young women like. No tradespeople get into her house; she has no maid or servant who's not afraid of her; so there's no chance for bribery.

SIRO. What do you think you can do then?

CAL. Nothing is ever so hopeless that there isn't some means that lets one hope for it, and even though it's poor and weak, still a man's resolve and eagerness to carry the affair through keep it from seeming so.

SIRO. Well then, what makes you hope?

CAL. Two things. One is Messer Nicia's stupidity, for though he's a judge, he's the stupidest and silliest man in Florence. The other is that both of them long to have children, for after being married six years and still not having any, and being very rich,[1] they are so eager for them that they are dying of it. There's a third thing, that her mother has been a lively dame, but she's rich,[2] so I don't know how to handle her.

---

1. *Their riches made them well able to provide for children. Poor families often felt daughters a burden because of the dowries required to marry them well.*

2. *Hence bribes won't interest her.*

SIRO. Up to now have you tried to do anything about it?

CAL. Yes, I have, but not of much account.

SIRO. In what way?

CAL. You know Ligurio, who's always coming to eat with me. He was once a marriage broker and later took to begging suppers and dinners. And because he's an amusing man, Messer Nicia is very intimate with him—though Ligurio bamboozles him—and even if he doesn't invite him to eat with him, he does sometimes lend him money. I've made myself his friend and told him about my love. He's promised to help me with all his might.

SIRO. Watch out that he doesn't trick you; these gluttons usually aren't very reliable.

CAL. That's true. All the same, when a thing's to a man's advantage, you can believe, if you take him into your confidence, that he'll give you honest service. I've promised, if he succeeds, to give him a lot of money; if he doesn't succeed, he'll get a luncheon and a supper out of it, which anyhow I wouldn't have eaten alone.

SIRO. What's he promised to do, so far?

CAL. He's promised to induce Messer Nicia to take his wife to the baths this May.

SIRO. How does that help you?

CAL. How does it help me? That place might change her nature, because in such spots people do nothing but amuse themselves. I should go there and take part in amusements of every sort I could, and shouldn't omit any sort of display. I should get on good terms with her and her husband. How can I tell? One thing brings on another, and Time works wonders.[3]

SIRO. It doesn't seem bad to me.

CAL. Ligurio left me this morning and said he'd interview Messer Nicia on the subject and let me know about it.

SIRO. There they come together.

CAL. I want to step to one side, so as to be ready to talk with Ligurio when he gets away from the Judge. Meanwhile you go into the house about your business, and if I want you to do anything I'll tell you.

SIRO. I'll be ready.

3. *The Italian proverb,* Di cosa nasce cosa, e il Tempo la governa, *has no English equivalent. Literally: "A thing comes from a thing, and Time controls it." Callimaco hopes that Time will bring him an opportunity.*

## I.2

### MESSER NICIA, LIGURIO

MESSER NICIA. I believe your advice is good, and I spoke to my wife about it last evening. She said she'd answer me today, but to tell the truth, I shan't go there on willing legs.

LIGURIO. Why so?

MESSER N. Because I don't like to get off base.[1] Then to have to shift quarters with wife, servant, household things—it doesn't suit me. Besides that, I talked last evening with some doctors. One of them said I should go to San Filippo, another to Porretta, another to Villa; and they seem to me so many big fools; for to tell the truth these doctors of medicine don't know what they're fishing for.

LIG. Yet what you spoke of first is bound to worry you, for you aren't in the habit of letting the Cupola[2] out of your sight.

MESSER N. You're wrong. When I was younger, I was a great gadabout. Why, they never held the fair at Prato without my going there, and there isn't a single town all around where I haven't been. And I can say more too; I have been at Pisa and at Livorno—think of that.

LIG. You must have seen the *carrucola* of Pisa.[3]

MESSER N. You mean the Verrucola.[4]

LIG. Oh, yes, the Verrucola. At Livorno did you see the sea?

1. *A figure taken from a children's game, somewhat like prisoner's base. Cf. Pulci,* MORG- ANTE *1. 32; 2. 8; 19. 70; 27. 39.*

2. *The dome of the Cathedral, still the "Hupola" to Tuscans.*

3. *Apparently a joke at Nicia's expense, having some connection with the use of* carrucola *(literally, pulley) to mean a foolish man. Paulus Jovius, writing of the* MANDRAGOLA, *says that Nicia was turned into a* currucola *(a variant form of* carrucola*) by his young wife* (FRAGMENTUM TRIUM DIALOGORUM, *quoted by Tommasini,* MACHIAVELLI, *I, 645).*

4. *One of the summits of Monte Pisano, near Pisa, is Monte Verruca (the Wart), on the summit of which the ruins of a fortress, the Verrucola (the Little Wart), are still to be seen. Its importance to Florence in the campaigns against Pisa is indicated by the following on the operations in 1503 of the Florentine forces led by Giacomini: "They marched against the Verrucola, which, because of revealing the raids of the Florentines—since it was situated in a high place—and giving notice of them to the Pisans, had almost continually been a thorn in the eyes of the Republic, and therefore in all this war, though in vain, she had attempted with every effort to get it. But not at this time being able to withstand the artillery, which on account of the roughness of the mountains had been taken there with great difficulty (or this may have been an excuse to hide the cowardice of the defenders) the fortress surrendered." (Scipio Ammirato,* HISTORY OF FLORENCE, *bk. 28).*

*The Verrucola is indicated as blocking retreat toward Florence in Machiavelli's* HIS- TORICAL FRAGMENTS, *Dec., 1497. See also his* DISCOURSE ON PISAN AFFAIRS.

MESSER N. You know I did.

LIG. How much bigger than the Arno is it?

MESSER N. Than the Arno? It's four times, more than six, more than seven, you'll make me say; and you don't see anything but water, water, water.

LIG. I wonder, then, since you have pissed in so many snowbanks,⁵ that you make such a fuss about going to the baths.

MESSER N. Your mouth's full of milk.⁶ Does it seem to you just a joke to have to upset the whole house? Yet I'm so eager to have children that I'm ready to do anything. But talk about it a bit with these doctors; see where they advise me to go. Meanwhile I'll see my wife and come back here.

LIG. That's a good idea.

> 5. *pissed in so many snowbanks: visited so many places.*
> 6. *You talk like a baby.*

## I.3

### LIGURIO, CALLIMACO

LIGURIO [*to himself*]. I don't believe there's a stupider man in the world than this fellow; yet how Fortune has favored him! He's rich; he has a beautiful wife, virtuous, courteous, and fit to rule a kingdom. It seems to me that in marriages the proverb doesn't very often come true that says: God makes men, and they find their mates. Because often you see an able man chance upon an ass, and, vice versa, a sensible woman get a fool. But from this fellow's silliness we get the benefit that Callimaco can have hopes. But there he is. [*to Callimaco*] What are you looking for, Callimaco?

CALLIMACO. I saw you with the Judge and I was waiting until you got away from him, to find out what you've done.

LIG. You know what sort of man he is, of little sense, of less spirit, and he doesn't want to go away from Florence. Yet I urged him on, and at last he told me he'd do everything. And I believe that if his going away pleases us, we'll bring him to it, but I don't know whether we'll finish our business there.

CAL. Why?

LIG. How can I be sure? You know that all kinds of people go to these baths, and a man might come there who'd be as taken with

Madam Lucretia as you are, who would have more money than you do, would be more charming than you are. So there's danger of your going to this trouble for somebody else; and it may happen that the crowd of rivals will make her harder to get, or if she softens, she'll get a liking for some other man, not for you.

CAL. I know that what you say's true. But what can I do? What plan can I take up? Where shall I turn? I've got to try something, even if it's strange, risky, injurious, disgraceful. It's better to die than to live as I do. If I could sleep at night, if I could eat, if I could talk, if I could get pleasure out of anything, I'd wait for the right time with more patience. But now there's nothing I can do, and if I don't keep my hopes up by deciding on something, I shall certainly die, and seeing I've got to die, I'm not afraid of anything; I'll try any plan whatever, even if it's stupid, cruel, wicked.

LIG. Don't talk like that; check your runaway feelings.

CAL. You see well enough that I feed on such fancies because I'm trying to check them. So we've got to go ahead with sending him to the baths or try some other way, so I can feed myself with a little hope—if not true then false—that will let me keep alive some fancy that will do a little to lighten my sufferings.

LIG. You're right, and I'm in favor of doing it.

CAL. I believe it, though I know that such as you live by cheating men. Yet I believe I can't be counted among your dupes, for if you did cheat me and I found it out, I'd try to get revenge for it, and at once you'd lose the use of my house and the hope of getting what I've promised you for the future.

LIG. Don't be afraid that I'm not reliable, because even if there weren't as much profit in the business as I think and hope, you and I have a natural affinity, and I want you to carry out your wish almost as much as you do yourself. But enough of that. The Judge has engaged me to find a doctor and learn to what baths they'd better go. I want you to do as I suggest, and that is, say you've studied medicine and 've had some experience in Paris. He'll easily believe it, because he's so foolish and you're educated and can say something to him in Latin.

CAL. What help'll that be?

LIG. It'll help us send him to any baths we choose, and to apply some other schemes I've thought up, which will be shorter, more cer-tain, more likely to succeed than the baths.

CAL. What's that you're saying?

LIG. I'm saying that if you keep your spirits up and trust in me, I'll finish this business for you before tomorrow at this time. And even if he were the man he isn't and would investigate whether you're a doctor or not, the shortness of the time and the business itself will keep him from discussing it, or there'll not be time to spoil our plan even if he does discuss it.[1]

CAL. You're restoring me to life. This is too big a promise, and you're feeding me too much hope. What'll you do?

LIG. You'll find out when the time comes; just now I can't properly tell you, because there won't be time for doing, much less telling. You go into the house and wait for me there, and I'll go and find the Judge, and if I bring him to you, go along with what I say and adapt yourself to it.

CAL. I'll do it, though you fill me with hope that I'm afraid 'll go up in smoke.

1. *Ligurio guards against the revelation of this comic conspiracy.* Cf. DISCOURSES *3. 6.*

## CANZONE

### [*after the first act*]

He who makes no test, Oh Love,
of your great power,
must hope in vain ever to have true faith
in Heaven's highest worth.
He does not know how at the same time
one can live and die,
how one can search for ill and run away from good,
how one can love oneself less than some other,
how often the heart is frozen and melted by fear and hope;
he does not know how men and gods in equal measure
dread the weapons with which you're armed.

### II.1

### LIGURIO, MESSER NICIA, SIRO

LIGURIO. As I've told you, I believe God has sent him so you can have all you wish. He's given the strongest proofs in Paris, and you shouldn't think it strange he hasn't practiced his profession in Florence, because there are reasons for it. First, he's rich; second, at any moment he's likely to return to Paris.

MESSER NICIA. You're right, brother, that's very important; because I shouldn't like to have him take me into the woods and then leave me high and dry.

LIG. Don't worry about that; the only thing to be afraid of is that he won't accept the case; but if he does accept it, he certainly won't leave you until he sees it through.

MESSER N. For that part of it I'm willing to trust you. But as to his knowledge, I'll tell you myself, after I talk with him, whether he's a learned man, because he won't sell me any bubbles.[1]

LIG. And because I know what you are, I'm taking you to him so you can talk with him. And if after you've talked with him, it doesn't seem to you that in bearing, in learning, in speech he is a man in whose lap you can lay your head, say I'm not Ligurio.

MESSER N. So be it, in the name of the Holy Angel. Let's be going. But where does he live?

LIG. He lives on this square, at that door you see opposite yours.

MESSER N. Go ahead.

LIG. Done. [knocking]

SIRO. Who's there?

LIG. Is Callimaco at home?

SIRO. Yes, he is.

MESSER N. Why don't you say Doctor Callimaco?

LIG. He doesn't care about such nonsense.

MESSER N. Don't call it that; do the right thing yourself, and if he doesn't like it, let him loosen his belt.[2]

---

1. Or inflated bladders, or balloons. The expression is explained by Varchi (ERCOLANO 98) as meaning to tell as certain something not certain.

2. let him loosen his belt: seemingly equivalent to "let him lump it." Cf. THE [GOLDEN] ASS, chap. 1 end. In Lorenzo Lippi's MALMANTILE RACQUISTATO 3. 47, the saying occurs as "let him tighten his belt" (cinga for scinga), apparently with the same meaning as here.

## II.2

### CALLIMACO, MESSER NICIA, LIGURIO

CALLIMACO. Who is this man who wants me?

MESSER NICIA. *Bona dies, domine magister.*

CAL. *Et vobis bona, domine doctor.*[1]

LIGURIO [*to* NICIA]. How does he seem?

MESSER N. [*to* LIGURIO]. Fine, by the Apostles.

LIG. If you want me to stay here with you, you'll have to speak so I can understand you; otherwise we'll make two fires.[2]

CAL. Are you on pleasant business?

MESSER N. I don't know. I'm hunting for two things that another man most likely would run away from: that is, to make trouble for myself and for others. I haven't any children and want some, so in order to have such a trouble I come to worry you.

CAL. It'll never bother me to do a favor to you or to any man so able and worthy as you are. And I've not worked at my studies so many years in Paris for any other reason than to be able to help such men as you.

MESSER N. Many thanks. And when you're in need of my profession, I'll be glad to help you. But let's get back *ad rem nostram.* Have you thought what bath would be good to help my wife become pregnant? For I know Ligurio has told you what you need to know about this affair.

CAL. So he has. But in order to satisfy your wish, I must know the cause of your wife's sterility, for there can be many causes. *Nam causae sterilitatis sunt aut in semine, aut in matrice, aut in strumentis seminariis, aut in virga, aut in causa extrinseca.*[3]

MESSER N. This is the ablest man there is.

CAL. Besides these, you could be the cause of this sterility, through impotence; and if that were so, there would be nothing we could do.

MESSER N. Me impotent? Why, you make me laugh, I don't believe there is a tougher and healthier man in Florence than I am.

CAL. If that's not it, you can feel certain we shall find a cure.

MESSER N. Isn't there some other cure than baths? Because I don't want that bother, and my wife doesn't like going away from Florence.

LIG. Yes, there is. Let me give the answer. Callimaco is much too cautious. [*to* CALLIMACO] Haven't you told me you know how to make up some medicines that without any question will cause pregnancy?

---

1. *Bona dies, etc. How do you do, Doctor? And how do you do, Judge?*

2. *make two fires separate.*

3. *For the causes of sterility are either in the semen, or in the womb, or in the seminal organs, or in the penis, or in an extrinsic cause.*

CAL. Yes, I have. But I go slowly with men I don't know, because I don't want them to think I'm a quack.

MESSER N. Don't have any fears about me, because you've amazed me so much that there is nothing I wouldn't believe or do if you had a hand in it.

LIG. I believe you'll have to see a specimen.

CAL. Certainly; nothing can be done without one.

LIG. Call Siro, and let him go with the Judge to his house for it and come back here; and we'll wait for it in your house.

CAL. Siro, go with him. And if it's convenient, sir, come back here soon and we'll consider what's best.

MESSER N. What's that? If it's convenient! I'll be back in a minute, for I have more faith in you than the Hungarians have in their swords.[4]

4. *Apparently proverbial.*

## II.3

### MESSER NICIA, SIRO

MESSER NICIA. This master of yours is a wonderful man.

SIRO. Even more so than you say.

MESSER N. The King of France must set store by him.

SIRO. Much.

MESSER N. And for that reason he must be glad to live in France.

SIRO. Of course he is.

MESSER N. And he's right. In this city there's not a man who isn't a shitsticks; ability isn't valued. If he should stay here, there wouldn't be a man who would pay any attention to him. I'm in a position to talk about it, for I've shit out my guts in order to learn two aitches,[1] and if I had to live by it, I should be out in the cold, I can tell you.

SIRO. Do you make a hundred ducats a year?

MESSER N. Not a hundred lire, not a hundred grossi, believe it or not! And the reason is that a man who doesn't have a pull with the government of this city,[2] though of my standing, can't find a dog to

1. *Tommaseo's* DIZIONARIO *explains this as meaning to learn a little, since H is not important in Italian. Though this form, as well as the learning of four aitches, is said to be common, the only example given is this from* MANDRAGOLA.

2. *Nicia's words (*chi non ha lo stato in questa terra*) suggest a stronger meaning, such as* control the government, *hardly warranted by the situation. Lorenzo de'Medici, writing that*

bark at him, and we're good for nothing but to go to funerals and to meetings about some marriage, or to sit all day dawdling on the Proconsul's bench.³ But I don't pay any attention to them, I'm not dependent on anybody; let those do it who are worse off than I am. All the same, I don't want to be quoted, because I should certainly get some big tax or some leek in my tail⁴ that would make me sweat.

SIRO. Never fear.

MESSER N. This is my house. Wait here; I'll be back right away.

SIRO. Go ahead.

---

he accepted the direction of Florentine affairs in order to preserve his friends and his property, writes that one can hardly live in Florence without control of the government (si può mal vivere ricco senza lo stato) (Roscoe, LIFE OF LORENZO, Appendix 12).

3. This seems proverbial for long waiting on the convenience of an arbitrary bureaucrat.

4. leek in my tail: trouble would be made for me.

## II.4

### SIRO, alone

If the other judges were like this one, we should take stones for ovens.¹ Yes, for this wretched Ligurio and this crazy master of mine are getting him into a place where they'll disgrace him. And truly I'd wish it, if I thought it wouldn't be found out, because if it is found out, I'll be in danger of my life, and my master of his life and property. He's even become a doctor. I don't know what their plan is and where this trick is leading. But I see the Judge with a specimen bottle in his hand. Who wouldn't laugh at this big fool?

1. take stones for ovens: Machiavelli himself explained it in a letter to Guicciardini in Sept. 1525 (p. 983) as meaning "act like crazy men."

## II.5

### MESSER NICIA, SIRO

MESSER NICIA [to LUCRETIA, inside the house, and then to himself]. I've always done things your way; now I want you to do them in mine. If I'd thought I wasn't going to have children, I'd sooner have married a country girl, who—¹ [to SIRO] Is that you, Siro? Follow

1. I have followed what seems indicated by the first edition, not followed by modern editors. Nicia is mumbling to himself, and breaks off on seeing Siro. Girolamo Ruscelli, in his edition (Venice, 1554), gives a text to be translated: I'd sooner have married a country girl than you. Is that you, Siro?

me. What trouble I've gone through to make this silly woman give me this specimen! And that doesn't mean that she doesn't want to have children, for she's more anxious about it than I am, but when I try to get her to do some little thing, what a business!

SIRO. Be patient; with gentle words you can usually get a woman where you want her to go.

MESSER N. Gentle words! After she's riled me! Be quick, go and tell the Doctor and Ligurio that I'm here.

SIRO. There they are, coming out of the house.


## II.6

### LIGURIO, CALLIMACO, MESSER NICIA

LIGURIO [*to* CALLIMACO]. The judge'll be easy to persuade. His wife'll give trouble, but we'll find a way.

CALLIMACO [*to* NICIA]. Have you the specimen?

MESSER NICIA. Siro has it, under his cloak.

CAL. Give it here. Hmm, this specimen shows weakness of the kidneys.

MESSER N. It looks rather cloudy to me; yet she just passed it.

CAL. Don't think it strange. *Nam mulieris urinae sunt semper maioris grossitici et albedinis, et minoris pulchritudinis, quam virorum. Hujus autem, in caetera, causa est amplitudo canalium, mixtio eorum quae ex matrice exeunt cum urina.*[1]

MESSER N. [*aside*]. Uh, huh, San Puccio's cunt! This man gets better and better the more I deal with him; see how well he talks about these things.

CAL. I'm afraid she's poorly covered at night, and that makes her pass cloudy urine.

MESSER N. She always has a good blanket over her. But she does keep kneeling four hours to string off paternosters before she gets into bed, and acts like a fool about getting chilly.

CAL. Well then, Judge, either you have faith in me or you haven't; either I can tell you of a sure cure or I can't. On my side, I'll give you the medicine. If you have faith in me, you'll accept it. Then if,

---

1. *"For the urine of women is always of more thickness and whiteness and of less beauty than that of men. Now, among other things, the cause of this is the large size of the canals, the mixture of those things that go out of the womb with the urine."*

a year from today, your wife doesn't have her own son in her arms, I bind myself to pay you two thousand ducats.

MESSER N. Speak up, then, for I'm ready to believe you in everything and to trust you more than my confessor.

CAL. The fact is, there's nothing surer to make a woman pregnant than to have her take a medicine made of mandrake. This is something I've tested two pairs of times[2] and always found true. If it hadn't been for this, the Queen of France would be barren, as well as countless other princesses in that country.

MESSER N. It is possible?

CAL. It's as I tell you. And Fortune favors you so much that I've brought with me all the things that go into that medicine, and you can have it when you like.

MESSER N. When will she have to take it?

CAL. This evening after supper, because the moon is right and the time can't be more suitable.

MESSER N. This won't be much trouble. Get it ready by all means; I'll have her take it.

CAL. Now we've got to think about something else: namely, that the first man who has to do with her after she takes the medicine will die within eight days, and all the world can't save him.

MESSER N. Shit! I don't want this vinegar and sugar; you won't put it off on me. You've got me into a nice state.

CAL. Be calm, there's a way out.

MESSER N. What?

CAL. Get somebody to sleep with her right after it; if he's with her one night, he'll draw to himself all the poison of the mandrake.[3] Then you can lie with her without danger.

MESSER N. I won't do any such thing.

CAL. Why?

MESSER N. Because I won't turn my wife into a whore and myself into a cuckold.

CAL. You can't mean it, Judge. Why, you don't seem to me as wise as I was thinking you were. Is it possible that you hesitate to do

---

2. *two pairs of times: often.*

3. *The trick owes its persuasive power to the superstition that disease, especially syphilis and leprosy, can be got rid of by transfer to another person in sexual intercourse. Machiavelli's contemporary Bandello treats it as a fact in* NOVELLA *1. 37, and so does John Donne in* SATIRE *4. 134.*

what the King of France has done, and all the lords in that country?
MESSER N. Whom do you suppose I could find to do such a crazy
thing? If I tell him, he won't do it. If I don't tell him, I victimize
him, and that's a matter for the Eight.[4] I don't want to get into
trouble in that quarter.

CAL. If that's all you're worried about, let me take care of it for you.
MESSER N. How'll you do it?
CAL. I'll tell you. I'll give you the medicine this evening after
supper. You give it to her to take and put her to bed at once, which
will be about ten o'clock. Then we'll disguise ourselves, you, Ligurio, Siro, and myself, and we'll go hunting in the New Market, the
Old Market, all through such places. And as soon as we find an
idle young fellow, we'll pull a sack over his head, and to the music of
blows, we'll take him into your house and into your bedroom in the
dark. There we'll put him in the bed and tell him what he's got to
do, and there'll be no difficulty at all. Then in the morning you'll
send him off before day, have your wife bathe, and you can be with
her at your pleasure and without danger.

MESSER N. I'm satisfied, since you say that kings and princes and
lords have used this method. But above everything else, don't let it
be known, because of the Eight.

CAL. Who do you suppose will tell it?
MESSER N. One difficulty is left, and it's important.
CAL. What is it?
MESSER N. To get my wife to consent, for I don't believe she'll
ever make up her mind to it.
CAL. You're right. But I hope I shall never be a husband if I can't
get my wife to do what I want.
LIG. I've thought of a scheme.
MESSER N. What is it?
LIG. Through her confessor.
CAL. [to LIGURIO]. Who'll get the confessor to do it?
LIG. [to CALLIMACO]. You, I, money, our rascality, theirs.
MESSER N. If nothing more, I'm afraid that for anything I say she
won't be willing to talk with her confessor.
LIG. And there's a scheme for that too.
CAL. Out with it!
LIG. To have her mother take her to him.

    4. *for the Eight: for the Criminal Court.*

MESSER N. She has faith in her.

LIG. And I know her mother is on our side. Come on, let's not waste time; it's getting toward evening. You go and amuse yourself, Callimaco, and see to it that at eight o'clock we find you in your house with the medicine ready. We'll go to her mother's house, the Judge and I, to get her to help us, for I know her. Then we'll go to the Friar, and we'll report to you what we've done.

CAL. [*to* LIGURIO]. Oh, don't leave me alone.

LIG. [*to* CALLIMACO]. You act drunk.

CAL. [*to* LIGURIO]. Where do you want me to go now?

LIG. [*to* CALLIMACO]. This way, that way, along this street, along that one; Florence is a big town.

CAL. [*aside*]. This is killing me.

## CANZONE

[*after the second act*]

Everybody knows how happy he is
who is born stupid and believes everything.
Ambition does not disturb him,
fear does not upset him—
those two that ever are the seeds
of pain and discontent.
This judge of yours,
in hope to have children,
will believe that an ass can fly;
and everything else he has wholly forgotten,
and only on this has set his desire.

## III.1

### SOSTRATA, MESSER NICIA, LIGURIO

SOSTRATA. I've always heard that it's the part of a prudent man to take the best among bad choices.[1] If for having children you don't know any other way, then you'll have to accept this one, if it doesn't burden the conscience.

1. *Found in* PRINCE *21 and elsewhere. See Index:* Evils, choice of.

MESSER NICIA. Just so.

LIGURIO. Now you go and talk with your daughter, and the Judge and I'll go and talk with Fra Timoteo, her confessor, and tell him the story, so you'll not have to tell him. You'll see what he'll say to you.

SOST. All right, I'll do it. Your road takes you that way, but I'm going to see Lucretia, and I'll bring her to speak with the Friar, no matter what.

### III.2

#### MESSER NICIA, LIGURIO

MESSER NICIA. Perhaps you think it strange, Ligurio, that we have to tell so many stories to get my wife to consent, but if you knew everything you wouldn't think it strange.

LIGURIO. I believe the reason is that all women are timorous.

MESSER N. That's not it. She used to be the sweetest person in the world and the most accommodating, but a neighbor of ours told her she'd become pregnant if she vowed to hear the first mass at the Servi¹ for forty mornings, and she made her vow and went there twenty mornings or so. Then you know one of those nasty friars began to hang around her, so she didn't want to go back there any more. It certainly is a bad thing, though, that those who ought to set us good examples should be of that sort. Isn't that so?

LIG. Hell, yes, if it's true.

MESSER N. From that time on she's had ears like a rabbit, and when almost nothing is said to her, she finds a thousand difficulties in it.

LIG. I don't think it strange any more. But that vow, how was it carried out?

MESSER N. We had it dispensed.

LIG. That's good. But if you have them, give me twenty-five ducats, for in an affair like this, one has to spend money and make the Friar one's friend in a hurry and give him hope of more.

MESSER N. Here, take them. This doesn't worry me, I can economize somewhere.

1. *The church of the Servites (Servi di Maria), Santissima Annunziata. See* ARTICLES FOR A PLEASURE COMPANY, *par. 9.*

LIG. These friars are knavish, crafty, and it's not strange, because they know our sins and their own. A man who isn't used to them could make a mistake and fail to get one of them to do what he wants. So I hope you won't spoil everything by talking, because a man in your station, who sits all day in his study, understands just books, and can't manage practical affairs. [*aside*] This fellow is so stupid I'm afraid he'll spoil everything.

MESSER N. Tell me what you want me to do.

LIG. Leave the talking to me, and don't say a single word unless I give you a sign.

MESSER N. I agree. What sign will you make?

LIG. I'll close one eye, bite my lip. Oh, no. We'll do differently. How long is it since you spoke to the Friar?

MESSER N. More than ten years.

LIG. That's good: I'll tell him you've got deaf, and you'll not answer and never say anything unless we speak very loud.

MESSER N. I'll do it.

LIG. Don't be worried if I say some things that seem to you different from what we want, because it'll all fit in.

MESSER N. All right.

## III.3

### FRATE TIMOTEO, A WOMAN

FRATE TIMOTEO. If you want to confess, I'm at your service.

WOMAN. Not today. Somebody's waiting for me, and it's enough for me to have let out a bit right here like this. Have you said those masses of Our Lady?

FRATE. Yes, madam.

WOMAN. Now take this florin, and every Monday for two months say the mass of the dead for the soul of my husband. And though he was a bad one, yet the flesh does pull. I can't help mourning when I think about him. But do you believe he's in Purgatory?

FRATE. There's no doubt of it.

WOMAN. I'm not at all sure he is. You know what he did to me sometimes. Oh, how much I complained about him to you! I kept away from him as much as I could, but he was so pressing. Oh, good Lord!

FRATE. Have no fears. The mercy of God is great; if a man doesn't lack the will, time for repentance won't be lacking.

WOMAN. Do you believe the Turk is coming over into Italy this year?[1]

FRATE. Yes, if you don't say your prayers.

WOMAN. My goodness! God help us! such deviltries! I'm so afraid of that impaling.[2] But I see here in church a woman who has some thread of mine; I want to go and speak to her. Good bye!

FRATE. Good bye!

1. *Especially after the Turkish capture of Otronto in 1480, Italians could fear invasion by the Turks. Such popular fear is suited to the stupid woman who expresses it. In a letter to Guicciardini (18 May 1521, translated below) Machiavelli classes it among* novelle da pancacce *(stories told by gossips on public benches). One of Giovambattista dell'Ottonaio's* CARNIVAL SONGS *begins:*

> Chi vuol udir bugie o novellaccie,
> venga ascoltar costoro
> che stanno tutto il di su le pancaccie

*(Anybody wanting to hear lies and tall stories should go to listen to those who sit all day on the public benches).* (Charles S. Singleton, NUOVI CANTI CARNASCIALESCHI DEL RIN-ASCIMENTO, *Modena, 1940, p. 61; See also* CARNIVAL SONGS, *III. 34.)*

2. *A horrible Turkish method of execution given a bawdy suggestion.*

## III.4

### FRATE TIMOTEO, LIGURIO, MESSER NICIA

FRATE TIMOTEO [*to himself*]. The most liberal givers alive are the women, but the most vexing. Anybody who drives them away gets rid of vexation and profit; he who deals with them gets profit and vexation together. But it's a fact that there's no honey without flies. [*to* LIGURIO *and* NICIA] How goes it, my good men? Don't I recognize Messer Nicia?

LIGURIO. Speak loud, for he's got so deaf he can't hear anything now.

FRATE. You're welcome, sir.

LIG. Louder.

FRATE. Welcome.

MESSER NICIA. I'm glad to see you, Father.

FRATE. How goes it?

MESSER N. Very well.

LIG. Talk to me, Father, because you can't make him understand unless you fill the square with noise.

FRATE. What do you want with me?

LIG. Messer Nicia here and another worthy man, whom you'll hear about later, are going to have several hundred ducats laid out in charity.

MESSER N. A bloody flux on you!

LIG. [*aside to* NICIA]. Keep still, damn you; it won't be much. [*to* FRATE TIMOTEO] Don't be astonished, Father, at anything he says, because he doesn't hear, and sometimes he thinks he hears but his answers don't fit.

FRATE. Go ahead, then, and let him say what he wants to.

LIG. I have part of that money with me, and they've selected you to lay it out.

FRATE. I'll be delighted.

LIG. But it's necessary, before the money is turned over, for you to help us in a strange affair that has happened to Messer Nicia (and you are the only man who can help us) on which his family's reputation entirely depends.

FRATE. What is it?

LIG. I don't know whether you know Cammillo Calfucci, nephew to the Judge here.

FRATE. Yes, I know him.

LIG. A year ago, he went on business to France, and not having a wife (for she is dead), he left his daughter, old enough to get married, in the care of a convent; it isn't necessary now to give you its name.

FRATE. What happened?

LIG. It happened that either through the nuns' neglect or the girl's empty-headedness, she is now four months pregnant, so that if it isn't prudently seen to, the Judge, the nuns, the girl, Cammillo, and the Calfucci family will be disgraced. The Judge is so much concerned about this scandal that he has vowed, if it doesn't become known, to give three hundred ducats for the love of God,

MESSER N. What poppycock!

LIG. [*aside to* NICIA]. Keep still. [*to* FRATE TIMOTEO] and to give it through you. And nobody but you and the abbess can help us out.

FRATE. How?

LIG. By persuading the abbess to give the girl a medicine to make her miscarry.

FRATE. That's something to think about.

LIG. See how much good will result from doing this. You keep up the reputation of the nunnery, the girl, her relatives; you return a daughter to a father; you help out the Judge here and all his relatives; you carry on all that charitable work that these three hundred ducats'll make possible. And on the other side you injure only a piece of flesh not yet born, without sense, which can be lost in a thousand ways; and I believe that good is what does good to the largest number, and with which the largest number are pleased.¹

FRATE. So be it, in God's name! Do what you want to, and let it all be done for God and charity. Tell me the name of the nunnery, give me the medicine, and—if you want to—that money, so I can begin to do good works.

LIG. Now you seem to me the churchman I thought you were. Take this part of the money. The nunnery is . . . But wait, there's a woman in the church who's beckoning to me. I'll come back at once; don't leave Messer Nicia; I want to speak a word or two to her.

1. *Here, dramatically perverted for a low purpose, is Machiavelli's clearest statement of the principle of the greatest good to the greatest number. Cf. "the generality of the men of Italy" (*THE PRINCE *26, par. 1).*

## III.5

### FRATE TIMOTEO, MESSER NICIA

FRATE TIMOTEO. About this girl, how old is she?¹
MESSER NICIA [*to himself*]. I'm dizzy.
FRATE. I say, how old is this girl?
MESSER N. May God send him trouble!
FRATE. Why?
MESSER N. Because he ought to have it.
FRATE. [*aside*]. I seem to be in a mess. I'm dealing with a crazy man and a deaf one. One runs away; the other doesn't hear. Yet if these aren't lead florins, I can use them better than they can. But there's Ligurio coming back.

1. *In the translation of d'Avenel this speech runs: "Cette jeune fille, de combien est-elle enceinte?" Other renderings are to the same effect. Yet the preceding scene has given the answer: four months. Lexicons furnish no support for such a translation.*

## III.6

### LIGURIO, FRATE TIMOTEO, MESSER NICIA

LIGURIO [*to* NICIA]. Keep still, Sir. [*to the* FRATE] Oh, I have great news, Father.

FRATE TIMOTEO. What?

LIG. That woman I spoke with told me the girl has miscarried all of herself.

FRATE [*aside*]. For certain, that charity money will go off like grease.[1]

LIG. What is it you're saying?

FRATE. I'm saying you ought so much the more to give that money to charity.

LIG. The gift'll be made when you want it, but you'll have to do something else to help the Judge here.

FRATE. What's that?

LIG. Something that'll be less blamed and gossiped about, more pleasing to us, more profitable for you.

FRATE. What is it? I'm under contract to you, and I seem to have got so intimate that there is nothing I won't do.

LIG. I prefer to tell you in the church, between you and me, if the Judge will be so good as to wait here. We'll come back soon.

MESSER NICIA. As the toad said to the harrow.[2]

FRATE. Come along.

1. *grease: grease in the fire.*
2. *the toad said to the harrow. See Machiavelli's letter to Guicciardini (Sept. 1525, no. 198).*


## III.7

### MESSER NICIA *alone*

Is it day or night? Am I awake or asleep? Am I drunk (though so far today I haven't had a thing to drink), so that I go along with this poppycock? No sooner have we said one thing to the friar than he says something else. Then he told me to act deaf, and I should have to stop up my ears like the Dane[1] if I were to keep from hearing the silly things he's said, and God knows what they're for. I am out twenty-five ducats, and not a thing has been said on my business,

1. *Ogier the Dane, a hero of romance, stopped his ears like Ulysses.*

and now he has planted me here with a dibble like a numskull.'
But they're coming back, and the Devil take them if they haven't
talked about my business.

2. *with a dibble: like a planted seed, he can't go away. A zugo (translated numskull) is a sort of friedcake. The whole is a proverb applied to a person left waiting without consideration.*

## III.8

### FRATE TIMOTEO, LIGURIO, MESSER NICIA

FRATE TIMOTEO. Have the women come. I know what I've got
to do, and if my influence is enough, we'll finish this marriage
business this evening.[1]
LIGURIO. Messer Nicia, Fra Timoteo is going to do everything.
We must see that the women come.
MESSER NICIA. You make a new man of me. Will it be a boy?
LIG. A boy.
MESSER N. Love brings me to tears.
FRATE. Go on into the church; I'll wait here for the women. Stay
in some place where they won't see you, and when they've gone I'll
tell you what they said.

1. *Perhaps Fra Timoteo uses the word* marriage *as a euphemism, or perhaps Machiavelli intended it jocosely, as does Boccaccio in* DECAMERON 2. 7.

## III.9

### FRATE TIMOTEO *alone*

I don't know which of us has bamboozled the other. This rascally Ligurio came to me with that first story to test me, so that if I
didn't make a deal with him he wouldn't have told me this one.
Thus they wouldn't expose their plan without gaining anything, and
they didn't care about the false one. It's true that I've been bamboozled; but all the same this bamboozling brings me profit. Messer
Nicia and Callimaco are rich, and in different ways there is much to
be got from both of them. This affair is certain to be kept secret,
because the telling of it is as serious for them as for me. However
things go, I don't repent of it. It is true, though, that I fear there'll
be difficulty, because Madam Lucretia is cautious and good; but I'll
bamboozle her by using her goodness. For all women lack brains,

so when one of them knows enough to say two words, it makes her famous, because in a city of the blind, a man with one eye is Duke. But there she comes with her mother, who is certainly a bitch, and will be a great help to me in bringing her to what I want.

## III.10

### SOSTRATA, LUCRETIA

SOSTRATA. I believe you believe, my child, that I value your honor as much as anybody in the world, and I wouldn't advise you to do anything that isn't proper. I've said, and I say it again, that if Fra Timoteo tells you it isn't a thing to burden your conscience, you should do it without thinking about it.

LUCRETIA. I've always been afraid that Messer Nicia's wish to have children would make us commit some sin, and for this reason, whenever he's spoken to me of anything, I've always been suspicious and afraid, especially after what you know happened to me when I went to the Servi. But of all the things that have been tried, this seems to me the strangest, to have to submit my body to this shame, to be the cause that a man should die as the result of his shaming me, because if I were the only woman left in the world and the human race had to begin again from me, I can't believe that such a way to do it would be permitted to me.

SOST. I can't discuss so many things with you, my child. Talk with the Frate, see what he says, and then do what he recommends and we do, and everybody does who's interested in you.

LUCR. I'm sweating with anxiety.

## III.11

### FRATE TIMOTEO, LUCRETIA, SOSTRATA

FRATE TIMOTEO. You're welcome! I know what you want to learn from me, because Messer Nicia has spoken to me. In truth I've been at my books more than two hours, studying this case, and in my researches I've found many things that support us both in detail and in general.

LUCRETIA. Are you speaking seriously or are you joking?

FRATE. Oh, Madam Lucretia, are these things to be joked about?

Don't you know me yet?

LUCR. Yes, Father, but this seems to me the strangest thing that ever was heard of.

FRATE. Madam, I believe you, but I don't want you to say so any more. There are many things that at a distance seem terrible, un-bearable, strange, yet when you get close to them they seem mild, bearable, normal; hence, we say that fears are worse than evils them-selves; and this is one of that sort.

LUCR. God grant it!

FRATE. I want to go back to what I said earlier. You must, as to conscience, accept this rule: where a good is certain and an evil uncertain, you ought never to give up the good for fear of the evil. Here you have a certain good, that you will become pregnant, gain a soul for the Lord. The uncertain evil is that the man who lies with you after you take the medicine may die; yet there are also those who don't die. But because the matter is uncertain, it's not a good thing for Messer Nicia to run this risk. As to the action, the notion that it's a sin is a fairy story, because the will is what sins, not the body, and what would make it a sin would be your husband's displeasure, but you will be pleasing him; or if you should take pleasure in it, but you will get displeasure from it. Besides this, one's purpose must be considered in everything; your purpose is to fill a seat in paradise, to please your husband. The Bible says that Lot's daughters, thinking that they alone were left in the world, had to do with their father, and because their intention was good, they did not sin.

LUCR. What are you persuading me to?

SOST. Be persuaded, my child. Don't you see that a woman who doesn't have any children doesn't have any home? When her hus-band dies, she is left wretched, deserted by everybody.

FRATE. I swear to you, Madam, by this consecrated breast, that submitting to your husband in this affair is as much a matter of conscience as eating meat on Wednesday, which is a sin that goes away with holy water.[1]

LUCR. To what are you bringing me, Father?

FRATE. I am bringing you to what will give you reason always to pray to God for me, and you will be more pleased next year than now.

1. *Wednesdays are fast days during the four weeks of the season of Advent.*

SOST. She will do what you want. I am going to put her to bed this evening myself. [*to* LUCRETIA] What are you afraid of, snotty nose? There are fifty women in this city who would lift their hands to Heaven for it.[2]

LUCR. I consent; but I don't believe I shall be alive at all tomorrow morning.

FRATE. Do not fear, my daughter. I shall pray to God for you; I shall repeat the prayer of the angel Raphael, so he will be with you.[3] Go with assurance and get ready for this secret act, because it's now evening.

SOST. Good bye, Father.

LUCR. God and Our Lady help me and keep me from shame!

2. *In thanksgiving.*
3. *As, according to the Apocryphal book of Tobit, he was with Tobias.*

## III.12

### FRATE TIMOTEO, LIGURIO, MESSER NICIA

FRATE TIMOTEO. O Ligurio, come out.

LIGURIO. How goes it?

FRATE. Well. They've gone home ready to do everything, and there'll be no difficulty, because her mother'll go to stay with her, and intends to put her to bed herself.

MESSER NICIA. Are you telling the truth?

FRATE. Well, well, you're cured of your deafness.

LIG. San Clemente has shown him favor.

FRATE. It would be a good thing to put up a votive image there,[1] to start a crowd coming so I could share your gain with you.

MESSER N. We're getting off on trifles. Will my wife make any difficulty about doing what I want?

FRATE. No, I tell you.

MESSER N. I'm the happiest man in the world.

FRATE. I believe it. You will peck up a boy for yourself.[2] Who doesn't have, let him go without.[3]

LIG. Go to your prayers, Father, and if we need anything else, we'll

1. *A waxen image of an ear at San Clemente's altar, as a sign of thanksgiving for his cure.*
2. *An expression derived from a bird's use of its beak, meaning to gain with effort or shrewdness.*
3. *Proverbial for "Who wants a thing and cannot get it, let him go without."*

come for you. You, Sir, go to your wife, to keep her firm in this decision, and I'll tell Doctor Callimaco, so that he'll send you the medicine. And at seven o'clock let me see you again, to arrange what ought to be done at ten.

MESSER N. All right. Good bye.

FRATE. Good wishes.

# CANZONE

## [after the third act]

Pleasant indeed is the trick
carried on to the dear conclusion that has been dreamed of,
that takes one out of distress
and makes sweet every bitter thing that has been tasted.
Oh restorative splendid and rare,
you show the straight path to wandering souls;
you, O Love, with your great power
by making others blessed make them rich;
you conquer, with your sacred counsels alone,
rocks, enchantments, and poisons.

# IV.1

## CALLIMACO *alone*

I wish I could just know what those fellows have done. Can it be that I shan't see Ligurio again? It's not just five o'clock; it's six. How anxious I've been and still am! It's true that Fortune and Nature keep their account balanced; the first never does you a good turn that on the other side something bad doesn't come up. The more my hope has grown, the more my fear has grown. How wretched I am! How can I ever live in such distress and disturbed by these fears and hopes? I'm a ship tossed by two opposing winds, which is the more in danger the closer she comes to port. Messer Nicia's folly makes me hope; Lucretia's caution and firmness make me fear. Woe is me! I can't find rest anywhere! Sometimes I try to conquer my feelings; I reproach myself for this excitement and say to myself: "What are you doing? Are you crazy? When you get her, what'll it amount to? You'll recognize your mistake; you'll regret the labor and worry you've gone through. Don't you know how little good a man finds in the things he has longed for, compared with what he expected to find? On the other hand, the worst you can get from it is that you'll die and go to Hell. But how many others have died! And in Hell how many worthy men there are![1] Are you ashamed to go there? Face your fortune; run away from trouble, but if you can't run away from it, bear it like a man; don't be downcast; don't be a coward like a woman." And so I give myself courage, but not for long, because on every side I'm attacked by such a desire to be with her just once that I feel as though my whole body from the soles of my feet to my head has gone wrong: my legs tremble, my vitals are shaken, my heart is torn out of my breast, my arms lose their strength, my tongue falls silent, my eyes are dazzled, my brain whirls.[2] If I could only find Ligurio, I should have somebody to pour out my feelings to. But there he is coming toward me, fast. This man's report'll either make me live a little longer or die and be done with it.

1. *Compare one of the sayings of Castruccio Castracani, given at the end of his* LIFE.
2. *Callimaco's description is imitated from Catullus 51 (*Ille mi par).

## IV.2

### LIGURIO, CALLIMACO

LIGURIO [*to himself*]. I've never wanted to find Callimaco so much and I've never had so much trouble in finding him. If I were taking him bad news, I should have met him straight off. I have been at his house, in the Square, in the Market place, at the Spini Bench, at the Tornaquinci Loggia, and I haven't found him. These lovers walk on quicksilver; they can't stand still.

CALLIMACO [*to himself*]. There's Ligurio coming along looking this way; he must be hunting for me.[1] Why do I keep waiting, instead of calling him? He seems in good spirits too. [*to* LIGURIO] Oh, Ligurio, Ligurio!

LIG. Oh Callimaco, where've you been?

CAL. What's the news?

LIG. Good.

1. *Added by Ruscelli in his edition (Venice, 1554).*

CAL. Really good?

LIG. The very best.

CAL. Is Lucretia willing?

LIG. Yes.

CAL. The Friar did what was needed?

LIG. He did.

CAL. Oh, blessed Friar! I shall always pray to God for him.

LIG. Oh fine! As though God granted his grace in evil things as well as good ones! The Friar will want more than prayers.

CAL. What will he want?

LIG. Money.

CAL. Let him have it. How much have you promised him?

LIG. Three hundred ducats.

CAL. That was right.

LIG. The Judge has paid him twenty-five.

CAL. What?

LIG. It's enough for you that he's paid them.

CAL. What's Lucretia's mother done?

LIG. Pretty nearly all of it. When she got the idea that her daughter could have this pleasant night without sin, she didn't stop begging, ordering, encouraging Lucretia until she took her to the Friar, and there she acted in such a way that she consented.

CAL. Oh, God! For what merits of mine do I deserve so many good things? I'm ready to die for happiness.

LIG. What a man this is! Now for happiness, now for sorrow—this fellow wants to die no matter what. Have you the medicine ready?

CAL. Yes, I have.

LIG. What are you going to send him?

CAL. A glass of hypocras, that is good to settle the stomach, cheers the brain.—Oh! Oh! I am ruined.

LIG. What is it? what can it be?

CAL. There's no help for it.

LIG. What the devil is it?

CAL. We haven't done a thing; I've walled myself up in an oven.[2]

LIG. How? Why don't you tell? Take your hands away from your face.

2. *I am ruined by my own carelessness.*

CAL. Don't you know that I told Messer Nicia that you, he, Siro, and I would catch somebody to put in bed with his wife?

LIG. What of that?

CAL. How can you say "What of that?" If I'm with you, I can't be the one to be caught; if I'm not with you, he'll realize the trick.

LIG. You're right, but isn't there a way out?

CAL. I don't think so.

LIG. Of course there is.

CAL. How?

LIG. I want to think about it a little.

CAL. Here's a pretty how-de-do; I'm in fine shape if you've got to make plans now.

LIG. I have it.

CAL. What is it?

LIG. I'll make the Friar, who's helped us up to now, do this too.

CAL. In what way?

LIG. We've all got to disguise ourselves. I'll make the Friar disguise himself; he'll imitate your voice, your face, your dress; I'll tell the Judge it's you and he'll believe it.

CAL. It suits me, but what shall I do?

LIG. I count on you to put on a short jacket and come with a lute in your hand, near the corner of his house, singing a little song.

CAL. With my face uncovered?

LIG. Yes, for if you wear a mask, he'll get suspicious.

CAL. He'll know me.

LIG. He won't, because I expect you to twist your face, to open and stretch your mouth or show your teeth, and close one eye. Try a little.

CAL. Is this it?

LIG. No.

CAL. This?

LIG. It isn't enough.

CAL. Like this?

LIG. Yes, yes, remember that. I've a false nose at home; I want you to wear it.

CAL. All right, what then?

LIG. When you reach the corner, we'll be there, we'll snatch your lute, seize you, spin you around, take you into the house, put you in the bed. You're to do the rest for yourself.

CAL. It's certain to be carried through!

LIG. So far you will be carried, but to manage so you'll return later to the same place is your affair, not ours.

CAL. What?

LIG. You must win her over in the course of this night, and before you leave, let her know who you are, confess the trick to her, show her your love for her, tell her of the happiness you wish her, show her that without disgrace she can be your friend, and with great disgrace your enemy. It's impossible she'll not come to an understanding with you, and that she'll want this night to stand alone.

CAL. Do you believe that?

LIG. I'm sure of it. But let's not lose any more time; it's eight o'clock already. Call Siro, send the medicine to Messer Nicia, wait for me in your house. I'll go for the Friar, make him disguise himself and bring him here, and we'll find the Judge and do what's left.

CAL. That's good; go ahead.

## IV.3

### CALLIMACO, SIRO

CALLIMACO. Oh Siro!

SIRO. Sir!

CAL. Come here.

SIRO. Here I am.

CAL. Get that silver cup that's in the cupboard in my room, put a little cloth over it, bring it to me, and look out that you don't upset it on the way.

SIRO. Very good, sir. [*He goes for the cup.*]

CAL. [*to himself*]. This fellow's been with me for ten years and has always been a faithful servant. I believe he'll show fidelity in this business too, and though I haven't told him about this trick, he guesses it for himself, for he's something of a rascal, and I see that he's adapting himself to it.

SIRO. Here it is.

CAL. That's good. Be quick, go to Messer Nicia's house and say that this is the medicine his wife has to take right after supper—and the earlier she has supper the better—and that we'll be on the corner as arranged, at the time when he's going to be there. Hurry.

SIRO. Here I go.

CAL. Listen. If he wants you to wait for him, wait, and come here with him. If he doesn't want you, come back here to me, after you have given it to him and delivered the message.
SIRO. Yes, sir.

## IV.4

### CALLIMACO *alone*

I'm waiting until Ligurio comes back with the Friar. And any, body who says it's hard to wait is telling the truth. I'm losing ten pounds every hour, thinking where I am now and where it's possible I'll be two hours from now, and afraid something'll come up to spoil my plan. If that should happen, this'll be the last night of my life, for I'll throw myself into the Arno, or I'll hang myself, or I'll throw myself from these windows, or I'll stab myself with a knife at her door. I'll do something so I'll live no longer. But do I see Ligurio? It's he; he has a man with him that seems humpbacked, lame; it certainly must be the Friar disguised. Oh, friars! If you know one of them, you know them all. Who is the other man who's come up to them? It looks like Siro, who's already done my errand to the Judge. It's he. I'll wait for them here so as to join them.

## IV.5

### SIRO, LIGURIO, *the* FRATE *disguised*, CALLIMACO

SIRO [*to* LIGURIO; *the* FRATE *is just out of hearing*]. Who's that with you, Ligurio?
LIGURIO. A worthy man.
SIRO. Is he lame or is he pretending?
LIG. Look at something else.
SIRO. Oh, he has the face of a big rascal.
LIG. Oh, keep still; you're making a nuisance of yourself. Where's Callimaco?
CALLIMACO. Here I am. I'm glad to see you.
LIG. Oh Callimaco, give this little fool of a Siro some instructions; he has already said a thousand foolish things.
CAL. Siro, listen to me. This evening you must do everything Ligurio tells you to, and when he gives you an order, imagine that I

am speaking. And what you see, touch, or hear you must keep absolutely secret, in so far as you value my property, my honor, my life and your own welfare.

SIRO. Very good, sir.

CAL. Did you give the cup to the Judge?

SIRO. Yes, sir.

CAL. What did he say?

SIRO. That everything is now arranged.

FRATE TIMOTEO. Is this Callimaco?

CAL. I am, at your service. Let's consider our business settled; you can treat me and all my property as though they were your own.

FRATE. I understand, and I believe it, and I've undertaken to do something for you that I wouldn't have done for any other man in the world.

CAL. You'll not lose your labor.

FRATE. It's enough that you wish me well.

LIG. Let's have no more ceremonies. We'll go and disguise our-selves, Siro and I. You, Callimaco, come with us, so you can go and do your business. The Frate will wait for us here; we'll come back at once and go for Messer Nicia.

CAL. What you say's right. Let's go.

FRATE. I'll wait for you.


## IV.6

### *The* FRATE, *alone in disguise*

They tell the truth who say that bad company brings men to the gallows; and many times one comes to harm by being too accom-modating and too good, as well as by being too bad.[1] God knows I wasn't thinking of harming anybody; I was staying in my cell, saying my offices, dealing with my penitents. Then all at once this devil of a Ligurio turned up; he made me put my finger in a sin, then I have put in my arm and my whole body, and I don't know yet where I am going to end. Yet I comfort myself that when an affair's important to many, many have to be careful about it. But here are Ligurio and that servant coming back.

1. *Cf.* THE PRINCE *19. Good deeds may produce hatred.*

## IV.7

### FRATE TIMOTEO, LIGURIO, SIRO

FRATE TIMOTEO. Welcome back!

LIGURIO. Are we in good shape?

FRATE. Excellent.

LIG. We still don't have the Judge. Let's go to his house. It's after nine o'clock; come on.

SIRO. Who's that opening his door? Is it his servant?

LIG. No, it's he, himself. Ha, ha, ha, ha.

SIRO. What are you laughing at?

LIG. Who wouldn't laugh? He's wearing a little jacket that doesn't cover his ass. What the devil's he got on his head? It looks like one of those furs that canons wear. And he has a little sword at his belt. Um, um, he's muttering something or other. Let's move to one side, and we'll hear some hard-luck story about his wife.

## IV.8

### MESSER NICIA *disguised*

How many sickening things this crazy wife of mine has done! She's sent the maid to her mother's house, and the man to the country. I praise her for this, but I certainly don't praise her that before she made up her mind to go to bed she made so many squeamish objections: "I don't want . . . . What shall I do? . . . What are you making me do? . . . Oh me! mamma dear!" And if her mother hadn't talked the father of the leek to her,[1] she wouldn't have got into that bed. Plague take her! I like to see women pretty fussy, but not too much; for she's taken our heads off, kitten-witted as she is! Then if anybody should say: "Let the wisest woman in Florence be hanged," she would say: "What have I done?" I know that Pasquina will go into Arezzo,[2] and before I leave the game I

---

1. *talked the father of the leek.* *Varchi explains it as meaning "to rebuke one and accuse him freely and declare to him what is going to happen to him if he does not change" (*ERCOLANO *99). In one of Machiavelli's* EXTRACTS FROM LETTERS TO THE TEN OF BALIÀ, *it is said: "Fra Girolamo [Savonarola] returned from a visit to the King [of France]; he said he had read the King the father of the leek" (*OPERE, *ed. Passerini and Milanesi, 2. 251).*

2. *Pasquina will go into Arezzo: proverbial for "the thing will be done." But there seems to be a specific application to the coition of Callimaco and Lucretia. Cf. Messer Mazzo and Monte Nero in* DECAMERON *6, introd.*

shall be able to say like Monna Ghinga:³ "Because I've seen it, with these hands."⁴ I'm fine; who would recognize me? I seem bigger, younger, more agile; no woman anywhere would take bed-money from me. But where shall I find those fellows?

3. *Monna Ghinga: apparently a proverbial speaker.*

4. *A reference to the expression, "touch with the hands," meaning to make sure of. Cf. Act V, sc. 2.*

## IV.9

### LIGURIO, MESSER NICIA, *the* FRATE *disguised,* SIRO

LIGURIO. Good evening, sir.

MESSER NICIA. Oh, uh, uh.

LIG. Don't be afraid; we're the men you want.

MESSER N. Oh, here you all are. If I hadn't recognized you at once, I'd have given you as straight a thrust as I could, with this sword. You are Ligurio? and you are Siro? and that other, is he the Doctor, huh?

LIG. Yes, Sir.

MESSER N. Imagine. Oh! if he isn't well disguised! Vaquattù wouldn't know him.¹

LIG. I've had him put two nuts in his mouth so he won't be recognized by his voice.

MESSER N. You're careless.

LIG. Why?

MESSER N. Why didn't you tell me that earlier? For I'd have put two in my mouth as well, and you know whether it's important not to be recognized by our voices.

LIG. Take this and put it in your mouth.

MESSER N. What is it?

LIG. A ball of wax.

MESSER N. Oh wh——thu, thu, pu, pu, sp, sp——Plague take you, you big rascal!

LIG. I beg your pardon; I've given you the wrong one, without realizing it.

MESSER N. Pthu, pthu, pu, pu——What was it, what was it?

LIG. Aloes.

1. *Vaquattù: A proverbial man of great power and shrewdness. The name means "Come here, you."*

MESSER N. Damn you! Sp, sp, Pthu——Doctor, why don't you say anything.

FRATE. Ligurio has made me mad.

MESSER N. Oh! how well you diguise your voice!

LIG. Let's not lose any more time here. I'm going to be captain and draw up the army for battle. On the right horn Callimaco shall be in command, myself on the left, between the two horns will be the Judge here;[2] Siro will be the rear-guard and reinforce any squadron that falls back. The battle-cry will be Saint Cuckoo.[3]

MESSER N. Who is Saint Cuckoo?

LIG. He's the saint most honored in France. Let's march on and set our ambush at this corner. Keep still and listen; I hear a lute.

MESSER N. That's what it is. What's the best thing to do?

LIG. We ought to send a scout ahead to find out who it is, and we'll act according to his report.

MESSER N. Who'll go?

LIG. Go along, Siro. You know what you need to do. Be cautious, take a good look, hurry back, make your report.

SIRO. I understand.

MESSER N. I shouldn't like to catch a crab, such as some weak old fellow or invalid, and have to play this over again tomorrow night.

LIG. Never fear, Siro's a capable man. There he is, coming back. What have you found, Siro?

SIRO. He's the prettiest young chap you ever saw. He isn't twenty-five and he's coming along alone in a short jacket playing a lute.

MESSER N. He's what we want, if you're telling the truth. But take care that this broth isn't upset all over you.

SIRO. It's just as I've told you.

LIG. Wait till he gets by this corner and at once we'll be on him.

MESSER N. Come over here, Doctor; you seem to me to be made of wood. Here he is.

---

2. *horns:* In English more commonly wings. *It is fitting that the judge, who is to be cuckolded, should be between the horns.*

3.                 *The cuckoo then, on every tree,*
                   *Mocks married men; for thus sings he,*
                            *Cuckoo;*
                   *Cuckoo, cuckoo: O, word of fear,*
                   *Unpleasing to a married ear!*

(Love's Labour's Lost, end). *Nicia is too stupid to get the reference.*

CALLIMACO [*sings*]. May the devil manage to come to your bed,
    Since I cannot come there.
    And may he break two ribs in your chest
    And the other parts that God has made you.
    And may he drag you through mountains and
      valleys
    And take off the tops of your shoulders.[4]

LIG. Stand still. Give that lute here.

CAL. Oh! What have I done?

MESSER N. You'll find out. Cover his head, muffle him up.

LIG. Spin him around.

MESSER N. Give him another whirl; give him one more. Take him into the house.

FRATE. Messer Nicia, I'm going to bed, for my head aches fit to kill me. And if it isn't necessary, I'll not come back tomorrow morning.

MESSER N. Yes, Doctor; don't come back; we can get on by ourselves.

    4. *The texts give only two lines of this song. For the rest see Debenedetti's edition (Biblioteca Romanica), p. 78.*

## IV.10

### FRATE TIMOTEO *alone*

They're shut up in the house, and I'll go to the monastery. And you, spectators, don't find fault with us, because all night nobody here will get any sleep, so the acts aren't separated by time for it.[1] I'll repeat the office;[2] Ligurio and Siro will have supper, because they haven't eaten today; the Judge will go from the bedroom into the hall, so the kitchen will be clear. Callimaco and Madam Lucretia'll not get any sleep, because I know that if I were he and you were she, we wouldn't get any sleep.

    1. *Dramatic theory, here ridiculed by Machiavelli, required that actions such as journeys—in this instance, sleep—, that couldn't be represented on the stage, should be thought of as taking place between the acts, which might thus be separated by a number of hours, so long as the entire comedy was not prolonged beyond twenty-four. Actually, the action of the* MANDRAGOLA *is here interrupted.*

    2. *The church service.*

## CANZONE

*[after the fourth act]*

Oh sweet night, oh holy
and quiet hours of night,
you that couple yearning lovers;
in you all pleasures join,
so you are the only cause that renders souls blessed.
To the troops of lovers you give fit reward
for their long drudgery.
You, oh happy hours,
set every icy heart
afire with love.

## V.1

### FRATE TIMOTEO *alone*

All night I haven't shut an eye, I'm so eager to learn how Callimaco and the others have got on; I've been attending to various things to use up the time; I said matins, read a life of the Holy Fathers, went into the church and lit a lamp that had gone out, changed the veil of a Madonna who works miracles. How many times I have told these friars to keep her clean! And then they are puzzled if worship falls off. I remember when there were five hundred images here, and today there're not twenty. We're to blame, because we haven't known how to keep up her reputation. We used to go in procession before her every evening after compline, and have lauds sung for her every Saturday. We were always making vows to her then, so that folks would see new images before her; in confession we all the time encouraged men and women to make vows to her. Now none of these things is done, and then we are puzzled if business gets slack. Oh how few brains these friars of mine have! But I hear a big noise from Messer Nicia's house. There they come, sure enough. They are bringing out the prisoner. I've got here at the right time. They've really waited until the very last drop in the bottle;[1] it's just daybreak. I'm going to stand still and hear what they say, without showing myself.

1. *the last drop in the bottle: to the bitter end.*

## V.2

### MESSER NICIA, CALLIMACO, LIGURIO, SIRO

MESSER NICIA. You hold him on that side and I'll hold him on this one; and you, Siro, hang on to his coat from behind.

CALLIMACO. Don't hurt me.

LIGURIO. Don't be afraid, just take yourself away.

MESSER N. Let's not go any farther.

LIG. You're right; get rid of him here. Whirl him around twice, so he won't know where he's come from. Spin him, Siro.

SIRO. Here goes.

MESSER N. Spin him again.

SIRO. That's done.

CAL. My lute!

LIG. Be off, rascal, be off. If I hear of your talking, I'll cut your throat.

MESSER N. How he runs! Let's go and get out of these clothes. And it'll be a good thing for all of us to go out early, so it won't look as though we've been awake all night.

LIG. That's a good notion.

MESSER N. You and Siro find Doctor Callimaco and tell him how well the affair has come out.

LIG. What can we tell him? We don't know a thing. You remember that when we got into the house we went into the cellar to drink. You and your mother-in-law were busy with him, and we didn't see you again until now, when you called us to put him out.

MESSER N. That's true. Oh, I can tell you some fine things. My wife was in bed in the dark. Sostrata was waiting for me at the fire. I got there with this young fellow, and so that nothing should be done under a hood,[1] I took him into a store room I have off the hall where there was a shaded lamp; it threw out some light, but in such a way he couldn't get a look at my face.

LIG. You were clever about that.

MESSER N. I told him to undress; he held back; I turned on him like a dog, so that he thought it was taking him a thousand years to get his clothes off; and he stood naked. His face is ugly. He had a

---

1. *under a hood: unseen.*

great big nose, a twisted mouth; but you never saw finer skin, white, soft, smooth; and don't ask about the other things.

LIG. It's just as well not to talk about them. Why did you need to look him all over?

MESSER N. You're asking for the iambic.[2] Since I'd put my hands into the dough, I wanted to go to the bottom of it; then I wanted to see if he was healthy; if he had had syphilis, where would I have been? You're talking nonsense.

LIG. You're right.

MESSER N. When I had seen he was healthy, I had him follow me, and in the dark I took him into the bedroom; I put him in the bed, and before I would go away I wanted to touch with my hands how the thing was going,[3] for I am not used to being made to take fireflies for lanterns.[4]

LIG. What sense you've shown in managing this affair!

MESSER N. When I'd touched and made sure of everything, I went out of the bedroom and locked the door and went to my mother-in-law, who was by the fire, and we kept on talking all night.

LIG. What did you talk about?

MESSER N. Lucretia's stupidity, and how much better it would have been if she'd given in at first without so many goings and comings. Then we talked about the baby—for I imagine I have him in my arms all the time, the darling—until I heard the clock strike seven, and since I was afraid day would come on, I went into the bedchamber. And what do you think? I couldn't make that big rascal get up.

LIG. I believe you.

MESSER N. He'd liked his rich diet. Yet he got up, I called you, and we led him out.

LIG. The affair's gone well.

MESSER N. What do you think troubles me about it?

LIG. What?

2. *Varchi explains this as one of the things said to a person who is trying to persuade us of something that we aren't going to believe, to get him out of our sight and get that boredom out of our hearing* (ERCOLANO *134*).

3. *touch with my hands: a common figure for making sure of something. Here it becomes comically literal.*

4. *Explained by Varchi as to make what does not exist appear to exist, and to make small things big* (ERCOLANO *55*).

MESSER N. That poor boy, who's got to die so soon and whom this night is going to cost so dear.

LIG. Oh, don't worry about that. Let him take care of it.

MESSER N. That's true. But it does seem to me a thousand years until I can see Doctor Callimaco and tell him how glad I am.

LIG. He'll come out in an hour or so. But it's bright daylight. We'll go and undress; what'll you do?

MESSER N. I'll go into the house too and put on my best clothes. I'll have my wife get up and bathe and have her go to the church, so as to be churched.⁵ I should like you and Callimaco to be there, and all of us could speak to the Frate, to thank him and pay him back for the good he's done us.

LIG. That's a good suggestion; we'll do it.

5. *A formula for the ceremonies of the first visit to church after childbirth. Nicia anticipates.*

## V.3

### FRATE TIMOTEO *alone*

I've heard their talk and I like it, considering how stupid this judge is; the very last part was specially pleasing. And since they're coming to visit me at home, I won't stay here any longer but'll wait for them in the church, where my stock-in-trade'll fetch a higher price. But who's coming out of that house? I'm sure it's Ligurio, and that must be Callimaco with him. I don't want them to see me here, for the reasons I've given. Besides, if they don't come to my place, there'll always be time to go to theirs.

## V.4

### CALLIMACO, LIGURIO

CALLIMACO. As I told you, my Ligurio, I was anxious until three o'clock, and though I was having a very good time, it didn't seem to me right. But then I made myself known to her and made her understand my love for her, and how easily, because her husband is so stupid, we could live in happiness without any scandal, and promised her that when God removed him, I'd take her as my wife. Besides my sound reasons, too, she felt what a difference there is between the way I lie with her and the way Nicia does, and between the kisses of a young lover and those of an old husband. After some sighs she said: "Your cleverness, my husband's stupidity, my mother's folly, and my confessor's rascality have brought me to do what I never would have done of myself. So I'm forced to judge that it comes from Heaven's wish that has ordered it so, and I'm not strong enough to refuse what Heaven wills me to accept. I take you then for lord, master, guide; you are my father, you are my defender; I want you as my chief good; and what my husband has asked for one night, I intend him to have always. You'll make yourself his best friend; you'll go to the church this morning, and from there you'll come to have dinner with us; after that your comings and stayings'll be as you like, and we can be together at any time without sus picion." When I heard these words, I was ready to die with their sweetness. I couldn't answer with even a little of what I tried to. So I'm the happiest and most fortunate man who ever lived; and if I should never lose this happiness through either death or time, I should be more blissful than the blessed, happier than the saints above.

LIGURIO. I rejoice in all your happiness, and what I foretold has come about for you to the dot. But what'll we do now?

CAL. Let's go to the church, for I've promised to be there, and she'll be coming, and her mother and the Judge.

LIG. I see his door opening; there they are; they're coming out, and the Judge is behind them.

CAL. Let's go into the church and wait there.

## V.5

### MESSER NICIA, LUCRETIA, SOSTRATA

MESSER NICIA. Lucretia, I believe it's good to do things in the fear of God, not like a mad woman.

LUCRETIA. What's got to be done, now?

MESSER N. See how she answers. She acts like a fighting cock.

SOSTRATA. Don't be astonished at it; she is a bit indignant.

LUCR. What are you trying to say?

MESSER N. I'm saying I'd better go ahead and speak to the Frate and tell him to meet us at the church door, to lead you to the church ing, because this morning it's exactly as though you were born a second time.

LUCR. Why don't you go?

MESSER N. You're very lively this morning. [*to* SOSTRATA] Last evening she acted half dead.

LUCR. Thanks to you.

SOST. Go and find the Friar. But you don't need to; he's outside the church.

MESSER N. So he is.

## V.6

FRATE TIMOTEO, MESSER NICIA, LUCRETIA,
CALLIMACO, LIGURIO, SOSTRATA

FRATE TIMOTEO [*aside*]. I'm coming out here because Callimaco and Ligurio have told me that the Judge and the women are coming to church.

MESSER NICIA. *Bona dies*, Father.

FRATE. You're welcome, and may such happiness be yours, Madam, that God will give you a fine boy.

LUCRETIA. God grant it.

FRATE. Of course he'll grant it.

MESSER N. Do I see Ligurio and Doctor Callimaco in the church?

FRATE. Yes, sir.

MESSER N. Beckon to them.

FRATE. Come here.

CALLIMACO. God be with you!

MESSER N. Doctor, let me present you to my wife.

CAL. With pleasure.

MESSER N. Lucretia, this is the man who'll cause us to have a staff to support our old age.

LUCR. I'm delighted to meet him and want him to be our closest friend.

MESSER N. Now bless you. And I want him and Ligurio to come and have dinner with us this noon.

LUCR. Yes, indeed.

MESSER N. And I'm going to give them the key of the room on the ground floor in the loggia, so they can come there when it's convenient, because they don't have women at home and live like animals.

CAL. I accept it, to use it when I like.

FRATE. Am I going to get some money for charity?

MESSER N. Have no fears, domine; it will be sent to you today.

LIGURIO. Doesn't anybody remember Siro?

MESSER N. Let him ask; what I have is his. You, Lucretia, how many grossi are you going to give the Frate for your churching?

LUCR. You give him ten.

MESSER N. Deuce take me!

FRATE. Madam Sostrata, to my eye you've put a new shoot on the old tree.[1]

SOSTRATA. Who wouldn't be happy?

FRATE. Let's all go into the church; there we'll say the usual prayer. Then after the office you can have your dinner when you want to. [*to the audience*] You who're waiting, don't wait any longer for us to come out. The office is long; I'll be staying in the church, and they'll go home by the side door.[2] Good bye.

1. *a new shoot on the old tree: you look younger.*
2. *As at Florence from Santa Croce or Santa Maria del Fiore.*

# CLIZIA

## Dramatis Personae

CLEANDER, NICOMACO'S son
PALAMED, CLEANDER'S friend
NICOMACO, an old man
PIRRO, NICOMACO'S servant in the city
EUSTACE, NICOMACO'S servant on his farm

SOFRONIA, NICOMACO'S wife
DAMON, NICOMACO'S neighbor
DORIA, SOFRONIA'S servant
SOSTRATA, DAMON'S wife
RAYMOND, CLIZIA'S father

## CANZONE

How happy is the day
on which we can bring up old memories
and do them honor,
we now can see, because around us
all the friendly people
in this place have gathered.
We who in woods and forests
spend our lives
have come here too—
I a nymph and we who're shepherds—
and are singing together our loves.

Fair the days and quiet,
happy and beautiful the land
where of our songs the music is heard!
Hence, light-hearted and joyful,
these efforts of yours
we shall accompany with our songs,
with such sweet harmony
as never you have heard before.
And we shall take our leave then—
I a nymph and we who're shepherds—
and shall go back to our old loves.

## PROLOG

If into the world the same men should come back, just as the same events come back, never would a hundred years go by in which we should not find here a second time the very same things done as now.[1]

This is said because long ago in Athens, a splendid and ancient city in Greece, there was a gentleman who, having one son and no other children, by chance took into his house a little girl whom, until she reached the age of seventeen, he brought up very carefully. It then happened that all at once both he and his son fell in love with her. Their rivalry over this caused many strange and unexpected events. When these were settled, the son took her as his wife and for a long time lived with her very happily.

What would you say if, only a few years ago, this same thing happened in Florence? And our author, wishing to put one of these stories on the stage for you, has chosen the Florentine, thinking you would get more pleasure from it than from the other. For Athens has been destroyed; the streets, the public squares, the build-ings there cannot be recognized. Then, too, those citizens spoke Greek, and you do not understand that language. So take the event that happened in Florence, and do not expect to recognize the family or the people because, to avoid censure, the author has changed the real names to fictitious ones.

Before the comedy begins, he wants you to see the actors, so you will identify them better when they speak. [*to the actors*] Come out, all of you, so the people can see you. [*to the audience*] Here they are. Do you see how pleasantly they come along? [*to the actors*] Get yourselves into line there, one close to the other. [*to the audience*] Now look. This first one is Nicomaco, an old man overcome with love. By his side is Cleander, his son and rival. The next is named Palamed, Cleander's friend. Those two who come after them are Pirro, a servant, and Eustace, a foreman, each of whom wants to be husband to the lady-love of his master. That woman who comes next is Sofronia, the wife of Nicomaco. After her is Doria, her servant. Of the two remaining, one is Damon, the other is Sostrata, his wife. There is also another actor who, since he has still got to

1. *Cf.* DISCOURSES *3. 43.*

come from Naples,[2] will not show himself to you. I believe this is sufficient and you have looked at them enough. [*to the actors*] The people dismiss you; go in again. [*to the audience*] This story is called *Clizia*, because that is the name of the girl they are going to fight over. Do not expect to see her, because Sofronia, who has brought her up, does not, for modesty's sake, want her to come on the stage. Hence, if there is anybody here who wants to ogle her, he will have to be patient.

It remains for me to tell you that the author of this comedy is a man of great refinement, and he would take it badly if you should think, as you see it acted, that there is anything immodest in it. He does not believe there is. Yet if it should seem so to you, he excuses himself as follows. Comedies exist to benefit and to please the audience. It is certainly very helpful for anyone, and especially for young men, to observe an old man's avarice, a lover's madness, a servant's tricks, a parasite's gluttony, a poor man's distress, a rich man's ambition, a harlot's flatteries, all men's unreliability. Comedies are full of instances of these, and all these things can with the utmost propriety be put on the stage. But if comedies are to give pleasure, they must incite the audience to laughter, which cannot be done if they keep their language serious and solemn, for the words that cause laughter are either stupid, or biting, or amorous. It is necessary, therefore, to put on the stage persons who are stupid, or sarcastic, or in love, and for this reason comedies that are full of these three types of speech are full of laughter; those that lack them do not find anybody to laugh as he watches.

Since, then, our author wishes to give pleasure and in some places to make his audience laugh, and since he has not brought into his comedy stupid persons, and since he has abstained from sarcasm, he has been obliged to turn to persons in love and to the events that happen in love. If in this play anything immodest is said, it will be said in such a way that the ladies here can listen to it without blushing. Be so kind, then, as to give us a favorable hearing, and if you satisfy us by listening, we shall endeavor to satisfy you by acting.

2. *Machiavelli is poking fun at those who demand verisimilitude in the theatre. Raymond arrives in Florence in the fifth act, so cannot be present at the beginning.*

## I.1

### PALAMED, CLEANDER

PALAMED. Are you going out so early?

CLEANDER. Where are you coming from so early?

PAL. From attending to some business of mine.

CLE. And I wish to do some myself or, to put it better, to try to do some, for I don't feel at all sure I'll really do it.

PAL. Is it something that can be told?

CLE. I don't know. But I do know it's something hard to do.

PAL. Well, then, I'd better go away, because I see it annoys you to have anybody with you. And for this reason I've been keeping out of your way, because I've been finding you unfriendly and crotchety.

CLE. Crotchety? No. But in love? Yes.

PAL. You don't say. You're setting my cap straight on my head.[1]

CLE. My dear Palamed, you don't know half the masses.[2] I've been living in despair and now I live that way more than ever.

PAL. How's that?

CLE. What I've kept from you in the past I'm going to tell you now, since I'm brought to such a state that I need help from everybody.

PAL. If I wasn't willing to stay in your company before, I'm less willing now, because I've heard again and again that one ought to run away from three sorts of men: singers, old men, and lovers. For if you're with a singer and tell him some affair of yours, when you think he's listening to you, he lets out *ut, re, mi, fa, sol, la,* and gurgles a ballad in his throat. If you're with an old man, he sticks his head into every church he comes to and goes to all the altars to mumble a paternoster. But the lover's worse than both of these, because it's not enough that if you speak to him he's planting a vine,[3] for he fills your ears with complaints and with such a lot of his troubles that you're obliged to feel pity for him. For if he has to do with a cheating whore, either she wrongs him terribly or she's driven him out of her house; there's always some sort of thing to tell you. If he loves a respectable woman, a thousand envies, a thousand jealousies, a thousand hates upset him; he never lacks reason for lamenting. So, my

1. *setting my cap straight: making clear what puzzled me.*
2. *You haven't heard anything yet.*
3. *Woolgathering.*

dear Cleander, I'll stay with you as long as you need me; apart from that I'll run away from your sorrows.

CLE. I've kept these feelings of mine hidden up to now for those very reasons, so I'd not be avoided as crotchety or made game of as a laughingstock, because I know that under a show of kindness many get you to talk, and then snicker behind your back. But since Fortune has now brought me to a point where I believe there's little I can do, I'm going to talk with you about it, partly to relieve myself, and partly so that you'll help me if I need you.

PAL. I'm ready, when you want me, to listen to everything, and, besides, when I can aid you, I won't avoid troubles or dangers.

CLE. I'm sure of it. I believe you know about that girl we've brought up in our house.

PAL. I've seen her. Where did she come from?

CLE. I'll tell you. Twelve years ago, in 1494, when King Charles went through Florence, as he was going with his big army on his campaign against the Kingdom, there was quartered in our house a gentleman of Monsieur de Foix's regiment, named Beltramo of Gascony. My father treated him with respect, and, because he was a man of character, he in turn treated our family with respect and deference; and though many hated the French they had in their houses, my father and that man formed a very close friendship.

PAL. You had much better luck than the rest, for those who were put in our house did us all sorts of damage.

CLE. I believe it, but it didn't happen that way to us. This Beltramo went off with his king to Naples. And, as you know, when King Charles had conquered that kingdom, he was forced to leave, be-cause the Pope, the Emperor, the Venetians, and the Duke of Milan united against him. So, leaving part of his soldiers in Naples, he came toward Tuscany with the rest; and on reaching Siena, since he heard that the League had a very large force on the Taro to assail him as he came down from the mountains, he decided he oughtn't to lose time in Tuscany; for that reason he went into Lombardy not through Florence but by way of Pisa and Pontremoli. Beltramo heard the rumor about enemies and feared that, as really happened, the French would have to fight a battle with them. And since he had as part of the spoil he took at Naples this girl, who then must have been about five years old, pretty and winning, he decided to get her out of danger. So by one of his servants he sent her to my father, begging that he would do him the favor of keeping her until at some more convenient time he could send for her. He sent no word whether she was of high or low birth; he merely indicated that she was called Clizia. My father and my mother, because I was the only child they had, at once fell in love with her . . .

PAL. Aren't you the one who's in love with her?

CLE. (Let me go on.) and so they treated her like their own dear daughter. I, who then was ten years old, played with her, as children do, and developed a prodigious love for her, which kept on increasing with the years, so that when she reached the age of twelve, my father and my mother kept their eyes on my hands[4] in such a way that if I merely spoke to her the house was turned upside down. This strict-ness (because one always wants most what one can have least of) doubled my love; and it has given and is now giving me such distress that I'm more wretched than if I were in Hell.

PAL. Beltramo never sent for her?

CLE. He was never heard of again; we feel sure he was killed in the battle of the Taro.

PAL. That must have been it. But tell me, what are you going to do? What's your idea? Do you want to marry her, or do you want her for your mistress? What hinders you? she's in the house with you. Can it be that you've no way of dealing with it?

CLE. I've got to tell you some other things I'm ashamed of, because I want you to know everything.

PAL. Go ahead.

CLE. "I want to laugh," she said, "and I suffer."[5] My father is also in love with her.

PAL. Nicomaco?

CLE. Yes, Nicomaco.

PAL. For the love of God!

CLE. For the love of God and the Saints!

PAL. Oh, this is the strangest thing I ever heard of. Nothing is being ruined by it—except a family! How do you live together? What do you do? What do you plan to do? Your mother knows about it?

CLE. My mother knows, the maids know, the servants know; our situation is a mess.

4. *As though to watch one suspected of intending to steal. Cf.* ORLANDO FURIOSO, *3. 77.*
5. *Seemingly proverbial for something serious with a comic aspect.*

PAL. Tell me now; how far has the thing gone?

CLE. I'll tell you. My father, even if he weren't in love with her himself, would never give her to me as my wife, because he's stingy and she has no dowry. He's also afraid she's of humble birth. I, for my part, would take her as wife, as mistress, or in any way I could get her. But there's no point in talking about this now. I'll merely tell you the state we're in.

PAL. I wish you would.

CLE. As soon as my father fell in love with her, which must have been about a year ago, and wanted to satisfy this desire, which simply gives him fits, he decided there was no help for him except to marry her to somebody who then would share her with him, because to try to get her before she was married seemed to him something wicked and repulsive. And not knowing where to turn, he's selected as most reliable for this affair our servant Pirro; and he worked at this dream of his so secretly that he was within a hair's breadth of putting it through before anybody found out about it. But Sofronia my mother, who for some time had realized he was in love, discovered this trick and, driven by jealousy and anger, is working as hard as she can to spoil it. She's not been able to do any better than put another suitor in the field and find fault with the first; so she says she intends to give her to Eustace, the foreman on our farm. And though Nicomaco has more authority, nevertheless my mother's shrewdness and the help of the rest of us, which we give her without much exposing ourselves, have kept the affair hanging many weeks. All the same, Nicomaco presses us hard and has determined, in spite of sea and wind, to have this wedding today; he plans that Pirro marry her this evening, and he's rented that little house next to ours where Damon lives; he says he intends to buy it for him, furnish it with household goods, open a shop for him, and make him rich.

PAL. Does it matter to you if Eustace gets her rather than Pirro?

CLE. What's that? Does it matter to me? This Pirro's the worst rascal in Florence. It matters to me because, besides having made this bargain about her with my father, he's a man who's always hated me, so I should prefer to have the Devil from Hell get her. I wrote yesterday to our foreman to come to Florence. I can't imagine why he didn't come last evening. I'm going to stay here to see if I see him coming. What are you going to do?

PAL. I'll go and attend to my affairs.

CLE. Go along; good luck.
PAL. Good bye. Keep on the watch the best you can, and if you want any help, speak up.

## I.2

### CLEANDER *alone*

Certainly the man who said that the lover and the soldier are alike told the truth. The general wants his soldiers to be young; women don't want their lovers to be old. It's a repulsive thing to see an old man a soldier; it's most repulsive to see him in love. Soldiers fear their commander's anger; lovers fear no less that of their ladies. Soldiers sleep on the ground out of doors; lovers on the wall-ledges.[1] Soldiers pursue their enemies to the death; lovers, their rivals. Soldiers on the darkest nights in the dead of winter go through the mud, exposed to rain and wind, to carry out some undertaking that will bring them victory; lovers attempt in similar ways and with similar and greater sufferings to gain those they love. Equally in war and in love, secrecy is needed, and fidelity and courage. The dangers are alike, and most of the time the results are alike. The soldier dies in a ditch and the lover dies in despair.[2] So I'm afraid that's what'll happen to me. And I have the woman in the house with me, see her when I wish to, always eat with her!—which I believe is my greatest sorrow, because the nearer a man is to his wish, the more he wishes it, and if he doesn't have it, the more sorrow he feels. Now I must think about upsetting this marriage; after that new happenings will bring me new plans and new chances. Can it be that Eustace isn't coming from the farm? And I wrote to him to be here last evening. Oh, there I see him coming around that corner. Eustace, oh, Eustace.

1. *Extending around the base of a building and giving room for a lover to spend a vigil under his mistress's window.*
2. *From Ovid,* AMORES *1. 9. 1–20.*

## I.3

### EUSTACE, CLEANDER

EUSTACE. Who's calling me? Oh, Cleander.
CLEANDER. Why've you been so slow in coming?

Eus. I did come yesterday evening but haven't shown myself be⁄ cause, a little before I got your letter, I got one from Nicomaco that laid on me a mountain of things to do; and for that reason I didn't want to run into him unless I saw you first.

CLE. You've done right. I sent for you because Nicomaco is hur⁄ rying on this marriage with Pirro. You know my mother doesn't like it, because, if we're going to make some man of ours happy with this girl, she wants her to be given to the one who deserves her most; and truly your habits are quite different from Pirro's; between you and me, he's a rascal.

Eus. Thank you. For a fact, I've had no notion of marrying, but since you and the mistress want it, I want it too. It's also true that I don't want to make Nicomaco my enemy, because, after all, he's the boss.

CLE. Don't be afraid, because my mother and I aren't going to fail you and'll get you out of every danger. I wish very much you'd slick up a bit. You're wearing this cloak that's falling off your back; your cap's dusty; you need a shave. Go to the barber, wash your face, brush your clothes, so Clizia can't refuse you for being a hog.

Eus. I'm not very likely to bleach out.[1]

CLE. Go, do what I tell you to, and then go into that church near us and wait for me there. I'll go into the house and see what the old man's thinking of.

1. *He is tanned from his life on the farm.*

## CANZONE

He who makes no test, oh Love,
of your great power,
must hope in vain ever to have true faith
in Heaven's highest worth.
He does not know how at the same time
one can live and die,
how one can search for ill and run away from good,
how one can love oneself less than some other,
how often the heart is frozen and melted by fear and hope;
he does not know how men and gods in equal measure
dread the weapons with which you're armed.

## II.1

### NICOMACO *alone*

For God's sake, what's wrong with my eyes this morning? There seem to be some flashes in them that keep me from seeing light; and yesterday I could have seen the hair in an egg.[1] Have I drunk too much? Perhaps I have. Oh God! this old age brings with it all sorts of horrid defects. But I'm not yet so old that I can't break a lance with Clizia.[2] Can it be, though, that I've fallen in love like this? And what's worse, my wife's aware of it, and she guesses why I want to give this girl to Pirro. Altogether, my furrow doesn't run straight. Still I must try to win the match. Pirro! oh Pirro! come down; come outside.

1. Could have seen anything, however small. *Proverbial.*
2. See 4. 4 note, below.

## II.2

### PIRRO, NICOMACO

PIRRO. Here I am.
NICOMACO. Pirro, I want you to get married this evening, no matter what.
PIR. I'll get married now.
NIC. Hold up a bit. One thing at a time, as Mirra said.[1] Also we've got to do things in such a way that the house won't be turned upside down. You see, my wife doesn't like it; Eustace wants her too; I'm sure Cleander favors him; God and the Devil have turned against us. But you just hold right to it that you want her. Don't be afraid, for I'll be strong enough for all of them; if worst comes to worst, I'll give her to you in spite of them; and if anybody wants to grumble, let him grumble.
PIR. For God's sake, tell me what you want me to do.
NIC. I don't want you to leave this spot, so that if I need you, you'll be on hand.
PIR. I'll stay here. But I've forgotten to tell you something.
NIC. What is it?

1. *Proverbial.*

PIR. Eustace is in Florence.

NIC. What! in Florence? Who told you so?

PIR. Ser Ambrogio, our neighbor at the farm. He told me that he came through the gate with him yesterday evening.

NIC. What! yesterday evening? Where was he last night?

PIR. Who knows?

NIC. Let's hope it's all right. Go on, do what I've told you to. [PIRRO *goes.*] Sofronia's sent for Eustace, and that rascal's paid more attention to her letters than to mine, and I wrote him to do a thou-sand things that'll ruin me if they aren't done. By Heaven, I'll pay him for this. At least I wish I knew where he is and what he's doing. But here's Sofronia, coming out of the house.

## II.3

### SOFRONIA, NICOMACO

SOFRONIA [*aside*]. I've shut Clizia and Doria into their room. I have to protect that poor girl from my son, my husband, my servants; all of them have laid siege to her.

NICOMACO. Where are you going?

SOF. To mass.

NIC. And in Carnival time! Imagine what you'll be doing in Lent.

SOF. I believe one ought to do what's right at any time, and it pleases Heaven the more to do it in times when the rest are doing what's bad. But as to our doing what's right, it's my notion that we're working on the wrong side.

NIC. What's that? What do you want us to do?

SOF. We shouldn't think about nonsense. And since we have in our house a girl who's very good and pretty, whom we've brought up with a lot of trouble, we should take care that we don't throw her away now, so that even though earlier everybody praised us, now everybody will blame us, since we'll be giving her to a guzzler, with no brains, who doesn't know how to do anything except a little shaving, that a fly couldn't live on.

NIC. My Sofronia, you're wrong. He's a young man of good ap-pearance, and if he doesn't know, he can learn, and he's fond of her; those are three good points in a husband: youth, beauty, and love.

It seems to me we can't do better, and decisions on such things aren't found at every door. If he has no property, you know that property comes and goes; and he's one of those who're likely to make it come, and I'll not forsake him, for to tell you the truth, I'm thinking about buying for him that house I've taken on lease from Damon our neighbor, and furnishing it with household goods; and then, even though it may cost me four hundred florins to put him—

SOF. Ha, ha, ha.

NIC. What are you laughing at?

SOF. Who wouldn't laugh? Where are you planning to put him?

NIC. Well, what do you mean? —to put him into a shop, I'm not going to consider the expense.

SOF. Are you really intending to take from your son, with this wild plan, more than is right, and to give to this fellow more than he deserves? I don't know what to say; I suspect there's something else underneath.

NIC. What do you think there is?

SOF. If there were anybody who didn't know it, I'd tell him about it, but because you know it, I'll not tell you.

NIC. What do I know?

SOF. We won't bother about that. What induces you to give her to that fellow? With this dowry or a smaller one, couldn't we marry her better?

NIC. Yes, I'm sure of it. All the same, I'm moved by the love I feel for both of them, for, since I've brought them both up, I'm glad to help both of them at once.

SOF. If that affects you, didn't you also bring up Eustace, your foreman?

NIC. Yes, I did. But do you expect me to make her the wife of that fellow, who has no breeding and has always been on the farm with the cattle and sheep? Oh, if we should give her to him, she'd die of sorrow.

SOF. And with Pirro she'll die of hunger. Let me remind you that breeding in a man means that he has some capacity, knows how to do something, as Eustace does, who is in the habit of trading, of doing business, of being thrifty, of managing other people's affairs and his own, and is a man who could live on water;[1] you know he has laid up a nice property. Pirro, on the other hand, is never any-

---

1. *Industrious and economical.*

where except in the taverns or gambling; he's a shitwit who would die of hunger in Altopascio.[2]

NIC. Haven't I told you what I'm going to give him?

SOF. Haven't I answered that you'll be throwing it away? It comes to this, Nicomaco: you've spent money in bringing her up, and I've put labor into caring for her, and so, since I've a share in these things, I intend also to see for myself how they'll turn out—or I'll say so many bad things and stir up so much scandal that you'll think you're in a bad way, for I don't know how you can show your face. Go ahead, talk about these things with a mask on![3]

NIC. What's that you say? Are you crazy? Now you make me want to give her to him no matter what. And because I want to, I'm determined he shall marry her this evening, and he's going to marry her, though your eyes spout out water.

SOF. Either he'll marry her or he'll not marry her.

NIC. You can threaten me with chattering; try to keep me from speaking. Perhaps you believe I'm blind and don't recognize the sleight-of-hand tricks you're playing. I knew well enough that mothers wished well to their children, but I didn't believe they wished to lend a hand in their improper actions.

SOF. What's that you say? Improper?

NIC. Oh, don't make me tell. You understand and I understand; both of us know how far off San Biagio's day is.[4] Let's agree, on your honor, because if we keep up this nonsense, we'll be the laughingstock of the town.

SOF. Keep up what nonsense you want to. This girl's not going to be thrown away; before that, I'll turn not merely our house but Florence upside down.

NIC. Sofronia, Sofronia—the one who gave you that name wasn't asleep; you're a soffiona,[5] and you're full of wind.

SOF. In God's name, I want to go to mass. We'll see each other again.

NIC. Listen a bit. Isn't there any way for putting an end to this thing, and not making people think we're crazy?

2. *In Tuscany, about nine miles east of Lucca; here indicating a place where food is easy to raise.*

3. *Concealing something.*

4. *We know what's what.*

5. *A bellows; hence, a person swollen with presumption.*

SOF. Not crazy, but certainly low-down.

NIC. And there are in this city so many men of standing, we have so many relatives, and there are so many good clerics! Let's ask them about this matter we can't agree on, and in this way either you or I'll be found mistaken.

SOF. Do we want to go to advertising our follies?

NIC. If we don't want to choose either friends or relatives, let's choose a priest, and they'll not be advertised, and we can put the thing before him in confession.

SOF. Whom can we go to?

NIC. We can't possibly go to any one else than Frate Timoteo, who's our family confessor and a holy man and already has worked some miracles.

SOF. What miracles?

NIC. What's that? What miracles? Don't you know that through his prayers Madam Lucretia, the wife of Messer Nicia Calfucci,[6] who was sterile, became pregnant.

SOF. A fine miracle, a monk to make a woman pregnant! It would be a miracle if a nun should make her pregnant!

NIC. Won't you ever stop blocking my way with these chatterings?

SOF. I intend to go to mass and I don't intend to turn over my affairs to anybody.

NIC. Go ahead, then, and come back; I'll wait for you at home. [*to himself*] I believe it'll be well not to go very far off, so they can't carry Clizia away somewhere. [*He leaves.*]

6. *These are characters in Machiavelli's* MANDRAGOLA, *but the narrative is not the same. In the* MANDRAGOLA, *Frate Timoteo does not attempt to cause Lucretia's pregnancy.*

## II.4

### SOFRONIA *alone*

Anybody who knew Nicomaco a year ago and who has dealings with him now would have a right to be shocked on seeing the great change in him. For he was always serious, steadfast, cautious. He spent his time as a good man should. He got up early in the morning, heard mass, bought the provisions for the day. Then, if he had business in the public square, in the market, with the magistrates, he attended to it; if he didn't, he either joined with some citizen in serious conversation, or he went into his office at home, where he wrote up his ledger and straightened out his accounts. Then he dined pleasantly with his family, and after he had dined, he talked with his son, advised him, taught him to understand men, and by means of various examples, ancient and modern, showed him how to live. Then he went out. He spent the whole day either in business or in dignified and honorable pastimes. When it was evening, the Ave Maria always found him at home; he sat a little while with us by the fire, if it was winter, then went into his office to go over his affairs. At nine o'clock he had a cheerful supper. This ordering of his life was an example to all the others in the house, and everybody was ashamed not to imitate him. And so things went, orderly and pleasant. But since this infatuation for that girl has got into his head, his affairs are neglected, his farms are going to ruin, his business ventures fail; he's always scolding and doesn't know why; he comes into the house and goes out a thousand times a day without knowing what he's doing; he never comes back at such an hour that he can have dinner and supper on time; if you speak to him, he doesn't answer, or he doesn't answer to the point. The servants, seeing this, make game of him, and his son has given up respecting him; everybody does as he pleases, and, in short, nobody is afraid to do what he himself is seen doing. Hence I'm afraid, if God doesn't furnish us a cure, that this poor house will be ruined. Oh well, I'll go to mass and ask God's help the best I can. I see Eustace and Pirro; they're quarreling. What fine husbands are waiting for Clizia!

## II.5

### PIRRO, EUSTACE

PIRRO. What're you doing in Florence, you scamp?

EUSTACE. I don't have to tell you.

PIR. You're so closely shaved that you look to me like a scrubbed privy.

EUS. You have so little sense that I wonder the boys don't throw stones at you.

PIR. We'll soon see who has more sense, you or I.

EUS. Pray to God that the boss doesn't die; if he should, one of these days you'll be a beggar.

PIR. Have you seen Nicomaco?

EUS. Why do you want to know whether I've seen him or not?

PIR. It means a lot to you to know, because unless he's changed his mind, if you don't go back to the farm of your own accord, he'll have the police carry you there.

EUS. My being in Florence gives you a lot of trouble.

PIR. It'll give others more trouble than it does me.

EUS. And so let others worry about it.

PIR. Still, you'd like to keep a whole skin.¹

EUS. You watch and snicker.

PIR. I'm watching for you to be a fine husband.

EUS. Well now, do you know what I want to say to you? "And still the Duke kept on building walls."² But if she gets you, she'll have climbed on the wall-ledges.³ How much better it would be if Nicomaco would drown her in that well of his! At least the poor thing would die all at once.

PIR. Foh, wretched hayseed, perfumed in the dungheap! [*to the audience*] Do you think he has the right flesh for sleeping beside so delicate a girl?

EUS. She'll have plenty of flesh with you, for if her bitter fate gives her to you, either she'll be a whore in a year or she'll die of hardship. But the first of these will be all right with you, because for a cuckold who'll eat and keep still you're just the man.

PIR. That's all right, every man must sharpen his own tools; we'll see which one Fortune favors. I'm going into the house before I have to crack your skull.

EUS. And I'm going back into the church.

PIR. You'd better not get out of sanctuary.

1. *Literally: the flesh pulls.*

2. *"When somebody tries to persuade us of something we don't want to believe, to get rid of him, and to get that boredom out of our ears, we (Florentines) are in the habit of saying: 'Still the Duke was building a wall'" (Varchi, ERCOLANO 134).*

3. *An annotator suggests "in order to ask alms." What follows suggests "to act as a street-walker."*

## CANZONE

By just so much as love is fair in a youthful heart,
by so much it beseems not one
who has passed the flower of his years.

Love has power befitting the years,
and in early life it is greatly honored
but in late has little worth or none.
So, you aged lovers,
it is best to leave that affair to fiery youths,
who, eager for heavier toil,
can do more generous honor to their lord.

## III.1

### NICOMACO, CLEANDER

NICOMACO. Cleander, oh, Cleander!

CLEANDER. Sir?

NIC. Come down, come down, I say. What are you about in the house all this time? Aren't you ashamed of yourself? You're bringing a bad name on this girl. On carnival days young fellows like you generally amuse themselves seeing the masques or playing football. You're one of these men who can't do anything, and you seem to me neither dead nor alive.

CLE. I don't find pleasure in such things, and they never did please me; I had much rather be alone than with such company, and I'm the gladder to stay in the house when you stay here, so if you want anything, I can do it.

NIC. [*aside*]. Oh, see how he handles it! [*to* CLEANDER] You are a fine son. I don't need to have you close at hand all day; I keep two servants and a foreman so as not to have to call on you.

CLE. Good God! But all the same it isn't that I don't have good intentions in what I do.

NIC. I don't know why you do it. But I do know that your mother is crazy and will ruin this house. It would be better for you to mend matters.

CLE. Either she, or somebody else.

NIC. Who else?

CLE. I don't know.

NIC. It's clear to me that you don't. But what do you say about this affair of Clizia's?

CLE. [*aside*]. See where we land.

NIC. What did you say? Speak up, so I can hear you.

CLE. I say that I don't know what to say about it.

NIC. Doesn't it seem to you that this mother of yours is making a mistake in not wanting Clizia to marry Pirro?

CLE. I don't understand it.

NIC. It's plain to me. You've taken her side; there's something hidden there besides words. Does it seem to you, then, that she would be better with Eustace?

CLE. I don't know and I don't understand.

NIC. What the devil do you understand?

CLE. Not this.

NIC. You've understood, though, how to get Eustace to come to Florence and to hide him so I shouldn't see him, and to set traps for me in order to break off this wedding. But I'll throw you and him into the Stinche;[1] and I'll give her dowry back to Sofronia and send her away; for I intend to be master of my own house, and everybody can uncork his ears to that! I'm going to have this wedding come off this evening. Or if I can't find any other means, I'll set this house afire. I'll wait here for your mother, to see if I can come to terms with her; but if I can't, at least I'm going to keep my dignity, for I don't intend that the goslings shall lead the geese to drink. Go, then, if you're interested in your own good and in the peace of the family, and beg her to do as I wish. You'll find her in church, and I'll wait for you and her in the house here. And if you see that rascal Eustace, tell him to come to me; otherwise he'll never get on in his affairs. [*Exit*]

CLE. I'll go at once.

1. *A prison in Florence.*

### III.2

#### CLEANDER *alone*

Oh how wretched it is to be in love! In what misery I pass my days! I know well enough that a man who loves a girl as beautiful as Clizia has many rivals who cause him no end of pain, but I've never heard of anybody so unlucky as to have his father for a rival. And whereas many young men have some help from their fathers, I find in mine the ground and the cause of my troubles. And though my mother aids me, she does not do it to aid me but to hinder her husband's affair. And for that reason I can't show myself boldly in this business, because she would at once believe that I had made with Eustace the very bargain my father has made with Pirro. And if she should believe that, her conscience would make her let the water run down the hill, and she wouldn't take any more trouble; and I should be entirely done for and should be so grieved by it that I believe I wouldn't live any longer. I see my mother coming out of the church. I want to talk with her and understand her purpose and see what measures she's planning to use against the old man's schemes.

## III.3

### CLEANDER, SOFRONIA

CLEANDER. God be with you, mother.

SOFRONIA. O Cleander, have you just come from our house?

CLE. Yes, mother.

SOF. Have you been there all the time since I left you there?

CLE. I have.

SOF. Where's Nicomaco?

CLE. He's in the house and, in spite of what's happened, hasn't come out.

SOF. Let him be, for God's sake. The glutton thinks one thing about it and the tavern-keeper something else.[1] Has he said anything?

CLE. A mountain of rude things; and it seems to me the Devil's got into him. And he wants to put Eustace and me in the Stinche. As for you, he wants to return your dowry and drive you away. And he threatens, besides, to set the house afire. And he's ordered me to find you and induce you to agree to this marriage; otherwise things won't be pleasant for you.

SOF. What do you say about it?

CLE. I say what you do, for I love Clizia as a sister, and it would cut me to the heart if she fell into Pirro's hands.

SOF. I don't know how you love her. But I do say this to you, that if I believed I was taking her from Nicomaco's hands to put her in yours, I wouldn't trouble myself about it. But I think Eustace'll want her for himself, and you'll forget your love because of your wife (for we're soon going to give you one).

1. *Proverbial: equivalent to the English "He reckons without the host."*

CLE. You're right about it; and therefore I beg you to do everything to keep this wedding from coming off. And if you can't do anything else than give her to Eustace, give her to him. But if it's possible, it'd be better (as I see it) to leave things as they are, because she's still young and it's not getting late for her. It's possible Heaven may let us find her parents, and if they should be noble, they'd not thank you for having married her to a servant or a peasant.

SOF. You're right; I've thought of that myself. Yet the madness of this old man upsets me. But in spite of it, so many things are turning around in my head that I believe some of them will spoil his whole plan. I want to go into the house because I see Nicomaco loitering around the door. You go into the church and tell Eustace to come to the house and not to be afraid of anything.

CLE. All right.

### III.4

#### NICOMACO, SOFRONIA

NICOMACO. I see my wife coming back. I'll try to make a bit of a fool of her, to see if good words help me any. [*to* SOFRONIA] Now, my girl, are you going to keep acting so melancholy when you see your darling? Stay here with me a minute.

SOFRONIA. Let me go.

NIC. Wait, I say.

SOF. I shan't; I think you're drunk.

NIC. I'll catch you.

SOF. Are you crazy?

NIC. Crazy? because I'm so fond of you?

SOF. I don't want you to be so fond of me.

NIC. This can't be.

SOF. You're killing me. Uh, nuisance!

NIC. I wish you'd tell the truth.

SOF. I believe it.

NIC. Oh, look at me a little, my love.

SOF. I am looking at you, and I'm smelling you, too. What a good perfume! My! My! You do please me.

NIC. [*aside*]. Bother! She's noticed it. Damn the rascal that put it on me!

SOF. Where'd you get these perfumes you smell of, you old lunatic?
NIC. A man went along here selling them; I talked with him and some of the odor was left on me.
SOF. [*aside*]. Now he's come to lying; didn't I say so? [*to* NICOMACO] Now aren't you ashamed of what you've been doing for a year back? You're all the time with half a dozen young fellows,[1] you go to the tavern, you're often in the whorehouse and the gambling joint, you spend money recklessly. A fine example you set for your son! Give a wife to these mighty men!
NIC. Oh, wife, don't say all the bad things to me at once; save something for tomorrow. But isn't it right that you should act as I wish rather than I as you wish?
SOF. Yes, in proper things.
NIC. Isn't it proper to marry off a girl?
SOF. Yes, when she's married well.
NIC. Won't she be well off with Pirro?
SOF. No.
NIC. Why?
SOF. For the reasons I've given you at other times.
NIC. I understand these things better than you do. But suppose I should handle Eustace in such a way that he wouldn't want her?
SOF. And suppose I should handle Pirro in such a way that he wouldn't want her either?
NIC. From now on, it's a contest between us, and the one who persuades his man wins.
SOF. It suits me. I'm going into the house to talk with Pirro; and you'll speak with Eustace, whom I see coming out of the church.
NIC. All right.

1. *The Italian reading now favored gives* six, *which may be taken to mean a group; parallels are lacking.*

## III.5

### EUSTACE, NICOMACO

EUSTACE [*to himself*]. Cleander's told me to go into the house and not to be afraid, so I'll pluck up courage and go in.
NICOMACO [*to himself*]. I should like to read the riot act to this rascal, but I can't, since I've got to ask him for favors. [*shouting*] Eustace!

Eus. Oh! Your Honor.

Nic. When did you get to Florence?

Eus. Last night.

Nic. You've waited a long time before letting yourself be seen; where've you been so long?

Eus. I'll tell you. Yesterday morning I began to feel bad. My head ached, I had a swelling in the groin and felt as though I had fever; we're afraid of the plague just now, so I was badly scared. Last night I came to Florence and stayed at the inn; I didn't want to go to your house, for fear I'd harm you or your family if I did have the plague. But thank God, it's all gone away and I'm feeling well.

Nic. [*aside*]. I've got to act as though I believed him. [*to* Eus.] You've done the right thing. Are you entirely over it?

Eus. Yes sir.

Nic. [*aside*]. Not over being a scamp. [*to* Eus.] I'm glad you're here. You know there's a quarrel between my wife and me about giving Clizia a husband. She wants to give her to you, and I want to give her to Pirro.

Eus. Then you like Pirro better than you do me?

Nic. On the contrary, I like you better than him. Listen a bit. What do you want of a wife? You're now thirty-eight years old, and a girl isn't suited to you, and it's likely that after she'd been with you some months, she'd hunt for a younger man than you and you'd be wretched. Then I wouldn't be able to rely on you any longer; you'd lose your job, you'd grow poor, and you and she would go begging.

Eus. In this city a man who has a pretty wife can't be poor. You can be liberal to everybody with fire and with your wife, because the more you give, the more is left for you.

Nic. Then do you wish to marry this girl for the sake of displeasing me?

Eus. No, no, I want to do it to please myself.

Nic. Come on now, go into the house. [*aside*] I was crazy if I thought this bumpkin would give me an answer to suit me. [*to* Eus.] I'll change my tone with you. Get your accounts ready to hand over, and be off where God wills, and make up your mind that you'll be the worst enemy I have, and that I'll do you all the harm I can.

Eus. That doesn't worry me, if only I get Clizia.

Nic. You be hanged!

## III.6

### PIRRO, NICOMACO

PIRRO [to SOFRONIA inside]. Before I'll do what you want, I'll let myself be skinned.

NICOMACO [aside]. The affair is going well. Pirro is keeping his promise. [to PIRRO] What is it? Whom are you fighting with, Pirro?

PIR. I'm fighting now with the one you're always fighting with.

NIC. What does she say; what does she want?

PIR. She's begging me not to take Clizia for my wife.

NIC. What did you tell her?

PIR. That I'd let myself be killed before I'd give her up.

NIC. You said the right thing.

PIR. If I did say the right thing, I'm afraid I did the wrong one, because I've made enemies of your wife, your son, and all the others in the house.

NIC. What does that matter to you? Stand well with Christ, and laugh at the saints.

PIR. Yes, but if you should die, the saints'd give me pretty bad treatment.

NIC. Never fear; I'll make such a provision for you that the saints won't be able to give you much trouble; and if they try it, the magis⁄ trates and the laws'll protect you, if only through your help I get a chance to sleep with Clizia.

PIR. I'm afraid you won't be able to; I see the mistress so angry at you.

NIC. I've decided it'll be a good thing, in order once for all to get out of this mess, to draw lots for who shall have Clizia. My wife won't be able to refuse that.

PIR. But if the lot should go against you?

NIC. I trust in God it won't.

PIR. [aside]. Oh, crazy old man! He thinks God will lend a hand to this wickedness of his. [to NIC.] I believe that if God should worry about such things, Sofronia too might trust in God.

NIC. Let her trust! And even if the lot should go against me, I've thought of a remedy for it.  Go, call her, and tell her to come outside with Eustace.

PIR. Sofronia, you and Eustace come to the master.


### III.7

#### SOFRONIA, EUSTACE, NICOMACO, PIRRO

SOFRONIA. Here I am; what's up now?

NICOMACO. We certainly must handle this matter properly. You see that since these two don't agree, we'll have to agree.

SOF. You're in a very great hurry. What isn't done today'll be done tomorrow.

NIC. I want to do it today.

SOF. Then do it, if you want to.  Here are both the rivals.  But how do you plan to do it?

NIC. I've decided, since we aren't in accord with each other, that it must be turned over to Fortune,—

SOF. What's that?  To Fortune?

NIC. that we'll put their names in one bag, and in another Clizia's name and a blank slip, and that first the name of one of them'll be drawn, and the one to whom Clizia's name goes shall have her, and the other must have patience.  What do you think?  Won't you answer?

SOF. Go ahead, I'm willing.

EUSTACE. Watch what you do.

SOF. I am watching, and I know what I'm doing.  Go into the house, write the slips, and bring two bags, because I want to get out of this anxiety, or I'll get into worse.

EUS. Just as you say.

NIC. In this way we'll all agree.  Pray to God, Pirro, for yourself.

PIRRO. For you.

NIC. You're right in saying "for me."  It'll be a great consolation to me for you to get her.

EUS. Here are the bags and the lots.

NIC. Give them here.  What does this one say?  *Clizia.*  And this other one?  It's blank.  That's right.  Put 'em in this bag here.  What does this one say?  *Eustace.*  And this other?  *Pirro.*  Take 'em and put 'em in this other.  Shut 'em up.  Keep your eyes on 'em, Pirro, so nothing can happen to us under a hood;[1] there's somebody here who knows how to play swindling tricks.

SOF. Suspicious men aren't good.[2]

NIC. These are words. You know that the only one deceived is the one who's trusting. Whom do we want to draw?

SOF. Anybody you like.

NIC. Come here, boy.

SOF. It's necessary for him to be a virgin.

NIC. Virgin or not, I haven't looked into the matter.[3] Draw a slip from this bag, after I've said some prayers: 'O Saint Appolonia,[4] I pray you and all the saints and holy protectors of marriage that you grant Clizia such grace that out of this bag will come the slip of the man we prefer.' Draw, in God's name. Give it here. Oh, it has killed me! Eustace!

SOF. What is it? O God, bring about this miracle, so this man will lose hope.

NIC. Draw from the other one. Give it here. Blank. Oh, I'm alive again—we've won. Pirro, may it be a joy to you! Eustace has fallen dead. Sofronia, since God has decided that Clizia should be Pirro's, you must decide it too.

SOF. I do.

NIC. Prepare for the wedding.

SOF. You're in a big hurry; can't we wait until tomorrow?

NIC. No, no, no! Don't you hear me say No? What? Do you want to think up some trick?

SOF. Are we going to carry on the affair like heathens? Isn't she going to hear the wedding mass?

NIC. The bean mass![5] She can hear it some other day. Don't you know that absolution is given to one who confesses late as well as to one who confesses early?

SOF. I fear she has what is ordinary for women.[6]

1. As though under the shelter of a cowl, like that of a friar.
2. A Tuscan proverb.
3. Literally: I haven't held my hands there.
4. Saint Appolonia, patron of the toothless, is suitably invoked by the toothless Nicomaco (act 4, scene 2), as a comic actor would emphasize for his audience.
5. Probably merely an expression of contempt, though what follows suggests that the bean is here a male sexual symbol. Cf. Mauro, CAPITOLI DELLA FAVA.
6. The menses.

NIC. Let her apply the extraordinary of men.[7] I intend to have the wedding this evening. It seems you don't understand me.

SOF. Let him marry her and be the worse for it! Let's go into the house, and you'll have to make the announcement to this poor girl, and it'll not be hose-news.[8]

NIC. It'll be pants-news.[9] Let's go inside.

SOF. [*to herself*]. I'm not going now, because I want to find Cleander, and have him think up some way to deal with this bad business.

## CANZONE

He who once angers a woman,
rightly or wrongly, is a fool if he believes
to find in her, through prayers or laments, any mercy.
　　When she enters upon this mortal life,
along with her soul she brings
pride, anger, and disregard of pardon.
Deceit and cruelty escort her
and give to her such aid
that in every undertaking she gains her wish;
and if anger harsh and wicked
moves her, or jealousy, she labors and watches;
and her strength mortal strength surpasses.

## IV.1

### CLEANDER, EUSTACE

CLEANDER. How can my mother have been so little on the watch as to turn herself over to chance in this way, about a thing on which the honor of our house entirely depends?

EUSTACE. It's as I've told you.

CLE. How unlucky I am! How unhappy I am! See how I met exactly the person to delay me so long that, without my knowledge, the marriage has been decided on, the time for the ceremony set, and everything has gone to the old man's wish. O Fortune! because you're

7. *Apparently the penis.*
8. *Hose were a suitable present for a bringer of good news.*
9. *In the original, there is a play on* calze *(hose) and* calzoni *(pants).*

a woman, you've always had the habit of befriending young men; but this time you've befriended the old men. Why aren't you ashamed of arranging that such a delicate face will be beslavered by such a rank mouth, such delicate flesh touched by such trembling hands, by such frowzy and stinking limbs? For not Pirro but Nico-maco (as I believe) will have her. You couldn't have done me a greater injury, since with this blow you've taken from me at once my sweetheart and my money; for Nicomaco, if this love lasts, is going to leave more of his property to Pirro than to me. It seems a thou-sand years until I can see my mother, to pour out my sorrow, and lament with her about this decision.

Eus. Take comfort, Cleander; it struck me she went into the house grinning, so I believe you can feel sure the old man isn't going to gather this pear as neatly as he supposes. But look; he and Pirro are coming out, and they're both in good spirits.

Cle. Go into the house, Eustace. I'll stand aside with the hope of learning some of their schemes that may be to my advantage.

Eus. I'll go at once.

## IV.2

### NICOMACO, PIRRO, CLEANDER

NICOMACO. Oh, how well it's gone! Did you see how melan-choly the gang is, how hopeless my wife is? All those things add to my happiness, but I shall be still happier when I hold Clizia in my arms; when I touch her, kiss her, and squeeze her. Oh, happy night, shall I ever see you? And this obligation I have to you, I'm going to pay you double for.

CLEANDER [*aside*]. Oh crazy old man!

PIRRO. I believe it. But I don't believe you can do anything at all this evening; I don't see any chance for it.

NIC. Why not? I'll tell you how I've planned to manage the affair.

PIR. I'd like to know.

CLE. [*aside*]. And I much more, because I may be able to hear something that'll upset other people's affairs and straighten out my own again.

NIC. You know Damon our neighbor, from whom I've taken the house on lease for your benefit?

PIR. Yes, I know him.

NIC. I plan that you take her this evening to that house, even though he lives there and has not cleared it out; for I'll say I want you to take her to the house where she's going to live.

PIR. What then?

CLE. [*aside*]. Prick up your ears, Cleander.

NIC. I've directed my wife to ask Sostrata, Damon's wife, to help her manage this wedding and get the bride ready, and I'll tell Damon that you beg to have your wife go there. When this has been done, and we've had supper, this woman will take the bride to Damon's house and put her with you in the bedroom and in bed. And I'll say that I'm going to stay with Damon at the inn, and Sostrata'll be with Sofronia here in this house. You, when you're left alone in the chamber, will put out the light and loiter about the bedroom, acting as though you're undressing. Meanwhile I'll come on tiptoe into the bedroom and undress and get into bed with Clizia. You can easily lie on the truckle bed. In the morning before day I'll get out of bed, as though I wished to urinate, and put on my clothes, and you'll get into the bed.

CLE. [*aside*]. Oh, old rascal! What good luck that I've learned this plan of yours! What a misfortune for you that I've learned it!

PIR. It seems to me you've planned this affair very well. But you'll need to fortify yourself in such a way that you'll seem young, because I'm afraid your old age will be found out in the dark.

CLE. [*aside*]. What I've heard is enough for me; I'm going to tell my mother. [*exit*]

NIC. I've thought of everything, and I intend, to tell you the truth, to have supper with Damon, and I've planned a supper as I want it. First I'll take a dose of an electuary called satyrion.[1]

PIR. What a strange name that is!

NIC. It has stranger effects, for it is an electuary that, for this business, would make a man ninety years old turn young again, not merely one who's seventy, as I am. When I have taken this electuary, I shall sup on a few things, but all of them full of nourishment. First, a salad of cooked onions, then a mixture of beans and spices.

PIR. What do they do?

NIC. What do they do? These onions, beans, and spices, because they are hot and windy, would make a Genoese carrack make sail.

1. *An aphrodisiac.*

In addition to these things, I'll have a big pigeon roasted, so under-done it'll bleed a little.

PIR. Look out that you don't ruin your stomach, because that'll have to be chewed for you, or you'll have to swallow it whole. I don't see that you have very many or very strong teeth in your mouth.

NIC. I've no fears about that because, though I haven't many teeth, my gums are as strong as steel.

PIR. I'm thinking that when you've gone and I've got into the bed, I'll be able to get on without touching her, for I have a vision of finding that poor girl broken in pieces.

NIC. Let it be enough for you that I'll have done your office and that of a comrade.

PIR. I thank God for giving me a wife of such a sort that I shan't have to take any trouble either to get her with child or to pay her expenses.

NIC. Go into the house, hurry on the wedding, and I'll talk a bit with Damon, for I see him coming out of his house.

PIR. I'll set about it.


## IV.3

### NICOMACO, DAMON

NICOMACO. The time has come, Damon, when you can show me whether you love me. You must clear out of your house and not leave your wife or anybody else there, because I wish to run this affair as I've told you.

DAMON. I'm ready to do all that, if only I can please you.

NIC. I've told my wife to ask your Sostrata to come and help her get ready for the wedding. See to it that she comes as soon as she's called, and especially that your servant comes with her.

DAM. Everything's arranged. Send for her when you like.

NIC. I'm going down to the druggist's to attend to something, and'll be back at once. You wait here until my wife comes out and calls yours. There she comes; be ready. Good bye.

## IV.4

### SOFRONIA, DAMON

SOFRONIA. No wonder my husband urges me to ask Sostrata, Damon's wife, to help me! He's trying to get the house clear so he can tilt[1] to suit himself. There's Damon over there. Oh, mirror of this city and pillar of his precinct, who gives his house over to such a disgraceful and scandalous business! But I'll treat them in such a way that they'll always be ashamed of themselves; and now I'm going to begin making game of this man.

DAMON. I wonder why Sofronia stands still and doesn't come along to ask for my wife. But here she comes. God be with you, Sofronia!

SOF. And you, Damon. Where's your wife?

DAM. She's in the house and ready to come when you call for her, because your husband's asked me for her. Shall I go and call her?

SOF. No, no, she must be busy.

DAM. She isn't busy at all.

SOF. Let her be; I don't wish to trouble her. I'll call her when the time comes.

DAM. Aren't you getting ready for the wedding?

SOF. Yes, we're getting ready.

DAM. Don't you need somebody to help you?

SOF. A world of people has gathered there by now.

DAM. [*aside*]. What shall I do now? I've made a big mistake to help this crazy old man, slavering, watery-eyed, and toothless. He's made me offer my wife to aid this woman, who doesn't want her, in such a way that she'll believe I'm begging a meal, and'll think me a rascal. [*exit*]

SOF. I'm sending this fellow away all puzzled. See how he goes off shrunk into his cloak. Now it's my job to make game of my old man a bit. There he is, coming from the market. I hope to die if he hasn't bought something to make him seem spry, sweet-smelling!

1. *Common with sexual double meaning.* Cf. ORLANDO FURIOSO *35. 76.*

## IV.5

### NICOMACO, SOFRONIA

NICOMACO [to himself]. I have bought the electuary and a certain ointment just suited for rousing up my brigades.¹ When one goes armed to war, one goes with double courage. I see my wife. Oh dear, she has heard me.

SOFRONIA [aside]. Yes, I've heard you, and to your loss and shame, if I live until tomorrow.

NIC. Is everything ready? Have you asked this neighbor of yours to help you?

SOF. I asked her, as you told me to, but this dear friend of yours said I don't know what in her ear, so she answered that she wasn't able to come.

NIC. I don't wonder at it, because you're a little brusque and don't know how to be pleasant with people when you want something from them.

SOF. What do you expect, that I should chuck him under the chin? I'm not in the habit of caressing other women's husbands. Go on, ask her yourself, since you're good at running after other men's wives, and I'll go into the house to attend to the rest.

1. Seemingly a figure meaning physical forces.

## IV.6

### DAMON, NICOMACO

DAMON. I've come to see if this lover's got back from the market-place. But there he is, in front of the door. [to NICOMACO] I've met you right on time.

NICOMACO. And I have you, you no-account man! What have I begged you for? What have I asked from you? You've treated me nicely!

DAM. What's the matter?

NIC. You've sent your wife! You've emptied your house of people, and were so glad to do it! So because of you, I'm dead and undone.

DAM. Go and hang yourself. Didn't you tell me that your wife would ask mine?

Nic. She has asked her, and she didn't want to come.

Dam. Not at all! The offer was made to your wife. She didn't want her to come, and so you get me mocked and then you complain of me. May the Devil carry you away, and the wedding, and everybody.

Nic. In short, do you want her to come?

Dam. Yes, I do—plague take it!—she, and the servant, and the cat, and anyone else who's there. Go along, if you've anything to do. I'll go into the house and have her come at once through the garden.

Nic. Now he's my friend; now things 'll go well. Dear me! Dear me! What's the noise I hear in the house?


## IV.7

### DORIA, NICOMACO

Doria. I've been killed! I've been killed! Run, run, get that knife out of her hand. Run, Sofronia.

Nicomaco. What is it, Doria? what's up?

Dor. I've been killed.

Nic. How've you been killed?

Dor. I've been killed and you finished.

Nic. Tell me what's happened to you.

Dor. I can't because I'm so out of breath. I'm sweating. Give me a little breeze with your cloak.

Nic. Now, tell me what you know, or I'll break your head.

Dor. Oh sir, you're too cruel.

Nic. Tell me what you know, and what the noise in the house is.

Dor. Pirro had given Clizia the ring and gone to see the notary out at the back door. Well, don't you know? Clizia, upset by I can't imagine what craziness, seized a dagger, and with her hair flying loose, completely crazy, shrieked: "Where's Nicomaco? where's Pirro? I'm going to kill 'em." Cleander, Sofronia, all of us, tried to capture her and couldn't. She's posted herself in one corner of her bedroom and shouts that she's going to kill you no matter what; and they're so scared that one runs here and another runs there. Pirro's run into the kitchen and hidden behind the basket of capons. I'm sent here to warn you not to come into the house.

NIC. I'm the most wretched of men. Isn't it possible to get the dagger out of her hand?

DOR. Not yet.

NIC. Whom does she threaten?

DOR. You and Pirro.

NIC. Oh, what a misfortune this is! Now, my child, I beg you to go back into the house, and with good words see if you can get this foolishness out of her head, and have her put down the dagger. And I promise you I'll buy you a pair of slippers and a kerchief. Now go, my dear.

DOR. I'll go, but don't come into the house, unless I call you.

NIC. [aside]. Oh misery! Oh my bad luck! How many things go crosswise to make this night unhappy when I had hoped it would be so happy! [to DORIA] Has she laid down the dagger? Shall I come?

DOR. Not yet; don't come.

NIC. Oh God, what'll happen next? Can I come?

DOR. Yes, but don't go into the room where she is. Don't let her see you. Go into the kitchen with Pirro.

NIC. I'm going.

## IV.8

### DORIA alone

In how many ways we make game of this old man! What a circus it is to see the troubles of this house! The old man and Pirro are trembling in the kitchen; in the diningroom are the people who're getting the supper ready; and in the bedroom are the ladies, Cleander, and the rest of the household, and they have undressed Siro, our servant, and put his clothes on Clizia, and put Clizia's clothes on Siro, and they're going to have Siro act as bride in place of Clizia, and so that the old man and Pirro won't discover this fraud, they've shut them up in the kitchen, with the excuse that Clizia's raging. What a fine laugh! What a fine trick! But here are Nicomaco and Pirro outside.

## IV.9

### NICOMACO, DORIA, PIRRO

NICOMACO. What are you doing there, Doria? Has Clizia quieted down?

DORIA. Yes Sir, and has promised Sofronia that she's going to do what you want her to. It is true, though, that Sofronia thinks it'd be well for you and Pirro not to come into her sight, so her anger won't blaze up again. Later, when she is put in bed, if Pirro can't tame her, it'll be his fault.

NIC. Sofronia's advice is good; so we'll do. Now go into the house, and since everything's cooked, hurry along the supper. Pirro and I'll have supper at Damon's house. And when they've had supper, have her brought out. Hurry, Doria, for the love of God, because nine o'clock has struck already, and it's not good to be all night about these affairs.

DOR. That's right; I'll do it.

NIC. Pirro, stay here; I'm going to drink a while with Damon. Don't go into the house, so that Clizia won't get to raging again, and if anything happens, run and tell me.

PIRRO. Go on, I'll do all you order me to. [*in soliloquy*] Since this master of mine wants me to be without wife and without supper, I'm satisfied. I don't believe that in a year so many things could happen as have happened today, and I'm afraid others'll happen to me, because I've heard around the house some rumblings of laughter that I don't like. But look there; I see a torch showing; the procession must be leaving the house; the bride must be coming. I'm going to run for the old man. [*shouts*] Nicomaco! Oh, Damon! Come downstairs, downstairs. The bride's coming.

## IV.10

### NICOMACO, DAMON, SOFRONIA, SOSTRATA, and SIRO [*dressed like a woman and weeping*]

NICOMACO. Here they are. Go into the house, Pirro, because I think it'd be a good thing if she didn't see you. You, Damon, go ahead of me and speak with those women. There they all are, outside.

SOFRONIA. Oh, poor girl! She keeps weeping. You see she never takes her handkerchief from her eyes.

SOSTRATA. She'll laugh tomorrow. That's the way girls do. Good evening to you, Damon and Nicomaco.

DAMON. Welcome to you. Go upstairs, ladies, and put the girl to bed, and come back down. Meanwhile, Pirro'll get ready too.

SOST. Let's go, for God's sake.

### IV.11

#### NICOMACO, DAMON

NICOMACO. She acts very melancholy. And did you see how tall she is? She must've helped herself out with high heels.

DAMON. She seems taller than usual to me too. Oh Nicomaco! You're really lucky. The affair's gone just as you hoped. Handle yourself well; if you don't, it won't be easy for you to come back again.

NIC. Don't fear. I'm the man for doing the proper thing; since I've eaten that food, I feel myself as strong as a sword. But here are the women coming back.

### IV.12

#### NICOMACO, SOSTRATA, SOFRONIA, DAMON

NICOMACO. Have you put her to bed?

SOSTRATA. Yes, we have.

DAMON. That's good; we'll do the rest. You Sostrata, go and sleep with Sofronia, and Nicomaco'll stay here with me.

SOFRONIA. Let's go, because it seems to them a thousand years before they can get rid of us.

DAM. And it's the same for you. Watch out that you don't do yourselves any harm.

SOST. You watch out yourselves, because you have the weapons. We're unarmed.

DAM. Let's go into the house.

SOF. And we too. [*then, after* NICOMACO *goes in*] Go on there, Nicomaco; you'll strike obstacles, because this woman of yours will be like the pitchers from Santa Maria Impruneta.[1]

---

1. *Pitchers formerly made at Santa Maria Impruneta, near Florence. The spout is so placed*

## CANZONE

Pleasant indeed is the trick
carried on to the dear conclusion that has been dreamed of,
that takes one out of distress
and makes sweet every bitter thing that has been tasted.
Oh restorative splendid and rare!
You show the straight path to wandering souls;
you with your great power
by making others blessed make Love rich;
you conquer, with your sacred counsels alone,
rocks, enchantments, and poisons.

### V.1

#### DORIA *alone*

I never laughed so much before and I'm certain I'll never laugh
so much again; in our house there has been nothing but laughing all
night. Sofronia, Sostrata, Cleander, Eustace, everybody laughs.
And they have spent all night in measuring the time, and they say:
"Now Nicomaco's going into the room, now he's undressing, now
he's lying down by the bride, now he's attacking her, now he's
meeting strong resistance." And while we were thinking about
these things, Siro and Pirro came into the house and made our
laughter double. And what was still finer was to see how Pirro
laughed at Siro, so much that I don't believe anybody, this year, can
have had better fun or more of it. Those ladies have sent me out,
since it's already day, to see what the old man's doing and how he
bears this mishap. But see, he and Damon have come out of the
house. I'm going to step to one side and watch them, to get something else to laugh about.

---

*as to give an ithyphallic suggestion. Cf. the "tunne-dish" of Shakespeare's* MEASURE FOR
MEASURE *3. 2. 176.*

## V.2

### DAMON, NICOMACO, DORIA

DAMON. How've things been all night? how's it gone? You don't say a thing. What's been all this hurly-burly of dressing, opening the door, getting out of bed and getting in again, so that you've never been quiet? I was in bed on the ground floor under you, and haven't been able to sleep at all, so that I was indignant and got up, and now I find you going out all upset. You don't say anything; you seem to me dead. What the devil ails you?

NICOMACO. My brother, I don't know where I can escape, where I can hide, or where I can keep out of sight the shame I've brought on myself. I'm disgraced forever; there's no help for it; never again shall I be able to face my wife, my children, my relatives, my servants. I've struggled to disgrace myself, and my wife has helped me succeed, so I'm done for. And I'm the sorrier that you too share this discredit of mine, because everybody'll know you had a hand in it.

DAM. What happened? Have you broken something?

NIC. What do you suppose I've broken? I wish I'd broken my neck.

DAM. What's happened then? Why don't you tell me?

NIC. Boo, hoo, hoo! I feel so bad I don't think I can tell it.

DAM. Humph, you act like a baby. For God's sake, what is it?

NIC. You know what the plan was; I, following that plan, went into the room and without any noise undressed; and in place of Pirro, who'd laid himself to sleep on the truckle-bed, without there being any light, I lay down beside the bride.

DAM. Very well, what then?

NIC. Boo, hoo, hoo! I drew close to her. In the way of the newly married, I started to put my hands on her breast, and she seized my hand with hers and wouldn't let me. I tried to kiss her, and she with the other hand pushed my face away. I tried to put myself on top of her, and she punched me with her knee in such a way that she's broken a rib. When I saw that force wasn't enough, I turned to prayers, and with soft words and loving ones (yet in a whisper, so that she wouldn't recognize me), I asked her to be kind enough to allow me my pleasures, saying to her: "Now, my dear heart, why do you torture me so? Now, my love, why don't you allow gladly what other women gladly allow to their husbands?" Boo, hoo, hoo!

DAM. Dry your eyes a bit.

NIC. I feel so bad I can't be quiet; I can't help weeping. I kept chattering. She never gave a sign of being willing to speak to me, much less of granting anything further. Now seeing that, I turned to threats and began to say rude things to her, both what I'd do and what I'd say. Well, do you know, she all at once drew up her legs and gave me a couple of such kicks that, if the bed clothes hadn't held me, I'd have bounced into the middle of the floor.

DAM. Can it be?

NIC. Indeed it could be. After doing that, she turned on her face and held herself with her breast down on the bed, in such a way that all the levers in the workshop wouldn't have turned her over. When I saw that force, prayers, and threats did me no good, I gave up hope and turned my back on her, resolved to let her be, thinking that toward morning she might change her mind.

DAM. Oh, how well you did! You should have taken this way at the start; and if she didn't want you, you shouldn't have wanted her.

NIC. Wait a bit; that isn't the end; now we get to the real thing. Being all bewildered in that way, between my grief and the exertion I'd had, I drowsed a little. You know that all at once I felt myself stabbed in the side, and here under the rump five or six cursed hard strokes given me. Half asleep, I hurriedly put my hand there and found something hard and sharp; I was so scared that I jumped out of the bed, remembering that dagger Clizia had taken to stab me with. At this noise Pirro, who was asleep, roused up. I told him— for I was driven on more by fright than by reason—to run for a light, because she had a weapon to kill both of us. Pirro ran, and when he got back with the light, instead of Clizia we saw Siro, my servant, raised up on the bed all naked, and in contempt (boo, hoo, hoo,!) he was making faces at me (boo, hoo, hoo!) and finally the *manichetto*.[1]

DAM. Ha, ha, ha!

NIC. Oh, Damon, you are laughing at me?

DAM. I feel sorry enough about this affair; still it's impossible not to laugh.

DORIA [*aside*]. I'm going to report what I've heard to my mistress, so she can laugh twice as much.

1. *A gesture of contempt. The right arm with closed fist is raised and bent, and the left fist laid on the inside of the elbow, to simulate the ithyphallus.*

NIC. This is my misery, that everybody'll have to laugh about it, and I'll have to weep, and in my presence Pirro and Siro sometimes talked insultingly, sometimes laughed, and then, half-dressed as they were, they went off, and I believe they've gone to find the women, and they'll all laugh. And so everybody laughs, and Nicomaco weeps.

DAM. I know that you know I'm sorry for you and for myself, since for love of you I got into this trap.

NIC. What do you advise me to do? Don't abandon me, for the love of God.

DAM. It seems to me, if something better doesn't come up, that you'll have to give yourself into the hands of your Sofronia, and tell her that from now on she can do as she likes about Clizia and about yourself. She too'll have to think about your honor, because, since you are her husband, you can't be disgraced without her sharing in it. There she is, coming out. Go and speak to her, and meanwhile I'll go to the public square and the market-place to listen, and if I hear anything about this affair, I'll try to cover it up as well as I can.

NIC. I beg you to.

## V.3

### SOFRONIA, NICOMACO

SOFRONIA [to herself]. Doria, my servant, has told me that Nico-maco's come out of the house, and that he's a sight to feel sorry for. I want to speak to him, to see what he says to me about what's just been happening. There he is. [to NICOMACO] Oh Nicomaco!

NICOMACO. What do you want?

SOF. Where are you going so early? Are you coming out of the house without saying a word to the bride? Did you learn how she got on with Pirro last night?

NIC. I don't know.

SOF. Who does know, if you don't? You, who've turned half Florence upside down to bring about this marriage? Now that it's over, you act ignorant about it and dissatisfied.

NIC. Oh, let it go; don't worry me.

SOF. You're the one who worries me, because, though you ought to comfort me, I have to comfort you; and though you ought to provide for them, I have to do it, for you see I'm carrying 'em these eggs.'

NIC. I should think it'd be a good thing for you not to make a joke of me now. Let it be enough that you've done it all this year, and yesterday and last night more than ever.

SOF. I never wanted to make a joke of you; but you're the one who's wanted to do it to all the rest of us, and finally to yourself. Aren't you ashamed to have brought up a girl in your house with such care, and in every way as daughters of the best families are brought up, and then to try to marry her to a rascally and shiftless servant, because he's willing you should lie with her? Did you think you were dealing with blind people, or with those who couldn't upset these shameful plans of yours? I confess that I've managed all those tricks that have been played on you because, if I was to make you come to your senses, there was no other way than to get so many witnesses to your actions that you'd be ashamed, and then shame'd make you do what nothing else could. Now this is the point. If you wish to come back to your duty and be that Nicomaco you were a year ago and before, we'll all return to you, and the matter'll not be known. And if it is known, to err and to do better is common.

NIC. My Sofronia, do what you like; I'm prepared not to go beyond the limits you set, if only the thing doesn't get known.

SOF. If you agree to act like that, everything is settled.

NIC. Where is Clizia?

SOF. As soon as she'd had supper yesterday evening, I sent her off, dressed in Siro's clothes, to a nunnery.

NIC. What does Cleander say?

SOF. He's happy that this marriage is broken off, but he's very sad because he doesn't see how he can have Clizia.

NIC. I now give up to you all responsibility for Cleander's affairs. All the same, if we don't know who she is, I think it isn't right to give her to him.

SOF. I don't either. But we must put off marrying her until some-thing's known about her or until this fancy is out of his head. Meanwhile, the marriage with Pirro must be annulled.

NIC. Manage her as you like. I'm going into the house to rest, for on account of the bad night I've had, I can hardly stand, and also

1. *The customary nourishing breakfast for bride and groom.*

because I see Cleander and Eustace coming out, and I don't want to speak to them. You talk with 'em; tell 'em our decisions, and that it must satisfy 'em that they've won, and they're never to speak to me about this affair.

## V.4

### CLEANDER, SOFRONIA, EUSTACE

CLEANDER. You've heard that the old man has shut himself up in the house; and he must have got pardon from Sofronia for what he's done; he seems very meek. Let's go and learn about the affair from her. Good morning, Mother! What does Nicomaco say?

SOFRONIA. The poor man has entirely lost heart; it seems to him he's disgraced; he's given me a blank check, and in the future wants me to run everything according to my own notions.

EUSTACE. That's good. I'm going to have Clizia!

CLE. Slow up a bit. She isn't a morsel for your palate.

EUS. Oh, this is fine. Now that I thought I'd won, have I lost like Pirro?

SOF. Neither you nor Pirro's going to have her; nor are you, Cleander, because I've decided it'll be that way.

CLE. At least have her come back to the house, so I shan't be deprived of seeing her.

SOF. She'll come back, or she'll not come back, just as I decide. Let's go and put the house in order. And you, Cleander, try to see Damon, because it's a good thing to speak to him about doing what he can to cover up what's happened.

CLE. I'm not satisfied.

SOF. You'll be satisfied later.

## V.5

### CLEANDER alone

When I think my voyage is over, Fortune throws me once more into the midst of the sea, and among the roughest and stormiest waves. First I fought with my father's love; now I fight with my mother's ambition. In the first, I had her as a helper; in the second,

I am alone, so I see less light in the second than I did in the first. I lament my hard lot, since I was born to have nothing good. And I can say that from the time when this girl came into our house, I have known no other happiness than to think about her, and in that my pleasures have been so rare that their days are easily counted. But whom do I see coming toward me? Is it Damon? It is he, and he's in very good spirits. What is it, Damon? What news do you bring? What's the reason for such good spirits?

## V.6

### DAMON, CLEANDER

DAMON. I couldn't have heard better news, nor more lucky, nor that I'd bring more gladly.

CLEANDER. What is it?

DAM. Your Clizia's father has come to the city, and he's named Raymond, and he's a Neapolitan gentleman, and he's very rich, and he's come only to find this daughter of his.

CLE. How do you know?

DAM. I know it because I've talked with him and heard everything, and there's no doubt about it.

CLE. How did it happen? I'm crazy with joy.

DAM. I want you to hear it from him. Call Nicomaco and Sofronia your mother out of the house.

CLE. Sofronia, oh, Nicomaco! Come down to see Damon.

## V.7

### NICOMACO, DAMON, SOFRONIA, RAYMOND, CLEANDER

NICOMACO. Here we are; what's the good news?

DAMON. I say that the father of Clizia, named Raymond, a Neapolitan gentleman, is in Florence to find her; and I've talked with him, and have already persuaded him to marry her to Cleander, if you consent.

NIC. If this is so, I'm quite willing. But where is he?

DAM. At the Crown; and I've told him to come here. There he comes. He's the one with those servants behind him. Let's go to meet him.

NIC. Here we are. God be with you, worthy man!

DAM. Raymond, this is Nicomaco and this is his wife, who've brought up your daughter with such care; and this is their son and will be your son-in-law, if it suits you.

RAYMOND. I'm glad to meet you all. And I thank God he has been so gracious to me that, before I die, I shall see my daughter again, and be able to requite these noble people who have done her honor. As to the marriage, nothing can please me better, so that this friendship of ours which your deserts have begun, will be kept up by the marriage-alliance.

DAM. Let's go inside, where you'll learn from Raymond the whole thing in detail, and get ready for this happy wedding.

SOFRONIA. Let's go. And you, spectators, can go off home, because, without coming out again, we can arrange for the new wedding, which will be female, and not male, like Nicomaco's.

## CANZONE

You who with such attention and quiet,
fair souls, have listened
to a good and humble example,
a wise and noble teacher for our human life,
and through its means understand,
what things should be avoided and what sought for
if you are to rise direct to Heaven,
and under a flimsy veil have seen much more besides
that now would be too long to tell,
we pray that you will retain such profit
as your great courtesy deserves.

# ARTICLES FOR A PLEASURE COMPANY

*[There is an autograph manuscript, but the date is unknown. Like Swift's* RULES FOR POLITE CONVERSATION *and parts of Jonson's* CYNTHIA'S REVELS, *this is a satire on fashionable society.]*

WHEREAS MANY MEN AND WOMEN HAVE BEEN MEETING for a long time to gossip, and whereas it has happened that they have many times done pleasant things and many times disagreeable things, and whereas as yet no way has been found for making the pleasant things grow more pleasant and the disagreeable things less disagree-able, and whereas at times some schemes have been imagined but have had no result, because of lack of diligence by those who have imagined them, it has seemed good to those who have some brains and, in the affairs of men and women, some experience, to organize— that is, so to regulate—such a Company that each one would be able to imagine, and after imagining to do, those things that to men and women, or to any of them, in any way can give delight. There-fore it is decided that the said Company is and intends to be subject to the rules written below, signed and settled by common agreement. They are these, to wit:

No man younger than thirty can be of the said Company, and the women can be of any age.

That the said Company shall have a head—man or woman as it may be—to hold office eight days, and of the men the first head shall be he who has the longer nose, and so in succession, and of the women she who has the smallest feet, and so in succession.[1]

Anyone, either man or woman, who shall not repeat within a day the things done in the said Company, shall be punished in this way: if a woman, her slippers shall be fastened up in a place where everybody can see them, with a notice below them with her name; if a man his hose, wrong side out, shall be fastened up in a place that is conspicuous and seen by everybody.

1. *The nose was supposed to correspond directly and the feet contrarily to the size of the sexual parts.*

They shall always speak badly of each other; and of any strangers who happen there they shall tell all the faults and make them generally known without any hesitation.

No one of the said Company, whether man or woman, is to confess in other times than Holy Week, and anybody who violates this rule shall be obliged, if a woman to carry, and if a man, to be carried by, the head of the Company, in such way as seems good to him. A blind confessor is to be selected, and if he is hard of hearing, so much the better.

No one shall for any reason speak well of the others, and if anybody violates this, he shall be punished as above.

If any man or any woman should seem to himself very beautiful and two witnesses of this can be found, the woman shall be obliged to show her leg bare as far as four fingers above her knee; if he is a man, to make plain to the Company whether he has in his codpiece a handkerchief or something of the sort.

The women shall be obliged to go at least four times a month to the Servi,[2] and also at all times when they are asked to by the Company, under the penalty of twice as often.

When a man or a woman of the said Company begins to tell a thing and the others let him finish it, they shall be condemned to that penalty that shall seem proper to him or her who began the said narrative.

There shall be discussed in the said Company all those matters on which the lesser part of those assembled shall agree; and the fewer votes shall always have the decision.

If to any member of the Company some secret is told by one of his brothers or by anybody else, and within two days he has not made it public, he is to be understood, whether he be a man or a woman, to have incurred the penalty of having always to do everything backwards, without being able in any manner or way, direct or indirect, to free himself.

In the said Company there never should be or can be silence, but the more chattering there is, and the more at the same time, so much more approbation is deserved; he who is the first to stop chattering is to be contemptuously avoided by all the others of the Company until he gives a reason for stopping.

2. *For a reference to the bad character of the brothers at the Church of the Servi* (Santissima Annunziata) *see* MANDRAGOLA *3. 2.*

The members of the Company ought not to and cannot oblige each other in anything, but when they are asked by anybody to carry messages, they ought always to repeat them with the opposite meaning.

Each one shall be obliged to envy the good of the other, and for this reason to do him all the bad turns he can; if he is able to do one and does not, he shall be punished at the pleasure of the ruler.

That each one everywhere and at every time, without any regard, shall be obliged to turn around at any laugh or spitting or other sign, and to answer with the same under penalty of not being able to deny anything that may be asked of him for the entire month.

In order that each one may have his opportunity, it is enacted that each man and each woman shall sleep the one without his wife and the other without her husband, at least fifteen entire days every month, under the penalty that husband and wife shall sleep together two months without intermission.

He or she who speaks most words and least sense will be most honored and held in most esteem.

Both the men and women of the said Company are to go to all the pardonings, feasts and other affairs carried on in the churches, and to all the dinners, luncheons, suppers, comedies, parties and similar chatterings that go on in houses, under pain, if a woman, of being shut up in a house of friars, and if a man, in a nunnery.

It is required that the women spend three-quarters of the time at either the windows or the doors, front or rear as it seems good to them; and the men of the said Company are required to appear before them at least twelve times a day.

That the women of the said Company do not need to have mothers-in-law, and if any of them at this time has one, she is within six months, by using scammony or some such medicines, to get rid of her. This medicine they can also use against husbands who do not pay their debt.

Never shall the women of the said Company wear hoop skirts or anything underneath that may offer obstruction; and all the men are to go without laces,[3] and instead of them use pins, which the women are prohibited to wear, under the penalty of having to look with spectacles at the Giant of the Piazza.[4]

3. *Compare Ruggiero's embarrassment with the laces of his armor in* ORLANDO FURIOSO *10. 115.*

4. *The naked figure of David by Michelangelo, placed in the Piazza della Signoria in 1504.*

That each one, male as well as female, in order to give the place a reputation, is to boast of the things that he does not have and does not do; and whenever he tells the exact truth, through that truth showing either his poverty or some such thing, he shall be punished at the pleasure of the ruler.

That no one is ever to show by external signs the thoughts in his mind; rather the contrary shall be done, and he who best knows how to pretend or to tell lies merits most commendation.

That the greater part of one's time is to be spent in beautifying and cleaning oneself, with the penalty to anybody who violates the rule of never being looked at by the others in the Company.

Whoever in a dream shall repeat anything he has said or done that day shall be held for half an hour with his ass raised, and each one of the Company is to give him a cut with a whip.

Whoever when hearing mass does not often gaze all around, or who puts himself in a place where he cannot be seen by everybody, shall be punished for the sin of lese majesty.

No man or woman, especially one who wishes to have children, shall put a shoe first on the right foot, under penalty of having to go barefoot a month, or as much longer as the prince shall think good.

That nobody in going to sleep shall close both eyes at the same time, but first one and then the other; this is an excellent method for preserving the sight.

That the women in walking shall manage their feet in such a way that it will not be possible by means of them to know whether they are high or low necked.

That nobody shall ever be allowed to blow his nose when he is seen, except in case of necessity.

That each one is bound by the custom of the court to scratch himself when he itches.

That the nails of the feet as well as those of the hands are to be cleaned every four days.

That the women are to be obligated in sitting down always to put something under them in order to seem taller.

That they shall choose for the Company a medical man not more than twenty-four years old, so that he may have strength for fatigues and can surmount labor.

# BELFAGOR: THE DEVIL WHO MARRIED

[*The date is unknown; both early and late ones have been suggested. Though the handwriting of the autograph manuscript might furnish a clue, no one has attempted to use it.*

*According to Bandello (I Novelli 40) Machiavelli had some reputation for the narrating of stories; at least that storyteller speaks of him as a splendid and eloquent speaker of Tuscan, who on a certain occasion was begged to relate one of his pleasing stories. The only independent story that has come down to us is* BELFAGOR, *unprinted until after the author's death.*

*The simple plot is a variation of the old theme later stated by Ben Jonson as* THE DEVIL IS AN ASS. *Akin to Machiavelli's other writings is the satire on aspects of Florentine life—vividly presented—and the picture of Satan as the just and wise ruler of a well-regulated princedom.*]

ONE CAN READ IN THE ANCIENT RECORDS OF FLOREN-tine affairs, just as one can also hear the story told, about a very holy man whose life was praised by everybody who lived in those times; in the ecstasy of his prayers, he learned that as countless numbers of wretched souls who died under God's displeasure went to Hell, all or most of them complained that they were brought to such great misfortune by nothing else than by getting married. By this Minos and Radamanthus and the other judges of Hell were much aston-ished. And though they could not believe that such slanders as those men spoke against the female sex were true, and yet such com-plaints grew greater every day, they gave Pluto a proper report of it all. He resolved to make a full examination of the matter with all the princes of Hell, and then to decide on the method judged best for revealing its falsehood or completely finding out its truth.

Calling them therefore to council, Pluto spoke to this effect:

My dear friends, even though by Heaven's decrees and by de-cision of Fate, entirely beyond repeal, I possess this kingdom, and for it I cannot be under obligation to any judgment, either heavenly or earthly, yet, since it is the highest prudence for those who are most powerful to be most subject to the laws and most to esteem the judgment of others, I have determined, in an affair that might result in some shame to our empire, to get your advice on how I ought to conduct myself. Because, since the souls of all the men who come to our kingdom say that their wives caused it, and since this seems to us impossible, we fear that if we pronounce judgment in accord with this tale, we shall be slandered as too credulous, and if we do not pronounce it, as not severe enough and hardly lovers of justice. And because the first sin is that of light-minded men and the second of unjust ones, and since we wish to escape the reproaches that might result from either one, but have not found a way to do it, we have summoned you that you might aid us with your counsel and be the reason why this kingdom, as in the past it has been without infamy, may continue in the same way in the future.

To each of those princes the matter seemed very significant and of great consequence, but though they all came to the conclusion that it was necessary to find out the truth about it, they were divided on the method. For one advised that they should send one devil, others that they should send several, into the world, so that in the form of a man he could personally learn what was true. Many others supposed that it could be done without so much trouble, since by means of various tortures they could force various souls to reveal it; yet because the greater number advised that somebody be sent, they adopted that opinion. So, finding nobody who would volunteer for this mission, they determined to make their selection by lot. This fell on Belfagor, an archdevil, but earlier, before he fell from Heaven, an archangel. Though he undertook this duty very unwillingly, nevertheless, under the compulsion of Pluto's authority, he consented to carry out all that was decided in the council, and pledged himself to those conditions that were solemnly resolved on among them.

These were that the devil appointed for this business should at once receive a hundred thousand ducats, with which he was to go into the world, and in human form to take a wife and live with her ten years; then, pretending to die, he was to return and as a result of his experience testify to his superiors on the burdens and annoyances of marriage. The council also settled that during the said time he should be subject to all the troubles and evils to which men are subject, and which result in poverty, imprisonment, sickness and all the other misfortunes that men incur, unless he could free himself from them with fraud or with cleverness.

So Belfagor accepted the conditions and the money and came to the world; providing himself abundantly with horses and attendants, he entered Florence very honorably. This city before all others he chose as his home, because it seemed to him most fit to support one who employed his funds in money-lending. Taking the name of Roderigo of Castile, he rented a house in the Street of All Saints,[1] and so that his situation would not be found out, he said that when he was a child he had left Spain and gone to Syria, and in Aleppo had gained all his property; that he had left that place to come to Italy so he could take a wife in regions more civilized and more suited to a well-ordered life and to his own taste. Roderigo was a very handsome man and seemed to be about thirty years old; and in a few days, after he had made evident what great wealth he possessed and had given examples of his kindness and liberality, many noble citizens who had plenty of daughters and little money made proposals to him. Among all these women, Roderigo chose a very beautiful girl named Onesta, daughter of Amerigo Donati, who had three others—along with three grown-up sons—and these daughters were almost ready for marriage. Though this man was of a very important family and greatly respected in Florence, nonetheless, considering his bevy of children and his social position, he was very poor. Roderigo provided a magnificent and spectacular wedding, omitting nothing expected in such festivities. Moreover, since by the rules established for him when he left Hell, he was subject to all human passions, he at once began to take pleasure in the honors and splendors of the world and to set store on being praised by men— something that caused him no little expense.

Besides this, he had not been long married to his Madam Onesta before he fell excessively in love with her; he could not be contented if ever he saw her sad or displeased. Madam Onesta had brought into the house of Roderigo, along with her social position and her beauty, such great pride that Lucifer's was never so great; in fact Roderigo, who had tested both of them, considered that of his wife greater; yet it became far loftier as soon as she realized her husband's love for her, and since she felt she could in every way lord it over him, she gave him orders without any mercy or consideration and did not

1. *Borgo Ognisanti, in the western part of Florence.*

hesitate, when he denied her anything, to sting him with rude and offensive words. This caused Roderigo unimaginable distress. Yet nevertheless his father-in-law, her brothers, her family, the bonds of marriage, and above all, his great love for her, made him patient. I shall pass over the great expense that, in order to satisfy her, he incurred in dressing her in the latest fashions and in satisfying her with the latest designs—which our city, following the habits natural to it, incessantly varies—because he was forced, if he was to remain at peace with her, to help his father-in-law marry off his other daughters, on which he spent a huge sum of money. After that, if he wanted to get on well with her, he had to send one of her brothers into the Levant with woolens, another to the West with silks, and the third to open a goldbeater's shop in Florence. In these affairs he laid out the greater part of his fortune.

Beside this, at Carnival time and on Saint John's day, when all the city was celebrating according to its ancient custom and many noble and rich citizens were getting reputations with splendid banquets, Madam Onesta, so that she would not be inferior to other wives, wanted her Roderigo to outdo all the others in such feasts. He submitted to all these things for the reasons given above; and though they were very expensive, they would not have seemed expensive to him if they had produced tranquillity in his house and if in peace he had been able to wait for the time of his ruin. But the reverse happened; along with unbearable expenses, her arrogant disposition caused him countless difficulties. No servants or workers in his house could endure her even for a very few days, much less for a long time. This caused Roderigo great embarrassment because he could not keep any trusted servant who took a real interest in his affairs; it went so far that even those devils he had brought with him to act as servants chose to go back to Hell and live in the fire rather than stay in the world under her rule.

Since Roderigo, then, was leading this vexatious and unquiet life, and with his unregulated expenses had by now used up all the money he had reserved, he came to living on the hope of the remittances he was waiting for from the West and the East; and since he still had good credit, in order not to be without what he wanted, he borrowed money. Before long, then, so many of his notes were in circulation that they were observed by those engaged in that sort of business on the Exchange. And when his position was already delicate, at the same moment news came from the East and the West that one of Madam Onesta's brothers had gambled away all of Roderigo's money that he had, and that the other, returning on a ship loaded with his goods, entirely uninsured, had been drowned along with them. No sooner did these things become known than Roderigo's creditors held a meeting and, judging that he was bankrupt and yet that they could not act openly against him because the day of payment had not come, decided it would be prudent to watch him so closely that—following word with act—he could not get away secretly.

Roderigo, on the other hand, not seeing any way to better his case and knowing all that the laws of Hell required of him, determined to run away—no matter what. So one morning he mounted his horse and, since he lived near the Prato Gate,[2] went out through it. His departure was no sooner known than his creditors were in an uproar; applying to the magistrates, they set out in pursuit not merely with the police but with a crowd. Roderigo, when the outcry was raised behind him, was not a mile from the city. Hence, seeing that he was in a bad fix, he determined, in order to get away more secretly, to leave the road and try his fortune across the fields. But since he was impeded in doing this by the many ditches that cross the country and kept him from going on horseback, he tried to get away on foot, leaving his horse in the road and moving from field to field, concealed by the vines and canebrakes with which that country is covered. Near Peretola he came to the house of Gianmatteo del Brica, one of Giovanni del Bene's tenants, where by chance he found Gianmatteo, who had come home to feed his cattle. From this man Roderigo asked aid, promising that for saving him from the hands of his enemies, who were pursuing him to shut him up in prison until he died, he would make the farmer rich and would before he went away give such proof that Gianmatteo would believe him. If he did not carry out his promise, he was willing to let Gianmatteo put him in the hands of his enemies. Though Gianmatteo was a farmer, he was a man of resolution. Judging that he could not lose by deciding to save Roderigo, he gave his promise and, hurrying him to a great pile of stable manure he had in front of his house, covered him with reeds and other refuse that he had gathered to burn. Roderigo was

2. *The western gate north of the Arno; see the end-papers.*

scarcely well hidden when his pursuers arrived, but with all the threats they could make to Gianmatteo, they never got out of him that he had seen Roderigo. Hence, going farther on, and hunting for him in vain that day and the next, they returned worn out to Florence.

Then Gianmatteo, when the outcry was over and he had taken Roderigo from his hiding place, asked him to fulfill his promise. To this Roderigo answered: "My brother, I am under a great obliga' tion to you, and I fully intend to satisfy it, and that you may believe I can do so, I shall tell you who I am." Then he told him who he was and the conditions laid upon him when he left Hell and about the wife he took; and besides he told him how he intended to make him rich. In short, it was this: When Gianmatteo heard that any woman was possessed by a spirit, he might be sure that Roderigo was the devil possessing her; and he would never leave her until Gianmatteo came to drive him out. This would give the farmer a chance to ask whatever pay he wanted to from the relatives of the woman. Ending in that way, Roderigo disappeared.

Many days did not pass until it was reported all over Florence that one of Messer Ambruogio Amidei's daughters, whom he had given in marriage to Bonaiuto Tebalducci, was possessed by a de' mon; her relatives did not fail to employ all the remedies that are used in such cases, applying to her San Zanobi's skull and San Giovanni Gualberto's mantle. All these things were made ridiculous by Roderigo. And to make plain to everybody that the disease of the girl was a spirit and not something fanciful, she spoke in Latin and debated philosophical matters and revealed the sins of many; among these she revealed those of a frate who for four years had kept in his cell a woman dressed like a novice. These things made everybody wonder. Meanwhile Messer Ambruogio was very unhappy. Having in vain tried every remedy, he had lost all hope of curing her, when Gianmatteo came to see him and promised health for his daughter if he agreed to give him five hundred florins to buy a farm at Peretola. Messer Ambruogio took his offer. Then Gianmatteo, first having certain masses said and going through some ceremonies to give the affair a good appearance, came close to the ear of the girl and said: "Roderigo, I have come to see you, so you will keep your promise to me." To this Roderigo answered:

I am well pleased. But this is not enough to make you rich.
And for that reason, when I leave here I shall enter into the
daughter of Charles, King of Naples; and I shall never leave
except by your means. He then will see that you get a proper
reward. After that you will give me no more trouble.

And having said this, he left the girl, to the pleasure and wonder of
all Florence.

No long time passed by after that until news of the misfortune
that had come to the daughter of King Charles was spread all over
Italy. Finding no cure, the King, learning about Gianmatteo, sent
to Florence for him. When he got to Naples, after some feigned
ceremonies he cured her. But Roderigo, before he left, said:

You see, Gianmatteo, I have kept my promise to make you rich.
And since I have no further obligation, I am no longer liable
to you for anything. So be so kind as not to bother me any
more, because if up to now I have done you good, in the future
I shall do you harm.

Returning then to Florence very rich (for he had received from
the King above fifty thousand ducats), Gianmatteo planned to enjoy
his riches in peace, not at all expecting that Roderigo would plan to
molest him. But this notion of his was suddenly disturbed, for news
came that a daughter of Louis VII King of France was possessed by
a spirit. This news completely changed Gianmatteo's expectations,
as he reflected on the power of that king and the words Roderigo had
spoken to him. The king, then, finding no cure for his daughter and
learning of Gianmatteo's skill, first simply sent one of his officers to
ask his aid. But since the farmer indicated certain reasons against it,
the king was obliged to request the Signoria to send him. It com⁄
pelled Gianmatteo to obey. So when, completely disconsolate, he
had gone to Paris, he first explained to the king that it was certain
that in the past he had cured some who were possessed with demons,
but that it did not for that reason follow that he knew how or was
able to cure all such, because some of them were of such a rascally
disposition that they feared neither menaces nor incantations nor any
religious ceremony. But all the same he would do what he could,
and if he did not succeed he asked to be excused and pardoned. To
which the King answered in anger that if he did not cure her he
would be hanged. At this Gianmatteo was much distressed, yet,

plucking up his courage, he had the possessed princess come. Getting close to her ear, he humbly asked aid from Roderigo, emphasizing the benefit done him and the great ingratitude he would show by deserting Gianmatteo in such necessity. To which Roderigo answered:

> What! Wretched traitor, do you have the rashness to come before me? Do you suppose I can let you boast of being made rich by my power? I am going to show you and everybody that I know how to give and take away everything as I choose; and before you go away from here I shall certainly get you hanged.

Hence Gianmatteo, not seeing at the time any other resource, determined to try his fortune in another way. So having the possessed princess leave, he said to the King:

> Sire, as I have told you, there are many spirits so malicious that no proper dealings can be carried on with them, and this is one of that sort. Yet I am going to make a final effort; if it succeeds, Your Majesty and I shall have what we want; if it does not succeed, I shall be in your power, and you will have that mercy on me that my innocence deserves. So arrange to have set up in the square of Notre Dame a platform big enough to hold all your barons and all the clergy of this city; have the platform decorated with cloth of silk and of gold; set up in the middle of it an altar, and Sunday morning I want you and the clergy and all your princes and barons, with regal splendor, with gorgeous and rich costumes, to assemble there; after celebrating a solemn mass, have the possessed princess come to the place. Besides this, I need to have ready on one side of the square at least twenty persons with drums, horns, kettledrums, bagpipes, shawms, cymbals and noise-makers of every sort; these men, when I lift my hat, will strike up on their instruments and as they play will come toward the platform. These proceedings, along with certain other secret remedies, I believe will make this spirit go away.

Everything was at once arranged by the King, and when Sunday morning came and the platform was full of dignitaries and the square full of people, after mass was celebrated, the possessed princess was escorted to the platform by two bishops and many lords.

The expulsion of a devil from one possessed.   A wall painting by Taddeo di Bartolo from the Museo Communale—formerly the city hall—of San Gimignano.   Machia-velli visited the town at least twice (Ridolfi, Vita di Machiavelli, p. 148). (Fontenelli photograph)

When Roderigo saw such an assembly of people and such great preparation, he was almost stunned and said to himself:

> What does this vile coward think he can do? Does he believe he can awe me with this splendor? Doesn't he know that I am used to seeing the splendors of Heaven and the furies of Hell? I shall certainly punish him.

And when Gianmatteo came close and begged him to come out, he said:

> Oh, you have a fine idea! What do you think you can accomplish with these preparations of yours? Do you expect through them to escape my power and the wrath of the King? Vile rascal, I shall not fail to get you hanged.

So with one of them repeating his prayers and the other insulting him, Gianmatteo decided he could lose no more time. When he gave the signal with his hat, all those assigned to making noise struck up on their sound-makers, and with noises that rose to the sky came toward the platform. At the noise Roderigo pricked up his ears; not knowing what it could be and feeling greatly astonished, in a complete daze he asked Gianmatteo what it was. Gianmatteo in great excitement replied: "Alas, my Roderigo! That is your wife who is coming to get you." It was wonderful to observe what change of spirit came on Roderigo when he heard the word *wife* spoken. It was so great that, not thinking whether it were possible or reasonable that she was there, without answering further, full of terror he fled, leaving the girl free. He preferred to return to Hell to give an accounting for his deeds rather than again with such great annoyance, anxiety and danger to put his neck under the marriage yoke. Thus Belfagor, returning to Hell, gave assurance about the ills that a wife can bring into a house. And Gianmatteo, who was shrewder than the devil, in complete happiness returned home.

# CARNIVAL SONGS

*[Tommasini (VITA DI MACHIAVELLI 1.113 ff.) assigns three of the Carnival Songs to Machiavelli's youth; the LOVERS AND LADIES WITH-OUT HOPE (No. II) he puts in the middle of his career; he dates the BLESSED SPIRITS (No. III) soon after the election of Giulio de' Medici as Pope (19 November 1523), and the HERMITS (No. IV) in 1524. Ridolfi assigns No. III to the election of Leo X (VITA DI MACHIAVELLI, p. 210).*

*The type was a popular one in Florence; a number appear in the works of Lorenzo the Magnificent. They are avowedly light compositions, depending for much of their comic effect on bawdy double meanings difficult to reproduce in English. Because of this untranslatable quality I have omitted No. V, BY THE MEN' WHO SELL PINE CONES. Though Machiavelli generally conforms to the comic tradition of the carnival song, he sometimes moves toward the serious, as in BY THE BLESSED SPIRITS.*

## I. BY THE DEVILS DRIVEN OUT FROM HEAVEN

1 Once we were—but now no longer are—blessed spirits; because of our pride we all were driven from Heaven; and in this city of yours we have seized the rule, because here we find confusion and sorrow greater than in Hell.

8 And hunger and war and blood and ice and fire little by little we have brought into the world upon each mortal; and in this carnival we come to be with you, because of each ill we have been and will be decreed the beginning.

15 This is Pluto and that is Proserpina placing herself by his side—a woman beautiful above all earthly women. Love conquers all things; hence it conquered him, who never rests in his attempt to make all others do what he has done himself.

22 All pleasures and displeasures of Love by us are begotten, both weeping and laughter and joy and sorrow. All those who are in love should follow our will, and they will be pleased because in doing every evil we take delight.

## II. BY LOVERS AND LADIES WITHOUT HOPE

### [*Lovers*]

1 Listen, O lovers, to our lamentable grief; without hope, timid and filthy, in the deep center of Hell we are ruled by devils, because by such pains we were tormented at the time when we loved these ladies that we gave ourselves to the infernal powers in order to escape our afflictions.

8 Our prayers, our tears, our sobs and sighs were breathed to the winds, because we found them ever desiring our torment. Hence, laying aside those burning thoughts, in our new servitude we now judge that cruelty greater than theirs is not to be found.

### [*Ladies*]

15 However great has been your love, just as great ours too has been, but not having displayed it as you have, for the sake of our honor it has remained unspoken. Not through this is the lover injured, but men who have more fury than patience form in the world so foul an opinion.

22 But because to lose you is for us too great a sorrow, we continue to follow you, with music and songs and soft words calming the spirits, so that, releasing you from the road to Hell, to your friends they will restore you, or of both you and us they will make prey.

### [*Lovers*]

29 No further time for pity is granted; hence on silence we are deter' mined; and he who does not act when he has time, then repents and prays in vain. Because to these with one consent we give ourselves, all your prayers are wholly in vain. That which has pleased cannot displease.

### [*Ladies*]

36 Therefore, ladies, when you have bound some lover to your love, in order not to be wanderers like us, avoid all bashfulness; do not send then to the cursed kingdom, because one who brings damnation on another is to like pain condemned by Heaven.

l. 35 *To give a person what he wishes is not injustice.*

## III. BY THE BLESSED SPIRITS

1　Blessed spirits are we, who from the celestial benches come here to present ourselves on earth, because we see the world in so many afflictions, and for slight causes such cruel war; we come to show him who errs that our Lord is greatly pleased when arms are laid down and continue unused.

10　The pitiable and cruel affliction of miserable mortals, their long distress and suffering without remedy, their lament for countless ills that day and night make them complain, with sobs and distress, with loud voices and sorrowful outcry—each of these asks and beseeches compassion.

19　This to God is not pleasing, and cannot be to one who of humanity has even a touch. Therefore he has sent us to show you how just is his wrath and his anger, since he sees his kingdom—his flock—disappearing little by little, if the new shepherd does not control it.

28　So strong is your desire to ruin the city which once to all the world gave laws that you do not understand that your contests open the road to your enemies. The ruler of Turkey grinds his weapons and seems to be all burning with desire to overrun your pleasant fields.

37　Therefore, lift up your hands against the cruel enemy, relieving your afflicted people; lay down, Christians, this your ancient hatred, and against him turn your arms invincible; otherwise, your accustomed strength will be forbidden to you by Heaven, since in you religious zeal is exhausted.

46　May fear leave you, may enmities and rancors, avarice, pride, and cruelty; in you may the love of just and true honors rise up, and may the world return to that first age. So to you will be open the roads to heaven, leading to the blessed folk, and the flames of virtue will not be extinguished.

## IV. BY THE HERMITS

1　On the high ridges of our Apennines we are brothers and hermits; now we have come here into this city because all the

l. 1 *celestial benches: An echo of Dante,* PARADISO *32. 29, etc.*
l. 27 *the new shepherd: Pope Clement VII, Giulio de'Medici, or Leo X.*

astrologers and diviners have frightened you so (according to what we have heard from many) by saying that a season horrid and strange menaces every land with plague, flood and war, lightning, tempests, earthquakes and avalanches, as though already the world were at its end.

12 And they declare above all that the stars are overflowing with so many waters that the world, as great as it is, will wholly be covered. Therefore, gracious and fair ladies, if ever it pleased you to serve anything that is above you, let not one of you come forward to make defense against us. It is true that the sky is clear and promises us a glad carnival, but any man who tries to oppose us speaks falsely.

23 The waters will be the tears of those who die for you, O chosen ladies; the earthquakes, avalanches, and their terror will be the tempests and the wars of love; the lightnings and arrows will be your eyes, which make them die. Do not fear other harm; that will be which is wont to be. Heaven wishes to save us; and besides, he who sees the devil in very truth, sees him with smaller horns and not so black.

34 But still if Heaven should wish to avenge our mortal failings and offenses and to have our human race go down to the depths, it would have the Sun's chariot given anew into Phaeton's hands, that he might return to burn up the world. Meanwhile God in mercy secures you from water; have a care of fire. This judgment much more disturbs us, if in accord with our sin Heaven condemns.

45 Still, if you believe those vain rumors, come along with us to the summits of our high rocks; there you will make your hermitages, and then see it rain and form lakes in all the low places. There men have a good time as much as anywhere else, and we shall care little about the rain, for he who is taken up there will not fear the water below him.

*l. 11 Such were the prophecies of astrologers in 1523-1524 (Tommasini, VITA DI MACHIA-VELLI 1. 115).*

## VI. BY THE SNAKE CHARMERS

1 We are snake charmers who charm by nature, ladies, and go seeking our fortune.

3 We are descended from the house of Saint Paul, born far from these lands; but having come here, we have been taken by your loving nature.

7 We are all born with a sign underneath, and he who has the largest is the most learned; if you should see it you would see at a stroke the fine things nature knows how to make.

11 May it please you, then, to learn from us what evil these serpents can do you and how you must provide that every hour you do not suffer some mishap.

15 This snake, so short and knotted as you see, is called Hard Hide; when he is in heat and is angry, with his point he would pierce armor plate.

19 The adder that's deaf is a vicious animal, which assails everybody in front and behind, but when he comes in front he does less ill, though he causes much greater fear.

23 This lizard, large and well put together, takes pleasure in looking a man in the face; and about you, ladies, it does not trouble much—something that nature has granted to it.

27 Certain big lizards we have here inside, which assault people from behind by treachery, and if at first they do not cause terror, at last they execute their evil thrust.

31 As long as you look, this snake increases; if you squeeze it, it gets from between your fingers; then not much results from the test, nor can it, though it tries, do harm to your nature.

35 These serpents remain among the grass, or under a rock, or in some narrow crevice; only this large one delights in being in a swamp or in some great cleft.

39 Therefore great discretion is needed when one of you sits down that you be not struck on your buttocks by some blow of an evil sort.

43 But if you wish not to have fear of them, you must drink of this wine and keep this stone by you, and that it does not fall upon you you must take care.

47 So, when you are charmed, in all places you will sit down; the larger the snakes you find, the more it will seem to you that you have better fortune.

l. 3 *St. Paul, bitten by a viper, was unharmed (Acts 28: 3-6).*

# FAMILIAR LETTERS

[*Since these letters were not written for publication, literary polish is not to be expected. In their genuineness, giving glimpses of the author and his friends, they form the best of autobiographies. They have been printed so many times that the privacy to which they are entitled has long since been destroyed. Obviously many of the total number Niccolò wrote have not been preserved; many had already perished when his grandson collected what he could. The present collection, though not quite complete, gives most of the letters usually printed, enough to indicate Machiavelli the man and to supplement the works he intended to make public.*

*The numbering is that of Alvisi's edition (Firenze, 1883). Since he includes letters sent to Machiavelli, there are many gaps in the numbering here. For other texts used, see the list in vol. 1. I regret that Franco Gaeta's edition (Milano, 1961) came too late to be much used.*

*The place, date, and recipient's name precede the letter and are not repeated at its end, where they often appear in the originals. Information lacking in the original is put in square brackets. Machiavelli's name is given at the end of a letter only when it appears in the original or in the surviving copy.*]

## No. 3

9 March 1497-[1498], Florence
[*To Ricciardo Bechi, in Rome*]¹

### [*Savonarola*]

In order to give you a full account of affairs here about the Frate, according to your wish, I can tell you that after the two sermons were delivered, of which you have already had copies, he preached on the Sunday of the Carnival, and after saying many things, he invited his followers to receive Communion on the day of the Carnival in San Marco and said he was going to pray to God that if the things he had predicted did not come from Him, He would show a clear sign of it. And this he did, as some say, in order to unite his party and make it stronger to defend him, fearing that the Signoria newly chosen, but not announced, would be opposed to him. On the announcement on Monday of the Signoria, of which you must have had full notice, he judged it more than two-thirds hostile to him, and the Pope already had sent a letter summoning him, under penalty of interdiction. Hence, being afraid that the Signory would require him to

1. *A rough draft or copy, not the letter actually sent.*

obey at once, he determined, either on his own notion or advised by others, to give up preaching in Santa Reparata and go to San Marco. Therefore the Thursday morning when the Signory took office, he said, still in Santa Reparata, that to remove dissension and preserve the honor of God, he was going to draw back,² and that men should come to listen to him in San Marco, and women should go to San Lorenzo for Fra Domenico.

Our Frate being, therefore, in his own house, now to hear with what boldness he began his sermons, and with how much he continued them, would have caused you no little wonder. Because, fearing greatly for himself and believing that the new Signory would not be hesitant about harming him and having concluded that many citizens would be crushed by his fall, he began with great terrors, with reasons that for those who did not examine them were very convincing, showing that his followers were the best of men and his adversaries the most wicked, using every expression he could to weaken the adverse party and strengthen his own. Of these things, because I was present, I shall briefly run through a number.

The text of his first sermon in San Marco was this passage from Exodus: "The more they afflicted them, the more they multiplied and grew." And before he came to the explanation of these words, he showed for what reason he had drawn back, and said: "Prudence is straight thinking in practical matters." Then he said that all men have had and now have an end, but diverse. "For Christians, their end is Christ; for other men, both present and past, it has been and is something else, according to their religion. Being directed, then, we who are Christians, to this end which is Christ, we ought with the greatest prudence and observation of the times to preserve His honor; and when the time asks us to risk our lives, to risk them for Him; and when it is time for a man to conceal himself, to conceal ourselves, as we read of Christ and of Saint Paul; and so, he added, we ought to do and we have done.³ Therefore, when it was time to resist fury, we have done so, as happened on Ascension Day, because so the honor of God and the time demanded. Now that the honor of God requires that we yield to wrath, we have yielded."

And having given this short discourse, he indicated two companies: one which serves under God, namely, himself and his fol-

2. *From his defiant position.*
3. We *means Savonarola himself.*

lowers; the other under the Devil, namely, his opponents. And having spoken of it at length, he entered upon the exposition of the words of Exodus already given, and said that through tribulations good men grew in two ways, in spirit and in number: in spirit, because man unites himself more closely to God by overcoming adversity, and becomes stronger as nearer to his active cause, just as hot water brought close to the fire becomes hotter because nearer its active cause. They also grow in number, because there are three sorts of men, that is the good (and these are the ones who follow me), the perverse and obstinate (and these are my adversaries); and there is a further kind of men of free lives, given to pleasure, not stubborn in doing evil nor devoted to doing well, because they see neither of them clearly. But when between the good and the perverse there appears some practical difference, "since opposites when placed near one another stand out more clearly," they recognize the malice of the wicked and the simplicity of the good, and draw near to the latter and avoid the former, because naturally everybody avoids evil and follows good gladly; and therefore in adversities the wicked grow fewer and the good multiply, "and therefore the more," etc. I present it to you briefly, because the limits of a letter do not permit a long narrative. He said next—having entered into various discussions, as his custom is, further to weaken his adversaries, wishing to make a bridge to his next sermon—that our discords might cause a tyrant to rise up who would destroy our houses and lay waste our fields; and this was not at all opposed to what he had already said, that Florence was going to prosper and to master Italy, because the tyrant would remain there only a short time before being driven out. And with this he ended his sermon.

The next morning, again still explaining Exodus and coming to that passage where it is said that Moses killed an Egyptian, he said that the Egyptian stood for wicked men, and Moses for the preacher who killed them, by revealing their vices, and he said: "O Egyptian! I am going to give you a stab!" And then he turned the leaves of your books, O priests, and made such a mess of you that a dog would turn away from it. Then he added—and that was what he was driving at—that he intended to give the Egyptian another wound and a big one; and he said that God had told him that a man in Florence was trying to make himself tyrant and was negotiating and using ways for attaining it, and that his attempt to drive out the Frate, excommunicate the Frate, persecute the Frate, came to nothing else than that he wanted to make himself a tyrant, and that the laws should be kept. And he said so much about it that men later that day publicly guessed about a man who is as near to being a tyrant as you are to Heaven.

But after this, the Signoria wrote in his behalf to the Pope, and he saw that he no longer needed to fear his adversaries in Florence. Hence, though earlier he sought only to unite his party by speaking evil of his adversaries and to frighten them with the name of tyrant, now—believing that he no longer needs to do so—he has changed his cloak. So, encouraging them to share in the union that has begun, and making no further mention of the tyrant and of their wickedness, he tries to set all of them against the Supreme Pontiff and, biting him, says of him what could be said of the wickedest man you can think of. Thus, according to my judgment, he keeps on working with the times and making his lies plausible.

Now what the masses are saying, what men hope or fear, I leave you to judge, since you are prudent, because you can judge better than I can, since you know all about our factions and the nature of the times, and also, through being in Rome, know the Pontiff's intentions. Only this I beg of you, that if you have not felt that reading this letter of mine is burdensome, you will not find it a burden to tell me in answer what judgment in such a disposition of times and of purposes you make about our affairs. Farewell.

Your Niccolò son of M. Bernardo Machiavelli.

### No. 103

20 November 1509, Verona [*Isola della Scala*]
To the Honorable Luigi Guicciardini, as his dearest brother, in Mantua
Written in the house of G[*iovanni*] Borromeo

[*Personal matters; the difficulties of his mission to the Emperor*]

My dearest Luigi:

Today I have received your letter of the twenty-fifth, which has caused me more concern than if I had lost the lawsuit, since I learned that a little fever has come back to Jacopo. Still your prudence, the assiduity of Marco, the skill of the doctors, the patience and goodness of Jacopo give me confidence that you will drive it away like a filthy whore, an ass, a shameless pig. And from your first letter I expect to learn that in spite of it you have gone off completely happy toward Florence.

I am here in Isola, irritated like you, because here nothing is known about anything; and yet, in order to seem alive, I keep imagining endless letters to write to the Ten, and I am sending you their letter unsealed, which, when all of you have read it, you can give to Giovanni, who will send it by the first courier when Pandolfino writes, or as he thinks best. Give him my regards and tell him that I am here with his Stefano and am having a good time.

I would have gone to court, but Lang is not there, to whom I have the letter of introduction, and to the Emperor I have no letter, so that I might be arrested as a spy. Then every day it is said he is coming, and all those Mamelukes that follow the court are in control there.

I am glad you have sent those pledges to Florence, for which you deserve great praise from God and from the men of the world.

If you write to your Messer Francesco, tell him that I send my regards to the society. I am yours, very much yours; and as to writing, I think about it all the time. Good bye.

Niccolò Machiavegli
Secretary at Caesar's Court.

## No. 115

[*September 1512*], Florence
To an unidentified lady [*Alfonsina Orsini de' Medici?*][1]

[*The return of the Medici to Florence*]

Since Your Ladyship wishes, Noble Madam, to learn of the strange events in Tuscany which took place in recent days, I shall gladly relate them to you, both to please you and for the reason that their outcome honored the friends of Your Illustrious Ladyship and my masters, which two reasons cancel all the other unpleasant results, which are countless, as in the course of the matter Your Ladyship will understand.

1. *A draft or copy.*

It was decided at the Diet of Mantua to put the Medici back in Florence, and when the Viceroy left to return to Modena, it was much feared in Florence that the Spanish army would come into Tuscany. Nonetheless, there was no further assurance of it. The business of the Diet had been carried on secretly, and many could not believe that the Pope would want the Spanish army to upset that province, especially since they knew from letters from Rome that there was no great confidence between the Spanish and the Pope. Hence we remained with uncertain minds, making no preparation, until from Bologna came assurance of everything. But the hostile soldiers being already only a day's journey from our boundaries, all the city was at once disturbed by this sudden and almost unexpected attack. Having considered what ought to be done, we decided, since we were not in time to guard the passes of the mountains, to send with all possible speed to Firenzuola, a town on the borders between Florence and Bologna, two thousand infantry, in order that the Spaniards, so as not to leave behind them so large a force, would undertake the siege of that town and give us time to increase the number of our soldiers and resist their attacks with larger forces. At the beginning we thought we would not put our soldiers in the field, because we did not judge them powerful enough to resist the enemy, but would assemble them at Prato, a large town lying in the plain at the base of the mountains that come down from the Mugello, ten miles distant from Florence. We judged that place fit to hold our army, which could remain there in security, and because it was near Florence, we could at any time reinforce it if the Spaniards went in that direction.

When this decision was made, all the forces were moved into the places indicated. But the Viceroy, whose intention was not to attack the towns but to come to Florence to make a change in the government, hoping with the aid of the Party to do it easily, paid no attention to Firenzuola but, crossing the Apennines, came down to Barberino di Mugello, a town eighteen miles from Florence. All the towns of that region, being completely without garrisons, without resistance received his orders and furnished his army with food according to their ability. Meanwhile a good part of our soldiers were brought to Florence and the leaders of the menatarms met and considered defense against this attack. They advised that our soldiers should assemble not at Prato but at Florence, because they judged that if they were shut up in Prato they could not resist the Viceroy. Though his forces were not yet known, our commanders believed, since he came so boldly into this province, that they were such that their army could not resist them; and therefore they considered withdrawing them to Florence more secure, where with the help of the people they were enough to defend that city, and with this arrangement they could try to hold Prato, leaving there a garrison of three thousand soldiers.

This decision was pleasing, and especially to the Gonfalonier, since he judged himself more secure and stronger against the Party when he had more forces within the city near himself. And finding things in these conditions, the Viceroy sent ambassadors to Florence, who set forth to the Signoria that they did not come into this province as enemies and did not intend to make any change in the liberty of the city or in its government, but merely intended to make sure that she would leave the French party and join the League, which did not believe that as long as Piero Soderini was Gonfalonier it could be sure of the city or of any promises she made. They knew Soderini as a partisan of the French; therefore they wished that he would lay down his office and that the people of Florence would choose another gonfalonier as they wished.

To this the Gonfalonier replied that he had not come to that office with either deceit or force but that he had been put there by the people; and therefore if all the kings in the world united together should order him to lay it down, never would he lay it down; but if the Florentine people wished him to go, he would do it gladly, just as he gladly took it when, without any ambition of his, the people granted it to him. And in order to test the spirit of the populace, as soon as the ambassador had gone, he assembled all the Council and, putting before them the Viceroy's proposition, announced, if it pleased the people and they judged that his departure would bring about peace, that he was ready to go to his house, because since he had never thought of anything but benefiting the city, it would be a great grief to him if for love of him she should suffer. This thing with one accord everybody rejected, and he had offers from all to lay down even their lives for his defense.

It happened meanwhile that the Spanish army reached Prato and made a great attack; not taking her, His Excellency the Viceroy negotiated about an agreement with the Florentine envoy and sent him to Florence with one of his men, offering to be satisfied with a certain amount of money; as to the Medici, he would turn over their case to His Catholic Majesty, who might beg and not force the Florentines to receive them. The envoys having arrived with this proposal, and reporting the condition of the Spaniards bad, asserting that they would die of hunger and that Prato was going to be held, put so much confidence into the Gonfalonier and into the multitude, by which he was governed, that though that peace was advised by the wise, yet the Gonfalonier kept on delaying, until the next day news came that Prato was taken, for the Spaniards, having broken part of the wall, pressed back those who defended it and frightened them, so that after not much resistance all fled, and the Spanish, occupying the town, sacked it and killed the people in a miserable scene of distress. To Your Ladyship I shall not repeat the details in order not to cause you any depression of spirits. I shall say merely that more than four thousand men were killed and the others were prisoners and in different ways were forced to ransom themselves; and they did not spare virgins who were cloistered in the holy places, all of which they filled with rape and sacrilege.

This news caused great disturbance in Florence. Nonetheless, the Gonfalonier was not frightened, trusting in certain empty opin⁄ ions. He was counting on holding Florence and making an agree⁄ ment with the Spaniards for any sum of money whatever, if only the Medici were kept out. But his negotiators having gone and brought back the answer that it was necessary to receive the Medici or to be ready for war, everybody feared that the city would be sacked, on account of the cowardice of our soldiers in Prato. This fear was increased by all the nobility who wished to change the government, so that Monday evening, the thirtieth of August, at eight o'clock at night, our ambassadors received authority to agree with the Viceroy no matter what.

And so much did everybody's fear grow that the Palace and the usual protection by the soldiers of the government were given up; and since it was without guards, the Signoria was obliged to release many citizens who, being considered suspicious and friends of the Medici, had been held under strong guard many days in the Palace. They, along with many others of the most noble citizens of this city, who wished to get back their reputation, took courage. Hence on Tues⁄ day morning they came armed to the Palace, and having seized all the places in order to force the Gonfalonier to leave, were persuaded by some citizens not to use violence but to let him go by agreement. And so the Gonfalonier, accompanied by those same men, returned to his house, and the next night a large company, with the consent of the Signors, took him to Siena.

The magnificent Medici, after hearing what had happened, preferred not to come to Florence, unless first they settled the affairs of the city with the Viceroy, with whom after some difficulties they made an agreement; entering Florence, they were received by all the people with the utmost honor. There was established meanwhile in Florence a certain new order of government, in which it did not seem to the Viceroy that there was security for the house of Medici or for the League; therefore he indicated to the Signors of the city that it was necessary to put the government in the form it had during the lifetime of the Magnificent Lorenzo. The noble citizens wished to accede to this but feared that the multitude would not join in, and while they were carrying on this debate on how they would deal with these things, the Legate Giovanni de'Medici entered Florence; with His Lordship came many soldiers and especially Italians. And the Signors of the city brought together in the Palace on the sixteenth day of the present month many citizens—and with them was the Magnificent Giuliano—and talk was going on about the reform of the government, when a noise was made in the Public Square, because of which Ramazzotto with his soldiers and others seized the Palace, shouting: "Palle, palle."[2] And at once the whole city was under arms, and through every part of the city resounded that name, so that the Signors were obliged to summon the people to an assembly, which we call a parliament, where a law was passed by which the magnificent Medici were reinstated in all the honors and ranks of their ancestors. And this city remains very quiet and hopes not to live less honored with their aid than she lived in times gone by, when the Magnificent Lorenzo their father, of most happy memory, was ruling.

You have, then, Most Illustrious Madam, the detailed outcome of our affairs, among which I have not cared to include those matters that might distress you, as wretched and little necessary. On the others I have enlarged as much as the narrow limits of a letter permit. If I have satisfied you, I shall be very glad; if not, I pray that Your

2. *The cry of supporters of the Medici, derived from the three balls in their coat of arms.*

Most Illustrious Ladyship will excuse me.  Long and prosperously may you live.


## No. 116

[*January 1512–(1513), Florence*]
[*To Piero Soderini, in Ragusa*][1]

[*To the ruler driven from Florence by the Medici*]

A letter of yours came to me in a hood;[2] yet after ten words I recognized it.  I am sure the crowds at Piombino will recognize you, and of your hindrances and Filippo's I am certain, because I know one is harmed by a little light, the other by too much.  January does not trouble me, if only February supports me with his hands.  I am sorry about Filippo's suspicion, and in suspense wait for its end. [*He who does not know how to fence overcomes him who knows fencing.*]

Your letter was short but I by rereading it made it long.  It was pleasing to me because it gave me a chance to do what I feared to do and what you remind me that I should not do; and this part alone I have observed in it as without application.  At this I would wonder, if my fate had not shown me so many and such varied things that I am obliged to wonder but little, or to confess that I have not comprehended while reading and experiencing the actions of men and their methods of procedure.

I understand you and the compass by which you navigate; and if it could be condemned, which it cannot, I would not condemn it, seeing to what port it has taken you and with what hope it can feed you.  Consequently, I see, not with your mirror, where nothing is seen but prudence, but with that of the many, which is obliged in political affairs to judge the result when they are finished, and not the management while they are going on.  Each man according to his own imagination guides himself.  And I see various kinds of conduct bringing about the same thing, as by various roads one comes to the same place, and many who work differently attaining the same end.

1. *This letter is apparently a rough draft with notes for expansion and addition.  When a clause appears in two forms, I have given but one.  I have followed Mazzoni and Casella's text.*

2. *Disguised, perhaps not in his own hand.  Parts, especially of the first paragraph, were probably intended to be unintelligible except to writer and recipient.*

The actions of this Pontiff and their results have furnished anything needed to confirm this opinion.

Hannibal and Scipio were equally excellent in their military at/tainments; one of them with cruelty, treachery and lack of religion kept his armies united in Italy and made himself admired by the people, who to follow him rebelled against the Romans; the other, with mercy, loyalty and religion, in Spain got from those people the same effect; both of them won countless victories. But because it is not usual to bring up the Romans, Lorenzo de'Medici disarmed the people to hold Florence; Messer Giovanni Bentevoglio in order to hold Bologna armed them; the Vitelli in Città di Castello and the present Duke of Urbino in his territory destroyed the fortresses in order to retain those states; Count Francesco Sforza and many others built them in their states to make themselves sure of those states. [*To test Fortune, who is the friend of young men, and to change according to what you find. But it is not possible to have fortresses and not to have them, to be cruel and compassionate.*] Titus the Emperor believed he would lose his position on any day when he did not benefit somebody; some others might believe they would lose theirs on the day when they did anybody a favor. To many, weighing and measuring everything, suc/cess comes in their undertakings. [*As Fortune gets tired, anything is ruined. The family, the city, every man has his Fortune founded on his way of proceeding, and each Fortune gets tired, and when she is tired, she must be got back in another way. Comparison of the horse and the bridle about fortresses.*] This Pope Julius, who hasn't a pair of scales or a yard/stick in his house, gains through chance—although unarmed—what through organization and arms he scarcely could attain.

We have seen and see every day those I have mentioned, and countless others who could be used as instances, gaining kingdoms and sovereignties or falling, according to circumstances; and a man who was praised while he was gaining is reviled when he is losing; and frequently after long prosperity a man who finally loses does not in any way blame himself but accuses the heavens and the action of the Fates. But the reason why different ways of working are some/times equally effective and equally damaging I do not know, but I should much like to know. So in order to get your opinion I shall be so presuming as to give mine.

I believe that as Nature has given each man an individual face, so she has given him an individual disposition and an individual im-agination. From this it results that each man conducts himself according to his disposition and his imagination. On the other hand, because times vary and affairs are of varied types, one man's desires come out as he had prayed they would; he is fortunate who harmonizes his procedure with his time, but on the contrary he is not fortunate who in his actions is out of harmony with his time and with the type of its affairs. Hence it can well happen that two men working differently come to the same end, because each of them adapts himself to what he encounters, for affairs are of as many types as there are provinces and states. Thus, because times and affairs in general and individually change often, and men do not change their imaginings and their procedures, it happens that a man at one time has good fortune and at another time bad.

And certainly anybody wise enough to understand the times and the types of affairs and to adapt himself to them would have always good fortune, or he would protect himself always from bad, and it would come to be true that the wise man would rule the stars and the Fates. But because there never are such wise men, since men in the first place are shortsighted and in the second place cannot command their natures, it follows that Fortune varies and commands men and holds them under her yoke. And to verify this opinion, I think the instances given above, on which I have based it, are enough, and so I expect one to support the other.

To give reputation to a new ruler, cruelty, treachery and irreligion are enough in a province where humanity, loyalty and religion have for a long time been common. Yet in the same way humanity, loyalty and religion are sufficient where cruelty, treachery and ir-religion have dominated for a time, because, as bitter things disturb the taste and sweet ones cloy it, so men get bored with good and complain of ill. These causes, among others, opened Italy to Han-nibal and Spain to Scipio; thus both of them found times and things suited to their way of proceeding. At that very time a man like Scipio would not have been so successful in Italy, or one like Han-nibal so successful in Spain, as they both were in the provinces where they acted.

Niccolò Machiavelli.

## No. 117

13 March 1512-[*1513*], Florence
To the Magnificent Francesco Vettori, Most Worthy Florentine
Ambassador to the Supreme Pontiff, in Rome

### [*Longing for employment by the Medici*]

Magnificent Sir: As you have learned from Pagolo Vettori, I
have got out of prison amid the universal rejoicing of this city, even
though I hoped for it because of your doings and those of Pagolo, for
which I thank you. I won't go over again the long story of my
misfortune but will merely say that Luck has done everything to
cause me this trouble. Yet, thanks be to God! it is over. I hope I
won't run into it again, both because I shall be more careful and
because the times will be more liberal and not so suspicious.

You know in what condition I found our friend Messer Totto
[*Machiavelli*]. I ask favor for him from you and Pagolo [*Vettori*]
generally. He wants only, he and I, this special thing—that he may
be put among the servants of the Pope, and written in his record, and
have the patent for it. For these things we beg you.

Keep me, if it is possible, in the Signor Giuliano's memory, so
that, if it is possible, he or his family may employ me in something or
other, because I believe I would bring honor to him and profit
to myself.

Your Niccolò Machiavelli
in Florence.

## No. 119

18 March 1512-[*1513*], Florence
To the Magnificent Francesco Vettori, Florentine Ambassador to
the Supreme Pontiff, in Rome

### [*Bad Fortune resisted*]

Magnificent Ambassador:

Your very friendly letter has made me forget all my past troubles,
and though I was more than certain of the love you have for me, this
letter has been most pleasing to me. I thank you as much as I can

and pray to God that to your profit and benefit he will give me power to do something that will please you, because I can say that all of life that is left me I consider that I owe to the Magnificent Giuliano de'Medici and your Pagolo.

As to turning my face to resist Fortune, I want you to get this pleasure from my distresses, namely, that I have borne them so bravely that I love myself for it and feel that I am stronger than you believed. And if these masters of mine decide not to let me lie on the earth, I shall be glad of it, and believe I shall conduct myself in such a way that they too will have reason to approve. If they decide differently, I'll get on as when I came here, for I was born poor and I learned earlier to stint myself than to prosper. If you remain there, I'll come to pass some time with you, when you advise me to. But not to be more tedious, I send my regards to you and to Pagolo [*Vettori*], to whom I am not writing, because I don't know what further to say to him.

I related the story about Filippo Casavecchio to some of our friends, who rejoiced that he had got there safely. They were very sorry about the slight esteem and value that Giovanni Cavalcanti has for him. Considering the reason for this state of things, they have found that Giuliano Brancaccio told Messer Giovanni that Filippo had been instructed by his brother to recommend Giovanni, Ser Antonio's son, to the Pope, and for that reason Messer Giovanni was unwilling to admit him. They greatly blame Giuliano for spreading this scandal when it was not true;[1] if it had been true, they blame Filippo for taking certain desperate remedies, so advise him to be more cautious next time.

And tell Filippo that Niccolò degli Agli trumpets it throughout Florence, and I do not know the reason, but without scruple and without excusing anything, he blames him in such a way that there isn't a man who doesn't wonder at it. So caution Filippo that if he knows the cause of this enmity, he provide against it in some way; and just yesterday he came to see me with a list in his hand giving all the gossips in Florence, and he told me that he went recruiting those who would speak ill of Filippo, to get revenge on him. I wish to let you know, so you can mention it to him, and I send him my regards.

The whole group sends regards to you, beginning with Tom-

---

1. *I follow Mazzoni and Casella's text.*

maso del Bene and going as far as our Donato.² Every day we are in the house of some girls to recover our strength; only yesterday we were in the house of Sandra di Pero to see the procession pass; and so we go spending our time on these general rejoicings, getting pleasure from what is left of life, so that I feel as though I were dreaming.
Farewell.

Niccolò Machiavelli.

2. *Donato del Corno, a Florentine of some wealth but low rank, often mentioned in these letters.*

No. 120

April 9, 1513, Florence
To Francesco Vettori, in Rome

[I must discuss public affairs or be silent]

Magnificent Mr. Ambassador:

> And I, who had observed his color,
> Said: "How shall I go if you are trembling
> Who in my fear are wont to comfort me?"¹

This letter of yours terrified me more than the strappado; I grieve over any notion of yours that I am angry, not on my own account, because I am so trained that no longer do I passionately wish anything, but on yours. I beg you to imitate the others, who gain places for them-selves with persistence and craft rather than with ability and prudence. As to that story about Totto, it displeases me if it displeases you. Otherwise I am not bothering about it, and if we can't make the roll, let's whirl about.² Once for all let me tell you that you are not to take any trouble about anything I ever ask of you, because if I don't get what I ask, I shall not be disturbed.

If you are sick of discussing public affairs, after seeing many things turn out contrary to the notions and concepts you form, you are right; the like has happened to me. Yet if I could speak with you, I couldn't help filling your head with castles in Spain, because Fortune has determined that since I don't know how to talk about the silk business or the wool business or about profits and losses, I

1. *Dante,* INFERNO *4. 16–18.*
2. *A play on the Pope's roll or record of friends. Cf. No. 117, above.*

must talk about the government; I must either make a vow of silence or discuss that.

If I could get outside our territory, I should surely go, I too, to ask if the Pope is at home; but among so many favors, mine through my neglect was forgotten. I shall wait for September. I learn that Cardinal Soderini has a great deal of business with the Pope. I wish you would advise me if you think it wise for me to write him a letter asking that he recommend me to His Holiness; or if it would be better that by word of mouth you attend to this affair on my behalf with the Cardinal; or if nothing should be done—on which perhaps you will give me a word in reply.

As to the horse, you make me laugh by reminding me about it, because you are to pay me when I remember it and not otherwise.

Our archbishop [*Giovanni Salviati*] by this hour must be dead, and may God receive his soul and those of all his family. Farewell.

Niccolò Machiavelli, formerly Secretary.

No. 122

16 April 1513, Florence
To Francesco Vettori, His Patron and Benefactor, in Rome

[Florentine comedy; desire for employment]

Magnificent Ambassador:

Last Saturday I wrote to you, and though I haven't anything to say or to write, I don't want this Saturday to pass by without my writing.

The company that you know all about seems as though it were lost, because there isn't a dovecot that will hold us,[1] and all its leaders had a blowup. Tommaso del Bene has become queer, difficult, fussy, stingy to such an extent that when you return he will seem to you another man. And I want to tell you what has happened to me.

Last week he bought seven pounds of veal and sent it to Marione's house. Then he thought he had spent too much and wanted to find somebody who would share the cost, so he went hunting for somebody who would have dinner with him. Moved by pity, I

---

1. *Possibly proverbial, suggesting no meeting place.*

went with two others whom I hunted up for him. We had dinner, and when we came to figure the expense it amounted to fourteen soldi each. I had only ten with me, so I owed him four soldi; and every day he asks me for them, and just yesterday evening he dunned me on the Ponte Vecchio. You may not think he's wrong about that, but it is nothing to the other things he does.

Girolamo del Guanto's wife died, and for three or four days he was like a stupefied barbel.[2] Then he came to life and wanted to get another wife. So every evening we have been on the bench of the Capponi discussing this marriage. Count Orlando is all torn up again over a young fellow from Ragusa and is not able to get any kindness from him. Donato del Corno has opened another shop where they can sell doves, and he goes all day from the old to the new one and is like a crazy man, and now he goes off with Vincenzio, now with Pizzo, now with one of his boys, now with another; yet I have never seen that he is angry with Riccio. I don't know the cause of this; some think anything would be more to his purpose than the lot; I for my part can't make any sense out of it. Pier Filippo di Bastiano has returned to Florence and complains terribly of Brancaccino, but in general, and as yet has not come to any details. If he goes to Rome, I shall let you know, so you can warn him.

> So then if sometimes I laugh or sing, I do it because I have
> just this one way for expressing my anxious sorrow.[3]

If it is true that Jacopo Salviati and Matteo Strozzi have been let go, you will continue there as the public agent; and since Jacopo does not stay there, of those who are coming I see nobody who can stay there, so you can be sent away; hence I suppose that you will stay as long as you wish to. His Magnificence Giuliano will come there, and you will naturally find a chance to do me good, and the same thing for the Cardinal of Volterra.[4] So I cannot believe that if my affair is handled with some skill, I won't succeed in being employed at something, if not in behalf of Florence, at least in behalf of Rome and the Papacy, in respect to which I ought to be less suspected. Since I know you are firmly placed there, and you think I

2. *He acted dazed, as though lifeless. Perhaps the expression is derived, with change of adjective though not of meaning, from Pulci's* MORGANTE *20. 48.*

3. *Petrarch,* Cesare, poi che. *Machiavelli substitutes* express *for the* conceal *of the original.*

4. *Cardinal Soderini, brother of Piero Soderini, ex-gonfalonier of Florence.*

cannot make a move in any other way, and I may run into prejudices here, I ought to go there, and I cannot believe that, if His Holiness our Lord would employ me, I should not do myself good and bring profit and honor to all my friends. I don't write this to you because I want things too much, nor because I want you to undertake for my love any burden or trouble or expense or anxiety about anything, but in order that you may know my intention, and if you can help me, you may know that what benefits me always benefits you and your family, to which I owe all that is left me.

Niccolò Machiavelli in Florence.

No. 128

[*29 April 1513*]
[*To Francesco Vettori, in Rome*][1]

[*Ferdinand V of Spain, the Catholic; the new prince*]

Jesus Son of Mary

Magnificent Ambassador, Whom I Greatly Honor:

In the midst of my greatest good fortunes I never had anything that pleased me as much as your discussions, because from them I always learned something. Imagine, then, when I find myself now far from any other pleasure, how much I was pleased by your letter, to which nothing was wanting except your presence and the sound of your living voice; and as I have been reading it, for I have read it many times, I always have forgotten my unhappy situation, and I seem to have gone back to those affairs in which I have uselessly endured so many exertions and spent so much time. And even though I have vowed not to think any more on affairs of state nor to talk about them, as is proved by my coming to my farm and avoiding conversation, nevertheless, to answer your questions, I am forced to break every vow because I believe I am more obligated to the long-standing friendship I have with you than to any other obligation I have to any person; especially when you do me so much honor as you do at the end of your letter; to tell you the truth, I have taken a little pride in it, since it is true "that it is not a small thing to be praised by

1. For the text see Alvisi, letter no. 128; Lesca, letter no. 17; Villari (1914) 3.414; Tommasini 2.86, note 1. Alvisi puts this letter after Vettori's of 12 July; it is a copy or draft.

a praised man.""[2] I fear, though, that my notions may seem to you not to have their old flavor, for which I hope it will excuse me that I have deliberately given up such dealings altogether and, besides, that I have learned no details about what is now going on. And you know how well things can be judged in the dark, and especially these. So what I say to you will be based on either the foundation of your discourses or on my presuppositions, as to which, if they are false, I hope you will excuse me for the reason given above.

You would like to know, according to your letter of the twenty-first, what I believe has moved the King of Spain to make this truce with France, since you cannot see anything in it for him when everything is carefully gone over from all directions; so that on one side judging that the King is wise, and on the other being of the opinion that he has made a mistake, you are forced to believe that the truce hides some great thing which now neither you nor anybody understands. And truly your discourse could not be more careful or more prudent, nor do I believe that on this matter anything else could be said. Yet to act alive and to obey you, I shall say what occurs to me.

Nothing, I think, makes you hesitate more than the presupposition you lay down of the King of Spain's prudence. I answer that I have always thought Spain[3] more crafty and fortunate than wise and prudent. I do not intend to go over his affairs at length, but will deal with this expedition against France in Italy, made before England could move or Spain could be sure that he was going to move. I earlier thought and still think that in that expedition, notwithstanding its contrary end, without necessity Spain put into danger all his territories—which is a very rash thing in a prince. I say *without necessity*, because he had seen through signs of the year before, after so much harm that the Pope had done France (attacking his friends and trying to make Genoa rebel) and also after many provocations that he himself had given to France (by sending his soldiers with those of the Church to injure France's tributaries) that nevertheless France, when victorious (having driven away the Pope and deprived him of all his armies) and able to drive the Pope from Rome and Spain from Naples, did not wish to do so, but turned his mind to a treaty. So Spain could not fear France. Nor is there wisdom in the reason

2. Cicero, FAMILIAR LETTERS 5. 12. 7; 15. 6. 1.
3. *The King of Spain, as often in the* LETTERS. *Similarly, the King of England is* England, *and the King of France is* France.

brought forward for him, that he did it to make himself sure of the Kingdom,[4] since France had not intervened there, being tired out and beset with doubts. And if Spain should say that France did not come ahead then because of various reasons for hesitating which another time he would not have had, I answer that all those reasons for hesitation that France then had he was going to have always, because always the Pope was going to try to keep Naples from going back to France, and always France was going to be careful lest the Pope and the other powers should unite when they saw France ambitious.

And if someone says that Spain feared that if he did not unite with the Pope to make war on France, the Pope in anger would unite with France in order to carry on this war against him, since the Pope was a man so violent and full of the devil and therefore certain to make such a decision, I should answer that France always would have made a treaty with Spain sooner than with the Pope, if in those times France had been able to agree with either of them, both because the victory was more certain and he would not have had to use arms, and because then he believed himself greatly injured by the Pope and not by Spain. And to be revenged for that injury and to satisfy the Church with the Council, the King of Spain always could be either mediator of a solid peace or composer of a treaty secure for himself. Nevertheless he left behind all those plans and chose war. Yet in war he needed to fear that with one battle all his states would go, as he feared they would when he lost the day at Ravenna; indeed immediately after the news of that defeat he arranged to send Gonsalvo to Naples, for that kingdom was as though lost and the kingdom of Castile was tottering under him. And he had no reason to believe that the Swiss would avenge him and make him safe and restore to him his lost reputation as they did.

So if you will consider that whole action and the handling of those things, you will see in the King of Spain craft and good fortune rather than wisdom or prudence. And when I see a man making a mistake, I suppose he will make a thousand of them; and I do not believe that under this decision he has now made there is anything else than what is seen, because I don't drink the label on a bottle,[5]

4. *The Kingdom of Naples, in Italy the only Kingdom.*
5. *Literally, I do not drink districts, that is, I am not so impressed by the name of the region where a wine is produced that I forget to observe its quality.*

and in these matters I do not intend that any authority should move me without reason. Hence I hold to the conclusion that Spain may have made a mistake and understood badly and concluded worse.

But let us abandon my opinion and consider him prudent, and let us discuss his decision as that of a wise man. Making such a presupposition, then, I add that in trying properly to find the truth of this matter, I need to know whether this truce was made after the news of the Pontiff's death and the installation of the new Pope or before, because perhaps it would make some difference. But since I do not know, I shall assume it made before the Pope's death. If then I ask you what you think Spain should have done, being in the condition he is, you would answer what you have written to me, namely, that he could have made peace with France, restoring Lombardy, in order to put him under obligation and to remove all reason for bringing French armies into Italy.

To this I answer that to discuss this affair properly one must note that Spain made that expedition against the King of France with the hope of defeating him, perhaps relying too much on the Pope, on England and on the Emperor as foundations, as he learned when finally the test came, because he expected to get money enough from the Pope; and he believed that the Emperor would make a vigorous attack on Burgundy and that the King of England, being young and wealthy and correspondingly eager for glory, would be certain to come in great force whenever he embarked. Altogether, the King of Spain believed that France would be compelled both in Italy and at home to accept Spain's requirements.

Yet none of these things happened: Spain got money from the Pope only at first and sparingly; and later the Pope not merely did not give him money but every day sought to ruin him and carried on negotiations against him. From the Emperor came nothing further than the journey of the Bishop of Gurk, and slanders and reproaches. From England came a weak force which could not be combined with his own. Hence if it had not been for the seizure of Navarre, before France was in the field, both of those armies would have been disgraced, for they would have gained nothing but shame, because one never got out of the forests of Fonterabbia, the other retreated into Pampalona and with difficulty defended it. Hence Spain was exhausted in the midst of this confusion of friends, from whom he could expect nothing better, but rather every day something worse, because every day they negotiated for an agreement with France. As a result, seeing on the other side France bearing the expense, in agreement with the Venetians, and hoping in the Swiss, he decided that it would be better to be beforehand with the French King in whatever way he could, rather than to remain in such great uncertainty and confusion and under unbearable expense, because I have heard from a good source that a man now in Spain writes that there is no money and no way of getting it, and that the King's army is made up only of conscripts, who moreover are not obeying him.

So I believe his plan has been, in this truce, to make his allies realize their mistake and make them more forward in the war, as a result of his promising the ratification, etc., or to get the war away from his own country and away from such great expense and danger. (If in the spring Pampalona had been captured, he would without doubt have lost Castile, and it is not reasonable that he should wish any longer to run this risk.)

As to affairs in Italy, Spain may perhaps be relying more than is reasonable on his own soldiers; but I do not at all believe that he is putting reliance on the Swiss, or on the Pope, or on the Emperor, more than is necessary; and I believe he sees that in this affair eating may lead to drinking by the Emperor and the Italians.[6] And he should not have made a stricter agreement with France, to give him the Dukedom,[7] as you say he should have done, since he had not found France on his side, and also since he should not have judged it a useful decision. Indeed I believe France perhaps would not have made such a treaty, because already he must have made an agreement with the Venetians, and then as a result of not trusting in Spain or in his armies, France would have believed that Spain did not do it for the sake of an agreement with himself, but to ruin France's agreements with others.

As to Spain, I do not see any profit in it for him, because France would become in every way powerful in Italy, however he entered the Dukedom. And if to gain it Spanish arms were enough, to hold it he would need to send his own there, and in large numbers; such action could rouse the same suspicions in the Italians and in Spain that would be roused by armies coming to gain it by force. And of loyalty and of promises no one today makes any account. Hence

6. *Necessity and opportunity may teach them to make heavier demands.*
7. *Of Milan.*

Spain would not see in such conduct any security on one side, and on the other side would see this loss, because he would make this peace with France either with the consent of the allies or not. With their consent, he would judge it impossible, through not being able to bring to agreement Pope and France and Venetians and Emperor, so that to wish to do it by agreement with his allies would be a dream. Needing, then, to do it against their will, he would see in it an evident loss for himself, because he would be joined with a king—and making him powerful—who, every time he had opportunity for it, presumably would remember old injuries better than new benefits, and Spain would have excited against himself all the powerful Italians and those outside Italy because, since he was the sole rouser of all of them against France, to leave them now would be too great an injury. Therefore, as a result of this peace made as you would like to have had it made, he would have seen the greatness of the King of France sure, the anger of the allies against himself sure, and the loyalty of France uncertain; on the latter alone he must of necessity rely because, having made him powerful and the others angry, he would have to stand with France. But wise princes never, except through necessity, put themselves into the power of another man.

So I conclude that Spain has judged it a more secure plan to make a truce, because with this truce he shows his allies their mistake, so acts that they cannot complain, and gives them time to undo it if it does not please them; he gets the war away from home and again brings into dispute and confusion the affairs of Italy, where he sees that there is something to undo even yet, and a bone to gnaw. And as I said above, he hopes that eating will teach everybody to drink, believes that the Pope, the Emperor and the Swiss will take no pleasure in the greatness of the Venetians and France in Italy, and judges that if they are not enough to keep France from taking Lombardy, they will at least be enough with his help to keep France from going farther. For this reason Spain supposes that the Pope will have to throw himself entirely into his arms, because he can expect that the Pope will not unite with the Venetians or with their adherents, as the result of the affairs of Romagna. So with this truce he sees that French victory is uncertain and that he does not have to trust France and does not have to fear changes by the confederates. The Emperor and England will either ratify it or will not; if they ratify, they will consider that this truce is going to aid everybody and not hurt them; if they do not ratify, they will become more eager for war, and with forces greater and better arranged than in the past year will come to attack France. In every one of these cases Spain gains his purpose.

I believe, therefore, that his purpose has been this, and that he believes by means of this truce either to force the Emperor and England to make war in earnest or, by means of their reputation, with other ways than arms, to settle things to his advantage. And in every other procedure he would see danger, that is, either in continuing war or making peace against their will; and therefore he took a middle way, from which could come either war or peace.

If you have examined the plans and the advances of this king, you will be less astonished by this truce. This king from a slight and weak position has come to his present greatness, and has had always to struggle with new states and distrusted subjects. Yet one of the ways with which new states are held, and unsure minds are either made firm or are kept uncertain and unresolved, is to rouse great expectations about oneself, all the time keeping men's minds occupied in considering what is going to be the end of new decisions and new undertakings. Such a necessity this king has recognized and used well. It produced his war in Granada, his attacks on Africa, his entrance into the Kingdom, and all his other well-known, varied enterprises. He saw the end of none of these; indeed his end is not a particular gain or a particular victory but to give himself reputation among his people and to keep them uncertain among the great number of his affairs. Therefore he is a spirited maker of beginnings, to which he later gives the particular end that is placed before him by chance and that necessity teaches him, and up to now he has not been able to complain of his luck or of his courage. I prove to you this opinion of mine by the division he made with France of the Kingdom of Naples, about which he must have been sure that war would have to come of it between him and France, without seeing the end of it by a thousand miles; he could not have believed that he was going to defeat France in Apulia, in Calabria, and at the Garigliano. But it has been enough for him to begin, in order to give himself the reputation he sought, hoping either with fortune or with trickery to go ahead. So what he has done always, he will still do, and the end of all these plays will show you that such is the truth.

All the preceding things I have said assuming that Pope Julius was alive; but if King Ferdinand had learned of his death and the election of the present Pope, he would have done the same, because if he could not confide in Julius as being unstable, hasty, rash and stingy, in this one he cannot confide as being wise. And if Spain has any prudence at all, he is not going to be moved by any benefit that the Pontiff when of Lower rank conferred on him, or by any early connection, because the Pope then obeyed, now he commands; then he gambled with other men's property, now with his own; then he could profit from confusion, now from peace. And Spain must believe that His Holiness Our Lord will not use either his money or his armies against Christians unless he is coerced; and I believe everybody will hesitate to force him.

I realize that this letter must appear to you a *pastinacca* fish,[8] not of the flavor you expected. My excuse is that my mind is estranged from all these matters, as is shown by my going to my farm, far from every human face. Not knowing what is going on, I am forced to discuss in the dark, and have based everything on the information you have given me. Therefore I pray you to hold me excused. Give my regards to everybody there, especially to your Paolo, if he hasn't left.

Your friend<br>N. M.

8. *Having neither head nor tail.*

No. 124

20 June 1513, Florence
To . . . Francesco Vettori, in Rome.

[*France, England, Spain, the Swiss, and the Pope*]

Magnificent Ambassador:

I wrote some weeks ago in reply to a discussion of yours about the truce made between France and Spain. Since then I have had no letters from you, nor have I written, because, understanding that you were about to come home, I waited to speak to you directly. But since I now understand that your return has been put off and that you perhaps are going to stay there some days, I have decided to pay you a visit with this letter and to talk with you about all those things we would talk about if you were here. And though I can only talk wildly, because I am far away from secrets and from events, all the same I do not believe my opinions on affairs can do any harm either to me when I tell them to you, or to you when you hear them from me.

You have seen the result up to now of the French campaign in Italy, which has been for the most part contrary to all that could be believed or feared; and this outcome can be counted along with the other pieces of great good fortune that His Holiness the Pope and that splendid Family[1] have had. And because I believe that it is at all times the duty of a prudent man to reflect on what may harm him, and to foresee things when they are at a distance, and to assist what is good and to resist evil in time, I have put myself in the place of the Pope and have examined carefully what I should have to fear now, and what means I should use against them. This I shall write out for you, relying on what has been said by those who can do it better than I can, because of understanding these affairs more exactly.

If I were the Pontiff, I should think myself wholly dependent on Fortune until a truce were made through which arms would be laid down wholly or for the most part. I should think I was not safe from the Spaniards if they felt less apprehensive in Italy than they now do; nor safe from the Swiss if they were not apprehensive about France or Spain; nor safe from any other who might be dominant in Italy. So, on the other hand, I should not fear France if he remained on the other side of the mountains or if he returned to Lombardy on an agreement with me. And considering where things are at present, I should be as much afraid of a new agreement as of a new war.

As to the war that might make me return to those suspicions that I felt a few days ago, there is now no other fear except that France may win a great victory over the English. As to the agreement, it will take place when France makes an agreement with England or with Spain without me. And when I consider whether agreement with England will be easy or not, and also one with Spain, I decide that if one with England is difficult, this with Spain is possible and reasonable; and if we don't keep an eye on it, I greatly fear that it may come unexpectedly upon us, as did the truce between them.

1. *The Medici.*

The reasons that influence me are these. I have always believed and now believe that it would please and now pleases Spain to see the King of France out of Italy, provided that with his own arms and his own reputation he drove him out. I have never believed and do not believe that the victory the Swiss won last year over France was altogether pleasing to him. This opinion of mine is based on what is reasonable, since the Pope and the Swiss are too powerful in Italy, and on some reports from which I have learned that Spain complains also of the Pope, since he thinks the latter has given the Swiss too much power, and among the reasons that made him make a truce with France I believe this was one. Now if that first victory displeased Spain, this second that the Swiss have won will,[2] I believe, please him less, because he sees that he is alone in Italy, he sees that the Swiss have a high reputation there, he sees a Pope there who is young, rich and justly eager for glory and for not making a smaller display of himself than his predecessors have made, and he sees that he has brothers and nephews without territory. Spain therefore has good reason to fear him, for if he joins with the Swiss, Spain's possessions may be taken away from him, and not many obstacles can be seen to that if the Pope decides to do it. And Spain cannot provide against it more securely than by making an agreement with France, by which he could easily gain Navarre, and give France a state difficult to retain because of the nearness of the Swiss; and he could deprive the Swiss of their opening for easy passage into Italy, and could make the Pope's use of them less convenient. Such an agreement, when France is in his present situation, Spain—far from refusing it—should strive for.

So if I were the Pope and judged this likely to happen, I should try either to disturb it or to be leader in it; and I suspect that conditions may be such that a treaty can easily be concluded between France and Spain, the Pope and the Venetians. I do not put in it the Swiss or the Emperor or England, because I judge that England is going to let himself be ruled by Spain, and I do not see how the Emperor can be in agreement with the Venetians, or how France can come to terms with the Swiss; therefore I let them go and take those from whom the agreement is more to be hoped for; it seems to me that such an agreement would be enough for all four of them, because it ought to be enough for the Venetians to enjoy Verona,

2. *Novara, 6 June 1513.*

Vicenza, Padua and Treviso; for the King of France, Lombardy; for the Pope, his own territories; for Spain, the Kingdom. And to bring this about would cause injury merely to a counterfeit Duke of Milan, to the Swiss and to the Emperor, all of whom would be left ready to attack France. He to protect himself from them would have always to keep his corselet on, and this would make all the others safe from him, and the others would watch one another. Hence in this agreement I see great security and ease, because among them would be a common fear of the Germans that would be the glue to keep them stuck together, and there would not be among them any causes for complaint, except for the Venetians, who would be patient.

Taking it in any other way, I do not see any security, because I am of the opinion—and I don't believe I am deceiving myself—that when the King of France is dead, Spain will think about a campaign in Lombardy, and this will always be a reason for keeping his armies in the field. Otherwise I believe that in any case Spain will play a dirty trick on the others, and if the first victory of the Swiss made him make a truce, this second one will make him make peace; and I do not value negotiations he carries on, things that he says, or promises he makes. Such a peace, if it should be made, would be very dangerous, if made without the participation of the others.

Farewell,
Niccolò Machiavelli.

## No. 125

26 June 1513, Florence
To Master Giovanni di Francesco Vernacci[1] in Pera

*[Niccolò's misfortunes; God's help; business]*

Dearest Giovanni:

I have received several of your letters, and finally one of last April, in which and in the others you complain that you have not received mine. I answer that after your departure I had so many worries that it is no wonder I didn't write; it is rather a miracle that I am alive, because my office has been taken from me and I have been on the point of losing my life, which God and my innocence have saved

1. *A sister's son.*

for me. I have endured all sorts of evils, both of prison and other things. Yet by the grace of God I am well, and I manage to live as I can and so I'll try to do, until the heavens show themselves more favorable.[2]

You have written to me several times that I should see about lightening the taxes on your farm. On this I say that it is necessary for you to be here, and you will not be too late for the things that have to be done, because you will always be early enough.

Marietta[3] and all of us are well; try to keep well so that you can prosper in something.

Lorenzo Machiavelli complains about you and says that you do not explain clearly, because, as to one-half of the cloth that remains in your possession, you say that you have sold it for future payment and trusted it to I don't know whom, and you do not tell him the price, and the man to whom you say you have trusted it asserts that you are not correct. So I beg that you will write things out clearly and will go to the extreme of writing too much rather than too little, so that he can't rightfully complain about you.

Greet the consul on my behalf and tell him that I had his letter, and that I am alive and well, and have nothing else that is good. Christ keep you.

Niccolò Machiavelli in Florence.

2. *The remainder of this letter is printed in Lesca's edition, Florence, 1929.*
3. *Machiavelli's wife.*

### No. 129

4 August 1513, Florence
To Master Giovanni di Francesco Vernacci, in the Levant

*[Florentine commerce in the Levant]*

Dearest Giovanni:

I wrote to you about a month ago and told you what was happening to me and especially the reasons why I hadn't written to you before. I assume you got it, so I shall not repeat further. I received your letter of 26 May, to which it does not occur to me to say other than that we are all well; and Marietta had a baby girl that died after three days; Marietta is well.

I wrote to you before that Lorenzo Machiavelli did not feel satisfied with you, and especially with your reports, because he said you reported to him seldom and after delay, so that he did not get from your letters anything sure. I advise you therefore to write to those with whom you do business so clearly that when they have a letter of yours they may think they are there—in such detail it describes the thing to them. And as to sending you anything more, he has said to me that if he does not finish this piece of business entirely and come out clear, he intends not to undertake any other.

A certain Neri del Benino, brother-in-law of Giovanni Machiavelli, has come here, to whom Giovanni has given cloth; and therefore it is not proper that he should deal with anybody else. And Filippo [*Casavecchia*] wishes to sell it at the fair.

Try to keep healthy and attend to business, because I know that if you keep healthy and do your duty, you will not lack anything. I am well in body but in everything else ill. I have no other hope but that God will help me, and up to now he has indeed not abandoned me.

Remember me to the Consul Giuliano Lapi a thousand times, and tell him I am alive. I have nothing more to say. Christ watch over you.

Niccolò Machiavelli in Florence.

## No. 131

10 August 1513, Sant' Andrea in Percussina[1]
To Francesco Vettori [*in Rome?*]

*[Foreign powers in Italy; danger from the Swiss]*

Mr. Ambassador:

You do not want this poor King of France to have Lombardy again, and I do want it. I fear that your not wanting and my wanting have the same foundation of a natural affection or passion, which makes you say *no* and me, *yes*. You dignify your *no* by showing

1. At this village, about six miles south of Florence, can still be seen the house and farmland which Machiavelli inherited from his father. Their town house in Florence was on Via Guicciardini. After his loss of his secretaryship in 1512, he spent a good deal of time at Sant'Andrea, yet his letters are generally indicated as written in Florence. Florentine custom would have made the country house a usual summer residence.

that there would be more difficulty in bringing about peace if the King were to return to Lombardy; I have shown, in order to dignify my *yes*, that such is not the truth, and further that peace made in the method I indicate will be more secure and more solid.

And coming again to particulars, to answer your letter of the fifth, I say I am with you that, as to the King of England, it must always seem strange that he came into France with such great preparation and had to retire; it must be, then, that this retirement is founded on some necessity. I should judge that a necessity great enough would be that to which Spain and the Pope could force him, and I have been judging and now judge that if England should on one side find the attempt difficult and on the other should see the will of those two, he could easily be influenced. And if he should be discontented, it would seem to me pertinent, because the more the King of France is or will be weak, so long as he is between the hostile and dreaded English and Swiss, he cannot suppose that he can take other men's property; on the contrary, he will need to suppose that somebody else must protect his own for him. In that case the King of Spain will find his intention carried out, because I believe that in addition to making himself secure in his own states, he has been dreaming that with his armies he could continue as the cock of Italy. And in this situation they will all remain, because France, since he fears England and the Germans are hostile, cannot send a large army into Lombardy. He must therefore depend on Spanish armies in any case.

I do not see that the Swiss by themselves are in a position to make the English yield, because I do not believe that they can or will serve France except as hired soldiers. Because they are poor and do not border on England, France must pay them and at a high rate; moreover, he can hire Lanzknechts[2] and get the same service from them, and England would need to fear them quite as much. And if you say that England can get the Swiss to attack France in Burgundy, I answer that this method injures France, and if England is going to yield, France must find a way to injure England. I think Spain and the Pope will not now take up arms against France, but that on one side they will abandon him and on the other side will pretend that their reason for making war on France was consideration for the Church, and now that the King has desisted from harming her, they

2. *German mercenary infantrymen able to render much the same service as the Swiss soldiers.*

are not going to harm him. So I fully believe that without any stronger medicine England is going to retire, especially since, as I have said many times, he has found and is finding the expedition against France dangerous. And England has to keep in mind that if he comes to a battle and loses it, it could be that thus he would lose his own kingdom as well as France. And if you say to me that he will send money in large amounts to the Germans and will get France attacked from another side, I answer this with the opinion I have always held, that he will wish, both through pride and through glory, to spend his money on his own people; and, besides, anything he sent to the Emperor would be thrown away, and the Swiss would want too much.

I believe also that confidence between Spain and France can develop easily, because it is not to Spain's advantage to destroy the King in this way; and France has seen a test of it, for in the midst of his greatest dangers Spain has suspended arms. And so much the more France will trust in him, as on his side he sees that he is restored in Lombardy, for new benefits are wont to make men forget old injuries. On the other hand, Spain would not need to fear an old king,[3] worn out and sickly, placed between the English and the Germans, the one suspected and the other hostile; and he would not need to have the Pope's authority defend him, because it would be enough to keep that hostility alive.

Therefore I do not see, in attempting to bring about this peace through the means that I write of to you, greater difficulties than through those means of which you write; on the contrary, if there is an advantage, I see advantage in mine. On the other side, I do not see in your plan any safety, but in mine I do see some—of such a sort, though, as it is possible to get in these times.

He who wishes to see whether a peace is either durable or secure must among other things find out who are discontented with it, and from their discontent what may emerge. So considering your peace, I see England, France and the Emperor discontented, because not one of these has obtained his end. In mine, the discontented are England, the Swiss and the Emperor, for the same reasons. The discontents of yours can easily cause the ruin of Italy and of Spain, because as soon as this peace is made, even though France has approved it and England has not rejected it, both of these two will

3. *Louis XII of France, who died in 1515.*

again change their aim and their notion; and whereas France wished to go into Italy, and the other to master France, they will then turn to vengeance against Italy and against Spain. And reason requires that they will make a second agreement between themselves, in which they will have no difficulty in whatever they wish to do, when France is willing to reveal himself, because the Emperor with the aid of England and of France will leap the next day into Castile, will go into Italy when he wishes, will make France go there again, and so of a sudden these three together can upset and ruin everything. Neither the Spanish armies and the Swiss, nor the riches of the Pope are enough to hold this flood, because those three malcontents will have too much money and too many soldiers.

It is reasonable that Spain should see these dangers, and that he should try in every way to escape them, because France in this peace has no cause for loving him and much opportunity for damaging him; this opportunity France will be unlikely to give up in any way. Therefore if Spain has any eye at all for seeing things at a distance, he will not agree to it or carry it out, so that a peace will be made which will stir up a war greater and more dangerous. But on making such a peace as I have written about, in which the malcontents are England, the Emperor and the Swiss, these malcontents cannot, united or singly, easily injure an alliance of the other three [*the Pope, France, Spain*], because France, on this side and on the other side of the mountains, will continue to be an obstacle and, with the aid of the other two, will make such opposition that the allies will be safe, and England and the others will not undertake any enterprise, seeing its difficulty. There will be nothing through which the allies need to fear each other, since, as I have told you many times, each of them will have carried out his intention, and their enemies will be so powerful and dangerous as to keep them chained together.

There is in your peace another very serious danger to Italy, which is that every time there is a weak duke in Milan, Lombardy will belong not to that duke but to the Swiss. And though a thousand times those three [*England, France, the Emperor*] who are discontented at your peace fail to stir, I believe the nearness of the Swiss is very important and deserves to be more thoroughly considered than it is. You say that the Swiss will not stir because they have regard for France, because they will have the rest of Italy against them, and because it will satisfy them to give the country a raking[4] and go away. I cannot believe that you are right.

First, as I said above, France will desire to avenge himself, and having received harm from all Italy, will delight in seeing her ruined. Therefore he will secretly give the Swiss money, and feed this fire rather than otherwise.

As to union of the Italians, you make me laugh, first, because there never will be union here to do anything good. Even though the leaders should unite, they are not sufficient, because there are no armies here worth a farthing except the Spanish, who, because they are few, are not enough. Second, because the tails are not united with the heads. The people of this generation will compete in submitting to the Swiss before they will move a step to use any opportunity that arises.

As to its being enough for the Swiss to give a raking and go away, I tell you not to rest on or encourage others to rest on such an opinion, and I beg you to consider how men's affairs develop, and how the powers of the world, and especially republics, have developed. You will see that at first it is enough for men to defend themselves and not to be mastered by others; from this they go on to injure others and to try to master others. For the Swiss it was at first enough to defend themselves from the dukes of Austria; this defense made them esteemed at home. Then it was enough to defend themselves from Duke Charles, which gave them a name away from home. Then it was enough for them to take stipends from others, in order to keep their young men ready for war, and to get honor. This has given them a still greater name, has made them bolder, because they have learned and observed more countries and more men, and also has put in their minds an ambitious spirit and a desire to try carrying on war for themselves. And Pellegrino Lorini said to me long ago that when they came with Beaumont to Pisa, they often talked among themselves about the efficiency of their military organization and that it was like that of the Romans, and why could they not one day do as the Romans did? They were boasting that they had given France all the victories he had had up to that day, and that they did not know why one day they could not fight for themselves.

Now there has come this opportunity, and they have taken it, and they have entered Lombardy with the excuse of putting the present

4. *Rapid plundering, as distinguished from serious occupation.*

Duke back there, but in fact they themselves are the duke. On the first opportunity they will become complete masters of Milan, destroying the ducal family and all the nobility of that state; on the second, they will overrun all Italy, producing the same effect. Therefore I conclude that it will not be enough for them to give a raking and go away; instead one needs to be exceedingly afraid of them.

I know that to this opinion of mine is opposed a natural defect of man: first, wishing to live from day to day; second, not believing that anything can happen that has not happened; last, always reckoning about a person in the same way. Therefore there will be no one who will advise us to consider getting the Swiss out of Lombardy in order to put the French back there, because they are not willing to run the present risks that must be run in attempting it, nor will they believe in future ills, nor will they dream of being able to trust France. My friend, this German river is so large that it has need of a great dyke to hold it. If France had never been in Italy, and you were not newly aware of the arrogance, satiety,[5] and extortion of the French, which are the things that upset this consideration for us, you would already have run to France to ask him to come into Lombardy, because the precautions against this flood need to be taken now, before the Swiss put down roots in this land and commence to taste the sweetness of ruling. And if they settle themselves here, all Italy is ruined, because all the discontented will aid them and make them a ladder for their own greatness and the ruin of others. I fear them alone, and not them and the Emperor, as Casa[6] has written to us, though it would be easy for them to unite, because, just as the Emperor has been pleased that they should overrun Lombardy and become lords of Milan, which would not seem reasonable in any way for the very reasons that you wrote to me, so, notwithstanding those, they might be content that he should make some progress in Italy.

Mr. Ambassador, I write more to satisfy you than because I know what I ought to say, and therefore I beg you that by your next letter you will advise me how this world stands, and what is being done, and what is hoped, and what is feared, if you wish that in these weighty matters I am to support my opinions. Otherwise you

5. *Probably a textual error for insatiety (insazietà).*
6. *Filippo Casavecchia.*

will get hold of an ass's will and testament, or some of those things, like Brancaccino.[7] With my regards.

Niccolò Machiavelli, on his farm.

7. *Giuliano Brancaccio.*


## No. 133

25 August 1513, Florence
To Francesco Vettori [*in Rome?*]

[*Donato del Corno needs influence with the Medici*]

Magnificent Ambassador:

Because I know how much you love our Donato del Corno, and he knows it too, we have decided together with certainty to give you a bit of trouble, in order to see if by means of Signor Giuliano[1] we can satisfy him in this putting of his name in the bags that has to be done for the choice of officers.[2] You know with how much help Donato was assisted by the said Signor Giuliano in what was necessary to make him a voter. That was in a certain way to the astonishment of everybody, and must have resulted from Giuliano's great love for him, or from some great deserts. Now about these deserts I know something; and they are of such a sort that you or anybody might bring Donato's cause before His Lordship. And because we have done nothing, if there is no order that he is to be put in the bags and then recognized, it seems good to us now, since the couplers are engaged in putting names in the bags, to ask that Donato be put in. Therefore Donato writes the attached to His Lordship and reminds him simply of his idea, turning himself over to you for words; we beg you will be so good as to give His Lordship with your own hand the attached letter, and then to ask that he write instructing one or two couplers to put Donato in the bag among the first. I said two in order that there should be a clearer understanding of his will; but in whatever way he writes, the letter needs to indicate clearly that he wants it so, because you know the fussy people there are; and if it is

1. *Giuliano de' Medici, Duke of Nemours, then residing in Florence.*
2. *The bags contained the names of men considered eligible to hold office in Florence. When the offices were to be filled, names were drawn out. The Medici government saw to it that only names acceptable to it were put in the bags.*

not warm, we shall run into objections, and Donato will receive disgrace and harm. Because Donato trusts in Messer Francesco Pepi, you might arrange that one of the two to whom he writes should be Messer Francesco; and you might send the letter to Donato, so he can use it to his greatest advantage.

If I did not know how eager you are to help, and devoted to your friends, I would go to trouble in begging you, and so would Donato. May it be enough that he says he realizes for the most part this benefit is from you. I am yours to command.

Your Niccolò Machiavelli, in Florence.

## No. 134

26 August 1513, Florence
To Francesco Vettori, in Rome

[*France, England, Spain, and above all the Swiss; Mercenary Soldiers*]

Mr. Ambassador:

Your letter of the twentieth, now before me, bewildered me, because its arrangement, the multitude of its reasons, and all its other qualities so entangled me that in the beginning I was lost and con⁄fused; and if in the rereading I had not been a little reassured, I would have given you a bad card[1] and would have answered you about other things. But as I get used to it, the same thing has happened to me as did to the fox when he saw the lion: the first time he was ready to die for fear; the second time he stopped behind a bush to look at him; the third time he spoke to him; and so having reas⁄sured myself by getting used to it, I shall answer you.

And as to the state of things in the world, I draw this conclusion about them: that we are ruled by princes of such a sort that they have, either by nature or by accident, these qualities: we have a Pope who is wise, and therefore serious and cautious; an Emperor unstable and fickle; a King of France inclined to anger and timid; a King of Spain stingy and avaricious; a King of England rich, fiery, eager for glory; the Swiss brutal, victorious and arrogant; we in Italy poor, ambitious, cowardly; the rest of the kings I do not know about. Hence, con⁄sidering these qualities in connection with what is going on at

1. *Would not have replied.*

present, I believe the friar who said: "Peace, peace, and there will be no peace."[2] I admit to you that every peace is difficult, yours as well as mine. And if you hold that in mine there is more difficulty, I am satisfied; but I hope you will listen patiently, both where I fear that you deceive yourself, and where I feel sure that you deceive yourself.

Where I have doubts is, first, that you make this King of France of little importance too early, and this King of England a great thing. To me it does not seem reasonable that France should not have more than ten thousand infantry, because from his own country, if he did not have Germans, he is able to get many, and if not as experienced as the Germans, they are as experienced as the English. What makes me believe it is that I see that this King of England with so much energy, with so large an army, with so much desire to tear him up by the roots, as the Sienese say, has not yet taken Therouanne, a fortified town like Empoli, at the first attack and in a time when his soldiers are acting with such great energy. This alone is enough for me not to have so much fear of England and not to put so low a value on France. I judge this slow proceeding by France is choice and not fear, because he hopes, England[3] not getting a foothold in that state and the winter coming on, that he will be forced either to return to his island or to remain in France with danger, since those places are swampy and without a single tree, so that the English must already have suffered much. And therefore I should suppose that it would not be very difficult for the Pope and Spain to influence England. Besides, that France has not decided to give up the Council makes me continue in the opinion given above, because if he were so much distressed, he would need everybody, and would wish to be on good terms with everybody.

As to the money that England has sent to the Swiss, I believe it, but I am astonished that he sent it by the Emperor's hands, because I should believe the Emperor would have wanted to spend it on his own soldiers, not on the Swiss. And I am not able to settle it in my head that this Emperor is so thoughtless and the rest of Germany so careless as to allow the Swiss to rise to such influence. And when I see that it is so, I hesitate to judge anything, because this happens against every judgment a man can make. Not at all, too, do I know how it can be that the Swiss have held the Castle of Milan and have

2. *Savonarola.*
3. *Here, as usually in Machiavelli, England, France etc. mean the kings of those countries.*

not wanted to, because to me it appears that, having it, their intention has been carried out; and that they ought to do this rather than go to take Burgundy for the Emperor.

Where I believe you deceive yourself entirely is in the affairs of the Swiss, about fearing them more or less. Because I judge that they are to be feared exceedingly; and Casa knows and many of my friends, with whom I am in the habit of talking about these things, know that I had a low opinion of the Venetians, even at their greatest strength, because I always thought it a much greater miracle that they gained that empire and held it than that they lost it. But their ruin was too honorable, because what was done by a king of France could have been done by a Duke Valentino or any general of reputation who had appeared in Italy and had commanded fifteen thousand persons. What moved me was their way of proceeding without generals and soldiers of their own.

Now those reasons that made me not fear them make me fear the Swiss. I do not know what Aristotle says about states made up of detached pieces, but I do consider what reasonably can be, what is, and what has been; and I remember reading that the Lucumnians held all Italy as far as the Alps, until they were driven from Lombardy by the Gauls. If the Aetolians and the Achaeans did not make progress, it resulted more from their times than from themselves, because they had always upon them a Macedonian king of the greatest power, who did not let them get out of their nest, and after him the Romans; so it was more the power of others than their own constitution that did not let them expand. Now, the Swiss do not wish to make subjects because they do not see in it their own advantage; they say so now, because they do not see it now; but, as I said to you about something else, things go along gradually, and often men are led by necessity to do what it was not their intention to do, and the habit of bodies of people is to go slowly. Considering where the matter stands, they already have in Italy as their tributaries a Duke of Milan and a Pope; this tribute they have put with their income, and they will not wish it to fail; and when the time comes that one of them does fail, they will consider it rebellion, and will be at once at their pikes; on winning the contest, they will consider making themselves safe, and to do this they will put some additional bridles on those they have conquered; and so little by little they will come to assert full authority.

Do not trust at all in those armies which you say will one day produce some fruit in Italy, because that is impossible. First, with respect to them, there would be many leaders and those disunited, and I cannot see that a leader can be found who will keep them united. Second, with respect to the Swiss. For you need to understand this: the best armies are those of armed peoples; and they cannot be resisted except by armies similar to themselves. Remember some armies of renown: Romans, Lacedemonians, Athenians, Aetolians, Achaeans, swarms of Northerners. You see also that those who have done great things have armed their own people, as Ninus the Assyrians, Cyrus the Persians, Alexander the Macedonians. I find only Hannibal and Pyrrhus to represent those who with armies irregularly picked up have done big things. This came from the enormous ability of the leaders, and that was of such great influence that it gave their mixed armies the same spirit and discipline as are found in a ruler's own people.

And if you observe the defeats of France and his victories, you will see that he won as long as he fought against Italians and Spaniards, whose armies were like his own, but now that he has fought against armed peoples, such as the Swiss and the English, he has lost, and is in danger of losing more. Men of intelligence have always foreseen this calamity for France, inferring it from his not having his own infantry, and having disarmed his own people—which was contrary to every action and every precept of anyone who has been considered prudent and great. But this was not a defect of the early kings, but of King Louis, and from him on.

So do not, therefore, rely on Italian armies, if they are not either uniform like Swiss armies, or, being mixed, if they do not form one body like theirs.

And as to the divisions or disunions you mention, do not think they will produce an effect, so long as Swiss laws are observed; and they are going to be observed for a while. Because in that land there cannot be or appear heads that have tails, and heads without tails are destroyed soon and produce slight effect. And those whom they have killed probably have been some who as magistrates or otherwise have wished in unusual ways to favor the French party, who have been found out and killed, and they are not more important in that state than a number here who are hanged as thieves.

I do not, indeed, believe they will produce an empire like the

Romans, but I do believe they can become masters of Italy, by reason of their nearness and our disorders and vile conditions. And because this frightens me, I wish to remedy it, and if France does not suffice, I see no other resource; and I am now ready to weep with you over our ruin and servitude, which, if it does not come today or tomorrow, will come in our time. And Italy will owe that to Pope Julius and to those who do not protect us, if protection can now be found. Farewell.

Niccolò Machiavelli.

No. 135

*[August 1513, Florence]*
*[To Francesco Vettori, in Rome]*

*[The character of Lorenzo de' Medici, later Duke of Urbino]*[1]

I do not wish to omit giving you notice of the Magnificent Lorenzo's way of proceeding, for he has been up to now of such a quality that he has filled with good hopes all this city, and it seems that everybody finds in him happy recollection of his grandfather; because His Magnificence is attentive to business, liberal and pleasant in audience, slow and weighty in his answers. The method of his conversing differs so much from that of the others that no pride is seen in it; yet he does not mix in such a way that through too great familiarity he gains a low reputation. With young men of his age, he has such a manner that he neither alienates them from himself nor does he give them confidence to indulge in any youthful insolence. He makes himself, in short, both loved and revered, rather than feared, which as it is the more difficult to achieve, so it is more praiseworthy in him.

The management of his house is so arranged that, though we see there much splendor and liberality, nonetheless he does not abandon the life of a citizen. Thus in all his movements, outside and inside, nothing is seen that offends anybody or is to be censured; at which everybody appears to be much pleased. And though I know that from many you can learn this same thing, I have chosen to describe

1. *Grandson of Lorenzo the Magnificent. At this time he was residing in Florence as a sort of prince. To him* THE PRINCE *is dedicated. The text is a fragment of a letter.*

it, so that from my account of it you can get such pleasure as comes to all the rest of us who continually experience it; and you can when you have opportunity, give assurance of it to his Holiness, our ruler.

[*Niccolò Machiavelli.*]

## No. 137

10 December 1513, Florence
To Francesco Vettori, his benefactor, in Rome

[*Niccolò's life on his farm; the composition of* THE PRINCE*; desire to serve the Medici*]

Magnificent Ambassador:

"Never late were favors divine."[1] I say this because I seemed to have lost—no, rather mislaid—your good will; you had not written to me for a long time, and I was wondering what the reason could be. And of all those that came into my mind I took little account, except of one only, when I feared that you had stopped writing because somebody had written to you that I was not a good guardian of your letters, and I knew that, except Filippo and Pagolo,[2] nobody by my doing had seen them. I have found it again through your last one of the twenty-third of the past month, from which I learn with pleasure how regularly and quietly you carry on this public office, and I encourage you to continue so, because he who gives up his own convenience for the convenience of others, only loses his own and from them gets no gratitude. And since Fortune wants to do everything, she wishes us to let her do it, to be quiet, and not to give her trouble, and to wait for a time when she will allow something to be done by men; and then will be the time for you to work harder, to stir things up more, and for me to leave my farm and say: "Here I am." I cannot however, wishing to return equal favors, tell you in this letter anything else than what my life is; and if you judge it is to be swapped for yours, I shall be glad to change it.

I am living on my farm, and since I had my last bad luck, I have not spent twenty days, putting them all together, in Florence. I have until now been snaring thrushes with my own hands. I got up

---

1. Petrarch, TRIUMPH OF ETERNITY 13.
2. Filippo Casavecchia and Pagolo Vettori, *brother of the recipient of the letter.*

before day, prepared birdlime, went out with a bundle of cages on my back, so that I looked like Geta when he was returning from the harbor with Amphitryo's books.[3] I caught at least two thrushes and at most six. And so I did all September. Later this pastime, pitiful and strange as it is, gave out, to my displeasure. And of what sort my life is, I shall tell you.

I get up in the morning with the sun and go into a grove I am having cut down, where I remain two hours to look over the work of the past day and kill some time with the cutters, who have always some bad-luck story ready, about either themselves or their neigh-bors. And as to this grove I could tell you a thousand fine things that have happened to me, in dealing with Frosino da Panzano and others who wanted some of this firewood. And Frosino especially sent for a number of cords without saying a thing to me, and on payment he wanted to keep back from me ten lire, which he says he should have had from me four years ago, when he beat me at *cricca* at Antonio Guicciardini's. I raised the devil, and was going to prosecute as a thief the waggoner who came for the wood, but Giovanni Machiavelli came between us and got us to agree. Battista Guicciardini, Filippo Ginori, Tommaso del Bene and some other citizens, when that north wind was blowing, each ordered a cord from me. I made promises to all and sent one to Tommaso, which at Florence changed to half a cord, because it was piled up again by himself, his wife, his servant, his children, so that he looked like Gabburra when on Thursday with all his servants he cudgels an ox.[4] Hence, having seen for whom there was profit, I told the others I had no more wood, and all of them were angry about it, and espe-cially Battista, who counts this along with his misfortunes at Prato.[5]

Leaving the grove, I go to a spring, and thence to my aviary. I have a book in my pocket, either Dante or Petrarch, or one of the lesser poets, such as Tibullus, Ovid, and the like. I read of their tender passions and their loves, remember mine, enjoy myself a while in that sort of dreaming. Then I move along the road to the inn; I speak with those who pass, ask news of their villages, learn various

3. *A reference to a story founded on the* AMPHITRYO *of Plautus.*
4. *Gabburra, apparently a butcher, is unknown.*
5. *Battista Guicciardini was podesta of Prato when it was taken by the Spanish forces in 1512; as an immediate result the Medici were restored to Florence. It is remarkable that Machiavelli could use the fall of Prato in a est.*

things, and note the various tastes and different fancies of men. In the course of these things comes the hour for dinner, where with my family I eat such food as this poor farm of mine and my tiny property allow. Having eaten, I go back to the inn; there is the host, usually a butcher, a miller, two furnace tenders. With these I sink into vulgarity for the whole day, playing at *cricca* and at trich-trach, and then these games bring on a thousand disputes and countless insults with offensive words, and usually we are fighting over a penny, and nevertheless we are heard shouting as far as San Casciano. So, mixed up with these lice, I keep my brain from growing mouldy, and satisfy the malice of this fate of mine, being glad to have her drive me along this road, to see if she will be ashamed of it.

On the coming of evening, I return to my house and enter my study; and at the door I take off the day's clothing, covered with mud and dust, and put on garments regal and courtly; and reclothed appropriately, I enter the ancient courts of ancient men, where, received by them with affection, I feed on that food which only is mine and which I was born for, where I am not ashamed to speak with them and to ask them the reason for their actions; and they in their kindness answer me; and for four hours of time I do not feel boredom, I forget every trouble, I do not dread poverty, I am not frightened by death; entirely I give myself over to them.

And because Dante says it does not produce knowledge when we hear but do not remember, I have noted everything in their conversation which has profited me,[6] and have composed a little work *On Princedoms*, where I go as deeply as I can into considerations on this subject, debating what a princedom is, of what kinds they are, how they are gained, how they are kept, why they are lost. If ever you can find any of my fantasies pleasing, this one should not displease you; and by a prince, and especially by a new prince, it ought to be welcomed. Hence I am dedicating it to His Magnificence Giuliano.[7] Filippo Casavecchia has seen it; he can give you some account in part of the thing in itself and of the discussions I have had with him, though I am still enlarging and revising it.

You wish, Magnificent Ambassador, that I leave this life and

6. *This seems to be Machiavelli making notes on Livy's* History *for his own* Discourses, *out of which rose* The Prince.

7. *Giuliano de' Medici, later Duke of Nemours, son of Lorenzo the Magnificent. He resided in Florence after the restoration of the Medici in 1512, but in 1513 withdrew to Rome.*

come to enjoy yours with you. I shall do it in any case, but what tempts me now are certain affairs that within six weeks I shall finish. What makes me doubtful is that the Soderini we know so well are in the city, whom I should be obliged, on coming there, to visit and talk with. I should fear that on my return I could not hope to dismount at my house but should dismount at the Bargello, because though this government has mighty foundations and great security, yet it is new and therefore suspicious, and there is no lack of wiseacres who, to make a figure, like Pagolo Bertini, would place others at the dinner table and leave the reckoning to me.[8] I beg you to rid me of this fear, and then I shall come within the time mentioned to visit you in any case.

I have talked with Filippo about this little work of mine that I have spoken of, whether it is good to give it or not to give it; and if it is good to give it, whether it would be good to take it myself, or whether I should send it there. Not giving it would make me fear that at the least Giuliano will not read it and that this rascal Ardinghelli will get himself honor from this latest work of mine.[9] The giving of it is forced on me by the necessity that drives me, because I am using up my money, and I cannot remain as I am a long time without becoming despised through poverty.[10] In addition, there is my wish that our present Medici lords will make use of me, even if they begin by making me roll a stone; because then if I could not gain their favor, I should complain of myself; and through this thing, if it were read, they would see that for the fifteen years while I have been studying the art of the state, I have not slept or been playing; and well may anybody be glad to get the services of one who at the expense of others has become full of experience. Of my honesty there should be no doubt, because having always preserved my honesty, I shall hardly now learn to break it; he who has been honest and good for forty-three years, as I have, cannot change his nature; and as a witness to my honesty and goodness I have my poverty.

8. *Pagolo Bertini is unknown and the meaning of the sentence is uncertain.*

9. *Piero Ardinghelli was secretary to Pope Leo X. Machiavelli seems to have feared that, Giuliano had not read* THE PRINCE, *Ardinghelli would steal ideas from it and offer them as his own.*

10. *A reminiscence of Juvenal 3. 153 or Plautus,* STICHUS 1. 3. 20.

I should like, then, to have you also write me what you think best on this matter, and I give you my regards. Be happy.

Niccolò Machiavelli, in Florence.

## No. 138

19 December 1513, Florence
To Francesco Vettori [*in Rome?*]

[*Donato del Corno's contribution to the Medici; a Franciscan preacher*]

Magnificent Ambassador:

I wrote eight or ten days ago answering yours of the twenty-third of the past month and told you my doubts about my coming there. I wait for your opinion and then I shall do what you advise.

The present letter I am writing to you in behalf of our Donato del Corno.[1] You know how his affairs stand and that in the beginning he got a letter from His Magnificence Giuliano to the Magnificent Lorenzo. Then there was the death of Messer Francesco Pepi, who had taken the affair on his shoulders; this almost deprived Donato of hope. Yet not to give up entirely, we went—Donato and I—to see Jacopo Gianfigliazzi, who promised us vigorously that he would leave nothing undone; and just two days ago, with the letter you wrote him, we spoke to him again on this matter, and he promised better than the first time and concluded by saying that from now to the middle of January it could not be thought of, because he had to put the other names in the bags first. On our asking if he advised getting further letters from Giuliano, he said such action could be only good, but that we should delay until the last in order to get the letter when the thing is to be done, because if he had it now, it would, when the time came, be old, and the business would have to be done over from the beginning. Yet we need to act so that at the right time we will have this letter; and if you have not got that of which you last wrote to Donato, you could let it go. If you have got it, we would need to consider at the time of action what ought to be done.

We think, relying on our first experience, that a letter, unless there is somebody here who will remember it, will be a dead favor.

1. *See Letter no. 133, above.*

Hence we judge that you need to do something there, when you can, so that Ser Niccolò Michelozzi will receive this charge from Giu- liano. Here he will remind Lorenzo of it, either through a letter that Giuliano will write or through a letter that Piero Ardinghelli will write in Giuliano's name;[2] thus, whatever excuse Ser Niccolò may have, he will at the right time be made to remember the matter. Because we believe it will be easy for Piero Ardinghelli to attend to this thing, we suggest that you do some work on him, promising what you judge will be the best thing to offer him; Donato will be generous about it. The way for this is open, because Piero knows that His Magnificence Giuliano has caused favors to be done to Maestro Manente and some others whom Giuliano wished should be assisted, so it is proper for Donato to get some favors. If Piero is willing, I believe we can get everything. So we think this medicine of Piero should be used, and that all the favors that are coming should come from the eighth to the fifteenth of January, because Piero is at the business for the reasons given. In order that you may know everything and see if Donato deserves to be put in the number of the loving servitors of the most illustrious Medici Family, you should know that about a day after they returned to Florence, Donato carried to His Magnificence Giuliano five hundred ducats (they were lent freely and unasked), for which he is still creditor.[3] This is not told you so that you will tell it to anybody, but so that, knowing it, you will undertake this affair with more spirit.

Donato and I are not trying to annoy you and reannoy you in this matter, because, knowing how zealous a friend you are, we think to please you by asking it, and therefore he at the same time asks your aid and excuses himself to you, if it is at all necessary, and what we write we give as our opinion, but always we shall approve all the methods that you adopt as most prudent.

Those four verses that you write about Riccio in the beginning of the letter about Donato, we recited from memory to Giovanni Machiavelli; and in place of Machiavello and Pera, we inserted Giovanni Machiavelli. As a result he has a head like a basket,[4] and

2. *As secretary to Pope Leo X, head of the Medici family, Ardinghelli could write in the name of Giuliano de'Medici, then probably in Rome, to Lorenzo de'Medici, later Duke of Urbino, in charge of the family interests in Florence.*

3. *For Medici failure to repay this loan, see the letter of 17 Dec. 1517 (no. 166).*

4. *He is thoroughly confused.*

says that he does not know where you have found anyone whom it would concern, and that he is going to write to you about it in any case; for a while Filippo and I had a great deal of pleasure from it.

In this city of ours, which is a magnet for all the imposters in the world, there is a brother of Saint Francis who is half hermit, who, to get more belief for his preaching, claims to be a prophet; yesterday morning in Santa Croce, where he preaches, he said many great and wonderful things. First, before a long time passes, so that one who is ninety years old will be able to see it, an unjust pope will be set up against a just pope, and he will have his false prophets and will make cardinals and will divide the church. Likewise, he said that the King of France will be utterly destroyed and one of the house of Rouen will master Italy. Our city will be given to fire and plunder, the churches will be abandoned and ruined, the priests dispersed, and three years we shall be without divine service. There will be pestilence and famine of the worst sort; in the city ten men will not be left, and on the farms two will not be left. For eighteen years a devil has been in a human body and he has said mass. Some two million devils were unchained to be ministers of the things mentioned above, and they entered many bodies of dead men, and did not let those bodies decay, in order that false prophets and clergy might make the dead rise up, and be believed. These things frightened me yesterday to such an extent that this morning I was going to stay with *la Riccia*⁵ and I did not go; but I do not at all know whether, if I had had to stay with *il Riccio,* I should have paid any attention to that Franciscan. The preaching I did not hear, because I am not given to such doings, but I have heard it reported in this way by all Florence.

I give you my regards and ask that you will greet Casa on my behalf, and tell him that if he does not follow other customs than he followed here, he will lose his credit with the fellows there as he has lost it here. Farewell.

Niccolò Machiavelli, in Florence.

5. La Riccia *(the curly-haired), a Florentine harlot.* Il Riccio *(the curly-haired) is mentioned in the letter of 16 April 1513 (no. 122) as one of the servants of Donato del Corno. In a letter to Machiavelli, Vettori praises him as a faithful friend (9 Feb. 1513).*

## No. 140

5 January 1513-[*1514*], Florence
To Francesco Vettori . . . his most assiduous benefactor [*in Rome?*]

[*He who is held wise by day will never be held crazy by night*]

Magnificent Ambassador:

It is most certainly a great thing to consider how blind men are to the things in which they sin and what sharp persecutors they are of the vices they do not have. I could bring up as examples things Greek, Latin, Hebrew and Chaldean, and go off even to the land of the Sofi and Prester John and bring them before you, if instances right at home and recent were not enough. I believe Ser Sano[1] could have come into your house from one Jubilee to the next and that never would Filippo have thought that he gave you any trouble. Instead, he would have thought that you were glad to associate with him and that it was just the conduct suited to an ambassador, who, being obligated to countless serious doings, must necessarily have some recreations and pleasures; and this of Ser Sano would have appeared to him to fit exactly, and with everybody he would have praised your prudence and lauded you to the sky for such a choice. On the other side, I believe that if the whole brothel of Valenza had run through your house, Brancaccio never would have censured you for it; on the contrary he would have lauded you for this more than if he had heard you speaking better before the Pope than Demosthenes could.

If you had wished to see the proof of this reasoning, it would have been necessary for you, without either one's knowing of the admoni-tions of the other, that you should have given the appearance of believing them and wishing to carry out their advice. And if you had locked the door against the harlots and driven away Ser Sano and drawn back to serious behavior and been immersed in thought, there would by no means have passed four days before Filippo would have said: "What has become of Ser Sano? What is the reason he doesn't come here any more? I believe him a respectable man; I don't know what those groups are chattering about, and I am sure

1. *According to Vettori's letters, some of his friends demurred at his association with this man. Filippo Casavecchio and Giuliano Brancaccio, mentioned below, have appeared in earlier letters. See the index in vol. 3.*

he understands very well the habits of this court and is a useful thingamajig; you ought, Ambassador, to send for him." About Brancaccio, I'm not saying whether he is grieved and astonished by the absence of the women, and if he wouldn't have said it to you while he was keeping his ass turned to the fire, as Filippo would have done, he would have said it to you in your chamber when you were alone with him. And to explain to you better, when you were in such a puritanical frame of mind, I, who associate with and pay attention to women, should have needed to come in there. As soon as I got a notion of the thing, I would have said: "Ambassador, you will get sick, and it does not seem to me that you have any recreation; here there are no boys; here there are no women; what sort of a bitchin' house is this?"

Magnificent Ambassador, there are none here except crazy men; and few there are who know this world and who know that he who tries to act in the ways of others never does anything, because men never have the same opinions. These do not know that he who is held prudent by day will never be held crazy by night, and if anyone is thought a man of substance and effective, whatever he does to refresh his spirit and live happily will bring him honor and not blame; and instead of being called a bugger or a whoremaster, it will be said that he is tolerant, ready, and a good companion. They do not know also that he gives his own and does not take that of others and that he acts like the must when it boils, which gives its flavor to dishes that smell of mould and does not take mould from the dishes.

Therefore, Mr. Ambassador, do not be afraid of the mould of Ser Sano nor of the rot of Mona Smeria, and follow your habits, and let Brancaccio talk; for he does not realize that he is one of those hedge birds that is the first to squawk and shriek, and then on the coming of the owl is the first to be taken. And our Filippo is like a vulture, which when there is no carrion in the region, flies a hundred miles to find some, and when he has his crop full, he sits on a pine and laughs at the eagles, hawks, falcons and the like who, since they eat delicate foods, are for half the year almost dying of hunger. So Magnificent Ambassador, let one squawk and the other fill his crop, and you attend to your affairs in your own way.

Niccolò Machiavelli.

## No. 142

4 February 1513-[*1514*], Florence
To Francesco Vettori . . . his benefactor [*in Rome?*]

[*Amusement at Vettori's account of an evening in Rome*]

Magnificent Ambassador:

I came back yesterday from my farm, and your Pagolo gave me your letter of the eighteenth of the past month, which answered one of mine of I don't know when, in which I took great pleasure, seeing that Fortune has been so loving to you that she has been able to do so well that Filippo and Brancaccio have with you become one soul in two bodies, or rather two souls in one body, in order not to make a mistake. And when I consider from the beginning to the end the story you have told of them and of yourself—which in truth, if I had not lost my trifles, I would have inserted among the recollections of modern things—it seems to me as worthy to be recited to a prince as anything I have heard this year.

It seems to me that I see Brancaccio curled up on a seat to sit low in order better to observe the face of Costanza, and with words and with signs and with actions and with smiles and movement of mouth and of eyes and with spitting, I see him entirely poured out, entirely consumed and completely hanging upon the words, upon the breath, upon the look, upon the smell and upon the sweet ways and wom⁄anly kindness of Costanza.

> I turned to the right hand, and saw Casa,[1]
> who with that boy was closer to the mark,
> a bit grave⁄looking, and with shaven head.

I see him gesture and now shift himself toward one side, now toward the other; I see him sometimes shake his head at the halting and modest answers of the boy; I see him, as he speaks with him, taking now the function of the father, now of the teacher, now of the lover; and that poor boy remaining doubtful of the end to which he wants to bring him; and now he fears for his honor, now trusts in the gravity of the man, now has respect for his elegant and mature bearing. I see you, Mr. Ambassador, at close quarters with that widow and her brother, and having an eye on that boy, the right

1. *Filippo Casavecchia.*

however, and the other on that girl; and one ear for the words of the widow and the other to Casa and Brancaccio; I see you answering in general and to their last words, like Echo; and finally you cut off the talk and run to the fire with your quick little steps a finger long, and with your back a little bent. I see at your return Filippo, Brancaccio, the boy, the girl stand up, and you say: Sit down keep your seats, don't move, go on with what you were saying," and after many ceremonies, a little homely and slightly coarse, you get everybody seated and start some pleasant conversation. But above all I think I see Filippo when Piero del Bene came in; and if I knew how to paint, I would send him to you painted, because certain acts of his so familiar, certain glances oblique, certain pos, tures full of scorn cannot be written. I see you at table; I see the bread set out, the glasses, the table, and the trestles, and everybody showing or rather dripping gladness, and at last all plunging into a flood of joy. I see in the end Jove chained in front of the chariot; I see you in love; and because when fire is applied to green wood it is more powerful, so the flame in you is greater because it has found more resistance.  Here I should be permitted to exclaim in the words of Terence: "O heaven, O earth, O seas of Neptune!" I see you fighting within yourself, and since "Not easily agree or dwell in one place majesty and love,"[2] you would like to become a swan to lay an egg in her lap, now to become gold so that she might carry you off in her pocket, now one animal, now another, if only you are not separated from her.

Because you are terrified at my example, recalling what the arrows of Love have done to me, I am forced to tell you how I have con, ducted myself with him.  In short, I have let him go on and have followed him through valleys, groves, hills, and plains, and I have found that he has given me more pleasures than if I had treated him badly. Take off, then, the pack,saddle, pull out the bit, close your eyes, and say: "Go ahead, Love, guide me, lead me; if I come out well, may the praises be yours; if badly, may yours be the blame; I am your slave; you can gain nothing more by maltreating me, rather you will lose, maltreating your own property." With such and like words, enough to bore through a wall, you can make him com, passionate. So, my master, be happy; do not get frightened, show your face to Fortune, and continue to do what the revolutions of the

2. *Ovid*, METAMORPHOSES *2. 846.*

heavens, the conditions of the times and of men bring before you, and do not doubt that you will break every snare and overcome every difficulty. Then if you wish to make a serenade, I offer myself to come there with some fine invention to make her fall in love.

This is all that occurs to me in response to yours. About this place there is nothing to say, except prophecies and announcements of misfortunes, which God, if they speak falsely, I hope will cancel; if they speak the truth, I hope will turn to good.

When I am in Florence, I divide my time between the shop of Donato del Corno and la Riccia, and it seems to me I am boring both of them, for he calls me shop-nuisance, and she house-nuisance. Yet with both I conduct myself as a man of wisdom, and up to now I have profited so much from this reputation that Donato has let me get warm at his fire and the other lets me sometimes kiss her just in passing. I believe that this favor will last only a little while, because I have given both of them certain advice and have not succeeded with it, so that just today la Riccia said about me in a certain conversation that she pretended to carry on with her servant: "These wise fellows, these wise fellows; I don't know where they live;³ it seems to me that all of them take things by contraries."

Magnificent Ambassador, you see where the devil I am. Still I should like to keep these friends; but for myself I have no resource. If to you or to Filippo or to Brancaccio there occurs anything, I should be glad if you would write it to me. Farewell.

Niccolò Machiavelli, in Florence.

3. *I don't understand how their minds work.*

## No. 144

25 February 1513-[*1514*], Florence
To Francesco Vettori, in Rome

### [*A Milesian tale of Florence*]

Magnificent Ambassador:

I received a letter of yours week before last, and I have delayed until now in answering because I wished to learn better the truth of a story that I shall write below; then I shall answer parts of yours fittingly. An amusing thing has happened, or rather, to call it by its proper name, a ridiculous metamorphosis, and worthy to be set down in ancient writings. Because I do not wish anybody to feel hurt, I shall relate it to you hidden under allegories.

Giuliano Brancaccio for example, eager to go bird-hunting, on one of the evenings of the past days, after the sounding of the Ave Maria in the evening, seeing the weather dark, the wind rising, and a little rain falling—each a sign for believing that all the birds would wait—returned to his house, pulled on his feet a pair of big shoes, strapped on a basket, took a fowling net, a little bell on his arm, and a good bird-swatter. He crossed the Bridge alla Carraia, and by way of the Canto de' Mozzi came to Santa Trinita, and having entered Borgo Santo Apostolo, went twisting around a bit in those alleys that surround it; not finding birds that waited for him, he turned toward your goldbeater, and near the Parte Guelfa crossed the Mercato and through the Calimala Francesca came under the Tetto de' Pisani,[1] where looking carefully at all those hiding places, he found a little thrush, which with the bird-swatter and the light and the bell he stopped, and cleverly brought it into the depth of the thicket near the cave where Panzano was living. Detaining his bird there, and finding its disposition generous, and kissing it many times, he straightened two feathers of its tail, and at last, as many say, put it in the bird-basket hanging behind him.

But because the wind compels me to come out from under cover, and allegories are not enough, and this metaphor no longer serves me, Brancaccio wished to know who this was; and the boy answered, for example, that he was Michele, grandson of Consiglio Costi. Said at once Brancaccio: "Let it be a good omen; you are the son of a man of standing, and if you are wise, you have found your fortune. Understand that I am Filippo di Casavecchia, and I have a shop in such a place; and because I do not have money with me, either you come or you send tomorrow to the shop, and I'll pay you." When the morning came, Michele, who was rather bad than merely of little account, sent one Zanni to Filippo with a note asking him for what was due and reminding him of his promise. To that fellow Filippo showed an unpleasant air, saying: "Who is this, or what does he want? I have no connection with him; tell him to come to me." After that, Zanni having gone back to Michele and told him

---

1. *The Palace of the Guelf Party is on Piazzo San Biagio. The other places mentioned were or are close by.*

about it, the boy was not at all frightened, but boldly going to see Filippo, charged him with the favors he had received, and ended by saying that if Filippo did not hesitate to deceive him, he would not hesitate to speak ill of Filippo. Seeing that he was excited, Filippo took him into his shop and said to him: "Michele, you have been tricked; I am a man of good habits and do not indulge in such vices; so it is better to consider how you can find out about this trick, and that he who has had pleasure from you should pay you, than to take this road and without any benefit to yourself speak ill of me. There fore act in my way; go home, and tomorrow come to me and I'll tell you what I have decided on." The boy went off all confused; yet since he was to return, he remained patient. And when Filippo was alone, he was vexed by the strangeness of the thing, and without expedients, he fluctuated like the sea of Pisa when a hard southwest wind blows on it in the river mouth. Because he said: "If I keep still and satisfy Michele with a florin, I become his vineyard, make myself his debtor, confess the sin, and instead of innocent become guilty; if I deny it without finding out the truth of the thing, I have to stand in comparison with a boy; I have to justify myself to him; I have to justify myself to the others;[2] all the harm will be mine. If I try to find the truth, I must blame somebody for it; I may guess wrong; I shall bring on hostility over it, and with it all I shall not be justified."

And being in this anxiety, as the least bad decision he took the last; and he was to such an extent favored by Fortune that the first aim he took was directed at the correct target; for he inferred that Brancaccio had done him that rascally deed, considering that he was one who often went bird-hunting and that at other times he had played him some tricks when he made a vow at the Servi. And he went thereupon to find Alberto Lotti, for example, and told him the affair, and gave him his opinion, and begged him to summon Michele, who was his relative, and see if he could find out anything. Alberto, as an active and perceptive man, judged that Filippo had a good eye, and having promised him his services freely, sent for Michele, and after sifting him a while came to this end: "Would you be sure, if you heard the man speak who said he was Filippo, that you could recognize him by his voice?" To which the boy having answered yes, he took him to Santo Ilario, where he knew Bran caccio resorted, and coming up from behind, having seen Bran

2. *This seems the meaning though the original says "to justify the others."*

caccio, who was sitting in the middle of a big crowd telling stories, he managed that the boy got so close to him that he heard him speak; and on turning around and seeing him, Brancaccio, all confused, made off. So to everybody the affair seemed plain, in such a way that Filippo is now cleared and Brancaccio spoken ill of. And in Florence in this carnival nothing else is said than "Are you Brancaccio or are you Casa?" "And the story was well known under the whole heaven."[3] I believe you have had this account by other hands, but I wish to tell it more in detail, because so appears to me my obligation.

To your letter I have nothing to reply except that you should continue your love with loose reins, and the pleasure you take today, you will not have to take tomorrow; and if the thing stands as you have written to me, I envy you more than I do the King of England. I beg you to follow your star, and not to let an iota go for the things of the world, because I believe, have believed, and will always believe that it is true, as Boccaccio said, that it is better to act and repent than not to act and repent.

Niccolò Machiavelli, in Florence.

3. *Ovid,* ART OF LOVE *2. 561 (modified).*

## No. 145

16 April 1514, Florence
To Francesco Vettori [*in Rome?*]

[*Foreign powers in Italy; Swiss power; Machiavelli's finances*]

Magnificent Ambassador, Francesco Vettori:

Will it be, then, after a thousand years, a reprehensible thing to write something else than stories? I believe not. And therefore I have decided, laying aside every irrational hesitation, to beg you to straighten out for me a confusion I have in my head.

I see the King of Spain, who, since he came into Italy, has always been the first mover of all disturbances among Christians, put in the middle, just now, of many difficulties. It seems to me, first, that it does not advantage him that Italy should continue with her present face, and that he cannot bear that the Church and the Swiss shall have so much power in her. He appears to have more fear about the state of Naples now than when the French were there, because at that time the Pope was between Milan and Naples, for the Pope did not wish the French to get control of the Kingdom, in order not to be in the middle. But now between the Pope, the Swiss, and Spain there is no middle. It seems to me also that for things on the other side of the mountains to be in the midst of war does not advantage him, because not always can a war come out in a stale‑mate, as in the past year. And it would be necessary in the long run that the King of France should either win or lose; in neither of these lies the safety of Spain; so unless a third thing happens, so that the others are ruined, they all might turn to harming the cause of their trouble, because certainly Spain's tricks are known and they must have produced disgust and hatred in the minds of his friends and his enemies.

I conclude, then, that since things in their present state do not advantage him, it must be that he will try to change them. In attempting to change those of Italy with great safety, he must get the Swiss out of Milan, and not put France there. In this he has two difficulties: one, without France he cannot get the Swiss out; two, whom can he put there? Considering the first case, I do not believe that France ever will agree to come with all his forces into Lombardy except to be master. If there were agreements, either that he would come there or would give Milan to the second son of King Philip, as his son‑in‑law, or to some other, I do not know how he would observe them, since his armies would be more powerful than those of anyone else, if he were not always a ninny; and I do not see how Spain can trust in these promises. That the Swiss can be got out without France, I think everybody will say *no*. Considering who they are, where they are, how many they are, and the purpose they have formed, anybody will judge that without the French forces they cannot be got out. As to the second difficulty, that of giving Milan to someone, to the Church I do not believe that he will give it, to the Venetians much less; for himself he cannot take her. He might give her, as I have said, to his grandson, as is more reasonable, yet there is no security for him there, because now that is the same thing as to give it to the Emperor; and when the Emperor saw himself ruler of Milan, he quickly would get the desire to be emperor of Italy, and would begin at Naples, where the Germans had a claim before the Spaniards.

So I see in Milan, when she is taken for the Archduke against the will of the Swiss, difficulties in holding her, especially without French weapons, because if the Swiss cannot resist the flood when it comes, they will let it pass, and when it is passed, they will come back there; because they know that if a duke does not keep always twenty thousand infantry and six thousand cavalry at least, he will never be safe from them; and to keep so many, Spain and the Emperor do not have resources. As a result, the Swiss, notwithstanding the negotiations they learn are being held—which would result in giving that dukedom to the Archduke—stand firm against the French; and for these negotiations they show that they do not care, because they consider that others than the French cannot hold that dukedom against their will, and therefore they oppose the French, and the others they ridicule.

I should be glad, Mr. Ambassador, that you first would answer me, telling whether these presuppositions of mine seem to you true, and, if they do, that you would solve them for me; and if you wish to understand my solution, I shall write to you at length very gladly.

The present officers of the *Monte*[1] are the *Magnifico* Lorenzo [*de' Medici*], Lorenzo Strozzi, Lorenzo Pitti, Ruberto de' Ricci and Matteo Cini. They have not appointed officers for sales; arrangement remains with them; and I have to come under their jurisdiction with nine florins of *decima*, and four and a half of *arbitrio*, so that in a year I run to forty florins, and I have ninety as my income, or less. I worry along here as well as I can. If you think it wise to write a letter to any of these officials and to assure them that my condition is impossible, I turn myself over to you. To the *Magnifico* there is no use in writing, because to that business he does not attend; it is enough to address one or two of the others.

Niccolò Machiavelli, in Florence.

1. *A body dealing with public finances, and carrying on some banking business. See the next letter.*

## No. 146

20 April 1514, Florence
To Giovanni Vernacci, in Pera

[*A marriage of convenience*]

My dearest Giovanni:

I have your two letters of this last month, in which you instruct me to see to withdrawing that nun's money from the Monte; I shall attend to it as soon as possible, but cannot until after the octave of Easter, because it is not possible to go to the officials. I shall attend to it after that and give you notice of the results.

I shall find out from Lorenzo and others if I can turn any business to you, and if I can shall let you know.

There is an artisan here, a very rich man, who has one daughter a little lame but otherwise beautiful, good, and worthy; in comparison with other artisans he is of good family because he can hold office. I have thought that if he would offer two thousand sealed florins in ready money and promise to open for you a shop in the art of wool, making you active partner in it, perhaps it would fit your need to take her as wife. I believe he would advance fifteen hundred florins, and with these and the aid of your father-in-law you could gain honor and profit. I have spoken in this way in general and decided to write so you can consider it. Advise me in your first letter, and if you like it, give me power to act. Christ guard you.

Niccolò Machiavelli.

It would be possible to arrange to wait two or three years before marrying her, if you wished to remain some time out there.

## No. 148

10 June 1514, [*Florence*]
To Francesco Vettori, [*in Rome?*]

[*Machiavelli's finances; love*]

Magnificent Ambassador:

I received your two letters when I was on my farm, where I stay with my family, for Donato sent them to me on behalf of Brancaccio.

I made such reply as seemed suitable, both about my private affairs and about your love, and other things. But coming two days ago to Florence, I forgot them, so that since it seems to me a labor to rewrite them, I shall send them to you at another time. And for now I write this, so that you may know that yours have arrived safely, and I say that I have not gone to Rome, being held back by those causes which you now make clear to me and which I already understood for myself.

I shall continue, then, among my lousy doings¹, without finding a man who remembers my service or who believes that I can be good for anything. But it is impossible that I can remain long in this way because I am using up my money, and if God does not show himself more favorable to me, I see that I shall be one day forced to leave home and hire out as a tutor or a secretary to a constable, since I can do nothing else, or fix myself in some desert land to teach reading to boys, leaving my family here. They could reckon that I am dead, and would get on much better without me because I am an expense to them, being used to spending and unable to get on without spending. I do not write this because I want you to undertake for me something troublesome or annoying, but merely to express myself and in order not to write more of this matter, which is as hateful as it can be.

About your love, I remind you that those are afflicted by Love who, when he flies into their bosoms, try to clip his wings or bind him. For such, because he is a boy and unsettled, he digs out their eyes, their liver, and their heart. But those who, when he comes, are pleased and caress him, and when he goes away let him go, and when he comes back, receive him gladly, he always honors and holds dear, and under his command they triumph. Therefore, my friend, do not try to regulate one who flies, or to clip one who puts back, for one feather, a thousand; and you will be happy.

Niccolò Machiavelli.

1. *Literally* live.

## No. 150

3 August 1514, Florence
To Francesco Vettori

### [*Niccolò's new love, probably fictitious*]

You, my friend, have with many accounts of your love at Rome kept me full of rejoicing, and by letting me read and think of your pleasures and your angers, you have removed from my mind count﹁ less worries, because one is not good without the other. And truly Fortune has brought me to a place where I can render you just recompense, because while at my farm I have encountered a creature so gracious, so delicate, so noble, both by nature and happy chance, that I cannot praise her so much or love her so much that she would not deserve more. I ought to tell you, as you did me, the first acts of this Love, with what nets he took me, where he spread them, of what sort they were; and you would see that they were nets of gold, spread among flowers, woven by Venus, so pleasant and easy that though a villainous heart might have broken them, nonetheless I did not wish to, and for a bit I enjoyed myself in them, until the tender threads grew hard and were secured with knots beyond untying.

You should not believe that in taking me Love has used ordinary methods, because knowing that they would not have been enough for him, he used extraordinary ones of which I knew nothing, and from which I could not protect myself. May it be enough for you that, though I am close to fifty, these hot suns do not harm me, nor do rough roads tire me, nor the dark hours of the night frighten me. Everything to me seems level, and to all her desires, even though unlike mine and opposed to what mine ought to be, I adapt myself. And though I seem to have entered into great labor, nevertheless I feel in it such sweetness, both through what that face so wonderful and soft brings me, and also through having laid aside the memory of all my troubles, that for anything in the world, being able to free myself, I would not wish it. I have abandoned, then, the thoughts of affairs that are great and serious; I do not any more take delight in reading ancient things or in discussing modern ones; they all are turned into soft conversations, for which I thank Venus and all Cyprus.[1] So if it occurs to you to write anything about the lady,

1. *The island of Cyprus was the realm of Venus.*

write it, and of the other things talk with those who estimate them higher and understand them better, because I never have found in them anything but harm, and in these of love always good and pleasure. Farewell.

Your Niccolò Machiavelli.

## No. 152

4 December 1514, [*Sant' Andrea in*] Percussina
To Francesco Vettori, [*in Rome?*]

[*The marriage troubles of a friend's sister*]

Magnificent Ambassador:

The presenter of these words will be Niccolò Tafano, my friend. The cause of his journey is his sister, whom some time ago he gave in matrimony to a certain Giovanni. Though he was held by the bond of a ring, yet despising all oaths and despising the laws of marriage, Giovanni went to Rome, where for a long time he has lived and still lives, paying no attention to his marriage and his wife. Therefore this friend of mine wishes one of these two things: either Giovanni shall join his wife here or, returning the portion of dower he received, shall legally repudiate her, for he judges all such things can easily be done there where the Vicar of Christ lives. In this matter, therefore, we ask your aid and ask that you will approach that disloyal husband, and with such authority as you can, force him to satisfy the two Niccolòs who so heartily ask it. I am moved both by justice, which strengthens our case, and by the eagerness of the man himself and of his whole family, than which nothing in this rural region is pleasanter.

But enough on Tafano. As to what pertains to me, if you wish to know what I am doing, you can learn from this same Tafano the whole course of my life, and will realize how sordid and inglorious it is—not without anger, if as in the past you love me. For this I suffer and lament the more when I see that amid so many and so great instances of prosperity for the Magnificent Family and for Florence, to me alone Troy remains.[1]

Niccolò Machiavelli.

1. Ovid, METAMOPHOSES 13. 507. *Machiavelli expected his friend to cap the quotation, which continues: My woe still runs its course.*

## No. 154

20 December 1514 [*Letter No. 1*], [*Florence*]
[*To Francesco Vettori, in Rome?*]

> [*The wisest policy for the Pope is a French alliance; the Swiss as rulers of Italy; neutrality*]

You ask me what decision His Holiness Our Lord should make in order to keep the Church in the position of influence where he found her, since France with the assistance of England and the Venetians wishes by all means to recover the state of Milan, and on the other side the Swiss, Spain, and the Emperor unite to defend it. This is really the most important of your questions, because all the others depend on it, and they must be explained if this one is to be explained properly. I do not believe that for twenty years there has been a more serious question than this, nor do I know a thing among those past so difficult to understand, so uncertain to judge, and so dangerous to decide and carry out; yet, being forced by you, I will enter into this matter, discussing it honestly at least, if not adequately.

When a prince wishes to know what is going to be the fortune of two who fight each other, he must first measure the forces and the vigor of both. The forces, in this matter of France and of England, are those preparations that those kings are said to have made for this conquest, namely, to attack the Swiss in Burgundy with twenty thousand men, to attack Milan with a greater number, and with a much greater number to attack Navarre, in order to cause rebellion and change in the states of Spain; to put a great fleet on the sea and attack Genoa or the Kingdom, or wherever it may be to their advantage. These preparations which I mention are possible for these two kings and, if they intend to win, necessary; and therefore I suppose them true. Though the possibility relates to your last question, and we may imagine that England will detach himself from France, being displeased by his greatness in Italy, I prefer to debate that matter now, because if England does so detach himself, every question will be answered.

I believe that the reason why England sticks with France is to avenge himself on Spain for the injuries done to him in the French war. His anger is reasonable, and I do not see anything that so quickly could cancel this and destroy the love resulting from the marriage contracted between those two kings. I am not moved by the ancient hostility between the English and the French, which moves many, because the people wish what the kings do, and not the kings what the people do. As to his being caused annoyance by the power of France in Italy, evidently this must be the result either of envy or of fear. Envy could appear if England too did not have a place where he could get honor, and would have to remain idle, but when he can make himself famous in Spain, the cause of the envy ceases. As to fear, you must understand that many times a ruler gains territory but not forces, and if you consider well, you will see that for the King of France the gaining of cities in Italy is, with respect to England, a gaining of territory and not forces; because with as large an army he could attack that island without holding the states of Italy as with them. As to diversions because France has Milan, England no longer needs to fear France, who has a disloyal state, and there is nothing to keep England from moving the Swiss against him by paying them, for they, being injured by France, would be truly his enemies, and not as the other time. And because it also could happen, while France was gaining Milan, that England would upset the state of Castile, England with that conquest might harm France more than France could harm him with the conquest of Milan, for the reasons given. Therefore I do not see why England in this first rush of the war should need to detach himself from France, and therefore I affirm these unions and preparations of forces mentioned above to be necessary and possible.

We have remaining the Venetians, who are of the same importance to the forces of these two kings as are the forces of Milan to that other side; I judge them few and weak, and to be held back by half of the soldiers who are in Lombardy. Considering now the defenders of Milan, I see the Swiss in condition to put two armies together that can fight with any French that may come into Burgundy, and with those who come against Italy, because if in this case all the Swiss unite and with the cantons are joined the Grisons and the Vaudois, they can bring together more than twenty thousand men to an army.

As to the Emperor, because I do not know what he will do at any time, I do not care to discuss what he can do now. But uniting Spain, the Emperor, Milan and Genoa, I do not believe they exceed fifteen thousand men fit for war, Spain not being able to furnish new forces, because of expecting war at home.

As to the sea, if they do not lack money, I believe that between the Genoese and Spain they can form a fleet that to some extent can delay that of their opponents. I believe, then, that these are the forces of the two.

Trying at present to see to which side victory may incline, I say that the two kings, having money, can for a long time keep their armies together; the others, being poor, cannot. Hence, considering the armies, the condition and the money of the two, I believe it can be said that if they come quickly to a battle, the victory will be on Italy's side; if the war drags on, it will go to the other side. It is said, and seems reasonable, that the Swiss, knowing this difficulty and planning to come to battle quickly, intend to meet the French armies on the mountains of Savoy in order that the latter, if they try to cross, will be forced to fight or, if they do not fight, to turn back because of the narrowness of the position and the lack of supplies. Whether the Swiss are likely to succeed would have to be judged by someone experienced in the region and in war.[1] Nevertheless, I shall say this: that never in ancient history have I found that anyone has succeeded in holding mountain passes; but I have surely seen many who have abandoned the passes and waited for the enemy in open places, judging that they could better defend themselves, and with less disorder tempt the fortune of war—all their fortune and not all their forces.[2] And though I might give some reasons showing why this happens, I prefer to omit them, since this subject does not demand their discussion.

Considering everything, then, I see on this side the single hope of coming to a battle quickly, which also might be lost. On the side of France, I see him likely to win the battle and unable to lose the war, if he drags it out. On this side I see in the management of the war two obvious perils, among others. One is that either by force or by treaty the French will bring their fleet into the territory of Genoa or

1. *In 1515 the usual passes were guarded against the French. They suddenly crossed by an unusual one that was left unguarded, to the consternation of their adversaries. In this instance Machiavelli was a prophet.*

2. *So the detached words as they stand in all texts must be rendered. The texts depend on a copy or draft, not on a letter actually sent. At least it is plain that Machiavelli is referring to his belief that a ruler should not risk all his fortune when using only part of his forces. See* DIS-COURSES *1. 23.*

into Tuscany. They will no sooner land than all the province of Lombardy will be theirs, and many others—some timid and some discontented—will run to join them, in such a way that the French, finding that they are received, can dally with and wear out the Swiss at their pleasure. The other danger is that the cantons on the borders of Burgundy, on whom will fall the weight of the war made in those regions, if they see it last too long, will force the others to make peace with France. I am led to fear this by the example of Charles, Duke of Burgundy, who by making war and raiding on that side so tired them out that they sent him a blank sheet of paper, and he would have ruined them entirely if he had not been suddenly forced into battle. Whereas some hope or fear that the Swiss through their disloyalty will turn and make agreements with England and France and give the others up as booty, I do not fear it because they are fighting now for their own ambition; and if none of the aforesaid necessities compels them, I believe that in the war they will be loyal.

If then His Holiness the Pope is forced to make a decision and should choose the party on this side, I see victory doubtful for the reasons given above: both because his joining them does not altogether secure them and because his action, though it does take away convenience and influence from the French, does not give the others forces enough to enable them to hold the French. Indeed, since the King has a great fleet on the sea and the Venetians also can arm some ships, the Pope will find such difficulty in guarding his shores above and below[3] that his soldiers and yours here will scarcely be enough. His Holiness may indeed escape a present danger, if they are willing to rely on him, and will find also a present profit, since at present he can honor his friends.

If His Holiness takes the side of France, provided he does it so cautiously that he can without danger wait for France, I judge victory sure, because, by means of the fleet, he can put in Tuscany a great army along with his own. Thus he would at once cause a great uproar in Lombardy by acting with the Venetian soldiers there. The Swiss and the Spaniards could not resist two different armies from different sides and defend themselves from the rebellion of the people, which would be instantaneous. Altogether I do not see that it would be possible to deprive the French King of victory.

3. *The Adriatic and the Mediterranean.*

You wish, besides, to learn which would be less burdensome to the Pope: alliance with the French or with the Swiss, if either one could win with his alliance. I answer that I believe the Swiss as victors and their associates and allies, if they conquer, would at present observe an agreement with the Pope and would give him his states. But on the other hand he would have to bear the arrogance of the victor, and because I should not recognize as victors any but the Swiss, he would have to bear injuries by them, which would be of two sorts: first, they would deprive him of money; second, of friends. As to money, which the Swiss say they do not want now, when they are carrying on the war, you may believe they will be sure to want it when the war is finished, and they will begin with some tax, which will be heavy, and in order to appear honest and for fear of irritating them in the first heat of their victory, the Pope will not refuse it. As to friends, I believe—or rather I am certain—that the Duke of Ferrara, the Lucchese, and the like, will run to make themselves their dependents. When the Swiss have taken one of them, it will be all over with Italy's liberty, because every day with a thousand excuses they will tax and plunder, and they will change governments, and what they judge they cannot do now, they will put off until there comes a time to do it. Nor should anybody assure himself that they do not think of this, because they must think of it, and if they do not think of it, they will be made to think of it by the course of events; for the truth is that one conquest, one victory, causes thirst for another.

No one should be astonished that they have not openly taken Milan and have not gone farther than they have, because their system of government—which at home differs from that of others—likewise differs away from home, and has its analogy in all the ancient histories. Therefore if up to now they have gained associates, in the future they will gain dependents and tributaries, not troubling to command them or to manage them in details, but being satisfied if these dependents hold by them in wars and pay an annual tribute. These things the Swiss will keep up with the reputation of their armies at home and by punishing those who deviate from them. In this way, and quickly, if they continue this contest, they will give laws to you, to the Pope and to all other Italian princes, and when you see that they assume a protectorate, "you may know that the summer is at hand."[4] And if you say: "For that there will be a cure,

4. Matthew 24. 32.

because we shall unite against them," I say that this will be a second error and a second deception, because the union of many leaders against one is difficult to bring about and, once made, is difficult to maintain.

I give you as an example France, against whom everybody had entered into an alliance; but suddenly Spain made a truce, the Venetians became his friends, and the Swiss attacked him feebly; the Emperor was not seen again, and finally England joined with him. If that man against whom an alliance is made is of so much vigor that he does not at once go up in smoke, as the Venetians did, he always finds his advantage in many opinions,⁵ as France has done and as we see the Venetians would have done if they could have kept up that war for two months. But their weakness could not await the disunion of the allies—something that would not happen to the Swiss, who either with France or with the Emperor or with Spain or with the potentates of Italy would always find a way either to keep them all from uniting or, if they did unite, to disunite them. I know that many will poke fun at this opinion, and I fear it so much, and so much believe it that, if the Swiss succeed in checking this flood, and we both live seven years, I expect to remind you of it.

Since you wish to know what the Pope has to fear from the Swiss if they win when he is their ally, I say that he must fear some immediate taxes and, in a short time, servitude for himself and for all Italy without hope of redemption, since they have a republic, armed beyond comparison with any prince or potentate. But if the Pope were the ally of France and should win, I believe France would still keep his agreement, if the conditions were suitable and too much eagerness had not made the Pope ask too much and the King yield too much. I believe he would not lay tribute on the Church but on you,⁶ and that he would have consideration for her on account of his alliance with England, and on account of the Swiss, who would not all be dead, and on account of Spain, who, even though driven out of Naples, would be of some importance as long as he lived. Therefore it seems reasonable that France for his part would wish the Church influential and friendly, and also wish the Venetians so. Altogether, in any outcome of these victories, I see that the Church must be in someone's power; therefore I judge it better to be in the

5. *The conflicting opinions of allies each of whom is seeking his own advantage.*
6. *The Florentines.*

power of those who will be most reasonable and whom she knows from other times, and not in the power of those whose wants she does not know, since she does not know them well.

If the side to which His Holiness Our Lord adheres should lose, I fear his being brought into every extreme necessity of flight and of exile and of everything that a pope can fear. When a prince is forced to take one of two courses, he ought to consider among other things where the bad fortune of either of these can bring him. Then always, other things being equal, he ought to take that course which, if in the end it is bad, will be least bitter. Without doubt defeat would be less bitter with France as an ally than with the others as allies, because if His Holiness has France as ally, and loses, he has left the country of France, which is able to uphold a pontiff's honor; he remains with a fortune that through the power of that kingdom can rise up in many ways; he remains in his own house, and where many popes have had their seat.[7] If he is with those others and loses, he will need to go either into Switzerland to die of hunger, or into Germany to be laughed at, or into Spain to be swindled. Thus the first cannot be compared with the second in the evil its bad outcome will produce.

As to remaining neutral, I do not believe that it is ever advanta-geous to anybody when he is in such a situation, namely, when he is less powerful than any of those who are fighting and when his states are scattered among the states of one who is fighting. And you must realize, first, that nothing is more necessary to a prince than to govern himself in such a way in dealing with his subjects and with his allies and neighbors that he does not become either hated or despised; and if indeed he must neglect one of these two, he should not pay atten-tion to hatred but should look out for contempt. Pope Julius did not trouble about being hated, if only he was feared and respected; and by means of that fear he turned the world upside down and brought the Church where she is. I say that he who remains neutral is sure to be hated by him who loses, and despised by him who wins; as one who is thought of no account and considered a useless ally and an undreaded enemy, he needs to fear that every sort of injury will be done him and every sort of destruction planned for him. Indeed the victor will never lack excuses, because the neutral prince,

7. *At Avignon.*

with his states mixed among those at war, is forced to receive into his gates now this one, now that, to receive them into his house, to aid them with shelter, with food; and always everyone will imagine he is being deceived, and countless things will happen to cause countless complaints. Even though in the prosecution of the war nothing comes up—which is impossible—it will come up after the victory, because the lesser powers and those who fear you run quickly to the shelter of the victor and give him opportunity to hurt you. Hence to him who says, "It is true that one thing can be taken away from us and another thing left to us," I answer that it is better to lose every/ thing nobly than a part shamefully, and a part cannot be lost without the whole's tottering. He who considers therefore all the states of His Holiness Our Lord, and where they are, and the nature of the lesser powers included in them, and who they are who are fighting, will judge His Holiness one of those who in no way can continue such neutrality, but who will be forced, by making such a choice, to be hostile to both the winner and the loser, since everybody will wish to harm him, one for vengeance and another for profit.

You also ask me if, when the Pope allies himself with the Swiss, the Emperor and Spain, it would advantage Spain and the Emperor to deceive him and join France. I believe that a treaty between Spain and France is impossible and that it cannot be made without Eng/ land's consent, and that England cannot consent unless he plans to attack France; for that reason France could not think of it, because the English King, being young and eager for war, has nowhere to go with his armies except into France or into Spain, and as peace with France would bring war upon Spain, so peace with Spain would bring war upon France. Therefore the King of France, in order not to lose England, in order not to bring upon himself that war, and having a thousand reasons for hating Spain, is not going to give ear to peace; for if France wished or was able to make it, it would have been done—so many plans for the damage of others that King could have brought forward. Hence as far as Spain is concerned, I believe that the Pope would have reason to fear everything; but so far as France is concerned, he would be safe. And as to the Emperor, since he is shifting and unstable, every change is to be feared, whether it would advantage him or would not advantage him, since in these variations he has always lived and been nourished. If the Venetians should join the anti/French party, it would be of great moment, not so much because of the addition of their forces as through this group's remaining more simply an enemy of France, and if the Pope also joined it, there would be for the French, both in coming and in establishing themselves in Italy, countless difficulties. But I do not believe the Venetians will adopt this plan, because I believe they have had better terms from France than they have had from these others, and having followed a French Fortune when she was almost dead, it does not seem reasonable that they will abandon her now that she is about to rise up again, and I fear that they are offering empty words, as they usually do, for their own advantage.

I conclude, then, to come to the end of this discourse, that since there are more indications of victory on the French side than on that of the others, and since the Pope by joining can give the victory to France with certainty, and not to these others, and France is less to be feared and more bearable as friend and conqueror than these others, and loss is less hard with France as ally than with these others, and since he cannot securely remain neutral, that His Holiness Our Lord ought either to join France, or to join the others if the Venetians also join them, and not otherwise.

## No. 155

20 December 1514 [*No. 2*], Florence
To Francesco Vettori, in Rome

### [*More on neutrality*]

Magnificent Ambassador:

Since you have given me a strong desire, if I weary you with writing, say: "Let the injury be mine, since I wrote to him." I fear you will think that in my reply to your questions I passed too hastily over the part on neutrality and also over the part where I had to debate what he would have to fear from the conqueror if that party which he joined should lose, because in both it seems there are many things to consider. So I have gone at writing to you again on the same matter. And as to neutrality, a choice that many seem to approve, it cannot please me, because I do not recall, either in what I have seen or in what I have read, that it has ever been good, rather that it has always been very injurious, because it is certain to lose; and though you understand the reasons better than I do, yet I am going to recall them to you.

You know that the chief duty of every prince is to keep himself from being hated and despised, to avoid in his conduct contempt and hatred; whenever he does that well, everything must go well. This policy he must practice as much with his allies as with his subjects; and whenever a prince does not avoid at least contempt, he is done for. To me it seems that to remain neutral between two who are fighting is nothing else than to seek to be hated and despised, because always there will be one of them to whom it will appear, by reason of benefits received from him or through long-standing alliance with him, that you are obligated to follow his fortune, and when you do not join him, he at once hates you. That other despises you, because he finds you timid and irresolute, and quickly you get the name of a useless friend and an enemy not to be dreaded, so that whoever conquers does you harm without hesitation. Titus Livius in a few words from the mouth of Titus Flaminius gives this opinion, when he said to the Achaians, who were exhorted by Antiochus to remain neutral: "Nothing is farther from your interests; without favor, without dignity, you will be the booty of the winner."

It is also inevitable that in the conduct of the war between two powers, countless reasons for hate against you will appear, because most of the time the third is put in such a place that he can in many ways hinder or help one or the other. So always in a short time, beginning with the day when the war is started, you are brought to such a pass that the declaration you have not been willing to make openly and with credit, you are obliged to make secretly and without thanks; and if you do not do it, some still believe that you have done it. When Fortune is so generous in favor of the neutral that in the conduct of the war there rises no just cause for hatred on the part of either belligerent, it must appear when the war is ended, because all those who have been injured by him who has been third[1] and all those afraid of him, running to the shelter of the victor, give him cause for hatred and discord with you.

If somebody answers that the Pope, through the reverence felt for his person and through the authority of the Church, is in another situation, and will always have a refuge in which to save himself, I answer that such a reply deserves some consideration, and that then

1. *The neutral.*

building on some foundation is possible. Nevertheless it is a foundation not to be relied on; on the contrary I believe that if the Pope is
well advised, he will not think of it, that such a thought will not
cause him to make a bad choice. Because all the things that have
been I believe can be again; and I know that pontiffs have fled, gone
into exile, been pursued, suffered to the utmost, like temporal rulers,
and in times when the Church in spiritual matters was more revered
than she is today.

If then His Holiness Our Lord will consider where his states are
situated, who they are who are fighting together, who they are who
can take refuge with the winner, I believe His Holiness will not at
all rest on being neutral, and that he will think it advantages him
more to join, no matter what, so that, as to neutrality, to explain it at
greater length than the other time, I have nothing more to say to you.
And as to what he would have to fear from him who would win the
victory and conquer that party which he had joined, I shall say
nothing further about it, because I have said it all above.

I believe you may infer from the letter I wrote you that I would
depend on France, and that anybody who read it would fear that
affection had influenced me to some extent. That would displease
me, because I try always to keep my judgment firm, especially in
these things, and not to let it be corrupted by a vain contest, as do
many others. Because, if I have depended somewhat on France, I
think I have not been deceived, I wish again to run over what moved
me, which will be a sort of epilogue to what I have written.

When two potentates fight together, in order to judge who is
likely to win, it is necessary, besides measuring the forces of the two,
to see in how many ways the victory can come to one and in how
many to the other. I see nothing for the party on this side to do
except come to battle quickly; but for the French party there are all
the other methods, as I wrote at length. This is the first reason that
makes me believe more in France than in the others. Besides, if I
have to declare myself ally to one of the two, and I see that by joining
one I give him the victory with certainty, and by joining the other I
give it to him doubtfully, I believe that it will always be right to take
the certain, laying aside every obligation, every interest, every fear and
everything else that may displease me. I believe that if the
Pope joins the French, there will be no dispute on this, but if he
joins those others there will be plenty of them, for those reasons that

just now I wrote to you. Besides this, all wise men, when it is possible for them not to gamble all their property, are glad not to do so, and considering the worst that can come of it, they consider where in the evil before them the smallest evil appears. Because the things of Fortune are all doubtful, they join willingly that Fortune who, doing the worst she can, will bring the least harsh end.

His Holiness Our Lord has two dwellings, one in Italy, the other in France. If he joins France, he risks one of them; if he joins the others, he risks both. If he is an enemy to France and France wins, he is obliged to follow the Fortune of these others, and to go into Switzerland to die of hunger, or into Germany to live in despair, or into Spain to be swindled and turned into profit. If he joins France and loses, France remains to him, he lives in his dwelling, and with a kingdom at his service that is a papacy, and with a prince who, either through treaty or through war, may in a thousand ways rise up again. Farewell. And a thousand times I greet you.

Niccolò Machiavelli, in Florence.

## No. 156

20 December 1514 [*No. 3*], [*Florence*]
To Francesco Vettori, [*in Rome?*]

[Donato's affairs, and Niccolò's own]

Magnificent Ambassador:

When I had written the attached, I received yours of the fifteenth, which I will answer only in the part pertaining to Donato, to whom I read the section; and at once he was filled with such hope that his shirt doesn't touch his enterprise.[1] Because he has decided that in order to obtain this favor he will not be stingy in anything, he had the letter to Beni rewritten, through which, inside of six months, there will be paid to you when you wish a hundred ducats. And he has said to me that, besides these, when you need others, you should not spare anything or have regard to anything. The letters will be included in this; you will make use of them when convenient[2] and as is usual for such letters. About being sparing with them or not,

1. *Apparently bowdlerized by some early editor.*
2. *Some texts leave a blank at this point, e.g., Italia, 1813.*

Donato did not wish me to write anything, yet as from myself I bring it to you, especially since the act of a friend does not need more in any way, because if there is nothing more to be written in this affair, I suppose it can neither hinder nor help. Yet Donato does not wish that this be thought of or that anything be regarded, if only once he can get out of the plebeian class.

I thank you again for all the work and all the thoughts you have had for love of me. I do not promise you any recompense for it, because I do not believe I can ever do good either to myself or to others. And if Fortune had wished that the Medici, either in affairs in Florence or abroad, or in their private business or in that of the public, had only once employed me, I should be satisfied. Nevertheless, I do not yet mistrust myself in reality. And when this happens and I do not know how to sustain myself, you may grieve for me; but that which has to be, let it be. And I realize every day that what you say Pontanus writes is true; "and when Fortune decides to please us, she puts before us either present utility or present fear, or both together;" which two things I believe are the greatest enemies of that opinion I have defended in my letters.³ Farewell.

Niccolò Machiavelli.

3. *They are opposed to the courage and prudence that can resist and even overcome Fortune.*

No. 159

31 January 1514–[*1515*], Florence
To Francesco Vettori, in Rome

[*Grave men at leisure; the new prince*]

The boyish archer had already many times attempted to wound my breast with his arrows, for in hatred and in the injury of others he takes pleasure.

And though they were, those arrows, sharp and biting, so that a rock of adamant would not have warded them off, nonetheless they struck so strong an object that I little regard all their power.

So he, possessed with anger and fury, in order to show his lofty power, changed quiver, changed bow and arrow; and he shot one with such great force that still I feel the pain of its wound, and I confess and acknowledge his power.

I should not know how to answer your last letter on the passion of love with other words that seem to me more fitting than with this sonnet, from which you can see how much effort that little thief Love has spent in order to chain me; and they are, those he has put on me, such strong chains that I am wholly in despair of my liberty. I cannot think of any way in which I can unchain myself; and even if chance or some human stratagem should open to me some way for getting out of them, perchance I should not wish to take it; so much now sweet, now light, now heavy do I find those chains, and they make a mixture of such a sort that I judge I cannot live contented without that kind of life. And because I know how much such thoughts and news about such a life delight you, I regret that you are not here to laugh, now at my complaints, now at my laughter; and all that pleasure you might have, our Donato carries away, who together with the woman of whom I earlier wrote, are my only ports and the refuges for my boat, which in the unceasing storm long has been without rudder and without sails. And it is not two evenings ago that it happened that I could say, like Phoebus to Daphne:

O Nymph of Peneus, I pray, await me; I do not pursue as an enemy; Nymph, await. So the lamb from the wolf, so the deer from the lion, so the doves with trembling wing flee from the eagle, each one from his enemies.[1]

And just as to Phoebus these verses profited little, so to me the same words with her who was fleeing were of no moment, of no force.

Anybody who saw our letters, honored friend, and saw their diversity, would wonder greatly, because he would suppose now that we were grave men, wholly concerned with important matters, and that into our breasts no thought could fall that did not have in itself honor and greatness. But then, turning the page, he would judge that we, the very same persons, were lightminded, inconstant, lascivious, concerned with empty things. And this way of proceeding, if to some it may appear censurable, to me seems praiseworthy, because we are imitating Nature, who is variable; and he who imitates her cannot be rebuked. And though we have been accustomed to give this variety in a number of letters, I wish to give

1. Ovid, METAMORPHOSES 1. 504-507.

it this time in one, as you will see, if you will read the other page. Now spit.

Your Pagolo has been here with the Magnificent,[2] and in the course of his discussions with me on his hopes, he said His Lordship has promised to make him governor of one of those cities of which he now is taking the sovereignty. And having heard, not from Pagolo but by common report, that he is becoming lord of Parma, Piacenza, Modena and Reggio, it seems to me that this dominion is good and strong and such that under any conditions he can hold it, if in the beginning it be well governed. And if he is going to govern it well, he needs to understand well the nature of the subject. These new states, taken by a new ruler, offer, if they are to be kept, countless difficulties. And if there is difficulty in keeping those that are used to being all in one body, as, for instance, the dukedom of Ferrara, much more difficulty is found in keeping those that are newly made up of different members, as will be this of Lord Giuliano, because one part of it is a member of Milan, another of Ferrara. He ought therefore who becomes prince of it to consider making them into a single body and accustoming them to recognize one ruler as soon as possible. This can be done in two ways, either by living there in person, or by setting up there a deputy who will rule them all; so that those subjects, though of different cities and divided among various opinions, may look to one only and regard him as prince. And if his Lordship, wishing to remain for the present in Rome, should put there one who knew well the nature of things and the conditions of the places, he would lay a strong foundation for his new state. But if he puts into every city its own head, and His Lordship does not live there, that state will always be disunited, without reputation for him, and without bringing the prince respect or fear. Duke Valentino,[3] whose works I should always imitate if I were a new prince, realizing this necessity, made Messer Rimirro President in Romagna; that decision made those peoples united, fearful of his authority, fond of his power, and trustful in it; and all the love they felt for him, which was great, considering his newness, resulted from this decision. I believe this thing can easily be demon-

2. *Giuliano de'Medici, the Duke of Nemours, for whom his brother, Pope Leo X, was believed to be preparing a principality in northern Italy.*

3. *Cesare Borgia. See* THE PRINCE *7, for his management of the territory secured for him by his father, Pope Alexander VI.*

strated, because it is true; and if it should happen to your Pagolo, this would be a step in making him known not merely to the Magnificent but to all Italy; and with honor and profit to His Lord- ship, he could give reputation to himself, to you, and to your family. I spoke of it with him; it pleased him, and he will consider making use of it. I have thought it well to write about it, so that you will know our discussions and, wherever it is necessary, can pave the way to this thing.

And in the proud rascal's fall, he nevertheless did not forget Mahomet.[4]

Our Donato sends his regards.

Niccolò Machiavelli, in Florence.

4. *Luigi Pulci*, MORGANTE *1. 38.*

## No. 160

18 August 1515, Florence
To Giovanni Vernacci, in Pera

[*Niccolò's affection*]

Dearest Giovanni:

If I have not written to you in the past, I do not want you to blame either me or others, but only the times, which have been of such a sort that they have made me forget myself. Not, however, on that account have I really forgotten you, because always I shall look upon you as a son, and I and my affairs will be always at your disposal. Try to keep healthy and to do good, because from your good there can come nothing but good to whoever wishes you well.

Niccolò Machiavelli, in Florence.

## No. 161

19 November 1515, Florence
To Giovanni Vernacci, in Pera

[*Hopes for prosperity*]

Dearest Giovanni:

I have written to you twice during the last four months, and I am sorry that you have not received them, because I fear that you think

I do not write through being unmindful of you, which is not at all true, because Fortune has left me nothing else than relatives and friends, and I make capital of them, and especially of those who are closest to me, as you are, from whom I hope, when Fortune brings you to some honorable position, that you will render to my children a return for my doings for you. Keep well.

Niccolò Machiavelli, in Florence.

## No. 162

15 February 1515–[*1516*], Florence
To Giovanni Vernacci, in Pera

[*Waiting for Fortune*]

Dearest Giovanni:

You never write to me of not getting my letters that you do not strike me with a knife, because in the past year I have written to you six times and given the letters to Marietta to be sent to Alberto. She says she has sent them; you say you have not received them, at which I am vexed. So the last I wrote to you two months ago I sent by Bartolomeo Federighi, who told me he gave it to somebody who was going there. I have learned through your other letter of your hardships. I thank God that they have calmed down to such an extent that you are left alive and do not need any more to be in a sad frame of mind. And if the death of those has taken from you some opportunities, your having behaved well ought to restore them to you; so do not lose your courage and keep in good spirits.

As to myself, I have become useless to myself, to my relatives, and to my friends, because such has been the decision of my sad fate. And I can say nothing better than that there has been left me no other good than health for myself and all my family. I continue to wait in order to be in time to take Good Fortune, when she comes, and if she does not come, to have patience. And whatever may happen to me, always I shall keep you in that place where I have had you up to now. I am yours. Christ watch over you!

Niccolò Machiavelli, in Florence.

## No. 163

10 October 1516, Livorno
To the Magnificent Paolo Vettori, Most Worthy Captain of the
Papal Triremes

### [Fever and bleeding]

Magnificent Sir:

We arrived here in Livorno today at ten A.M. This we inform
you of by Antonio your servant, that you may know of our situation,
and if before your[1] arrival here anything occurs to you that we can do,
you can let us know about it. Of the galleys of the Bashaw nothing
is heard. We have brought here your Vincenzio, with a double
tertian ague; and though he has lost a pound of blood from the nose,
nonetheless the fevers do not stop. If they grow a little lighter, I
believe it would be well to put him in a basket carriage, while the
night is less severe, and bring him there. If you have to defer coming
here, advise us of what is wanted by Your Lordship, to whom all
send their warm regards.

Niccolò Machiavelli, in Livorno.[2]

1. *The texts require* our.
2. *This visit to Livorno is unknown except for this letter. See Ridolfi,* VITA DI MACHIA-
VELLI *(1954), p. 247.*

## No. 164

8 June 1517, Sant' Andrea in Percussina
To Giovanni Vernacci, in Pera

### [Family news]

Dearest Giovanni:

As at other times I have written to you, I do not want you to
wonder if I do not write or if I am slow in answering, because the
reason is not that I have forgotten you and that I do not esteem you
as I once did, because I esteem you more, because men are esteemed
according to their ability; and since you have proved that you are a
good and able man, I must needs love you more than I did, and
altogether take pride in you, since I brought you up, and since my

house is the beginning of that good which you have and which you are going to have. But since I am reduced to living on my farm by the adversities that I have had and now have, I go sometimes a month without thinking about myself; so if I neglect answering you, it is not strange. I have received all your letters, and am pleased to learn that you have done and are doing well; for I can have no greater happiness than that. When you are through and return, my house will be always at your service, as it has been in the past, even though poor and wretched.

Bernardo and Lodovico are becoming men and I hope on your return to get employment for one of them through your means.[1]

Marietta and all the family are well. And Marietta wishes you would bring her on your return a piece of light-brown camlet and needles from Damascus, big and little. And she says they must shine, for those you sent the other time were not very good. Christ watch over you.

Niccolò Machiavelli, on his farm.

1. *Niccolò's older sons.*

## No. 166

17 December 1517, [*Florence*]
To Lodovico Alamanni, at Rome

[Donato del Corno's affairs; ORLANDO FURIOSO]

My honored Lodovico:

I know that I do not need to take much trouble to show you how much I love Donato del Corno, and how much I desire to do anything that is a pleasure to him. Hence I know that you will not wonder if I make you some trouble for love of him, which I shall do so much the more without hesitation so far as I believe you can do it, and also as the case is just and in a sense pitiable. The said Donato, after the Medici lords had been back in Florence about a month, partly on account of his obligations to the Lord Giuliano, partly on account of his good nature, without being asked, took Lord Giuliano five hundred ducats of gold, and told him to use it and return it when convenient.[1] Since then five years have passed, and, in

1. *For this loan to Giuliano de'Medici, Duke of Nemours, see the letter of 19 Dec. 1513, above. Giuliano died 17 March 1516.*

spite of the great good fortune of the said lords, he has not been repaid; and being at present in some need, and knowing also that in recent days similar creditors have had their loans repaid, he has taken courage to ask for it, and has written about it to Domenico Buoninsegni and sent him the copy of the receipt he has in Giuliano's hand. But because with such a man as Domenico, through the great number of his duties, such errands are likely to die unless they have on their side some special influence, I have decided, in order that this one may live, to take courage to write about it, begging you will not think it an annoyance to speak about it to Domenico, and also to inquire about the way in which such money can be made ready. I hope it will not trouble you for love of me to deal with this business among your others; in fact, besides being pitiable and just, it will not be without profit to you, and I beg you to answer with a line about it.

I have just been reading *Orlando Furioso* by Ariosto, and truly the poem is fine throughout, and in many places is wonderful. If he is there, give him my regards, and tell him I am sorry only that, having spoken of so many poets, he has left me out like a dog, and has done to me in his *Orlando* what I shall not do to him in my *Ass.*[2]

I know that there you are all day in the company of the Most Reverend de' Salviati, Filippo Nerli, Cosimo Rucellai, Cristofano Carnesecchi, and sometimes Anton Francesco degli Albizzi, and you give yourself to having a good time and remember little of us here, poor unfortunates dead with cold and sleep. Yet, in order to seem alive, we meet sometimes—Zanobi Buondelmonti, Amerigo Morelli, Batista della Palla, and I—and we talk of that journey to France with so much vividness that it seems to us we are on the road, so that of the pleasures we would have there we have already used up half, and to be able to do it with better order, we plan to make a little model of it, and to go on this last Thursday of Carnival as far as Venice; but we are in doubt whether we should get an early start and journey from there, or if we should wait until our return and go by the straight road. I wish at any rate you would consult with Cosimo and write us what is best to do. I am at your disposal. May Christ watch over you.

2. *Machiavelli's unfinished poem commonly called* L'ASINO D'ORO, THE [GOLDEN] ASS. *Tommasini* (VITA DI MACHIAVELLI *2. 319, n. 3*) *says, correctly I believe, that the proper title is merely, as in this letter,* L'ASINO, THE ASS.

Give my regards to Messer Piero Ardinghelli, because I forgot to ask you to. Again farewell all.

Of the friendship and humanity of Your Excellence

The servant
Niccolò Machiavelli.


## No. 167

5 January 1517–[*1518*], Florence
To Giovanni Vernacci, in Pera

[*Marriage advised*]

Dearest Giovanni:

I am astonished when you say in your last letter that you have not had mine, because four months ago I wrote to you and had letters to you written by Lodovico and Bernardo, who asked you I do not know what absurdities, and the letters were given to Alberto Canigiani. As I said to you in that, if you had had it, you would not need to wonder if I have written to you seldom, because since you left I have had countless troubles, and of such a sort that they have brought me to a place where I can do little good to others and less to myself. Nevertheless, as I told you in that letter, my house and what remains to me are at your service, because aside from my own children, there is no man that I think so much of as I do of you. I believe your affairs have much improved in the position you have made for yourself there; and if they are in the shape I have heard, I should advise you to marry, and to marry a woman through whom you will strengthen your connection with me, and who is beautiful and has a good dower, and is of excellent standing. So I should be glad if, having to remain out there, either you would write to me or would have Alberto Canigiani tell me what your opinion is; and if you intend to take one, inform me in some way about your condition.

We are all in good health and send our regards to you. May Christ watch over you.

Niccolò Machiavelli, in Florence.

No. 168

25 January 1517–[1518], Florence
To Giovanni Vernacci, in Pera

[*More on marriage*]

Dearest Giovanni:

Perhaps twenty days ago I wrote you two letters with the same contents and gave them to two persons so that you would have at least one of them. Since then I have received yours dated the fourth of November. And I am grieved to the heart that you have not had my letters, because six months ago I wrote to you and had a letter written by each of my sons, and in order that you may have one of them, I shall also make a copy of this.

As in many of my letters I have said to you, Chance, since you left, has done the worst for me that she can, so that I am brought down to a condition enabling me to do little good to myself and less to others. And if I am careless in answering you, I have become so in other things; yet, while I am I, I and my house are at your disposal, as they have been always.

Many thanks for the caviar. And Marietta says that on your return you may bring her a piece of light-brown camlet.

By my other letter I wrote to you that when your affairs were in better shape, in the way I hear of and am convinced of, I should encourage you to take a wife, and if you decide to do so, there are at present some things at hand such that you would not be able to do better; so that I should be glad if in this matter you would give me some answer.

We are all in good health, and I am yours.

Your Niccolò Machiavelli, in Florence.

No. 169

15 April 1520, Florence
To Giovanni Vernacci, in Pera

[*Legal troubles in Florence*]

In the name of God.

Dearest Giovanni:

Since I wrote to you about the death of Alberto Canigiani, I have not had any letters from you, and also I have not written because I thought you would return every hour, but seeing that you have not returned, I am moved to write these few lines to do my duty by you, seeing how your things are going to ruin here. You know that Piero Venturi filed a complaint against you by which you were compelled to remit his balance, so that you suffered damage from it of sixty florins, as I am told by Piero Corsali. Besides this, there is likelihood of complaints being filed against you by Giovan Luigi Arrighetti, Giorgio Bartoli, and many others, who all have judgments against you, through there not being here anybody who can answer them or knows how to. I for my part am of no use there, because I should do you harm and not good, on account of the conditions in which I find myself. Your uncles and your father's cousins have not been willing to speak, if nothing else, to one of the six, and of friends you have nobody here who has been willing to take this trouble; so that if you do not return, you will lose property and honor. Piero Corsali has made excuses to me and tells me he has written to you. By all means, my Giovanni, consider well what is better and how much, because if you stay a year more out there, you will lose everything here and will remain the prey of those who have committed you. I write this to do my duty, and so that you cannot say that it has not been written to you. May Christ watch over you.

Your Niccolò Machiavelli, in Florence.

## No. 175

[*About 8 November 1520, Florence*]
To Francesco del Nero, [*Florence?*]

[*The contract for writing the* HISTORY OF FLORENCE][1]

To my honored brother-in-law, Francesco del Nero
Honored Sir:

The substance of the contract will be this:

He is to be hired for———years with an annual salary of———,
with the obligation that he must and will be held to write the annals
or history of the things done by the state and city of Florence, beginning with the date that seems to him suitable, and in that language—
whether Latin or Tuscan—that seems to him best.

Niccolò Machiavelli.

1. *Officially this employment came from the University of Pisa, of which Francesco del Nero
was commissioner. It was approved by Giulio de' Medici, later Pope Clement VII.*

## No. 179

17 May 1521, Carpi
To his Magnificent Master Francesco Guicciardini, J.U.D., Governor of Modena and Reggio, most worthy and especially to be most
honored, [*in Modena?*]

[*A preacher for Florence; the comedy of business*]

Magnificent Sir, Ruler to be Most Respected:

I was on the privy seat when your messenger came, and just then
I was thinking of the absurdities of this world, and I was giving all
my attention to imagining for myself a preacher after my mind for the
place at Florence, and he would be just what would please me, because in this I intend to be as obstinate as in my other opinions. And
because I never failed that city by not benefiting her when I could—
if not with deeds, with words, if not with words, with gestures—I
do not intend to fail her this time either. It is true that I know I am
opposed, as in many other things, to the opinion of the citizens there:
they would like a preacher who would show them the road to
Paradise, and I should like to find one who would teach them the

way to go to the house of the Devil; they would like, besides, that he should be a man prudent, blameless and true; and I should like to find one crazier than Ponzo, more crafty than Fra Girolamo, more of a hypocrite than Frate Alberto,[1] because it would seem to me a fine thing, worthy of the goodness of these times, that all we have experienced in many friars should be experienced in one, because I believe the true way of going to Paradise would be to learn the road to Hell in order to avoid it. Seeing, besides this, how much credit a bad man has who conceals himself under the cloak of religion, I can easily conjecture how much of it a good man would have who in truth and not in pretense continued to tread muddy places like St. Francis. So since my fancy seemed to me good, I have planned to take Rovaio,[2] and I believe that if he is like his brothers and sisters, he will be just right. I should be glad if, next time you write, you will give me your opinion.

I continue in idleness here because I cannot carry out my commission until the general and the assessors are chosen, and I keep ruminating on how I can sow so much discord among them that either here or elsewhere they may go to hitting each other with their sandals; and if I do not lose my wits, I believe I am going to succeed; and I believe that the advice and help of Your Lordship would assist greatly. So if you would come as far as this with the excuse of a pleasure jaunt, it would not be a bad thing, or at least by writing give me some master strokes. If you once every day would send me a servant just for this purpose, as you have today, you would do several good things: for one, you would give me light on some things quite to my purpose; for another, you would make me more esteemed by those in the house, seeing the messages come thick. And I can tell you that on the arrival of this arbalester with the letter, making a bow down to the earth, and with his saying that he was sent specially and in haste, everybody rose up with so many signs of respect and such a noise that everything was turned upside down, and I was asked by several about the news. I, that its reputation might grow, said that the Emperor was expected at Trent, and that the Swiss had summoned new diets, and that the King of France wanted to go in person to speak with that king, but that his councilors advised him

1. *Ponzo is obscure; Fra Girolamo is Savonarola; Frate Alberto is from the* DECAM-
ERON 4. 2.

2. *Giovan Gualberto, a Florentine, and a Franciscan.*

against it; so that they all stood with open mouths and with their caps in their hands; and while I write I have a circle of them around me, and seeing me write at length they are astonished, and look on me as inspired; and I, to make them wonder more, sometimes hold my pen still and swell up, and then they slaver at the mouth, but if they could see what I am writing, they would marvel at it more. Your Lordship knows that these friars say that when one is confirmed in grace, the Devil has no more power to tempt him. So I have no more fear that these friars will make me a hypocrite, because I believe I am very well confirmed.

As to the lies of the Carpigiani, I should like a contest in that matter with all of them, because quite a while ago I trained myself in such a way that I do not need Francesco Martelli[3] for a servant, because for a long time I have not said what I believed, nor do I ever believe what I say, and if indeed sometimes I do happen to tell the truth, I hide it among so many lies that it is hard to find.

To that governor I did not speak, because having found lodgings, I thought speaking to him useless. It is true that this morning in church I stared at him a bit while he was standing to look at some paintings. He did seem to me well set up, and I can believe that the whole corresponds to the part, and that he is what he seems, and that his crooked back is not a liar;[4] hence that if I had your letter with me, I should have made an attempt at drawing a bucketful out of him. At any rate no, damage has been done, and I except tomorrow some advice from you on my affairs and that you will send one of the same arbalesters and that he will hurry and get here all sweaty, so that the household will be amazed; for by so doing you will bring me honor, and at the same time your arbalester will get a little excerise, which for the horses on these spring days is very wholesome.

I might write to you also some other things, if I were willing to weary my fancy, but I wish for tomorrow to keep it as fresh as I can. I send my regards to Your Lordship, and may you ever prosper as you desire.

Your faithful Niccolò Machiavelli,
Ambassador to the Minor Friars.

3. *Unknown.*
4. *The original of this sentence is not clear.*

## No. 182

18 May 1521, [*Carpi*]
To Francesco Guicciardini, at Modena

[*The comedy of the friars; Rovaio as preacher*]

I can tell you that the smoke of it has gone up to the sky, because between the panting of the carrier and the great bundle of letters, there is not a man in this house and in this neighborhood who is not overcome with fear; and in order not to seem ungrateful to Messer Gismondo, I showed him those sections about the Swiss and the King. He thought it a great thing. I spoke to him of the sickness of Caesar and of the states he wished to buy in France, in such a way that it made him drool. But I believe that with all this he fears being made to act, because he keeps considering and does not see why it is necessary to write such long bibles in these deserts of Arabia, and where there is no one except friars; and I do not think I appear to him that unusual man of whom you have written to him, because I remain here in the house, or I sleep or I read or I keep quiet; so that I believe he concludes that you wish to play a joke on both me and him. Still he keeps testing, and I reply to him in a few words and badly put together, and rely on the flood that is to come, or on the Turk who is going to cross over,[1] and if it would be a good thing to carry on a Crusade in these days, and similar stories for tavern benches; so that I believe it seems to him a thousand years until he can talk with you yourself, in order to have things explained better, and to raise questions with you who have put this grease on his hands, because I disturb his house and keep him obligated here. Yet I believe he is very sure that the play can last but a short time, and therefore he continues putting a good face on it and making the meals good; and I gobble them up like six dogs and three wolves, and say when I dine: "This morning I gain two *giulii*." And when I have supper: "This evening I gain four of them." Yet all the same I am under obligation to you and to him, and if he ever comes to Florence I will make it up to him, and you meanwhile will give him words.[2]

This traitor Rovaio wants to be urged and keeps finding fault

1. *A common and comic source of fear at the time.*
2. *Procured for him this profit. Ironical.*

and says he is afraid he cannot come, because he does not know what methods he could then use in preaching, and he fears to be sent to the galley as though he were Pope Angelico;[3] and he says that he is not now honored in Florentine affairs, for they made a law when he preached there the other time that whores would have to appear in Florence with yellow veils, and that he has a letter from his sister that they appear as they please, and that they flourish their tails more than ever; and he was very sorry about this thing. Still I kept on consoling him, saying that he should not be astonished at it, that it was the custom of great cities not to stand firm long in a decision, and to do today a thing and tomorrow to undo it; and I brought up Rome and Athens, so that he was entirely consoled and almost promised me. By my next you will learn the rest.

This morning these friars here have elected their Minister General, who is Soncino; he was first a man, secondly a friar, humane and good. This evening I must appear before their paternities, and to- morrow I believe I shall be entirely finished, so that every hour seems to me a thousand, and I shall remain one day with Your Lordship, who I hope will live and reign for ages of ages.

> Niccolò Machiavelli
> Ambassador of the Florentine State
> to the Minor Friars.

3. *Pope Angelico, the angelic pope, is the ideally good pontiff of popular verse. Rovaio believes he will be sent to the galley (to prison) because opposed to the ambitions of influential clerics.*

## No. 183

19 May 1521, [*Carpi*]
To Francesco Guicciardini, [*in Modena?*]

[*More difficulty about the preacher; the friars*]

Catso! One needs to manage cleverly in dealing with that fel- low, because he is as tricky as thirty thousand devils. I believe he's aware you are making game of him, because when the messenger came, he said: "Whew! this must be some big affair; the messengers come fast." Then, after reading your letter, he said: "I believe the governor is making fools of me and you." I acted Albanese, Mes-

sere,[1] and said that I left certain business at Florence in a matter that
pertained to you and me, and I had asked that you would keep me
informed when you learned from there anything about it, and that
this was the chief cause for the writing; so my ass goes "Lappe,
Lappe,"[2] because I am afraid all the time he will make a clean sweep
and send me back to the inn; hence I beg that tomorrow you will
take a holiday, so that this sport will not become injurious, though
the good I have received cannot be taken from my body: splendid
food, glorious beds and such things, in which I have for three days
now been rejuvenated.

This morning I have made a beginning on the case of the division;[3] today I have to be attending to it; tomorrow I believe I shall
finish it.

As to the preacher, I do not expect to get any honor from it,
because this fellow holds off; the father in charge says he is promised
to others, so I believe I shall go back in disgrace; and I don't like it
at all, because I don't know how to appear before Francesco Vettori
and Filippo Strozzi, who wrote about it to me especially, begging
me to do everything, in order that this Lent they could feed on
spiritual food that would do them good. And they will be sure to
say that in everything I serve them in one way, because this winter
just past, when I was with them one Saturday evening at the villa of
Giovan Francesco Ridolfi, they gave me the duty of getting the
priest for the mass of next morning; and then the thing went in such
a way that that blessed priest arrived after they had dined, so everything there was upside down, and I got the blame for it. Now if in
this second commission I rebottle the wine on the dregs, imagine
what an angry face they will turn on me. Yet I am reckoning that
you will write them two lines and excuse me in this affair as well
as you can.

About the *History*[4] and the Wooden-Sandal State,[5] I do not

1. *He tried not to give a direct reply. Cf. the end of Burchiello's* SONNET *1. 73 (*LA
VIOLENTE CASA*).*
2. *Cf. Pulci,* MORGANTE *24. 125. A comic way of referring to noises in the bowels
produced by fear. Gluttony is indicated by* lappe, lappe *in the throat (*MALMANTILE RAC-
QUISTATO *5. 62).*
3. *Machiavelli's mission was to get the Minor Friars to divide their province so that Tuscany
would be separately administered.*
4. *Machiavelli's* HISTORY OF FLORENCE. *His visit to Carpi could be thought to
interrupt work on it.*
5. *The Franciscans were called Wooden-Sandal Brothers. Machiavelli is amused that he,*

believe that by coming here I have lost anything, because I have learned about many good laws and regulations of theirs and believe I can make good use of this knowledge, especially in comparisons: where I need to speak of silence I can say: "They were keeping more quiet than the brothers when they eat," and so I can bring forward many other things taught me by this bit of experience.

Your Niccolò Machiavelli.

------

*who had had missions to the Court of France, should now have this mission to the Franciscans, whose organization he absurdly magnifies into a sovereign state. Cf. the signature of the preceding letter.*

No. 185

26 September 1523, Sant' Andrea in Percussina
To Francesco del Nero, in Florence

[*Some business matters*]

Honored brother-in-law:

Patience with the troubles I make you. The churches are interdicted, as you will see by the enclosed. And for the sake of the study, I beg you to send me by Bologna the release, which I am sending to you by messenger; otherwise I shall have that chimney relaid. And I shall give your regards to the fowls.[1] I am yours.

Niccolò Machiavelli, on his farm.

1. *Machiavelli addresses this letter (like no. 175) to Francesco del Nero as his brother-in-law. Francesco similarly addresses Niccolò (Alvisi, letter no. 190). The details of this relation are unexplained; was Del Nero the husband of one of Niccolò's sisters?*

*Since Del Nero was connected with the administration of the University or Studio at Pisa, the word rendered study (studio) has been interpreted as referring to that institution. The fowls have been taken as referring to those that laid golden eggs (Machiavel,* TOUTES LES LETTRES, *... par Edmond Barincou, Paris 1955, II. 572). The simplest explanation is that Machiavelli is referring to business about his property at Sant' Andrea in Percussina, that the studio is his study there, the release is a legal document, and the fowls those on his farm.*

## No. 186

30 August 1524, [*Sant' Andrea in Percussina*]
[*To Francesco Guicciardini, in Modena?*]

### [*At work on the* HISTORY OF FLORENCE]

[*The beginning is lacking*] I have been staying and now stay on my farm to write the *History,* and I would pay ten soldi—I do not intend to say more—to have you by my side so that I could show you where I am, because, having to come to certain particulars, I need to learn from you if I give too much offense either by raising or by lowering these things.[1] But I shall keep on taking counsel with myself and shall try to act in such a way that, since I tell the truth, nobody will be able to complain.

Your Niccolò Machiavelli.

1. *A reference to what he might say about the ancestors of the Medici and of other Florentines as well. On this subject in the Preface to the* HISTORY OF FLORENCE, *he suggests that if ancestors are made famous the quality of their actions matters little.*

## No. 192

3 August 1525, Florence
To Francesco Guicciardini, [*in Faenza*]

### [*Tuscan farms*]

Mr. President:

I have put off writing until today, because before today I could not go to see the property of Colombaia, so I trust Your Lordship will excuse me for this delay.

I shall begin everything from Finocchieto.[1] And I must tell you as the first thing this: for three miles around one sees nothing pleasing; stony Arabia is not different. The house cannot be called bad, but I would never call it good, because it is without those conveniences that are sought for; the rooms are small, the windows are high; a dungeon is not made differently. It has in front a rough meadow; all the exits go off downward, except one that has level ground for perhaps two hundred feet; and with all this it is buried among the

1. Finccchieto, *the name of the farm, is the diminutive of* finocchio *(fennel). This was proverbially the last thing to come on the dining table. See Pulci,* MORGANTE *18. 198; 19. 62; 25. 291. Machiavelli is amused at his reversal of the normal order.*

mountains in such a way that the longest view does not exceed half
a mile. As to the farms, what they pay Your Lordship knows, but
they are in danger of paying every year less, because they have many
fields that the water washes in such a way that if great diligence is not
used there to hold the soil with ditches, in a short time nothing but the
bones of those fields will be left; this demands the master, and you
are too far away. I hear the Bartolini have made a purchase in that
region and that they lack a house for guests. If you could get rid of
it to them, I should encourage you to do so, because it is a good thing
for them and ought to save you loss. If they do not come into your
hands, whether you wish to hold it or to sell it, I would encourage
you to spend one hundred ducats, with which you could complete
work on the meadow, encircle with vines almost all of the hill where
the house is placed, and make eight or ten ditches in those fields that
are between your house and that of your first farm, which fields are
called la Chiusa. In these ditches I would put winter fruits and
figs; I would make a fountain at a fine spring that is in the middle of
those fields at the foot of some rows of vines, which is the only fine
thing there. This improvement will serve you for one of two things:
the first is that, if you decide to sell, anybody who comes to see it sees
something that pleases him, and perhaps will then wish to talk about
buying; for if you keep it as it is, and the Bartolini do not buy it, I do
not believe you will ever sell it, except to someone who does not come
to see it, like yourself. If you decide to keep it, the said improvements
will serve to get you more vines, which are good, and will keep you
from dying of sorrow when you go to see it. So enough about
Finocchieto.

Of Colombaia, I confirm, so far as I can observe with the eye,
all that Jacopo has written you and Girolamo has said. The farm
lies well, has its roads and ditches around the villa,[2] and faces between south and east. The fields seem good because all the fruit
trees, old and young, have much vigor and life in them. It has all
conveniences of church, of butcher, of road, of post, that a farm near
Florence can have. It has a great many fruit trees, and nevertheless
there is space to double them. The house is made like this: you enter
a court that is on each side about forty feet; it has in front, opposite
the door, a loggia with a balcony above, and it is as long as the size
of the court and about twenty-seven feet broad. This loggia has on the

2. *The texts print* valla. *I have ventured the emendation of* villa.

right hand of him who looks toward it a room with an anteroom; and on the left hand a hall, with room and anteroom; all these rooms with the loggia are habitable and not undignified; it has in this court a kitchen, a stable, a vatroom and another little court for poultry and for cleaning the house. It has underneath two wine cellars of excellent design; it has many rooms above, of which there are three that for ten ducats could be prepared for lodging men of some rank. The roofs are neither bad nor good. In short, I assure you of this, that with an expense of 150 ducats you could live comfortably, pleasantly, and not at all without dignity. These 150 ducats you would need to spend in remaking doors, paving courts, remaking some parapets, replacing a beam, repairing a stair, remaking the eaves of the roof, renovating and rearranging a kitchen, and similar small matters that give appearance and cheerfulness to a house; and so with this expense you can live as well as you could even by entering into a great sea.[3]

As to the rents, I have not yet examined them to suit me, since a man to whom I wish to speak was not there. In another letter I shall give Your Lordship a detailed account.

This morning I received yours, informing me that I am in high favor with the Maliscotta; in that I take more pleasure than in anything I have in this world. I shall be pleased to have you give her my regards.

On the affairs of the kings, the emperors, and the popes, I have nothing to write; perhaps for another letter I shall have something, and I shall write.

I pray Your Lordship to tell your Lady that I have given her greetings to all her friends, men and women, and especially to Averardo, all of whom send regards to Your Lordship and to her. And to Your Lordship I send numberless regards and offers of service.

Your Niccolò Machiavelli, in Florence.

3. *Great expenses.*

## No. 196

17 August 1525, Florence
To Francesco Guicciardini, [*in Faenza*]

[MANDRAGOLA; *pills for stomach and head; a marriage negotiation*]

Mr. President:

Yesterday I had yours of the twelfth, and in reply will tell you that Capponi returned, and this trouble of asking him has been taken on by your Jacopo; so, as you say, I believe he will be sufficiently understood. You can at least make them an offer, to let them see that you wish it if they do not depart from what is honorable. Girolamo and I think that you cannot offer less than three thousand ducats; yet for this you can give him such a commission as you like.

It pleases me that *Messer Nicia*[1] pleases you, and if you have it presented in this Carnival, we will come to help you. I thank you for the commendations given and beg you to continue them.

These overseers of the affairs of the Levant intend to send me to Venice for the recovery of some lost funds. If I go, I shall leave within three days, and in returning shall come where you are to spend an evening with Your Lordship and to see my friends.

I send you twenty-five pills made four days ago in your name; the recipe will be written at the end of this letter. I tell you that they have restored me. Begin by taking one of them after supper; if that causes a movement, do not take any more of them; if it does not cause a movement, two or three, and at most five; but I never took more than two, and in a week only once, and when I feel myself heavy in the stomach or the head.

Two days ago I spoke on that affair with our friend; I said that if I was going too far into his important business he should excuse me for it, since he was the one who had given me courage, and briefly I asked him his intention about giving his son a wife. He answered me, after some ceremonies, that he thought things had come to such a pass that young men nowadays think it disgraceful not to have an extraordinary dower, and he did not believe it in his power to bring his son to an ordinary one. Then having stood for a little while considering: "I believe I know for what reason you speak to me, because I know where you have been, and this discussion has

1. *An alternative title for Machiavelli's comedy now called* MANDRAGOLA.

been brought before me by other means." To which I answered that I did not know whether he guessed well or not, but that the truth was that between you and me there had never been any such discussion, which I demonstrated to him with all sorts of effective words. If I was acting, I was acting for myself and because of the good I wished to him and to me. Here I took the mask off from him and from you and from your situation and from the nature of present and future times, and said so many things that I made him uncertain. At last he admitted that if the Magnificent should decide to take a Florentine as his wife, he would be badly advised if he did not take her from your house. Hence I said I did not see how a man of sense like himself could swap you for some other citizen in order to get two or three thousand ducats more; moreover, since you have no sons and your wife has ceased bearing, chance might make the dower turn out larger than that of some one else he might take, from whom he could not get anything further than the dower. Since in the course of this discussion we walked to the Servi, I stopped at the door and said to him: "I wish to speak this last word to you in a place to be remembered, so that you will recall it. May God grant that you be not obliged to repent of it, and may your son not be forced to feel that he has little obligation to you." So he said: "In God's name, this is the first time we have talked about it; we must speak of it every day." To which I said that I was not ever again going to say about it a single thing, because it was enough for me to have paid my debt. In this way I have managed my spear, for I could not conceal what I was certain he was going to find out. I am now prepared to wait for him and not to miss any opportunity, and with discussions general and particular to hammer on this mark.

But let us turn to the recipe for the pills.

### Recipe

| | | |
|---|---|---|
| Hepatic Aloes | Dram. | 1½ |
| Germander | " | 1- |
| Saffron | " | -½ |
| Selected Myrrh | " | -½ |
| Betony | " | -½ |
| Pimpernel | " | -½ |
| Armenian Bole | " | -½ |

Niccolò Machiavelli, in Florence.

No. 198

[*September 1525, Florence*]
To Francesco Guicciardini, [*in Faenza*]

[*Some words in Machiavelli's comedy,* MANDRAGOLA]

Mr. President:

Since immediately on arriving I went to my farm and found my Bernardo sick with a double tertian, I have not written to you. But on returning this morning from the farm to speak with the doctor, I found one from Your Lordship of the thirteenth, through which I see into what distress of mind you have been brought by the foolish-ness of *Messer Nicia* and the ignorance of those fellows. And though I believe your doubts are many, nevertheless since you make plain that you wish the explanation of not more than two, I shall try to satisfy you.

*To take stones for ovens* does not mean anything other than to do something fit for mad men, and therefore that character of mine says that if all were like Messer Nicia, "We would take stones for ovens," that is, we would all do things fit for mad men, and this is enough for the first doubt.[1]

As to the toad and the harrow,[2] this has indeed need for greater consideration. And truly I have thumbed through many books, like Fra Timoteo, to find the foundation of this harrow, and at last I have found in Burchiello a text that supports me, where in one of his sonnets he says:

> Fearing that the sovereignty would pass away,
> There was sent as ambassador a kettle of thread,
> The tongs and the shovel were pursued,
> So that he found himself thereby poorer by
>     four ropes,
> But the harrow of Fiesole drew there . . .

This sonnet seems to me full of mystery; and I believe he who con-siders it well may continue to stir up our times. There is only this difference, that if now any one sends a kettle of thread, that thread is changed into macaroni, so that it seems to me that all times return

1. MANDRAGOLA *II. 4.*
2. MANDRAGOLA *III. 6.*

and that we are always the same people. The harrow is a construc‑ tion of square wood that has certain teeth, and our farmers use it when they wish to prepare the fields for seeds, in order to plant them. Burchiello brings forward the harrow of Fiesole as the most ancient in Tuscany, because the Fiesolani, as Titus Livius says in his second decade,[3] were the first to invent this instrument. And one day when a farmer was leveling his field, a toad that was not used to seeing such great labor, while she wondered and gaped to see what was up there, was run over by the harrow, which scratched her back in such a way that she put her paw there more than twice. Hence, as the harrow passed over her, when the toad felt herself hit hard, she said to him: "Without coming back." This word gave rise to the proverb that runs, when one wishes a person will not return, "As the toad said to the harrow." This is all I have found of value, and if Your Lordship has any uncertainty, let me know.

While you are active there, we here also do not sleep, because Lodovico Alamanni and I sup these evenings with the Barbera and talk of the comedy, so that she offers to come with her singers to furnish the chorus between the acts; and I offer myself to make the songs in harmony with the acts, and Lodovico offers to give lodging there in the house of the Buosi to her and her singers. So you see if we are attending to business, in order that this festival may have all its fitting parts. With my regards, etc.

Your Niccolò Machiavelli.

3. *A jocose touch; the second decade of Livy is not extant.*

## No. 199

[*After 21 October 1525, Florence*]
To Francesco Guicciardini, [*in Faenza*]

[*More on the marriages of Guicciardini's daughters; how to get money from princes*]

Mr. President:

I never remember Your Lordship (and I remember you every hour) that I do not reflect on the way for doing something to fulfil your wish in the thing that, as I know, among the others most presses upon you; and among the many fantasies that have come to my mind, there has been one which I have determined to write, not in order to advise you but to open for you a door, through which you will know better than anyone else how to pass. Filippo Strozzi finds himself burdened with sons and daughters, and as he seeks to honor his sons, so he believes it proper to honor his daughters, and he also believes, as all wise men believe, that the first ought to show the way to the others. He tried, among various young men, to give her to a son of Giuliano Capponi with four thousand florins of dowry, but he did not get what he wished, because Giuliano did not approve; so Filippo, despairing of doing anything good by himself, unless with the dowry he went so far that he afterward could not keep it up, applied to the Pope for support and aid, and through his suggestion took up the business with Lorenzo Ridolfi, and concluded it with eight thousand florins of dowry, because four thousand were paid by the Pope and four thousand by himself. Pagolo Vettori, wishing to make an honorable marriage, and not seeing any prospect for giving a dowry that would be enough, also applied to the Pope, and he, to please Pagolo, put there along with his influence two thousand ducats of his own.

My dear President, if you were the first who had to break this ice to travel in this direction, I should be one of those who perhaps would go slowly in advising you to enter it, but having had the way already prepared for you by two men who, for qualities, merits, and every other human consideration, are not your superiors, I shall always advise that you courageously and without any hesitation do what they have done. Filippo has gained with the aid of the Pope a hundred and fifty thousand ducats, and he has not hesitated to ask the Pope to aid him in that necessity; much less do you need to hesitate who have not gained twenty thousand. Pagolo has been aided countless times and in countless ways, not with offices but with money itself, and then without hesitation has asked the Pope to aid him in that need. Much less hesitation in doing it is proper for you, who have been aided not with trouble to the Pope but with honor and profit to him. I need not remind you of Palla Rucellai, or Bartolommeo Valori, or of a great many others who in their necessities have been aided from the Pope's purse; these examples I believe should make you bold in asking and confident of obtaining what you ask. Hence if I were in your position, I should write a letter to your agent at Rome, who would read it to the Pope, or I would write it to the Pope and have it presented to him by the agent, and to him in secret I should send a copy of it and should instruct him that he should see that he got a reply to it. I suggest that the letter should show that you have worked ten years to gain honor and profit, and that it seems to you that in both you have very well satisfied such a desire, though with very great hardships and dangers, for which you thank God first and then the blessed memory of Pope Leo and His Holiness,[1] to whom you owe the whole. It is true that you know very well that if men do ten things with honor and then fail in one, especially when that one is of some importance, it has power to blot out all the others; and therefore since you feel that in many things you have carried out the part of a man of ability, you would wish not to be lacking in anything. Having written such a preamble, I would show him what your condition is, and that you are without sons, but have four daughters, and that it is time to marry off one of them; if you do not marry her in such a way that this act corresponds with your other achievements, you will feel that you have never done anything of value. And then you can show that to this desire of yours nothing is opposed except the wicked ways and corrupt customs of the present time, since the matter is brought to such a pass that in proportion as a young man is nobler and richer, laying aside all other considerations, he wishes a larger dower; indeed, when they do not receive dowers great beyond all reason, they think themselves disgraced. You do not know how to overcome this difficulty, because if you give three thousand florins, that will be as far as you could go, and it is so much that four daughters would require twelve thousand, which is all the profit made by your dangers and labors. Not being able to go higher, you recognize such a dower as only half of what young men demand. Hence, as the only remedy, you have plucked up courage to do what his better friends, among whom you account yourself, have done, that is, to go for support and aid to His Holiness, not believing that what he has done for others he will deny you. And at this point I should name to him the young man you have planned on and show your certainty that the dower and nothing else thwarts you; therefore it is necessary that His Holiness overcome this difficulty. Here press him and bear him down with the most effective words you know how to find, to show him how important you think the matter. I feel sure, if it is dealt with at

1. *Pope Clement VII.*

Rome in the right way, that you will succeed. So do not fail yourself, and if time and the season permit it, I should encourage you to
send there for this purpose your Girolamo, because the whole thing
consists in asking boldly and showing great discontent if you do not
receive. Princes easily bend themselves to do new favors for those for
whom they have done old ones, or rather they are so afraid of losing
the benefits of their earlier favors if they refuse, that they always hasten
to confer new ones, when they are asked in such a way as I hope you
will ask this. You are prudent.

Morone was seized, and the dukedom of Milan is overthrown;
and as he has waited for the hood,[2] all the other princes will wait for
it, and there is no further recourse. Thus it is imposed from above.[3]

> I see into Alagna the fleur-de-lis entering,
> And in his vicar, etc.[4]

You know the verses; read the rest for yourself. Let us make for
once a gay Carnival; prepare for the Barbera a lodging among those
friars we know of, and if they don't go mad, I don't want any money
from it; and give my regards to Maliscotta, and let me know how far
along the comedy is and when you plan to present it.

I received that addition, making a total of a hundred ducats for
the *History*.[5] I am now beginning to write again, and I relieve myself
by blaming the princes, who have all done everything to bring us
here. Farewell.

Niccolò Machiavelli
Historian, comic writer, and tragic writer.[6]

2. *A figure of speech, taken from the gentle falcon that waits for its hood to be put on, meaning*
to submit tamely.

3. *Seemingly a quotation.*

4. *Dante,* PURGATORIO 20. 86. *I have translated Dante's text; the form usual in editions
of Machiavelli is perhaps a misprint.*

5. *Machiavelli was first paid in sealed florins, depreciated nearly one-half. The ducat had
not depreciated.*

6. *The first two parts of this description are literal. Figuratively, Machiavelli could think of
himself as a tragic writer because dealing with the sorrows of Italy, referred to in the closing
sentence of the letter.*

## No. 200

19 December 1525, Florence
To Francesco Guicciardini, [*in Faenza*]

[*More on the dowers for Guicciardini's daughters*]

Mr. President:

I have put off answering your last until this day, both because it did not seem to me pressing and because I have not been much in Florence. Now having seen there your master of the stables and thinking I can send a letter securely, I have not put it off longer. I cannot deny that your hesitation, on whether it is good to attempt that business or not in such a way, is good and wisely presented; nonetheless I shall give you my opinion, which is that one can make a mistake in being too prudent as much as in being too stirring; indeed to be of the latter sort many times is better. If Filippo and Pagolo had had these qualms, they would not have done what they wanted to, and if Pagolo does not have daughters that will lay out their course to the others, Filippo has some, but he hasn't thought about them, if only he can settle the first to his mind. I do not know if there is truth in what you say, that you will put the first in Heaven only to put the others in Hell, since this action will not with the others put you in a worse condition than you are in now with all of them; rather it will put you in a better one, because the other sons-in-law, besides having you, will have an honorable brother-in-law, and you will find some who are less avaricious and more honorable; in fact, even if you do not find them, for the other daughters those chances that you now find for this one will not fail you. So then I should try the Pope in any case, and if I did not come to half sword the first time, I should speak of it to him in general, tell him broadly my desire, beg him to help me, see where I find him, go ahead and draw back, according as it went. I remind you of the advice that Romeo gave to the Duke of Provence, who had four daughters: he encouraged him to marry the first honorably, telling him that she would give the others a norm and precedent. So he married her to the King of France, and gave him half Provence as a dower. As a result, with small dowers he married the others to three other kings, as Dante says:

Four daughters he had, and each one a queen, of which thing the sole cause was Romeo, a humble man and a foreigner.[1]

I am pleased to learn the queries of these friars, which I do not wish to decide here, but there, in that place, and we shall go with him who will do best for us. But I can tell you, though, that if the rumor upsets them, presence sets them to fighting.

Of the things of the world I have nothing to tell you, since everybody cooled down on the Duke of Pescara's death,[2] because before his death they talked of new restrictions and similar things; but now that he is dead, each man is a little reassured, and since he seems to have time, he gives time to his enemy. I conclude at last that on this side there is no possibility for doing, ever, anything honorable or vigorous about living or dying with justice, so much fear I observe in our citizens, and so unwilling they are to oppose him who is getting ready to swallow them up, nor do I see any exception to this, so that he who has to act after consulting with them will not do anything other than has been done up to now.

Your Niccolò Machiavelli, in Florence.

1. PARADISO 6. *133–135, modified.*
2. *The Marquis of Pescara was probably the most important general in the army of the Emperor Charles V which defeated and captured Francis I of France at the battle of Pavia in 1525. He negotiated with Morone (see letter no. 199) as though to betray the Emperor and make himself King of Naples, but revealed the negotiations to Charles V. On 3 Dec. 1525 he died.*

No. 202

3 January 1525–[1526], Florence
To Francesco Guicciardini, [*in Faenza*]

[MANDRAGOLA; *Charles V and Francis I*]

Mr. President:

I believed that I could begin this letter of mine in reply to your last in happiness, and I have to begin it in sorrow, since your nephew is so greatly mourned by everybody, and soon after has come the death of his mother—a blow truly not expected, and deserved neither by her nor by Girolamo. Nonetheless, since God has willed it so, it must be so, and there being no defense, we must think of it as little as possible.

As to the letter from Your Lordship, I shall begin where you do, in order in the midst of such disturbances to live happily. I can say this, that I shall come no matter what, and nothing can hinder me other than sickness, from which may God protect me, and I shall come when this month is over and at the time that you set. As to the Barbera and the singers, if some other consideration does not restrain you, I believe I can bring her for fifteen soldi to the lira. I say this because she has certain lovers who may impede it; yet, if I am diligent, they can be quieted. And that she and I have decided to come, this assures you, that we have made five new canzone suited to the comedy—and they are set to music to be sung between acts—of which I send you, enclosed with this, the words, so that Your Lordship can consider them; the music either all of us or I alone will bring you. You will need, though, if she is going to come, to send here a servant of yours with two or three animals. So much for the comedy.

I have always been of the opinion that if the Emperor intends to become master of affairs, he will never release the King,[1] because by keeping him he keeps all his opponents weak, so that for this reason they are giving him and will give him as much time as he wishes to organize. Thus he keeps now France and now the Pope in hope of truce, and does not break off the negotiations and does not finish them; and when he sees that the Italians are about to unite with France, he limits his discussions with France, so that France does not decide. Hence he gains, as with these tricks we see he already has gained Milan and was on the point of gaining Ferrara; he would have succeeded if he had gone there; and if that had happened, Italy would have been finished. And if I may speak of these Spanish brothers of ours, they have erred this time, for when the Duke passed through Lombardy to go there, they should have held him and made him go to Spain by sea and not have trusted him to go there by himself, because they should have known that many chances could come up, as there have, through which he would not go there.

We heard four days ago of closer relations between Italy and France, and it is credible because—Pescara being dead, Antonio da Leva being sick, the Duke having returned to Ferrara, the castles of Milan and Cremona still being held, the Venetians not put under obligation, and everybody clear about the ambition of the Emperor—

1. *Charles V will not release Francis I, captured at the battle of Pavia.*

we suppose that everybody will try to secure himself and that the chance is very good. But thereupon news comes that the Emperor and France have made an agreement: France yields Burgundy and takes as wife the sister of the Emperor; he abandons four hundred thousand ducats she has of dower, and dowers her with as much; he gives as hostages either his two younger sons or the Dauphin; he cedes to the Emperor all the territories of Naples, Milan, etc. Many believe in such an agreement and many do not, for the reasons given above; I believe he has made it to hinder those closer relations men⁄ tioned above, and later he will find fault with it and break it. Now we shall wait to see what will happen.

I understand what you tell me of your business, and that you think you have time for reflection, since the times are not suitable. To this I shall answer in a few words with that sincerity which the love and reverence I bear you require. Always, during my recollec⁄ tion, either war has been going on or it has been talked of. Now it is being talked of; in a short time it will be carried on; and when it is finished it will be talked of again, so that there never will be a time for thinking of anything; to me it seems that these times more ad⁄ vantage your business than do quiet ones, because if the Pope plans to take trouble or fears that trouble will be made for him, he must consider that he has need, and great need, of you; consequently he must wish to please you.

Your Niccolò Machiavelli, in Florence.

## No. 204

15 March 1525–[*1526*], [*Florence*]
To Francesco Guicciardini, [*in Faenza*]

[*Will Charles V release his prisoner, Francis I? Giovanni of the Black Bands*]

Magnificent and Honorable Messer Francesco:

I have delayed writing so long that Your Lordship has got ahead of me. The cause of my delay has been that since it seemed peace would be made, I believed you would soon be returning into Ro⁄ magna, and I held back in order to speak to you by word of mouth, though I had my head full of fantasies, of which I poured out part five or six days ago to Filippo Strozzi. Writing to him about some-thing else, I got myself started in the dance, and I debated three propositions: one, in spite of the treaty the King will not be free; two, if the King is freed, he will keep the treaty; three, he will not observe it. I did not say which of these three I believed, but I did decide that from any of these Italy would have war, and for this war I offered no preventive. Now, seeing from your letter your wish, I shall discuss with you what I was silent about with him, and so much the more willingly, since you have asked it.

If you should ask me which of these three things I believe, I cannot get away from the settled opinion I have always held, that the King is not going to be free, because everybody knows that if the King should do what he can do, he would cut off from the Emperor all the ways by which the latter can rise to the level he has planned for himself. I do not see any cause or reason strong enough to move him to let the King go. Hence, in my view, it must be that he will let him go either because his council has been bribed (something in which the French are masters), or because he sees that closer relations are certain between the Italians and the kingdom,[1] and it does not appear to him that he has time or means for breaking them up with-out the release of the King. He must believe, too, that the King, if released, will have to keep the terms, and the King in this matter must have been a large promiser, and shown in every way the causes of the hatred he has for the Italians, and other reasons he could bring forward to assure the Emperor of observance.

Nevertheless, all the reasons that can be brought forward do not guard the Emperor from being stupid, if the King intends to be wise; but I do not believe he intends to be wise. The first reason is that up to now I have seen that whatever bad decisions the Emperor makes do not injure him, and all the good ones the King makes do not benefit him. It will be, as I have said, a bad plan for the Emper-or to release the King; it will be a good one for the King to promise everything in order to be free. Nevertheless, because the King will keep it, the plan of the King will turn out bad and that of the Em-peror good. The causes that will make him observe it I have written to Filippo; they are these: he will have to leave his sons in prison; if he does not keep it, he will need to burden his kingdom, which is already burdened; he will need to burden the barons by sending them

1. *Of France.*

into Italy; he will have to turn at once to labors that, from past examples, are enough to terrify him; moreover he will be doing these things to aid the Church and the Venetians, who have helped to ruin him. Earlier I wrote to you, and I write again, that great is the anger the King must feel against the Spaniards, but that cannot be much less which he must feel against the Italians. I know well it can be said, and it would be true, that if through this hatred he lets Italy be ruined, he might then lose his kingdom. But the matter stands that he intends it thus, for as soon as he is free, he will be in the midst of two difficulties: one, having Burgundy taken from him and losing Italy and being in the Emperor's power; the second, in order to escape the first, to become almost a parricide and a breaker of faith. He would get into the above-mentioned difficulties in order to aid men who are disloyal and unstable, who for the slightest cause, after he had won, would make him lose again. So I lean to the opinion either that the King will not be free, or that, if he is free, he will keep his word. Dread of losing his kingdom if Italy is lost— since he has, as you say, a French brain—is not going to move him in the way in which it might move some other man.

The second reason for believing that the King is not going to be wise is that he will not believe that Italy will go up in smoke, but perhaps will believe he can aid her, since she will have purged some of her sins, and he would not have got his sons back and gained new strength. And if between them there were treaties for the division of spoil, so much the more the King would observe the treaties, but so much more the Emperor would be a crazy man to put back into Italy one whom he had got out of her, so that then he can chase out the Emperor himself.

I am telling you what I believe may be, but I do not at all say that for the King it would be a wiser plan, because he would have to imperil anew himself, his sons, and his kingdom in order to humble so hateful, feared, and dangerous a power. The remedies for it seem to me these: to see that the King, as soon as he gets out, has near him one who, with his influence and his arguments and those of him who sends him, will make him forget past things and think of new ones, show him the unanimity of Italy, show him his plan as successful, if he decides to be that free king that he ought to wish to be. I believe that arguments and requests can have effect, but I believe that there would be much more effect in deeds.

I judge, in whatever way affairs go on, that there will be war, and soon, in Italy; therefore the Italians must see to it that they have France with them, and if they cannot have her, must consider how they are going to manage. I believe that in this situation we can make one of two decisions: either be subject to the will of whoever comes and meet him with money and buy ourselves out; or truly arm ourselves and with arms help ourselves as well as we can. I for my part do not expect that buying ourselves out and money will be enough, because if they would be enough, I should say, "Let us stop here, and not consider further," but they will not be enough, because either I am entirely blind or he will take from you first money and then life. If so, it will be a sort of vengeance on him for us to make sure that he will find us poor and used up, if we get nothing more from defending ourselves. Therefore I believe we should not defer arming ourselves and should not wait for the decision of France, because the Emperor has leaders for his soldiers, has them in their places, can start war on his own terms when he pleases. It is necessary for us to prepare a force, whether hidden or open; otherwise we shall wake up one morning all bewildered. I should praise assembling forces secretly.

I say one thing that will seem to you crazy; I shall bring forward a plan that will seem to you either foolhardy or ridiculous; nonetheless these times demand decisions that are bold, unusual and strange. You know, and everybody knows it who can think about this world, that the people are uncertain and foolish; nevertheless, even though they are, often they say that something is being done that should be done. A few days ago it was said throughout Florence that the Lord Giovanni de'Medici was raising the flag of a soldier of fortune[2] to make war where he had the best opportunity. This rumor stirred up my spirit to imagine that the people were saying what ought to be done. I believe anyone who believes that among the Italians there is no leader whom the soldiers would more gladly follow[3] and whom the Spanish more fear and more respect; everybody also thinks that Lord Giovanni is bold, prompt, has great

2. *Giovanni de'Medici, known to history as Giovanni of the Black Bands, was the great-great-grandson of Giovanni, father of Cosimo, Pater Patriae, as was Pope Clement VII. His mother was Caterina Sforza, the Duchess of Forlì mentioned in* THE PRINCE *20. Machiavelli gives in this letter the general opinion of his military qualities. Mortally wounded in battle against the Emperor's forces, he died 30 Nov. 1526.*

3. *Cf.* THE PRINCE *26.*

ideas, is a maker of great plans. We could then, secretly making him strong, have him raise this flag, putting under him as many cavalry and as many infantry as we can. The Spanish would think this done craftily and perhaps would suspect both the King and the Pope, since Giovanni is retained by the King; and if this happened, it would soon make the brains of the Spanish spin around and they would change their plans, though perhaps they have counted on ruining Tuscany and the Church without any hindrance. It could make the King change his opinion and turn him toward abandoning the treaty and choosing war, since he would see that he has to do with people who are alive and, in addition to arguments, show him deeds. If we cannot use this method and yet are to make war, I don't know what we can do, and nothing else occurs to me. But tie a string around your finger for this: if the King is not moved by force and authority and by things that are being done, he will keep the treaty and leave you in the lurch because, after he has come to Italy many times and you have either acted against him or stood looking on, he will not intend that this time also the same thing will happen to him.

The Barbera is there. If you can help her, I ask your interest, because I think much more of her than I do of the Emperor.

Niccolò Machiavelli.

## No. 206

4 April 1526, [*Florence*]
To Francesco Guicciardini, [*in Rome*]

[*The walls of Florence*]

Your Magnificence My Honored Superior:

I received today about four o'clock yours of the first of the present month, and in the absence of Ruberto Acciaioli, who has gone to Monte Gufoni, I went at once to the Cardinal[1] and told him the intention of Our Ruler the Pope about the matters dealt with by Pietro Navarra[2] and that His Holiness wished Pietro to make so

1. *Cardinal Passerini, representing Pope Clement VII in Florence.*
2. *Pietro Navarra, Count of Alvito, a Spanish veteran. When Ferdinand King of Spain refused to ransom him after he was taken prisoner at the battle of Ravenna in 1512, he entered the*

great and splendid a plan that it would give heart to a people like this one, so they could hope to defend themselves against any serious and vigorous attack. His Most Reverend Lord said that he would have Pietro come to him again this evening, and would make the request and charge him as effectively as he could to produce such a thing. Nevertheless, having talked together of the plans presented, we conclude that, wishing to retain the old circuit, we can do no better, and that it is impossible not to retain that circuit; deciding not to retain it, we must either increase Florence in the way known to His Holiness Our Lord, or take away the quarter of Santo Spirito[3] and cut the city down to the level part only. The first method is made weak by the great garrison you would need, for which the people of Cairo would be too few.[4] The second method is partly weak and partly pitiless. It would be weak if you left the houses of that quarter standing, because you would leave a city to an enemy more powerful than you are, who could make use of the country more than you could, so that he would vex you instead of your vexing him. As to the other way of destroying the quarter, everybody knows how difficult and harsh that would be. Therefore we must fortify the quarter as it stands. The method of doing so I do not wish to write to you as yet, both because it is not actually settled and in order not to go ahead of my superiors. Let this be enough, that of the walls of the said quarter on the other side of Arno, part should be cut off, part advanced, part drawn back. I believe and Signor Vitelli, who has come for this purpose, believes that part of the city would then be very strong, stronger than the level portion; and so says and declares Count Pietro, declaring with oaths that this city, prepared in such a way, would become the strongest place in Italy. We are going to meet tomorrow morning to go over it all, especially the larger plan. Then those who are assigned will meet and consider what has been ordered, and all will be put in writing and in a drawing and will be sent to Rome to His Holiness Our Lord. My opinion is that it will satisfy him, and especially that of the hill, where the unusual provisions are made. That of the plain does not

French service and later that of the allies against the Emperor Charles V. His expert opinion on the walls of Florence was desired by Pope Clement VII.

3. *South of Arno.*

4. *For the huge size of Cairo, see Ariosto,* ORLANDO FURIOSO *15. 63. Machiavelli read the poem in 1517 (letter no. 166).*

depart from the ordinary, but because everybody knows how to make
such sites strong, it matters little. Count Pietro will be here tomorrow and the next day, and we shall endeavor to get out of his head
anything else that is there, and I have delayed in order to hear, so that
it will not happen to me as to that Greek with Hannibal.⁵ I thank
you, etc.

Niccolò Machiavelli.

5. *An inexperienced Greek talked on military matters in Hannibal's presence (Cicero, DE ORATORE 2. 18).*

No. 207

17 May 1526, [*Florence*]
To Francesco Guicciardini, [*in Rome*]

[*The Pope's delays; the walls of Florence*]

Magnificent Mr. President:

I have not written to you since I left there because my head is so
full of bastions that nothing else can come into it. The law is managed ordinarily in the way and with the method that in Rome is
directed by His Holiness Our Lord. There is a delay in publishing
the magistracy and in going ahead with the affair, until there comes
from Rome a substitute for Chimenti Sciarpelloni, who they say is
in such bad health that he cannot attend to such things. It will be
necessary also to have a supply for Antonio da Filicaia, who day
before yesterday had an attack of apoplexy and is in bad condition.
It is strange that the Cardinal has not had a reply about Chimenti,
and we fear some impediment; yet that is unlikely, since the matter
is so far advanced.

I have heard the rumors from Lombardy, and it is recognized on
every side how easy it would be to get some rascals from that region.
This opportunity, for the love of God, should not be lost, and remember that Fortune, our bad advice and our worse officials would
have brought not merely the King but the Pope to prison; he has
been taken out by the bad advice of others and the same Fortune.
Provide now, for the love of God, in such a way that His Holiness
will not go back into the same dangers, from which you will never
be secure until the Spanish are so completely taken out of Lombardy

that they cannot return. I have a notion that the Emperor, seeing the King fail him, will make great offers to the Pope, which ought to find your ears stopped, if you remember the ills you have borne and the threats that in the past have been made to you. Remember that the Duke of Sessa was accustomed to say that the Pope too late began to fear Caesar. Now God has brought things back to such a state that the Pope is in time to hold him, if this time is not let go. You know how many opportunities have been lost; do not lose this one or trust any more in standing still, turning yourself over to Fortune and to Time, because with Time there do not come always the same things, and Fortune is not always the same. I would speak further, if I were talking with a man who did not know secrets and did not understand the world. Free Italy from long anxiety; root out these frightful beasts, which beyond the appearance and the voice have nothing human.

Here it is thought, if the fortifications go ahead, that I am to have the position of overseer and of secretary, and I am to be aided by one of my sons, and Daniello de' Ricci is to handle the money and all the records.

Niccolò Machiavelli.

No. 209

2 June 1526 [*first letter*], [*Florence*]
To Francesco Guicciardini, [*in Rome*]

[*The Pope favors including more land within the walls of Florence*]

Magnificent Mr. President:

I have not written to you for many days about the wall; now I shall tell you what comes to mind about it. Here it seems that the Pope has returned to the notion of the mountains, moved by the opinion of Giovanni del Bene, who in his letter says that in including all those hills there is more strength and less expense. As to strength, no city very large is ever strong, because its largeness confuses those who guard it, and many troubles can appear—which in those of convenient size does not happen. As to less expense, that is chatter, because he makes many presuppositions that are not true. First, he says that all those mountains can be cut into for the space extending from the house of Bonciano to that of Matteo Bartoli outside the walls (which is, according to him, nineteen hundred feet, but is really over three thousand), so it is merely necessary to wall all the others. He says the cuts can be brought into use as a wall, and above them can be built a bank eight feet high and sixteen thick. This is not true, because there are countless places where because it is level there can be no cutting; further, all that cutting would not stand by itself and would wash down, so that it would have to be held up with a wall; then the banks around would cost a world, would be disgraceful to this city and in a very few years would have to be redone; so that the expense would be great and continuous, and bring little honor. He says that the city treasury could avail itself of eighty thousand ducats in value added to property, which is a fable, and he does not know what he is talking about nor from where this added value could be got; so to everybody it seems not to be thought of. Nonetheless we shall make the model the Pope has asked for and send it to him.

Until some special appropriation is made for this undertaking, it is necessary to spend the money that is here, and therefore the law lays down that the treasurer of the Signors should pay what money is now in the hands of the city—on whatever account any of it, both by the Signors and the officials, has been deposited with him. Nevertheless, Francesco del Nero will make trouble about paying if His Holiness Our Lord does not write to him to pay it. The office has written about it to the ambassador. I beg you to aid in the matter so that the Pope will write to him.

Niccolò Machiavelli.

### No. 210

2 June 1526 [*second letter*], [*Florence*]
To Francesco Guicciardini, [*in Rome*]

[*San Miniato as a fortress dangerous to Florentine liberty*]

Though I know that your Luigi has written to you his opinion about putting the hill of San Miniato inside the wall, I too do not intend to omit writing you a word about it, because I think the matter very important.

The most harmful thing a republic can undertake is to make within herself something strong or that easily can be made strong. If you put before you the model that was left there, you will see that when San Miniato is taken in and that bastion made up there, a fortress is made, because from the San Miniato Gate to that of San Niccolò the distance is so short that in a single day a hundred men could by digging a ditch make it into a strong fortress. Then if ever through any misfortune a powerful man should come to Florence, as the King of France did in 1494,[1] you would become slaves without any protection,[2] because, since he would find the place open, you could not keep him from going in there, and since he could close it easily, you could not keep him from closing it. Consider it well and forestall it with what skill you can, and advise that cutting-off, which is strong and not dangerous, because if the taking in of San Miniato is begun, I fear the cutting off would be too displeasing.

I have written these three letters separately, so that you can use all of them as is convenient.

Niccolò Machiavelli.

1. *Charles VIII entered Florence as a conquered city.*
2. *If a tyrant held the fortress of San Miniato, he could control the city. For such a possibility see* THE PRINCE *20.*

## No. 211

2 June 1526 [*third letter*], [*Florence*]
To Francesco Guicciardini, [*in Rome*]

[*The marriage negotiations once more*]

Until last Saturday I did not have a chance to speak with L[*orenzo*] S[*trozzi*], but being with him and discussing a number of things, he touched on his son, so I had an opportunity to complain of his paying little attention to the matter that I earlier brought before him, and said I was certain that as once a rich marriage escaped him, now one very honorable and not poor was going to escape him; I did not know, if he intended to give his son a Florentine girl, where else he could go. He freely confessed that I was telling the truth and that you had approached him, and nothing could please him more; it pleased him so much that even if the thing could not be done now, he could suppose, since you have four, that he would be in time for

one. His reasons for putting it off are that his wife's health is improved, and the boy has changed his ways for the better, associating
with educated men and studying hard; he had thoughts of marrying
him because earlier he did neither of these two things. The third
reason is his daughter, whom he wishes to marry off first. But the
idea nevertheless pleases him so much that he already has talked
many times with the boy about you. When he returned from Loreto,
he took the opportunity of being in Romagna two days with your
Jacopo, who showed the greatness of your position and with what
dignity you hold it and the name you have, and exalted your capacities to the sky. All this worked to make the thing easy when it was
to be discussed, because he feared his son would get the notion of a
big dower. Altogether he spoke on the affair in such a way that I
could not wish more. I did not fail to show him that his hesitation
is baseless—because the girl is of such an age that she can be kept
unmarried four or five years—and that this match would aid him in
marrying his daughter, because he who wants unusual dowers has
to give them. I labored with him a bit, so if he were not a man a
little set in his ways, I should have great hope in the matter.

Niccolò Machiavelli.

No. 219

5 November 1526, [*Florence*]
To Francesco Guicciardini, [*in Piacenza*]

[*Machiavelli in Modena. Political ineptitude*]

Mr. Deputy:

From Modena[1] I wrote Your Lordship a letter more fitted to
amuse Filicciafo than to do anything else;[2] so I write what happened
next.

So beginning at Modena, when I arrived Filippo [*de'Nerli*] met
me and said: "Can it be that I have never done a thing that is right?"
I replied with a laugh: "Mr. Governor, don't be astonished at that;
you are not at fault, but this year is, because not a person has done one

---

1. *In a letter of 30 Oct. Guicciardini acknowledged Machiavelli's letter from Modena, which apparently is not now extant. In Alvisi's text a misprint makes Guicciardini Deputy of Modena and hides the place where Machiavelli wrote. Lesca corrects the misprint.*
2. *Mentioned by Guicciardini in a letter of 12 Nov. 1526.*

thing well, nor is anything as it should be. The Emperor could not have conducted himself worse, not having for so long a time sent his men any aid, though he could easily have done so; the Spanish could now and then have played some big tricks on us, and have not known how; we could have won the war and have not known how; the Pope has trusted more in one penful of ink than in a thousand infantrymen, who would have been enough to guard him; the Sie- nese alone have conducted themselves well. It is no marvel if in a crazy time the crazy come out well.[3] So, my Lord Governor, it would be a worse sign to have carried through some good action than to have done a bad one." "Since that's the state of things," said Filippo, "I'm going to stop worrying and be quite happy." And so ended the first act of the comedy. Soon after came Count Guido Rangone, and when he saw me, he said: "Is the Deputy still angry?" I answered that he was not, because he no longer had near him the one who was the reason for his anger. And not to tell all the details, we talked a little of this blessed wrath of yours; and he said he would sooner go into exile in Egypt than serve in an army where you were. On that I said what was proper, and especially debated the bad and the good that your presence had brought about, so that easily every- body granted that it had done more good than harm. I remained in Modena two days and conversed with a prophet who said, bringing up witnesses, that he had foretold the flight of the Pope and the use- lessness of the enterprise, and again he says that not yet are we through with all the bad times, in which the Pope and we will suffer a great deal.

We came finally to Florence, and the greatest blame that I have heard given to you is that in letters written here to the Cardinal, you have shown the ease of the undertaking and its certain victory, whereupon I have said that this is not possible, because I believe I have seen all the important letters Your Lordship has written, in which there were opinions entirely against certain victory.

Niccolò Machiavelli.

3. *For an instance of Sienese madness, see* THE [GOLDEN] ASS *1. 23.*

## No. 219 B

[*November 1526,*[1] *Florence?*]
To Bartolomeo [*Cavalcanti, in ?*]

[*The military mistakes of Pope Clement VII*]

Dearest Bartolomeo:

The reason why the Pope started this war before the King of France sent his soldiers into Italy and took action in Spain according to his agreement, and before all the Swiss arrived, was his hope in the people of Milan and his belief that six thousand Swiss, whom the Venetians and the Pope had sent on learning of the first rebellions in Milan, would be so prompt that they would arrive at the same time as the Venetians arrived with their army. Besides, he believed that the King's soldiers, if they were not so prompt, would at least be early enough to aid in carrying through the undertaking. To these hopes were joined the needs of the Castle,[2] which was showing that it required aid. All these things, then, made the Pope hasten, and with such hope that we believed this war would end in fifteen days; this hope was increased by the capture of Lodi. The armies of the Venetians and of the Pope did unite, then; but of the presuppositions above, two of the most important were lacking, because the Swiss did not come, and the people of Milan were of no value. Hence, when we appeared before Milan, the people did not stir, and not having the Swiss, we did not have courage to stay there; we retired to Marignano, and did not return to Milan until five thousand Swiss had come. Their coming, as earlier it would have been useful, was then harmful, because it gave us courage to return to Milan in order to relieve the Castle, and it was not relieved, and we committed ourselves to remaining there; since the first retirement was shameful, nobody advised the second.

This caused the attempt on Cremona to be made with part of the infantry and not with all, as it would have been made if on the loss of the Castle we had been at Marignano. For these reasons,

1. *The reference to All Saints' Day near the end of the letter puts its date after 1 Nov. 1526. The Spanish fleet, mentioned just before as not yet arrived, reached Naples on Dec. 1. This letter, not in Alvisi's edition, is given by Tommasini,* VITA DI MACHIAVELLI *2. 1251. Ridolfi* (MACHIAVELLI, *p. 469) dates it about 6 Oct.

2. *Of Milan.*

then, and also since we expected it to be easy, we carried on the affair of Cremona weakly. This was contrary to a rule of mine that says it is not a wise plan to risk all one's Fortune and not all one's forces. They believed, because of the fortress, that four thousand soldiers would be enough to capture her. This attack, because it was weak, made Cremona more difficult, because those forces did not assail, but did point out, the weak places; as a result those inside did not lose them but strengthened them. Furthermore, they settled their courage to the defense; hence, although later the Duke of Urbino went there, and there were fourteen thousand soldiers round about, they were not enough; while if he had been there early with the whole army—able at one time to make several attacks—of necessity they would have taken her in six days, and perhaps this campaign would have been won, because we would have had the prestige of the capture, along with a very large army. Because, since thirteen thousand Swiss came, either Milan or Genoa, or perhaps both of them, would have been mastered. The enemy would have had no recourse; the troubles at Rome would not have occurred; the reinforcements, which have not yet come, would not have been in time. We have spent fifty days hoping for Milan, and the capture of Cremona comes too late, when all our affairs are in ruins.

We have then on our side lost this war twice: once when we went to Milan and did not stay there; the second time when we sent and did not go to Cremona. The reason for the first was the timidity of the Duke; for the second, the vanity of us all, because, feeling disgraced by the first retreat, nobody dared advise the second; and the Duke [*of Urbino*] could do badly against the will of all, and against the will of all he could not do well. These are the errors that have taken victory away from us; I say *taken it away* through our not having conquered early; because we might have deferred but not lost the campaign, if our bad arrangements had not been added. These also have been two: the first is that the Pope has not raised money in times when he could with reputation have done so, and in the ways used by other popes. The other is that he remained in Rome in such a condition that he could be captured like a baby—something that has snarled this skein up in such a way that Christ could not straighten it out; because the Pope has taken his soldiers from the field, and Messer Francesco [*Guicciardini*] is still in the field, and today the Duke of Urbino must have arrived there. Many leaders, of many opinions, are left, but all ambitious and unbearable; and lacking anybody who knows how to assuage their factions and keep them united, they will be a chorus of dogs.[3] From this results a confusion in our doings that is very great, and already Lord Giovanni [*de' Medici*] does not intend to remain there; I believe that today he will leave. These bad arrangements were all corrected by the eagerness and effort of Messer Francesco [*Guicciardini*]. Besides this, if money has been coming sparingly from Rome, now it will fail entirely. So I see little order in our houses, and if God does not aid us to the south, as he has done to the north, we have few resources left.

As God with the ruin of Hungary impeded aid from Germany for the northerners, so he will need to impede aid from Spain with the ruin of the fleet; hence we need to have Juno go to beseech Aeolus for us and promise him *la Contessa* and all the ladies in Florence,[4] so that he will give full freedom to the winds in our favor. Without doubt, if it were not for the Turk, I believe the Spanish would have come to celebrate All Saints' Day with us.

I, having seen the Castle of Milan lost and observed how the Spaniards have established themselves in three or four of those cities and made themselves sure of the people, judged that this war was going to be long, and through its length dangerous. I know with what difficulty cities are taken when there is somebody inside who means to defend them, and that a province is taken in a day, but a city requires months and years to take, as is shown by many ancient narratives and in modern times by Rhodes and Hungary. For that reason I wrote to Francesco Vettori that I believed we could not support this undertaking, except to bring about that the King of France should take Milan for his, and we should give him that state, or except as a diversion through which we would leave the frontiers of these states guarded, so that the Spanish could not make progress. The Pope then with all his forces should attack the Kingdom, which I believe could be taken before one of these cities here, because there would be neither obstinate defenders nor peoples conquered[5] . . ., such as a man would like. Besides this, the war would feed itself,[6] because in addition to the assistance he could have from the

---

3. *Cf. the quarrelsome leaders of* THE PRINCE *26.*

4. AENEID *1. 65 ff.*

5. *Something is lacking from the MS.*

6. *I have accepted Tommasini's emendation of the MS reading (*contesa*) to* se stessa.

cities, he would have tribute, and the richness of the country, not ravaged, would make assistance more lasting. Also the Pope without new expense would live securely in Rome, and we would see which the Emperor estimated higher, Lombardy or the Kingdom, If this is not done, I look on the war as lost, because its length is sure. and in length dangers can be reckoned as certain, either through lack of money or through other accidents such as those that have come up. I have thought it a strange plan to wear ourselves out in the field, leaving the enemy at ease in the city, so that, when at last his reinforcements came, finding us worn out, he should ruin us like the Admiral and the King.

## No. 222

2 April 1527, Imola
To Guido Machiavelli, in Florence

[*The study of letters and music; a rural problem; the family*]

My dearest son Guido:

I have received your letter, which has been a great pleasure to me, especially since you write that you are completely cured, because I could not have better news. For if God grants life to you and to me, I believe I can make you a man of standing, if you wish to play your part as you should, because, beside the great friendships I have, I have made a new friendship with the Cardinal Cibo (it is so great that I myself wonder at it), which will be of service to you. But it is necessary for you to learn and, since you no longer have the excuse of sickness, to work hard to learn letters and music, since you see how much I am aided by the little skill I have. So, my son, if you wish to give pleasure to me and bring prosperity and honor to yourself, do well and learn, because if you help yourself, everybody will help you.

The little mule, though he is crazy, needs to be treated quite differently from other crazy creatures, because the other crazy ones are tied up, and I want you to untie him. Give him to Vangelo and tell him to lead him onto Monte Pugliano and then take off his bridle and halter and let him go where he will to get his living and rid himself of his madness. The territory is large; the animal is small;

he can't do any harm. And so without taking any trouble about it, we can see what he wants to do, and you will be in time, whenever he gets his wits back, to catch him again. With the horses do what Lodovico has told you to do; he, I thank God, has got well, and he has sold out. And I know that he has prospered, since he has sent money, but I wonder and feel bad because he has not written.

Greet Mona Marietta[1] and tell her that I have been on the point of leaving here every day, and still I remain; and I never had so much desire to be in Florence as now; but I can do nothing else. Merely say to her that for anything I hear she can be sure that I shall be there before there is any trouble. Kiss Baccina, Piero and Totto,[2] if he is there, and I would have been glad to know whether his eyes are cured. Be happy and spend as little as you can. And remind Bernardo that he should try to do well; to whom within fifteen days I have written two letters and have had no reply. Christ watch over you all.

Niccolò Machiavelli, in Imola.

1. *Machiavelli's wife.*
2. *Machiavelli's youngest children. See Ridolfi,* VITA DI MACHIAVELLI *358, 472.*

No. 223

5 April 1527, Forlì
To Francesco Vettori, in Florence

[*What policy for Pope Clement VII?*]

My honored Francesco:

Since the truce was made at Rome, and we saw that the Emperor's soldiers did not intend to keep it, Messer Francesco [*Guicciardini*] wrote to Rome that it was necessary to take one of three courses: either go back to war in such a way that all the world should understand that never more were we going to discuss peace, in order that France, the Venetians, and everybody, without hesitation or suspicion, should do his duty (in his letter he showed that there were also many possibilities, especially in an attempt to aid the Pope). Or if this did not suit, we should adopt the second, which would be wholly contrary to the first, namely, enter into this peace with complete effort, and put our heads in the lap of this Viceroy,[1]

1. *Lannoy, the viceroy of Naples.*

and so let ourselves be controlled by Fortune. Or indeed, if worn out in the first of these two courses and disgraced by the second, we might take a third course, which does not matter and need not be mentioned now. Today Messer Francesco has received a reply from Rome, that the Pope has turned to take this second course of throwing himself wholly into the lap of the Viceroy and of peace, which if it succeeds will be now our safety; if it does not succeed, it will cause us to be wholly abandoned by everybody. If it is going to succeed or not, you can judge as well as we can; but I say to you only this, that Messer Francesco has taken in any event this decision, to aid in the affairs of Romagna, while he sees that at sixteen soldi to the lira they can be defended,[2] but when he sees them indefensible, without any hesitation he will abandon them, and with those Italian forces he can find and with such money as is left to him, he will come in this direction to save Florence and her state in any way he can. So be in good hope, for it will be defended no matter what.

This imperial army is strong and large; nevertheless, if it should not encounter men who have given up their courage, it would not capture a bake oven. But there is danger that through weakness one town at the beginning will yield to it, and when one does so, all the others will go up in smoke; this is one of the things that make the defense of this province risky. Nonetheless, though it may be lost, you can save yourselves if you do not give up your courage; and by defending Pisa, Pistoia, Prato and Florence, you will get an agree-ment with them that, if heavy, will not at the end be mortal. Because that decision by the Pope is still secret with respect to these allies, and for every other respect, I pray you not to make public this letter. Farewell.

Niccolò Machiavelli, in Forlì.

2. *The lira was made up of twenty soldi. Hence* sixteen to the lira *means* cheaply, or here, with probability of success.

## No. 224

14 April 1527, Forlì
To Francesco Vettori, in Florence

*[An unsatisfactory peace]*

Magnificent Sir:

The agreement has always been advised here for the same reasons for which you there have always advised it: having seen the conduct of France and of the Venetians, having seen the poor discipline of our soldiers, having seen that the Pope lacked all hope of being able to keep up the war in the Kingdom, having seen the power and obstinacy of the enemy, we judged the war lost, as you yourself, when I left there, judged it. This has led us always to advise agree-ment, but we meant an agreement which would be solid, and not uncertain and confused like this, which is made in Rome and not kept in Lombardy, and that there should be a little money here. That little we would need to keep to use in such an uncertain agree-ment, and we would continue unarmed; or in order to arm ourselves, we would spend the money and be left without any for the agree-ment. And so, whereas we thought that a clear agreement would bring safety, a confused one is wholly pernicious and our ruin.

From there it is now written that the agreement is almost settled, and because the first pay is sixty thousand scudi, we rely for the greater part on the money that is here. Here we have thirteen thou-sand ducats in cash and seven to our credit with the Venetians. If the enemy advance toward Tuscany, the money must be spent in maintaining our soldiers, in order to try to hold this poor city, so that if you rely on the agreement, you will have to rely on an agree-ment that will end these armies and these expenses. Otherwise, if we keep up a confused agreement that requires us to provide for both the agreement and the war, we shall not provide for either of them, and the result will be evil for us and good for our enemies, who, marching toward us, are giving their attention to war and letting you confuse yourselves between war and agreements. I am yours.

Your Niccolò Machiavelli, in Forlì.

## No. 225

16 April 1527, Forlì
To Francesco Vettori, in Florence

["I love my native city more than my soul"]

Magnificent, etc.:

Monseigneur de la Motte has been today in the camp of the imperials with the final form of the agreement made there. If Bourbon accepts, he must halt his army; if he moves, it is a sign that he does not wish any agreement. So tomorrow will be the judge of our affairs. Therefore the decision here, if tomorrow he moves, is to think on war completely, without having a hair that thinks further of peace; if he does not move, it is to think of peace and to lay aside all thought of war. With this north wind we too must sail and, if we decide on war, we must cut off all the affairs of peace, and in such a way that the allies will come on without any hesitation, because now we cannot hobble any more but must go like mad; often desperation finds remedies that choice has been unable to find.

They are coming without artillery into a difficult region. Hence if, with what little life remains to us, we unite with the forces of the League that are ready, either they will leave this province with shame or they will come down to reasonable terms.

I love Messer Francesco Guicciardini; I love my native city more than my soul; and I tell you this through the experience which sixty years have given me, namely, that I do not believe that ever more difficult articles than these were struggled with, where peace is necessary and war cannot be abandoned; and to have on our hands a prince who scarcely is able to deal with peace alone or with war alone.

I send you my regards.

Niccolò Machiavelli, in Forlì.

## No. 227

18 April 1527, Brisighella
To Francesco Vettori, in Florence

[*Those who gain from war will not praise peace*]

Honored Francesco:

These French soldiers have been miraculously brought here to Brisighella; and likewise it will be a miracle if the Duke of Urbino comes to Pianoro tomorrow (as it seems that the Legate of Bologna writes from there); here we shall wait, as I believe, to learn what he does. For the love of God, if you cannot obtain this agreement, cut off the negotiation right now and in such a way, with letters and with actions, that these allies will aid us; as the agreement, if it were observed, would be in every way the certainty of our safety, so to negotiate about it without carrying it through will be the certainty of our ruin. That the agreement was necessary will be seen if it is not made; and if Count Guido [*Rangone*] says something else, he is a fool. This only I wish to argue with him: You ask him if it is possible to keep them from coming into Tuscany, and he will say it is not, if he says what he has always said in the past; and similarly the Duke of Urbino. If it is true that they cannot be kept out, ask him how they can be got out without fighting a battle, and how fit this city is to endure two armies in her territory, when the friendly army is more unbearable than the hostile one. If he settles this for you, tell him he is right. But they who profit from war, as these soldiers do, would be fools if they praised peace. But God will give them more war than we shall want.

Niccolò Machiavelli, in Brisighella.

# A SONNET TO MESSER BERNARDO HIS FATHER ON THE FARM AT SAN CASCIANO

*[This bit of domestic foolery must have been written before the death of Bernardo Machiavelli in 1500.]*

THOSE FELLOWS HAVE BEEN LIVING A MONTH OR more on nuts, on figs, on beans, on smokedried meat, so it will be an evil and not a joke to make so long a stay up there.

5 As the thirsty ox of Fiesole looks on the Arno below and licks away its drivel, so they do about the eggs that the hucksterwoman has and, at the butcher's shop, about the mutton and the beef.

9 But in order not to make the maggots starve, we shall repeat a word after Daniel, since perhaps already there is something that he reads,

12 because, eating only bread and knife, we have got beaks that seem like those of woodcocks, and hardly hold our eyes half open.

15 Say to that brother of mine that he must come to enjoy with us the goose we had from you Thursday.

18 At the end of the play then, my Messer Bernardo, you will buy ducks and geese and will not eat them.

*l. 9 The maggots in the meat that the brothers of Machiavelli are eating in the city.*
*l. 10 Daniel is unknown.*
*l. 16 I follow Ridolfi, VITA DI MACHIAVELLI, p. 397.*

# TWO SONNETS TO GIULIANO, SON OF LORENZO DE'MEDICI

[*The dramatic date of these tailed sonnets is determined by Machiavelli's arrest after the conspiracy of Boscoli and Capponi in 1513. Since they came to light only in 1828, their real date can only be inferred; probably, though not necessarily, they were composed while Giuliano was residing in Florence in 1513, almost certainly before his death in 1516. Obviously, they were not intended to be sent to him.*

*They present the unquenchable humor with which Machiavelli accepted his misfortunes. When serious about them (in his Familiar Letter of 13 March 1512–1513), he is very brief.*]

### 1.

I HAVE, GIULIANO, ON MY LEGS A SET OF FETTERS, with six pulls of the cord on my shoulders; my other miseries I do not intend to recount to you, since so the poets are treated!

5 These broken walls generate lice so swollen that they look like flies; never was there such a stench at Roncesvalles, or in Sardinia among those groves,

9 as in my so dainty hospice; with noise such as if truly Jove on earth were thundering, and all Mongibello.

12 One is chained up and another is unironed with a pounding of locks, keys and bars; another shrieks he is too high above the ground!

15 What gave me most torment was that, sleeping near dawn, I heard them chanting the words: "We are praying for you."

18 Now let them go away, I beg, if only your pity may turn itself toward me, good father, and loosen these cruel bonds.

*l. 2 In the torture of the rack.*
*l. 8 Between the Arno and the western part of the wall of Florence, where dead horses and asses were skinned. See the end-papers.*
*l. 14 Raised up in the torture of the rack.*
*l. 17 For those being taken to execution.*

### 2.

LAST NIGHT, BESEECHING THE MUSES THAT WITH
their sweet cither and sweet songs they would, to console me,
visit Your Magnificence and make my excuses,

5 one appeared who embarrassed me, saying: "Who are you, who
dare to call me?" I told her my name; and she, to torture me, hit
me in the face and closed my mouth for me,

9 saying: "You are not Niccolò but Dazzo, since you have your
legs and your heels bound and you sit here chained like a mad-
man."

12 I wished to give her my arguments; she replied to me and said:
"Go like a fool with that comedy of yours in rags."

15 Give her proofs, Magnifico Giuliano, in the name of high God,
that I am not Dazzo, but am myself.

*l. 9 Apparently a man whose name had become proverbial in Florence.*
*l. 14 Rags* (guazzeroni)*: cf. Burchiello,* SONNET 1. 71 *(*GUARDARE I MERLI*).*

# A THIRD SONNET TO GIULIANO, SON OF LORENZO DE'MEDICI

[*A playful tailed sonnet with seriousness close to its surface.*

*Desire for employment and fear that somebody may get ahead of him suggest the date and situation of the letter on the composition of* THE PRINCE *(10 December 1513). The thrushes that, in the letter, he says he caught daily, here become, in his imagination, his poor present to Giuliano.*]

I SEND YOU, GIULIANO, SOME THRUSHES, NOT because this gift is good or fine, but that for a bit Your Magnificence may recollect your poor Machiavelli.

5 And if you have near you somebody who bites, you can hit him in the teeth with it, so that, while he eats this bird, to rend others he may forget.

9 But you say: "Perhaps they will not have the effect you speak of, because they are not good and are not fat; backbiters will not eat them."

12 I will answer such words that I am thin, even I, as my enemies are aware, and yet they get off me some good mouthfuls.

15 Won't Your Magnificence give up your opinions, and feel and touch, and judge by the hands and not by the eyes?

l. 5 *The Italian word* mordere *means to bite* both literally and figuratively; *the latter sense, to speak evil of, is now obsolete for English* bite *except in* backbite. *Machiavelli plays with the two senses throughout the poem.*
l. 17 *Investigate thoroughly.*

# SERENADE

[*Could Machiavelli have written these verses at the time when he offered Vettori a serenade that would make a lady fall in love (*FAMILIAR LETTERS, *4 February 1513–1514)? Some weeks earlier he began the letter of 10 December 1513 with the quotation from Petrarch: "Slow were never divine graces"; in the poem he adapts it in line 120. In the same epistle he tells of reading Ovid, more than once quoted in the letters of the period. From Ovid's* METAMORPHOSES, *XIV. 623–771, is taken the narrative of this serenade, lines 25–232. Perhaps, then, these octaves were composed in the winter of 1513–1514.*

*The framework of the narrative may be compared with the verses beginning the* FAMILIAR LETTER *of 31 January 1514–1515, the only other instance of Machiavelli's love poetry in this present collection.*]

HAIL, LADY, CHOSEN AMONG OTHER LADIES, RARE instance of beauty on earth; O one only phoenix, perfect soul, in which every beauty is enclosed and shut in, listen to what your servant utters to you, since with your eyes you make such war on him, and believe, if you wish to be happy, the true words he says to you.

9 It does not avail to be of great and lofty ability, it does not avail to have power, to have valor, if one does not yield to the noble kingdom of Venus the fair and of her son Amor. Of them alone the ire is to be feared, and the anger and implacable rage, because one is a woman, the other young and agile, and they have taken from many their individual being.

17 Wherefore, not to soften my dire lot, nor to mitigate the afflictions I bear, nor to show the fire that circles about my heart, which I put out with tears, but to beseech you to flee the rage of this goddess, I come with an example, in order that you may learn to flee the cruel net wherein Anaxarete was taken.

25 Before Italian valor put its auspicious nest on the seven hills and the Romans' deeds were known, and their fame and their renown, the valleys round about were held by various kings, until

in that region Palatinus came to the crown, under whom lived the fair Pomona.

33 There was no nymph on that shore who loved fruits as much as she did—so that her name from fruits [*pomi*] takes origin, because she sometimes grafts this one with her sickle, pours over that one living water when the hot sun is attacking its roots, trims from another branches dry and twisted—and she loved only fruits and gardens.

41 On these alone she had fixed her love, avoiding completely the snares of Venus and the arrows of the cruel ruler, despising his prayers and his menaces; and because, being a woman, she feared that some man would do her violence, with a wall she surrounds and encircles her garden, where for no reason does she ever allow a man to enter.

49 The young satyrs around her made various dances to appease her; Pan and Silenus, enamored of her, went many times to visit her, and always hard and cold they found her; but among them all he who loved her most hotly was Vertumnus and he was not more successful than they.

57 And because Nature had granted him power to change himself into varied shapes, he was wont sometimes to make himself into a farmer who just then had loosed the cattle from their yoke, and then to change himself into a soldier; and now it seemed that he had gathered fruits; and so he would change his nature only to see Pomona.

65 Then, to quiet the kindled flames and to come to the end of all his desire, he took the form of an aged woman with wrinkled brow and snowy hair, and descended into Pomona's garden among trees and fruits that seemed divine, and saluted her and said: "My fair daughter, and much more fair if you had any pity,

73 blessed indeed above all others you can be called, because in these fruits you take delight." Then he kissed her, and she could feel that these were not an old woman's kisses. Pretending he could not go any farther, he placed himself on a rock and said: "Rest, daughter, if you please, with me a while, and on this elm that is here put your mind meanwhile.

81 See also that vine that he keeps close among his branches and holds and gathers up; without that elm she would be on the earth and would not be beautified with so many spoils. The

elm without the vine that he holds would have nothing else for himself but branches and leaves; thus the one without the other in a short time a useless trunk, useless wood must be.

*89* You, nevertheless, continue disdainful and hard and are un-moved by their example, and you have no thought of accepting a lover who could give worthy support to your years. Though many because of your beauty feel great distress, sorrow and suffering, if you are willing to trust to my councils, I advise that you take Vertumnus for your lover.

*97* Believe me, who know him; that man loves you more than his life, and you only he desires; only you in this world he wishes and longs for, and he seeks nothing else under the sun; your servant in every way he names himself, of you only he speaks, you only he honors and cherishes; you are his first love and, if you allow it, to you he has dedicated all his years.

*105* Besides this, he is a young lover and is able to take the form that most pleases him; when you wish, you will see him before you, if only you yield to the love-torch. He loves as you do the garden and the trees, and like you he delights in fruit; and this valley here and these springs he has always visited often, and these mountains.

*113* And though he loves greatly the fruit and the gardens, every delight nevertheless he abandons to see you, and seeing, takes comfort and assuages the flame that envelops him. Be sure that he himself exhorts you to do this, not an old woman whom already time is overthrowing; have mercy on him who burns; love-graces were never slow.

*121* And if ever cruelty holds you or held you, filling your bosom with bitter poison, I shall tell you what happened in Cyprus to a woman for being cruel. As opposed to the kingdom of Love, she showed herself hard, wicked, iniquitous, evil, untrue; but vengeance so terrible and strange gives every woman the power to learn at her expense.

*129* Iphis, a graceful youth, was in love with the fair and the cruel Anaxarete; with fire his heart burned in his breast just as a little torch burns; he had always that face as the object which kindled his amorous thirst; and he made many attempts to see if by himself he could put out that fire.

*137* But when he could not by using reason in part soften such fury, before her doors on his knees he came weeping to confess his love, and with humble and piteous speech sought to lighten his sorrow; sometimes to her servants, sometimes to her nurse he told his sufferings and his sorrows.

145 Now and again he wrote letters, and his pains written out in detail he sent to her; often at her gate at night he put flowers and garlands wet with his tears; often, to show how much he burned, he chose to sleep close by her house, where of a cold rock he made a bed for his wretched body, his loving bosom.

153 But she was more cruel than the sea when it is moved by winds and tempests, and much harder than iron that by Norican fire is made red, and more so than the rock that above the surface does not show, but remains still underground, hard and huge; with words and with deeds she belittles him—so bad was this woman's natural bent.

161 This youth could not endure his long drawn-out pain and his torture; so weeping he stood at his lady's door in the utmost fear. Then as he wept he uttered these words: 'You conquer, Anax- arete. I am happy to die, that you may not longer endure the trouble I cause and may carry off the victory.

169 Deck your temples with green laurel; celebrate your triumph for the war that I waged against you; you are happy and I die happy, since in any other way I cannot please you. Since my suffering does not move you, rejoice as if you were of iron or hard rock, because my fate brings me now to lose both one light and the other.

177 And so that no one will need to tell you the happy news of my death, you will see me hanging with your own eyes, which will give you much greater delight. Take, cruel one, this cruel pres- ent deserved by your iniquity. But you, heavenly beings who see this, perhaps on me will have some pity.

185 If anyone's prayer was ever pleasing to you, if ever you yield to our human wills, cause the memory long to endure of this my death, of these my griefs, and by report at least let that be given me which callousness and cruelty take away.' Thus having spoken, by such madness he was overcome that about his neck he fastened a rope.

193 Then, full of hot and tearful imaginings, in the utmost pain he raised his eyes and said: 'Cruel woman, these are the flowers,

these are the garlands you want.' At last, to end so many sorrows, he let himself go, hanging free; at his fall it seemed that the
door made for his fate a sound of mourning.

201 His dead body they carried to his mother, who bewailed him
miserably, complaining against Heaven that did her injury, on
seeing her son so cruelly dead; she would not listen to entreaty
and comfort, so unresigned she was in her sorrow for his death
so premature. Yet she arranged to give him burial.

209 As the body was going to the grave, it reached the house of
Anaxarete; hearing that the body was passing by, she did not
keep back from the window. And when she looked on his
face, at once to stone the cruel woman turned, for all her body,
with great horror, turned to the rock she had in her heart.

217 In memory, then, of such a fate, put away that pride of yours;
follow Venus' kingdom and her court if, Pomona, in my way
you will act. Open to your lover the bolted doors; show pity,
and pity you will receive." And when the old woman had
spoken, she made herself a fair and noble youth.

225 Therefore Pomona, partly through fear, partly moved by so
pleasing a face, was not even a little obstinate or hard, but drove
all cruelty from her breast, and into Vertumnus' arms, happy
and confident, willingly put herself. And with him she long
lived happy, if he tells the truth who writes of this.

233 Happy woman, to whom we sing and play music, and you
round about who listen to this, imitate Pomona's example and
not Anaxarete's cruelty. Here is your servant who weeps and
argues, and only to see your face he thirsts; he prays that in the
glass of another's ill you will see yourself and to his prayers for a
bit will lend your ears.

241 His age is not so great and so advanced, nor is his life so strange,
nor has nature made him so ugly that you should be adverse to
his desires. You see his starving body and the tears he pours
from his eyes, enough to rouse pity in a heart though ignoble and
to move of themselves a Hyrcan tiger.

249 You are able with art and with craft to take him in amorous nets,
hence it is right that quickly you give him some gracious and
pleasing sign; otherwise, full of rage and of anger, dead at your
door he must grow cold as ice. Then for your amorous deceit
will the goddess Venus exact the penalty to your shame and loss.

257 From all directions, then, you are forced, O lady, to answer him who calls you: from one side you are driven by vengeance against her who does not love when she is loved; from the other side, the reward that awaits her who chooses to yield to Love's sovereignty. Therefore lay aside every proud and disdainful desire; live with him a fortunate and happy life.

www.ingramcontent.com/pod-product-compliance
Lightning Source LLC
Chambersburg PA
CBHW051946270326
41929CB00015B/2549